THE ARTS
OF MANKIND

EDITED BY ANDRÉ MALRAUX
AND GEORGES SALLES

THE ARTS OF THE SOUTH PACIFIC

JEAN GUIART

THE ARTS OF THE
SOUTH PACIFIC

TRANSLATED BY ANTHONY CHRISTIE

THAMES AND HUDSON

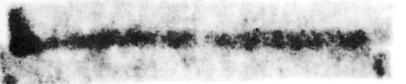

To Claude Lévi-Strauss
in recognition of his lucidity and insight
which have contributed so much
to the survival and renewal of Anthropology.

Printed in France © 1963 Editions Gallimard
This edition © Thames and Hudson 1963
This book must not be imported for sale into the U.S.A. or Canada

CONTENTS

PART THREE

Introduction

Of all the parts of the world, Oceania is the emptiest of land and people. Water is the commonest element by far, and fire is rarely absent. Yet people have made their home here on thousands of islands, large and small, many of them over-populated, and for two centuries the 'glamorous' way of life of these islanders has fired the imagination of writers, missionaries and romantic-minded tourists. But there is a dark side to the picture; ever since the first Europeans came on the scene, there have been unscrupulous adventurers who made, if on a small scale, in some of the Pacific islands, some of the earliest modern experiments in genocide.

Oceania is a region of contrasts—between the idyllic aspect of so many islands and the precariousness of human existence on them; for on the Micronesian atolls the spectre of famine is never absent even in surroundings of enchanting beauty. Today we find another contrast: between the easy life (how long, one wonders, will it last?) of the white minority, and the low standard of living among the natives, a standard resulting in part from the 'land-grabbing' methods of the white man in the nineteenth century. Sometimes there is also a contrast between the poverty of the dwellers in the highlands, where a primitive existence is the rule, and the relative prosperity of some of the coastal groups who have succeeded in keeping their land and adapting themselves to the exigencies of modern commerce.

The Pacific islands might be described as a human laboratory in which a great variety of traditions and cultures have given rise to very different social structures, the easier to study because of their small dimensions. Here, too, we find all types of colonization, from the harshest to the most liberal; a diversity of types of Christianity, from the most conventional to the most eccentric; and an equal diversity of spontaneous political activities, ranging from messianic utopian crusades to appeals to the United Nations. Thus Oceania fulfils at once the poet's dream and illustrates the all too often self-regarding 'realism' of certain business men and mining engineers.

Here we find all that is needed to excite men's curiosity and passions, to lure them into sometimes foolhardy ventures, to sap or to destroy their will-power, and to wither minds obsessed with the possibility of making a fortune in copra, mines or cocoa. But there are others who develop in the islands an epicurean attitude to life; like Tennyson's Lotus Eaters, indifferent to high ambitions and the outside world, they dream the hours away, basking in cool sea-breezes, and lead a life without complexes, deliberately restricted to immediate satisfactions. Almost all that has been written about Oceania is (or once was) true, at the moment of writing at least, and for the individual writer. Generalizations, on the other hand, are always unreliable.

Oceania does not lend itself to statistical analysis; figures there have only a relative significance. Averages are bound to be misleading when applied to an ecology that is essentially unstable, composite and everywhere limited. This aggregate of teeming microcosms is one of the human groups least understood by its administrators and the facts are often garbled by arm-chair specialists over-eager to present a logical, coherent picture of the Oceanian scene. Despite a veneer of Europeanized life, and despite well-defined (and new) material aspirations, we still catch glimpses of vestiges of the ancient social order. It survives chiefly in unspectacular forms, hardly perceptible to foreigners, and deliberately leads a semi-clandestine existence or, rather, one that is misunderstood, even in its religious manifestations.

Yet modern Oceania is not a relic of the past. After concerted massacres, the ravages of imported epidemics, kidnappings of men and women with a view to providing forced labour on the plantations of Queensland or in the potash mines of Chile, social equilibrium has been gradually restored thanks to the spread of Christianity, to an efficient health service seconded by recent improvements in education, more flexible methods of administration and to steps that are now being taken towards political emancipation.

In most of the area (with the exception of New Guinea) there is less illiteracy than in the southern parts of Europe and the manner of living has been adjusted to modern conditions. We also find a new collective urge towards a better life and a prevalent belief that the future lies with the natives. A new type of leader is coming to the fore, level-headed and practical-minded, with a gift for exploiting, sometimes creating, opportunities for advancement, and above all for dealing with complex situations in which Europeans are often involved, upon a realistic basis that keeps them always within the limitations of the feasible. Here, again, we have a multiplicity of interesting developments, on a small scale but none the less significant, in which races that were regarded until a few years ago as 'backward' are giving administrators lessons in the art of keeping to the point and in the diplomatic handling of prickly situations.

Oceanian art, so glorious in the past, has necessarily been affected by this evolutionary process. Now that the islander is forced to adapt himself to the changes taking place around him and to ever more intricate developments on the social and economic planes, he no longer has leisure to devote, during the agricultural slack season, to collective ritual or aesthetic activities. The notion of production, even of productivity, allied with the emergence of a will-to-power, has become something of an obsession, with the result that only the minor arts, practised by women, have survived: basket and mat-weaving and making tapa-cloth. Carving, for instance, has either completely died out or is rapidly disappearing almost everywhere.

By now the finest specimens of Oceanian art have found their way into private collections or the museums of Europe and America. What were once objects of veneration, cult symbols or adornments of daily life have now become counters in a speculative market. If the artists who were paid a few paltry francs or shillings for their works (when official pressure was not brought to bear to procure them gratis) could have shared in the present-day commercial value of these objects, there would have been less to regret. The contemporary vogue of so-called primitive works of art has its ugly side. For though these are duly admired, hardly anyone has a thought to spare for the men who made them.

Few, indeed, are those who try to understand the social conditions, the place and period, that were the background of these works. A rough-and-ready classification, for convenience sake, of the larger geographical areas is thought to be enough. The forms of Oceanian art have become dead letters, empty signs, into which every would-be connoisseur reads his personal reactions and any significance he desires. Or they are made objects of merely intellectual speculation, all the more sterile the more their true values are disregarded. The vogue for South Seas art began in France when the Surrealists claimed to find in it a dreamworld similar to their own. Subsequently it was explained as being an art directed to exclusively religious or magic ends. But this interpretation left out of account the complex of individual and collective motivations entering into it. Pieces of strictly anthropological interest served as pretexts for attractive but far-fetched theories, and in the process they were so to say dismembered, estranged from their creators and the men who saw in them a mirror of themselves.

Briefly, the present work might be described as a protest against the prevailing, over-simplified notion of the Oceanian world as one of thoroughgoing primitivity. But also, and above all, a conscientious attempt, however inadequate, to cast light on the diverse facets of a many-sided reality, to determine the true values of certain works of art, to illustrate the variety of possible contexts and to free the subject from the strait-jacket of attractive but inapt generalizations. The attempt may not satisfy all our readers; yet it could not be otherwise, if we were not to resort to the over-simplifications mentioned above.

Another need we felt was to approach the subject, hitherto treated on geographical lines, from a new angle. Even in our survey of styles we have tried to escape the constraints of geographical proximity, so as to arrive at an essentially functional classification. Needless to say, this study does not claim to be definitive. The stock-taking of Oceanian art has only just begun and for certain regions no iconographical documentation covering all existing (often widely dispersed) works is as yet available. The work that has been done *in situ* is often inadequate, especially as regards aesthetic symbolism. Malinowski, for instance, despite the vast range of his work, fails to tell us anything about the significance of the motifs carved on the prows of Trobriand canoes. Several years' research will be needed to complete our knowledge of the arts and culture of Melanesia and New Guinea; for the present, our only resource is to hunt through the mass of existing literature and unpublished records for information which may, perhaps, throw light on the many points that still remain obscure. Thus there still is ample scope for research-work, and only when this has been carried through can a new synthesis be attempted.

THE MATERIAL CONDITIONS
OF OCEANIAN LIFE

A myriad islands of every shape and size: such is the face of Oceania. They range in size from large land masses like Australia and New Guinea (with peaks rising to 16,000 feet above sea level) to small, sandy atolls covered with sparse vegetation, the haunt of crabs and occasionally of colonies of fishermen. The difference in size is paralleled by that of altitude; hence the conventional distinction between 'high' and 'low' islands.

But this distinction does not take us far. For the islands are also grouped in archipelagos, of varying dimensions, containing both high and low islands, the latter on the outskirts of the former. The differentiation between 'windward' and 'leeward' islands holds good only for islands that are fairly near each other. On the other hand, this question of 'exposure' is of prime importance for an understanding of the variety of local Micronesian climates. A northerly exposure means an absence of dew in the dry season, whereas a weather-side exposure ensures a permanently damp climate, with an abundant rainfall brought by the south-east trade-winds; the lee-side receives less rain and in some cases, when the natural factor is supplemented by the action of fire, the only vegetation is a low scrub.

In short the popular conception of the richness of the soil and the luxuriant vegetation of the islands has little foundation in fact. Under certain circumstances the tropical climate may equally well favour the growth of a relatively thick flora (provided no one interferes with it) and lead to conditions speeding up erosion and sterilization of the soil. Moreover, on the flat islands we find signs of a dangerous process of lateritization.

Thus the ecological conditions to which the inhabitants are subjected vary greatly in terms of the rainfall, copious in certain high islands and practically nil in some low islands, though both lie on the same latitude; also in terms of the prevailing currents, of the varying geological structure, of the presence or absence of forests, of the nature of the flora, whether scant and acidifying or lush and preservative, and, hence, of the degree of fertility or deterioration of the soil.

The nature of the vegetation is revealing to an expert eye. The effect of luxuriance so often remarked on by travellers is due to two causes. The coastal vegetation on high calcareous or volcanic beaches is usually dense; most noticeable are the Barringtonias, and in some places mangrove forests on the foreshore help to create the aspect of an impenetrable jungle. In the high islands where the humid virgin forests have not been disturbed, the vegetation, seen from the air, seems very dense. Actually, however, unlike the coastal forests, it is easy to traverse at ground level, since there is little or no undergrowth between the tree-trunks. Often one has to climb to some three thousand feet before encountering a dense forest in which tangled, mossy roots make progress difficult. Except in the coastal areas, lianas present no difficulty and the only obstacle, a relatively slight one, consists of certain plants with stinging leaves against

4

which the traveller has to be always on his guard. On the coral islands, on the other hand, the trees, though often lower and with less compact leafage, grow so close together that, when off the beaten tracks, one has often to hack one's way through with a machete.

Man has played havoc with this natural environment. The practice of slash-and-burn cultivation, the use of fire-arms for hunting, the activities of European stock-breeders operating on a large scale and of mining engineers who have to strip the soil when prospecting for mineral deposits, have led to the destruction by fire of almost all the vegetation on certain islands, sometimes on several occasions in the same year. True, the process of erosion and the impoverishment of the soil had set in before the coming of the Europeans. But they speeded it up and, except in modern states like Australia and New Zealand, no effective steps have been taken to counteract the process.

Another serious handicap, even in the high islands, is the frequent lack of water. Even where there is an abundant rainfall at certain times of the year, it is inadequate to provide a steady supply. Though some valleys are so thoroughly saturated that water spurts up at every step when we walk along their edges, some become completely waterless in the dry season, and others remain full for only an hour or two after showers.

For the coral islands have no surface water. At sea-level, however, a film of fresh water overlies the salt water which, seeping up through the porous coral substructure, holds it in suspension. This layer of drinking water, whose level sinks and rises with the tides, is tapped by means of wells (a recent development) and in some places comes to the surface at the bottom of natural caves.

The soil of the more recently formed volcanic islands, being no less porous than coral, freely absorbs rain-water and renders it back in the form of springs (sometimes hot springs), which become active at low tide. These conditions necessitate an organized suspension of hostilities—a sort of gentlemen's agreement—between the groups possessing springs and those having none.

There are also cases of large tracts of islands formed of limestone (not always coralline limestone) which rise to heights of several hundred feet above sea-level and in which the rivers flow underground for most of their course. Then, again, there are places where the distances between rivers are very great and it is sometimes necessary to make a long journey up-country to get other than brackish water—with the result that villages in the intervening regions may be completely without water for a great part of the year.

This aspect of the material conditions of life on the islands is apt to be overlooked; the prevalent conception of springs gushing forth from the slopes of the Tahitian mountains and memories of the 'Bath of Loti' tend to obscure the far less agreeable reality. Few are aware that, for example, vast areas of New Guinea are covered with mangrove swamps and that the large population has to exercise the utmost ingenuity in order to survive. The *farniente* life of the South Seas is an illusion—except for wealthy Europeans. Drought, endemic in many places, is nowadays largely remedied by wells and, provided it rains enough, by cisterns. Periods of drought seem to come in cycles lasting over several years and in the past this led to frequent famines, crops burnt up before maturity and the seeds 'taking' badly. In such times the only foodstuffs available were those procured by fishing and the gathering of edible wild roots.

5

1. New Caledonia, Isle of Pines. *Coral Landscape*.

2. New Caledonia. *Typical savanna, with paper-mulberries on fire*.

3. French Polynesia, Bora Bora. *Coral beach and volcanic relief.*

Famine is now less frequent than in the past. Iron tools enable fewer men to cultivate wider areas (provided enough land has been left at the disposal of the natives), with the result that it is possible to build up reserves of foodstuffs and there is a larger margin of safety in case of drought. But when the shortage is prolonged or a cyclone devastates the standing crops, the only remedy lies in official distributions of rice or the temporary migration of the males to other regions where they can find employment and earn enough to support their families until the next harvest. Formerly such catastrophes led to a state of long-lasting under-nutrition, the loss of many lives, and also to the making of individual or collective expeditions in canoes, in quest of better living conditions.

Thus the family played a considerable part in the social economy of the islanders. The precarious equilibrium between man and nature is illustrated by the following anecdote. No sooner had the puritan-minded missionaries of the Boston Missionary Society started operations in the Gilbert Islands (British Protectorate) than they were horrified by the prevailing drunkenness due to excessive indulgence in the local drink, fermented coconut toddy, and persuaded the authorities to prohibit its making and consumption. But after a time this prohibition had to be rescinded, the health officers having noticed that there was a marked rise in deficiency diseases. Analysis revealed the fact that coconut toddy, while extremely intoxicating, has a high vitamin content, indispensable in coral islands where there is practically no soil for growing vegetables and the staple foodstuffs consist almost exclusively of fish and coconut-meat.

To the other drawbacks of island life in early times was added a permanent sense of insecurity, causing the population to settle in small self-contained groups, each on its own land. This dispersal in small scattered hamlets—averaging twenty inhabitants—runs counter to the time-honoured anthropological theory that the inhabitants of dry countries, living under primitive conditions, always congregate near a supply of water. These settlements were usually of a more or less temporary order, in view of the large areas needed by a group practising slash-and-burn cultivation in which land had to be left fallow for two or three decades. Moreover, the quest of a reasonably cool climate led the islanders to avoid the foreshore and the beds of valleys and to settle on the crests of hills, on table-lands or outlying islets. On the low islands, where there were no such sites available, the villages were located just behind the beach; in other islands this location is a modern development, promoted by missionaries or government officials. In any case there is now a tendency for large villages to split up into smaller units, unless they are provided with such amenities as running water or communal reservoirs.

These settlements are as diverse in kind as widely scattered. In some parts of the Solomon and Fiji Islands the inhabitants live on artificial, man-made islands, built up on the barrier reefs. In New Caledonia, at the far end of a barren, uninhabited valley, we often find patches of greenery on ridges where a system of irrigated taro plantations (even if these have fallen into disuse) ensures a fairly regular water supply and a relative degree of coolness. In the New Hebrides

4. New Hebrides, Espiritu Santo. *Mountain region.*   5. New Caledonia, Gomen. *Hamlet in a poor region.*

(Espiritu Santo) platforms for small houses were cut out on the slopes of the steeper ridges, in places where the soil was unsuitable for cultivation. In the swamps of New Guinea even the smallest sandbanks emerging above the water have often been consolidated and used as sites for huts mounted on piles.

The structure of the dwelling-place is more often determined by ecological than by cultural conditions. Thus in mountainous regions, if the available space is limited and the population too scanty to provide an effective labour force, houses are stoutly constructed so as to resist the wind, protected against the cold by carefully made roofs and walls, and sometimes even have doors, if always very small ones. On the low islands near the Equator, where thick walls

6. French Polynesia, Huahine. *Fishing village on a lagoon.*

7. Loyalty Islands, Uvea. *Assembly Hall.*

and roofs would make them unbearably hot, dwellings are built of light materials and loosely constructed, the roofs and walls being made of coconut leaves, plaited in places but with enough interstices to let fresh air enter freely, while sheltering the occupants from the night winds. Further south, in regions exposed to cyclones, the dwellings on coastal zones or coral islands vary with the seasons; the fair weather residence being lightly built, the other, oblong or round, much more solid, with the thatch of walls and roof carefully sewn together, so as to enable the occupants to sleep in comfort during the cold season, and have a safe retreat in stormy weather.

The round house characteristic of the Loyalties and Caledonia (also found in New Britain and the highland valleys of New Guinea) has the merit of retaining the heat of a quite small fire all night; thus there is no need for any covering when sleeping—a great boon in the days before cotton or woollen blankets were available.

Thus it was not a case of races with an aptitude for building and others less endowed in this respect. Everywhere the dwelling-place was adapted to local requirements, but no unnecessary pains were taken over it. For large-scale building operations necessarily involved the employment of an army of workers who had to be fed, housed and given payment in one form or another. Naturally enough expenses were kept as low as possible; all the large buildings were the work of well-organized communities who, with an eye to prestige, were able to raise and support an extensive labour force for the duration of the work.

Island life is based on agriculture or fishing. The yield from rivers is relatively small. Formerly there was a practice of building temporary dams in the dry season, making it possible to empty partially a reach of the river and collect the fish in landing-nets. When there is a lagoon sheltered by a reef, it is here that the sea-fishing is done: by night with torches and harpoons; by day either with harpoons or lines. When the coastline abuts on the open sea, fishing is done by divers with spears; this dangerous form of sport is also practised on the seaward side of barrier reefs. In low islands, where constant fishing in the lagoon might lead to exhaustion of the food supply, the fishermen venture far out to sea in the tunny fish season; these expeditions call for nautical ability of no mean order. On the high islands we sometimes find communities exclusively composed of fishermen, who trade fish and shell-fish for other foodstuffs provided by up-country cultivators. These exchanges used to take place on fixed dates at prearranged spots, the barter sometimes being carried out in complete silence.

Agriculture was the basic activity, an extremely arduous one in the period when the only implement available was the digging stick. For, though loose volcanic soil was easy enough to work, the rocky soil of such islands as New Caledonia called for much hard labour before it could be made productive. According to the altitude and the degree of exposure of the arable land the principal cultivated plants were yams, bananas and taro.

For the tubers to fructify, yams require a certain warmth and a light soil. They cannot stand much cold and it is impossible to grow them above 1,500 feet, except on hillsides sheltered from the wind and relatively dry and warm. The banana grows best in damp, warm hollows; it, too, dreads wind and cold. As for taro, the more water there is, the better it thrives, and it stands up well to cold. It grows in the New Hebrides up to an altitude of 3,600 feet. In New Guinea we find it at even greater heights, exceeding 6,000 feet, where it shares the soil with sweet potatoes, a staple food in this island, but one cultivated only sporadically elsewhere in Oceania.

In the swamps of New Guinea the mangroves are interspersed with sago palms, but it is uncertain whether they were introduced by man. The trunk of the sago palm contains a large quantity of pith which when grated and moistened yields a flour that is one of the basic foodstuffs in New Guinea. It keeps remarkably well and is used as a stop-gap in this and many other islands, as far as the New Hebrides, in the intervals between other crops. In Melanesia sago palms are always planted in the vicinity of human habitations, since their leaves furnish excellent materials for roofs and walls.

Agricultural techniques vary, if only in detail, from one region to another. In the case of the numerous species of yam—with elongated or compact roots, with white or violet-hued flesh, with a smooth or bristly skin, with a fine-grained or fibrous texture—the methods of cultivation are everywhere much the same. The soil is carefully loosened up to a certain depth, thus providing a sort of nest of friable earth in which the seed is then embedded. Once it begins to sprout, the extremely fragile creeper calls for constant care. Sometimes it is trained on a vertical support, sometimes made to grow parallel to the slope of the hillside (New Caledonia). Another method is to provide a trellis of reeds on which the creeper can spread freely (New Hebrides). In the Loyalty Islands a criss-cross of bent sticks, each sunk in the ground, makes a sort of inverted basket over which the creepers can freely roam. There are other methods of yam cultivation, and sometimes a coat of mulch, whose thickness varies according to the weather, is added to protect the roots from abrupt changes of temperature.

Taro is a less sophisticated tuber. For its cultivation special methods of irrigation have been devised, as elaborate as those employed in Asiatic paddy-fields, but with this difference, that taro can be grown on very steep slopes and, given the relative sparseness of the population, it is not necessary to irrigate all available surfaces. In dry cultivation taro is almost the only food plant that grows well at high levels. In irrigated cultivation, when a steady supply of water is ensured by means of open channels (sometimes coming from a considerable distance), it is possible to make use of hillsides, even pebbly ones, with a dry exposure, where it would be hard to raise any other crop. In such cases it is desirable that the soil should not absorb water too readily, and that terraces should be given the gentlest possible slope, so that the water can flow over them without eroding the top-soil. The works carried out—notably in the south of New Caledonia—for canalizing water from great distances were engineering feats calling for much skill and careful planning. Ravines were spanned by hollowed-out tree-trunks, and a prolonged use of fire was often needed for splitting rock formations.

The existence of irrigated taro plantations has led some to infer the arrival of a higher civilization, but this is not borne out by the facts. No system of irrigation can be installed in regions where conditions are unfavourable to it. True, large-scale irrigation calls for skills associated with an 'advanced' civilization, but it is a matter of necessity where the soil is thin and arid. Though employed throughout New Caledonia, it prevails in the New Hebrides only in regions where it is feasible and necessary. Almost everywhere we find alternative solutions midway between the dry cultivation of taro and its cultivation on irrigated terraces. Sometimes it is grown in swamps provided with a system of drainage by intersecting ditches; sometimes in the moist depressions on the landward side of coastal dunes (on the atolls); and sometimes on the foreshore, at water level, where there is only a slight current or relative stagnation due to a counter-current. Given suitable conditions, every Oceanian people is quite capable of practising taro cultivation on terraces, but this is done only where absolutely necessary; for the irrigation system calls for greater man-power and far more elaborate planning than is needed for dry cultivation.

In the high valleys of New Guinea, when we find U-shaped glacier formations dating to the remote past, and on the margins of deep rivers or lakes, the soil needs constant draining. A labyrinthine network of deep ditches feeds a series of small channels serving individual fields.

Thanks to a geometric lay-out, with some of the alignments following the contours, it is possible both to drain off the water at the lowest levels and to provide for a better distribution of the water where there is a slope. This facilitates taro cultivation, which, however, is practised here on a smaller scale than that of the sweet potato.

In New Caledonia we find a different technique at once ensuring the humidity needed for crops on slopes and protecting the soil against erosion. Longitudinal ridges run up the hillsides, sometimes reaching to the summit and redescending the further slope, their parallel sides being protected by leguminous plants. The centre of the ridge is devoted to yams, and its sides to crops requiring more moisture, 'dry' cultivated taro, bananas, sugar-cane. A similar distribution of the cultivated plants is found on the peculiar crescent-shaped ridges built up on hillsides and consisting of masses of light soil held in by dry-stone walls.

There is no question that these elaborate structures (all the more remarkable when we remember that the only tools available were made of wood) have a definite aesthetic quality

8. New Caledonia, Huailu. *Yam cultivation on a hillside.*

and that the symmetry and perfection of their forms prove that their makers were not guided by purely practical considerations. Thus, when the irrigated terrace of a New Caledonian taro plantation ran round a hill, a vertical block of stone was set up on the edge of the terrace in line with the hilltop, so as to stress the movement of the parallel curves and add an ornamental touch to the lay-out.

Large-scale food production implies notions of agricultural economy, the planning of crops and the provision of a surplus so as to tide over periods of shortage and to ensure a margin of safety. Another reason for producing a food supply in excess of daily needs was the necessity of feeding a labour corps recruited from outside and also numerous guests at family or tribal feasts. How was the surplus constituted?

The storage of yams presents no difficulties. Once extracted from the earth, they keep perfectly for many months, if stored in a dry place. Large reserves could be laid by, enough to meet the needs of the community for a year or so. There is no special season for taro culti-

9. New Guinea, Baliem Valley. *Cultivation in an irrigated valley.*

vation. The tubers of this member of the *Araceae* family quickly deteriorate and have to be eaten within a few days after gathering, those grown in irrigated soil being the most fragile. If, then, a surplus is desired, it must be left in the ground; and the best system is to plant successive crops month by month, so as to be able to move from plot to plot and obtain a steady supply. The cultivation of bananas and sugar-cane raises exactly the same problems. Thus the yam is the most rewarding foodstuff from the agriculturist's point of view, since it is easiest to store and lasts longest. Taro and bananas do not lend themselves so well to barter, but their possessors often invite outsiders to consume them on the spot. Cooking bananas (plantains) are not appreciated at ceremonial feasts.

13

THE INHABITANTS

For two centuries the Pacific islanders have been a favourite theme of speculation and romantic literature, but this interest is largely misdirected, and the 'mystery' with which so many writers have chosen to invest them is largely fictitious. For, when all is said and done, the mentality of a peasant or fisherman of the South Seas differs very little from that of a Mediterranean peasant or fisherman. He is often said to be idle. But when driven by necessity or given an opportunity of showing his mettle (of which he seldom reaps the due reward), he is found to be both conscientious and hard-working.

Visitors to French Polynesia speak disdainfully of the Tahitian's laziness. But this is a superficial judgment. An objective, detailed study of the budget of a Tahitian family proves that its members exercise much skill in procuring remunerative part-time employment, and that their earnings, when pooled, ensure a quite adequate standard of living. Before blaming the Oceanians for neglecting this or that form of activity, it would be well to ascertain what is feasible under the prevailing technical and economic conditions, how much land is available, and so forth. Taking all these factors into account, we may well be amazed to see how well the inhabitants have succeeded, by dint of careful husbandry, in extracting from an often thankless soil the wherewithal for a life that, if far from idyllic, is reasonably secure.

So far, so good—but who exactly are these Oceanians? Ordinarily they are divided into four groups, corresponding to the four major geographical divisions of the area. They are Polynesians, Micronesians, Melanesians and Australians. Also, so as to distinguish them from the Melanesians living in the south-east extremity of New Guinea, the inhabitants of the greater part of the island are described as Papuans. The rough-and-ready division of Oceania into Polynesia, Micronesia, Melanesia and Australia is a convenient one—especially for the schoolteacher. But, viewed from the angle of human geography, this division hardly meets the case. For the physical geographer there is no real distinction to be made between Micronesia and Polynesia, while from the ethnic and cultural standpoint no break of continuity can be seen between Polynesia and Melanesia, any more than between Papua and Melanesia or between Melanesia and Micronesia. Australia alone is a case apart; yet we shall see how many affinities exist between North Australia and New Guinea.

The large land masses of Australia and New Guinea form an obvious contrast with the majority of Pacific islands. But how is one to differentiate between Melanesia and Polynesia, both alike composed of low and high, large and small islands? New Zealand, too, has semi-continental proportions and forms part of Polynesia. One might attempt a classification based on differences of size and structure, since Melanesia has a greater number of high islands of large dimensions than Polynesia. But in such a classification only the question of the relative dimensions of the big Melanesian islands could be taken into account, given the great number of high islands in Polynesia and even in Micronesia. When all is said and done, these divisions into large geographical areas are justified only by the positions of the various islands and groups of islands on the map of the Pacific Ocean.

Nor is the situation any clearer in the field of physical anthropology. The Polynesians are usually described as very tall, with an almost European appearance, round heads, black wavy (or straight) hair and fair skins. The Melanesians are described as dolichocephalic, with dark skins, long but frizzy hair, and often of a stature well below the average. Distinctive of the Papuans and the Melanesians are the respective shapes of their noses, convex in the case of the former and broad in that of the latter.

Based on limited local research-work, the existing statistics give little help towards establishing general laws. The Polynesians have come in for most attention and bulk large in comparative studies of the Oceanian scene. Traces of Mongoloid strains have been detected in the Polynesians, and these can also be seen, in a general way, in most of Melanesia and even in New Guinea. A contrast has been drawn between the flat or wavy hair of certain human types and the frizzy hair of others. Among the Polynesians we find people (but these are exceptional cases) whose hair is far more than wavy, almost frizzy in fact. In Melanesia nearly all the inhabitants of the Loyalties have flat or, oftener, wavy hair; the same types of hair are found in the southern portions of the New Hebrides group and, sporadically but persistently, in the rest of Melanesia.

The distinction sometimes made between the full but 'European' lips of the Polynesians and the thick, somewhat everted lips of the Melanesians has little to commend it. From New Guinea to New Caledonia we find people with thin lips, and also in Polynesia. The so-called Papuan nose exists in the Solomons, the New Hebrides, the Loyalties and Fiji, and it is not unknown in Polynesia and Micronesia. Straight noses can be seen everywhere in Oceania; particularly in the Solomons, New Hebrides, Fiji, the Loyalties and New Caledonia.

Not all Polynesians are tall, the stature of the Melanesians seems to vary greatly, and any generalizations in this respect would be unsafe. In the mountains of New Guinea and the New Hebrides are tribes of very small stature, but not true pygmies, the proportion of head to body being normal when compared with that among their neighbours. The members of many groups in New Caledonia, the Loyalties, the Hebrides and the Solomons are relatively tall.

Polynesian brachycephaly is much less marked in New Zealand, and the Melanesians are far from being uniformly dolichocephalic. Prognathism, more or less pronounced, is everywhere apparent. The colour of the skin is one of the least reliable criteria; if Polynesian flesh-tints vary greatly, these variations are largely determined by exposure to sunlight. It is common knowledge that women of the upper class were encouraged to stay indoors to keep a fair complexion. In Melanesia, however, we find marked differences in the natural tint of the skin, both in coastal areas of the islands and up-country.

Strongly projecting brows, common enough among the Melanesians, are, despite the many types of facial structure prevailing in Polynesia, rarely found there. It is often thought to be a result of contacts with ancient peoples similar to the present-day Australians. Anyhow in the south and centre of Australia the aborigines display a remarkable homogeneity: all are tall

and lanky, extremely hirsute (in the case of the men), with black wavy or slightly frizzed hair, fairly pale skin, and long heads with vizor-like jutting brow-ridges below which the eyes and nose seem remarkably deep-set. We find, however, shades of difference. In North Australia the skin tends to be darker, there is less pilosity, and hair is often completely frizzy. The Australian physical type of man (except in the matter of height) is met with in New Guinea, in southwest New Caledonia and even, here and there, in islands regarded as definitely Polynesian, such as Uvea in the Loyalties.

There is no question that the population of Oceania is extraordinarily mixed, this intermixture being more pronounced in the central area (New Guinea, Melanesia) than in the outlying regions where a certain homogeneity has been achieved (Australia, Polynesia). The western portion of New Guinea has always maintained contacts with Indonesia and Asiatic strains are evident in Micronesia. The numerous blood tests that have recently been made do not seem to throw much light on the problem; their results are often contradictory and hard to interpret. Actually, if paradoxically, this very diversity of blood types, none strictly localized, tends to give an impression (Australia excepted) of an over-all unity.

What view, then, should be taken of the prehistory of the Oceanians? Much has been written on the subject since the publication of the classic work by J.L.A. de Quatrefages nearly a hundred years ago. His speculations seem, for the most part, highly judicious (for the period). The most that has been done, subsequently, is to qualify and amplify them. Our present knowledge is in many respects inadequate to solve the various problems. Certain broad general outlines seem to emerge, but they call for detailed examination and any judgment professing to be definitive would be premature, not to say pretentious.

What, in fact, are our sources of information? To begin with, the results of archæological research and, in particular, a certain number of dates obtained by radioactive-carbon tests. Next come comparative studies of the material culture, sociology and myths of Oceania. In

10. Cook Islands. *Mangaian.*
11. New Guinea, Wahgi tribe. *Woman with her face painted white as a sign of mourning.*
12. *Fijian.*

this field stress was often laid on hypothetical relations of cause and effect, as when there was talk of a 'migration' whenever specific objects or techniques simultaneously existed in different places. But this involved an over-simplification. When men travel, it is often with a view to returning to their starting point. Objects, skills, art forms and institutions also travel and are transmitted by exchanges from one group to another, in all directions. The only determinant factors of this distribution were winds and currents and the maritime ability of the navigators, whenever it so happened that the voyagers were out of sight of land for several days.

Once the technique of long-distance voyages had been mastered—in Micronesia, Polynesia and a large part of Melanesia—there was nothing to prevent the transport of men and cargoes to far-distant islands. This proliferation and dissemination of physical types was paralleled by a great diversity of hybrid material cultures and social patterns, none exactly like its neighbours. One of Oceania's fascinations for the modern anthropologist is that it constitutes a sort of living laboratory in which all types of human society in their infinite variety can be studied *in situ*. No other field of inquiry is so rewarding for the researcher who desires to escape uniformity and, more unusual still, everything is on a scale that he can cope with single-handed.

The domestic utensils uncovered by excavation are, however, far from being as varied as those one would expect from a living material culture. They consist principally of fragments of pottery found in Polynesia as well as Melanesia; beads and fish-hooks in mother-of-pearl or common shell; implements in cut or polished stone; articles in bone or shell; cook-house debris (bones and shells) and remains of fireplaces. An examination of these objects suggests the possibility of working out chronological sequences, determined for example by the shapes of the blades of adzes and of fish-hooks, and by the ornamentation of the pottery. But datings based on these factors can be no more than conjectural for, so far anyhow, few object-yielding levels separated by sterile layers have been discovered. A noteworthy case is New Caledonia where the earliest date of human habitation is 347 B.C. ($\pm$ 350) and only one rich stratum has

17

13. New Guinea, Sepik.
Man's head with ceremonial decoration.

been disclosed. In Fiji there are sometimes two such strata, the earlier dating to 46 B.C. ($\pm$ 500).

A chronological table can, however, be drawn up based on data now available and showing the (provisional) dates of the first appearance of man in some archipelagos.

ARCHIPELAGO	ISLAND	AUTHOR	B.C.	+	A.D.
South Australia		Tindale	8700		
Marianas	Saipan	Spoehr	1527		
New Caledonia		Gifford	847		
Marquesas	Nuku Hiva	Suggs	122		
Fiji	Viti Levu	Gifford	46		
Samoa		Golson			9
Palau	Yap	Gifford			176
Marianas	Tinian	Spoehr			345
Austral Islands	Rapa	Heyerdahl			620
Easter Island		Malloy			858
Hawaii	Oahu	Emory			957
New Zealand		Duff			1150

None of these datings conflicts with local traditions. They indicate that man's appearance in Polynesia (the Marquesas, Hawaii, New Zealand) took place earlier than was generally supposed. In any case this sequence of dates, decreasing in antiquity from West to East and from the heart of Polynesia to its outskirts, flatly contradicts the theory that Polynesia was colonized from America.

A new factor is the archeological discovery of pottery in the Marquesas and Samoa; hitherto it was assumed that no pottery existed in Polynesia, except in Tonga.

18

14. *Pulako, King of the Friendly Islands.*

15. New Guinea, Pirimapune. *Skull worn as a chest ornament.*
16. New Zealand. *Maori.*

Here we may quote the opinion of an archeologist who is one of the leading authorities on Polynesian prehistory, Dr Alexander Spoehr, formerly director of the Bernice P. Bishop Museum at Honolulu.

'My guess is that one of the earliest movements of Malayo-Polynesian canoe voyagers was along the northern coast of New Guinea and into the Bismarck Archipelago, that they interbred with peoples already resident there, and that they pushed southward along the Solomons, the New Hebrides, and finally to New Caledonia, the southernmost major island in Melanesia.'

Elsewhere Dr Spoehr writes:

'In a previous paper, I committed the indiscretion of stating that the Polynesians probably came through Micronesia. This view is not sustained by convincing evidence and the question must remain open.'

This strikes a very different note from that of the Polynesian saga so brilliantly, if over-confidently, expounded in that fascinating volume *Vikings of the Sunrise,* by the late Sir Peter Buck (under his Maori pseudonym, Te Rangi Hiroa), who believed that all Polynesia was colonized by way of the Micronesian atolls.

The anthropological survey of Oceania is far from being complete, but work on it is still proceeding and the blank spots on the map are growing steadily fewer. For some years all authors dealing with Melanesia have agreed that it is necessary to take into account its relations with the Marianas and the Marshalls in Micronesia. This approach will certainly lead to a better understanding of the exact significance of the islands hitherto regarded as Polynesian outposts. The fact that islands exist on the southern, eastern and northern fringes of Melanesia, which can be classified as Polynesian, seems to present a far more complex phenomenon than that of a 'backwash' of Polynesians.

The generally accepted list is quite inadequate. To it must be added not only the small groups living in up-country districts of the large Melanesian islands, who have always claimed

21

to be of Polynesian descent—actually this is not claimed even by the inhabitants of Rennel Island or Ontong Java, for example—but also the groups speaking a Polynesian language. A table can be drawn up (necessarily provisional and incomplete) as follows:

ARCHIPELAGO	TRADITIONAL POLYNESIAN ORIGIN	STARTING POINT	SPEAKING A POLYNESIAN LANGUAGE
Loyalty Islands	North Coast of Uvea	Samoa	
	North and South Uvea	Wallis	
	Muli and Heo Islands	Wallis	
	Some clans in Loesi (Lifu)	Wallis	
	Some clans in Lifu and Mare	Tonga	
New Caledonia	Coastal groups at Hienghene, Balade and Kumac	Wallis	
	Some clans in Huailu and Burai	Samoa	
	Some clans in Isle of Pines	Tonga	
New Hebrides	Mele, Erakor, Vila (Efate)	Samoa	
			Aniwa
			Futuna
			Emae (Makata)
Solomons			Tikopia
			Anuda
			Duff
			Sikaiana
			Bellona
			Rennell
			Ontong Java
			Taku
			Kilinailau
New Guinea			Ninigo Islands
			Nissan
			Tonga
			Nuguria
Micronesia	Ellice Islands		Nukuoro
			Samoa
	South Gilbert Islands		Kapingamarangi

To the above should be added the Matty (Wavulu) and Durour (Aua) Islands (north of New Guinea), distinctively Micronesian from the viewpoint of their material culture. On examination, a similar Micronesian predominance can be detected in most of the so-called Polynesian islands on the outskirts of the Solomons. Other Micronesian elements are found in the Banks Islands and in the north-west of Espiritu Santo. Moreover, study of the social structure of Aniwa, Futuna and Emae in the New Hebrides proves that though the vocabulary is seemingly Polynesian, the local customs are precisely similar to those in near-by groups speaking Melanesian languages. Thus we have yet to elucidate the exact relations between these outlying communities. In the present state of our knowledge it is almost impossible to arrive at any definite conclusion on this point. But it would be regrettable to leave this problem in suspense.

17. New Guinea, Wahgi. *Facial tattooing of a young woman.*

18. New Guinea, Sepik. *Overmodelled skull of an ancestor.*

19. New Guinea, Asmat. *Nose ornament*.

Why not, then, attempt to formulate a tentative solution, taking into account all the known elements?

The source area of the Melanesian and Polynesian peoples may be located, from the linguistic viewpoint at any rate, somewhere in south-eastern China. The many strings of islands dotting the map of Indonesia lent themselves to the possibility of relatively short 'hops', enabling early voyagers to travel to New Guinea, and thence to Australia, without ever losing sight of land—hence the possibility of these journeys having been made on rafts. The first settled regions, on this view, were New Guinea, Australia and perhaps the Bismarck Archipelago. Probably akin to the present-day Australians, these early inhabitants of the islands were fishermen, hunters and food-gatherers, not agriculturists. Some authorities claim to distinguish two distinct groups: first, the so-called Murray or Ainoid type, physically akin to the Ainu of Japan, to which group may be assigned the aborigines of south-eastern Australia and some of the inhabitants of the highlands of New Guinea; secondly, the Veddoids—so named because of their resemblance to the Vedda population of India—who settled around the Gulf of Carpentaria in Australia and on the north and south coasts of New Guinea.

It is believed that a Negroid Oceanian type can be dated to about the same period, and that these Negroids settled in a tract of central New Guinea and on the Cape York peninsula of Australia. Intermixing of these three components must have given rise, even in these early times, to a complex ethnic situation; various groups stemming from this racial mélange may well have colonized the greater part of Melanesia, New Caledonia included. And this process may well have continued over a good many centuries.

The methods of cultivation employed today are thought to have been introduced by newcomers, not in the course of a mass migration, but by way of a gradual infiltration from archipelago to archipelago. Their means of navigation—outrigger canoes—enabled them to make longer voyages and to fan out in all directions from their starting point, New Guinea. Thus

24

20. *Man from the Sandwich Islands.*

there were off-shore expeditions in zigzags as well as those keeping to the 'classical' coastal routes along the Melanesian strings of islands. They could colonize Micronesia; then, feeling the need for more living-room, they travelled back along the northern outskirts of the Bismarck Archipelago and, after interbreeding more and more with their predecessors, occupied parts of the Solomon Islands, the New Hebrides, New Caledonia, the Loyalties and the Fiji Islands.

Recent studies of the sociology of eastern Melanesia indicate that it is impossible to draw any clean-cut racial distinction between this area and the nearer Polynesian archipelagos: Wallis, Futuna, Rotuma, Tonga and Samoa. We have here neither a purely Polynesian nor a purely Melanesian stock, but ethnic complexes whose common elements far outnumber differences. Hence, we are tempted to infer that what may be described as the Polynesian *ethnos* took form somewhere in this area, before spreading beyond Samoa, by way of the Cook and Austral Islands, to the Society Islands which, with 'Sacred Raiatea', were the secondary taking-off points of the Polynesians, in the direction of the Tuamotu Islands, the Gambiers and Easter Island in the east, the Marquesas and Hawaii in the north, and New Zealand in the south-west.

The existence of two population strains in Polynesia has been postulated on the strength of the legend of the *menehune* (black dwarfs). Most Oceanian folk tales tell of the presence of black, long-haired little men, genii of the backwoods or autochthonous denizens of the islands before the coming of the Polynesians. But the tales of elfs and goblins in European folklore do not justify us in identifying them with the Celts and Ligurians, and solid archaeological evidence is needed if we are to believe in the existence of this alleged primitive population. So far no such evidence has been forthcoming. That there were successive influxes, spaced out over a long period, seems at least equally probable.

Another theory has been put forward: that north-eastern Polynesia was colonized by des-

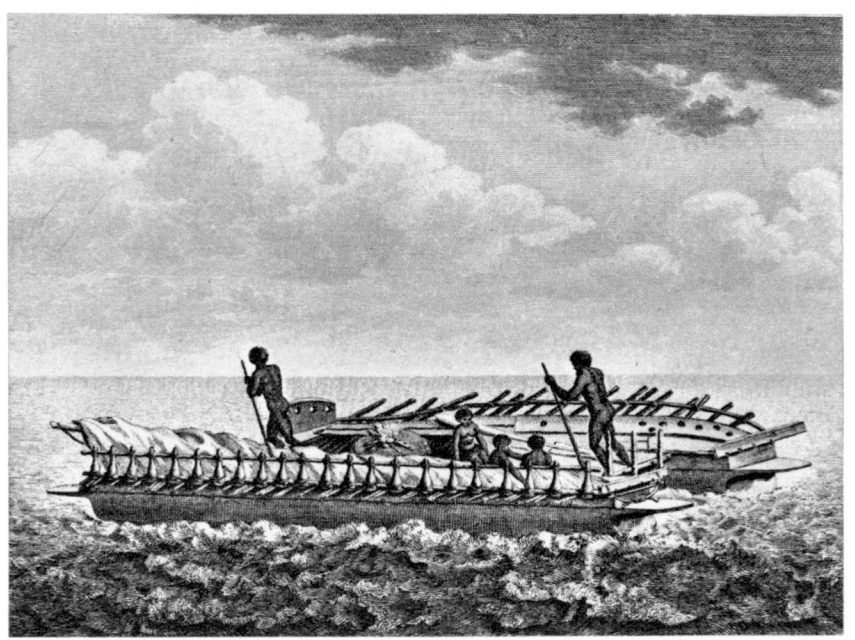

21. *Hawaiian double canoe.*

22. *New Caledonian double canoe.*

cendants of the first Viking settlers on the west coast of Canada. This romantic notion is the outcome of a long-standing desire to regard the Polynesians as a 'superior race'—superior, that is to say, to the other inhabitants of Oceania—with a complex, highly evolved civilization, ranking them beside Europeans. This esteem which the Polynesians have enjoyed since the days of the early Pacific explorers, and the 'glamour' they have exploited with such skill, are due to several causes. For one thing, an ethnological justification for their alleged superiority seemed to be called for. Thus there was talk of the Lost Tribes of Israel, of Sumerians, of the cultures in the Indus region and of Ancient Egypt. Today, Vikings or Incas are in favour.

The explanation of the presence in Polynesia of a culture styled superior (a quite unscientific notion) as being due to an influx of 'blond Aryans' calls up echoes that may jar on modern ears. It is based chiefly, not to say exclusively, on the presence of natural blonds in Polynesia. But apart from the fact that it is hard to distinguish in any of the islands between persons of pure ancestry, assuming such exist, and descendants of the white men—the fair- or red-haired English, Danish, Norwegian, Swedish, American and Norman sailors who have roamed the South Seas for some two centuries—another fact must be borne in mind: that persons with fair skin, dark- or light-red hair, and eyes that sometimes give the impression of being blue are met with in all parts of Oceania. Also we almost everywhere encounter albinos, whose skin and hair are almost completely bleached. It is but natural that, intermediary between the rest of the population and these albinos, there should exist specimens of humanity with fair or reddish hair and on occasion bluish, not merely colourless, eyes.

In any case most Polynesian and Melanesian new-born children have pale complexions and fair hair—which rapidly darken as they grow up. Finally, the custom prevailing throughout the islands of artificially bleaching the hair by means of lime is enough to discredit the accounts of fair-haired populations given by the earliest voyagers, who never stayed long enough to make a thorough study of local ways of life or to note this particular custom. When one has seen thousands of Oceanians with one's own eyes, one learns to take a cautious view of theories related to facts which, when studied at home in an arm-chair, may look mysterious.

According to the Norwegian author Thor Heyerdahl, a migration from the coast of South America lay at the origin of the Polynesian race. South America, according to one of the theories mentioned above, was one of the stopping-off places of the Nordic migrants. Heyerdahl does not go that far, but he comes near it. No praise is too high for the courage and determination of the leader of the Kon-Tiki expedition, but there would be little point in a detailed discussion of his theory. He employs the 'comparative' method which was in vogue half a century ago. Today no serious anthropologist draws conclusions from the simultaneous presence of implements or objects functionally alike in widely separated zones. What we now compare are no longer isolated elements but complexes and structures—and this, in the present state of our knowledge, can be done only progressively, step by cautious step.

All the same this question of the relations between Oceania and America is very much the order the of day and it is to the credit of Dr Paul Rivet (even if certain details of his hypotheses seem unacceptable) that he has given the matter serious study. It is quite possible that those remarkably seaworthy vessels, the Polynesian double-canoes, made landfalls at various points on the coast of North, Central and South America. Those famous White Indians of Darien may well be Polynesians rather than Nordics. But we are still awaiting the archæological campaign which will resolve the problem and it is for the 'Americanists' to clear the matter up.

In any case no definitive opinion is feasible as things stand. Claude Lévi-Strauss has recently drawn attention to the structural analogies existing between Chinese art, the art of the northwest coast of America, Maori (New Zealand) art and the tattooed ornamental motifs current among the Indians of Brazil. These analogies, certainly intriguing and so far unexplained, are not to be lightly dismissed.

Approaching the problem from another angle, Dr Rivet has laid stress on the simultaneous appearance of the sweet potato in Oceania and South America and on the fact that the name it bears both in Peru and in Polynesia appears to derive from the same word, *kumula* (or some very similar one). Indeed it seems that the starting point of this diffusion of the sweet potato must be located in South America. Its propagation in Oceania was apparently haphazard. While it is found almost everywhere in Polynesia, its presence in Melanesia has been brought to notice only quite recently; in many places it seems to have been introduced in the early nineteenth century by members of the London Missionary Society stationed in Samoa and Raratonga. In the centre of New Guinea, on the other hand, the dwellers in the high glacier valleys have made of it their staple crop. It thus seems reasonable to assume, with our colleague Jacques Barrau, that the diffusion of the sweet potato was gradual, by short stages, beginning with Indonesia, where it was probably brought in the first instance by the Portuguese.

The itineraries of the dispersal of cultivated plants reflect the desire, common to all peasant folks, to take from their neighbours whatever seems useful, or even merely agreeable to look at. When one has seen how often Melanesians setting out on a voyage take with them plants of nutritive or ornamental species carefully preserved in damp earth or bark, it is easy to understand how cultivated plants made their way from island to island. Some species of recent origin are even found in mountain villages none of whose inhabitants has ever set eye on a European.

Finally, we may turn to the problem of how the far-flung islands of the Pacific were successively populated. During the last few decades students of the subject have been inundated with theories of alleged 'migrations' (a term somewhat overworked in our opinion). They have been invited to study large wall-maps with arrows indicating the directions of these movements. Once again we do best to keep to the hard facts and then we find that there is no positive evidence of any migration in Oceania, except that of the peopling of New Zealand by emigrants from the Society and Cook Islands, which took place after the year 1000 of our era. Research made in New Zealand has proved that this was not a mass migration, but a steady trickle of voyagers lasting over a fairly long period and including occasional return trips.

The theory that in some unspecified period boat-loads of Polynesians deliberately set forth in quest of undiscovered lands is purely mythical. True, groups of sea-going canoes sometimes ventured on long voyages, but they always kept to well-known routes and were made for a specific (usually warlike) purpose. This was specially the case with the Tongan expeditions of three or four centuries ago, in the heyday of the Tongan empire, when it was a matter of exacting tribute from remote dependencies: Rotuma, the Ellice, Tokolu or Lau (Fiji) Islands; from Wallis and Futuna and even, for a time, Samoa. But the existence of a despotic, well-organized central power like that of Tonga was, it seems, unique in the history of the islands.

In the course of these often perilous off-shore voyages many canoes were swept off course by capricious currents and shifts in the trade-winds, and were lost forever, or else fetched up in Melanesia or Micronesia. Whether such unsolicited visitors were slaughtered or absorbed into the local population depended on their physical fitness, their numbers, their behaviour and the whim of their 'hosts'. There are grounds for thinking that some Melanesian chiefs are descendants of such accidental immigrants; in particular in islands along the route from Tonga to the southern New Hebrides (Futuna, Anatom), to the Loyalties (Lifu) and thence to New Caledonia (Isle of Pines). According to a local tradition there was a steady trade in pottery between Tonga and the Isle of Pines, and recent archeological finds do not seem to contradict this.

On the other hand, there is no question that a true migration took place towards the end of the eighteenth century, when a number of persons voyaged from Uvea in the Wallis Islands to the northernmost island of the Loyalty group, which, too, since then has borne the name Uvea. The descendants of these immigrants number, after two centuries, some four hundred persons. According to tradition the group was composed exclusively of men who enlisted in the armies of local chiefs; though they kept their language (with some distinctive archaisms), they were absorbed into the indigenous community. Assuming that European contacts and the resulting demographic losses ensured their numbers a relative stability, the original group cannot have numbered more than a hundred fighting men—the average crew of two double canoes of the old type. This gives an idea of the real scale of the Oceanian migrations.

A New Zealander, Andrew Sharp, has recently published an authoritative work in which he describes the authenticated voyages in canoes between the various Polynesian archipelagos. This list is, to my knowledge, incomplete, since it does not include numerous landfalls in Melanesia that took place in the same period. But his survey makes it clear that during two centuries canoes that had drifted off their course reached all the Polynesian archipelagos and that these drifts took place in all directions—though, needless to say, many failed to make land and were never heard of again. If we assume that they spanned a period of some two thousand years, these accidental voyages would account for the peopling of all Polynesia, starting from the source areas (Tonga and Samoa), given the geographic area covered by the islands and their respective population capacities. This applies, of course, only in a general way, and to inter-island voyages in which no land was sighted for many days.

The Tikopia islanders have long been acquainted with the route to the Banks Archipelago, to which they had a habit of migrating in times of food shortage, stopping off on the way at the rocky desert island of Vatganay, north-east of the New Hebrides. The voyage took five full days, and they still make this journey, in canoes, attracted by the high wages obtainable on the European plantations of the New Hebrides.

THE SOCIAL SYSTEM
AND ITS INSTITUTIONS

One of the hazards of sociological study in the Pacific is the variety of social patterns to be found there. The comparative investigation of these patterns is a difficult matter. For while in most societies there is one sector which presents a highly formalized aspect, the particular sector tends to vary from one society to another. In one it will be the kinship structure and marriage patterns, in another the form of chieftainship, in a third the system of magic, in another inter-tribal relations. Consequently it is not possible to construct syntheses which will hold good for the social organisation as a whole. It is as though in each social complex the need were felt for an area of freedom in which things were more fluid, less rigorously controlled and imposing less constraint on human relations.

We shall not be concerned here with kinship structure. This has little effect, as such, upon aesthetic matters, except insofar as the regularity and the abstract, quasi-mathematical aspect of the rules governing marriage and kinship may be considered an aesthetic achievement. Such an approach, though unconventional, would not be improper. These rules could be represented symbolically in a circular design—and native informants have been known to exhibit them in this form as a matter of course. We may indeed wonder whether certain geometric decorative motifs should not be connected with kinship structures, but even if it were correct, such a hypothesis would be difficult to verify. There is nothing less variable than a geometric design: the themes are by and large identical, and local variations, where they do exist, occur as much in the ways in which the themes as grouped as they do in the surfaces they are used to decorate.

The structure of the social system follows a limited number of patterns, each of which has a host of local variants. A detailed list of these (this has too rarely been attempted) would furnish an extraordinary wealth of material. There is, however, one area of Oceania which presents an instance of non-formalized organisation, even in terms of its descriptive vocabulary. Its social mechanism is difficult to determine but of the kind which has been described by one of the pioneers of modern Oceanian anthropology, Rivers, as 'gerontocracy'—government by the old. In this area the possession of young wives tends to be reserved to the elderly men. They are experts in the rites and in magical techniques which will ensure the success of such economic activities as hunting, fishing, food-gathering and agriculture. They have amassed large stores of traditional wealth. As a result young men have no opportunity for anything but irregular affairs which are either dangerous or involve heavy fines, payable in pigs, until they have attained a status which entitles them to acquire one or more wives.

This question of status is the key to the problem. But to what degree does it affect social

31

23. New Guinea, Wahgi. *Heavy ceremonial head-dress.*

mobility and what exactly are its modes of operation? Does it function within the society as a whole, or only within certain sectors of it?

In Australia gerontocracy occurs in a more or less pure form. Part of adulthood is devoted to a slow initiation—the pace is dictated by the oldest males—into the religious rites which assure the processes of human procreation, the multiplication of animals and plants and the beneficent co-operation of the weather. These rites are essentially aesthetic and involve either a figural representation of totemic myths or full-fledged dramatic performances in which the initiates are both participants and spectators. The ceremony consists in making the would-be initiate assume the personality of the ancestor or of the totem, or both at once, of making him mime their acts and follow the itinerary prescribed by the myth.

The prologue to the active part of the ceremony takes the form of painful surgical operations upon the sexual organs, incision and, especially, subincision: the opening of a certain length of the meatus. At the same time, the individual who has hitherto been a minor, is given instruction in the magical techniques which bring into play the positive forces ensuring human survival. The techniques consist of the recital of specific myths and the smearing of sacred objects in wood or stone (*churinga*) with red ochre or animal fat.

Marriage itself takes place at the end of a probationary period which may last several years and be interrupted by festivals at which sexual constraints are temporarily suspended. This gerontocracy operates on a relatively limited scale since each linguistically homogeneous tribe is subdivided, at least theoretically, into independent hunting districts and each district is in turn divided between small groups which keep to established routes. The initiation rites bring together the elders and young men of a district. Gatherings on a tribal scale are rare; when they do occur, they may include not only a whole tribe but its neighbours also. Systems of exchange maintain inter-tribal relations. There is no definite and recognizable control organization: at best we find 'Assemblies of the Elders.' Matrimonial organization in Australian gerontocracy, on the other hand, displays a complexity of mechanism which has been a treasure trove for many generations of students and research workers.

In New Guinea and Melanesia we find somewhat similar conditions among the farmers and pig-breeders whose life offers economic possibilities far superior to those of the nomads of Australia. Here not only does the existence of craft skills and facilities for preserving yams over several months encourage exchanges between groups and individuals, but pig-breeding provides the means for the accumulation of wealth. Personal wealth becomes a factor of social importance, offset in part by a system of tabus and obligations. It allows of polygamy and, because women have the task of rearing pigs, polygamy is a condition of wealth.

In addition to the movement of women from one group to another, there is an exchange of belongings, artifacts and pigs. Marriage, then, entails a preliminary accumulation of wealth, but since this is achieved by the group for the benefit of each of its members, the individual becomes dependent upon his 'classificatory brothers' and group solidarity has a material aspect overlapping the realm of myth and magic.

This is a situation which tends to create new tensions and which is maintained in a sometimes unstable equilibrium by certain more or less complex conventions embodying the notion of prestige. Prestige relates both to the individual and the group and operates in their relations

24. **Eastern Polynesias, Tahiti.** *Men's dance costumes.*

with the outside world. Within the group rivalry is confined to individuals, particularly in cases where the attributes of prestige are not clearly defined. As soon as there is systematization, rivalry exists with 'outsiders' while a fixed degree of equilibrium develops within the group.

Nowhere has technology advanced beyond the stage of polished stone tools, even in New Guinea where bronze axe-blades from Indonesia and antique Chinese porcelains are treated as treasures unutilized in everyday life. This is because the potential for economic development has been too limited to serve as an inducement or basis for a systematized division of labour and because material wealth provides few opportunities for exercising pressure, except insofar as it serves as a pretext for competitions in prestige between groups.

Typical of such a state of affairs is the development around a shrewd and wealthy individual of a group continually vying for prestige. In every case the group breaks up, at least partially, if the chief is seen to be losing ground vis-à-vis his principal rival. Duality, it would seem, is the general rule in such rivalries, since they invariably occur between two individuals or two groups. The protagonists do not remain the same, the temporary victor changing his opposite number progressively with each success. This duality can also be standardized, with the result that the rivalry is maintained between the same individuals.

The least formal pattern occurs among the Siuai in southeast Bougainville, Solomon Islands, and was studied by Douglas Oliver. The chief, *mumi*, is a man who has acquired reputation and prestige by his wealth and by the generous feasts he offers to his peers. By his intelligence and tact, and by the subtle manipulation to his own advantage of a series of loans constantly repaid and renewed, he has achieved a circle of dependants whose loyalty is conditioned by the continuance of his material success. Wealth, provided it is disbursed in a calculated and ostentatious manner, is thus a means of social mobility. But from the point of view of the *mumi* the slaughter of pigs to be given as food to a crowd of guests does not differ essentially from the destruction of blankets in the North American potlach. For even if food is given in exchange for food received, there is, nonetheless, the deliberate destruction of a potential for further enrichment.

The introduction of manufactured objects, whose relative scarcity makes them valuable, enables the process to be rationalized. Shell beads and cowries set in various ways on flexible mountings constitute treasures whose value never changes and they serve for ceremonial exchanges which have no economic implications on the occasion of births, marriages and deaths. But they can also be bartered for pigs and, at this level, acquire a commercial value and can be divided into exact parts, enabling them to be used as a measure of the *mumi's* generosity when making gifts to his guests. The process of accumulation thus shifts from a maximum to a minimum of risk, from a perishable product to one which stands the best chance of preservation. The surplus taro crop is used to rear pigs which can be used to acquire threaded beads. Clearly, however, beads are inanimate objects, whereas, despite the risks, the breeding of pigs offers the chance of a rapid multiplication of these fourfooted valuables.

On Maewo, in the New Hebrides, the problem has been solved by the storing of finely wrought mats, called 'money mats', inside a hut above a permanently burning green-wood fire whose smoke covers the mats with thick soot. The hut and its contents change hands and the value of the mats increases progressively with the thickness of the layer of soot.

The feasts given by the *mumi* to mark a step in his rise to importance provide an occasion for specific work performed under his orders and to his benefit, since he is responsible for the support of the workmen, the remuneration of the carvers and other expenses. The first stage is the construction of a great open pavilion which the male dependants use as a meeting place. Here they talk and even sleep. Next a set of big long drums is installed in the pavilion. These are used to summon the workers or simply as seats. Once these preliminaries are completed, and his followers firmly attached to his cause, the *mumi* sends an appropriate challenge to a rival, offering him a feast and gifts of such magnificence that if the latter cannot match them he will lose both face and his following. The career of a *mumi* proceeds in this manner from one challenge to another, with halts and temporary or lasting set-backs. This state of affairs is sufficiently general for the writer to have found it in southern central Malekula, where each village consists of a non-traditional structureless group established around a notable who has been able to construct a men's house, *nagamal*, and provide a dance-floor, *nasara*, surrounded by drums set in the ground. These drums, in Malekula, as among the Siuai, are of a simple, cylindrical type with a minimum of decoration.

It would seem that this arrangement, of a somewhat elastic order and open to all sorts of variants, often fails to come up to the exacting standards of the local theoreticians. A need was felt to build up more intricate systems and to devise more meticulous rituals so that each man's place could be largely predetermined. This would have the added advantage of making the situation more stable—but the evolutionary aspect of a society is never uniform. Several developments are actually found and in neighbouring districts these may overlap; but they can hardly be arranged, even tentatively, in a chronological sequence.

The hierarchy of grades

This unique institution, found in the centre and north of the New Hebrides, concerns essentially the men, though it has some echoes in the differences of rank among wives, differences which in almost every case are intended to emphasize, in a spectacular fashion, the social position acquired by the interested party in consequence of her husband's status.

The system is based upon the acquisition of a rank paid for in pigs at a fixed tariff. Payment is made to a group of elders, each member of which introduces the candidate to his own grade. These grades are arranged hierarchically: to each there pertains a series of privileges, not always pleasant. The essential difference between members of different grades is, in practice, that they cannot eat or cook together.

From the first grade of the series onwards, the eating of food prepared by women is forbidden. So is the use of products cultivated or even touched by women. Each member is obliged to cook his own food or to form a group with others of the same grade for this purpose. Life for elders at the top of the hierarchy can become extremely trying; they have to set up house with a younger man of the same grade whose function it is to help them abide by their own status regulations. Some of the huge buildings for men's reunions are divided into compartments, each with its own hearth, corresponding to a precise grade, where men having the same status come to eat and sleep. Those who are not allowed to partake together of cooked or raw food (fruit and the products of fishing or hunting) may not sit at the same level, nor sleep side by side, nor use the same implements.

Each grade has to have its own fields and also its own fruit-trees; these are forbidden to members of other grades by a distinctive sign cut in the bark. At ceremonies and at dances, its members paint motifs, appropriate to their grade, on their faces and fix in their hair, at the prescribed place, the special flower which they are privileged to use. They also thrust into their belts, at the level of the buttock fold, the bunches of coloured leaves which those of their rank use as body decorations.

This system calls for the accumulation of wealth, usually in terms of pigs. Here there is a new development. The upper canines of a pig are removed in its youth in order to allow the lower ones to develop into tusks without any wear on those of the upper jaw. The tusks then grow into a more or less protruding spiral until they come to form a complete circle. Some of them, the finest, curve on a single plane, with the point re-entering the root after penetrating the lower jaw and sometimes clamping both the jaws together. At this point in the growth of the tusk the animal suffers terribly and the women have to feed it with premasticated food. Such pigs are lean, skinny creatures which are kept alive only with difficulty, but this does not worry their owners, for their value lies in the degree of curvature of the tusks. The starting-point, in fact, is the concept of an 'ideal' tusk on which is based the value of the animal in question. Certain degrees of growth are defined by name and by particular markings on the curve. From the root to the tip the marks are further and further apart, in an irregular progression, the intervals corresponding to stages of growth recognised by breeders who are expert in such matters.

This method of fixing, for pigs, set values which increase steadily during their lifetime provides the basis for what might be termed a rationalisation of the trade in these animals. A borrowed pig will be repaid later with an animal whose value, calculated by the tusk, is not only that which the first animal's tusk would have acquired, had it lived, but includes a bonus as recompense for the owner. Since most people do not own enough pigs to attain a grade, animals have to be borrowed on all sides. Thanks to an intricate, memorised system of accounts, aided by a tally system marked on a cycas palm by breaking off an appropriate number of leaves at its base, each pig-owner can extend his holding indefinitely without much trouble. He is able, by numerous loans, to spread the risks which are assumed by the borrowers and to avoid much of the expense which he would incur if all the herd were permanently in his keeping, since this also requires a number of wives to rear them.

Each grade has a name which is also given to the group hearth assigned to it. Moreover, the acquisition of a grade involves a change in the initiate's name. The new name is announced publicly while the initiate takes part, with a spear, arrow or club, in the sacrifice of a pig of high value. This name is always in two parts, one of which consists of an invariable element corresponding to the grade and the other varying at the whim of the postulant or of the member who sponsors him. There is also a hierarchy of titles which corresponds to the hierarchy of grades.

This system is not, however, definitive, for although the higher grades and titles show a certain stability, the lower ones vary considerably in their number and duration from one village to another. Here we have one of the inevitable consequences of the practice of treating the pig as a unit of currency. Everything can be bought by means of pigs, from a pleasing song to an entire rite (with its material constituents, its songs and dances), or any part of it.

The village or the individual, after making such an acquisition, can use it to further personal

25. Polynesia, Cook Islands. *Chief's stool.* Museum of Primitive Art, New York.

prestige or split it into parts to be incorporated into various intricate ceremonies. The acquired rites can always be resold to any bidder, whether individual or group. Villages or districts, therefore, strive to make their hierarchical grades ever more complex and their rituals ever more elaborate by the incorporation of elements from outside, knowing that they will be able to recoup their expenses by allowing their neighbours to copy them.

Each ritual for the acquisition of a grade is completed by the erection of some kind of monument. There are various types ranging from a raised flat stone surrounded by ornamental plants to a carving on an upright stone or, more usually, one or more sculptures in wood or tree fern, painted and sheltered by a roof. These monuments, like the rituals, vary greatly, their execution ranging from the simplest to the most elaborate.

The rites last for several weeks, a part taking place usually every five days, and culminate on the day when the grade is assumed, which is also the day of payment. Each item has to be paid for: the title and the new personal name; the monument and each of its constituents:

materials, carving, paint, roof, ornaments, vegetables. A pig must be given for the right to mark the prohibition on the trees, another for the flower to be placed in the hair, another for the coloured leaves for bodily adornment, another for the facial painting, another for admission to the new hearth, several, in the higher grades, for the fence of wood and stone set up round the private hut, another to ensure that the drum call appropriate to the man's grade is used for his benefit and so forth. On such occasions, more than a hundred pigs may change hands. The dogged persistence that is required to advance in this social hierarchy can well be

26. New Caledonia, Huailu. *Ceremonial avenue, Tyibey clan.*

imagined. Many lose heart midway or lack the means necessary to complete their advancement.

Here it would appear that we have a form of government by the rich, since they occupy the highest grades and not only reap the greatest benefit from their prestige, but also exercise authority over their own and near-by villages, provided that there is no one of equal rank there to be a rival. This authority derives basically from a widespread fear of the magic power of members of the highest grades who are regarded as a species of supermen. But although accession to the grades is governed by a well-established, precisely defined system, involving individuals in a network of obligations and privileges, the extent of the authority which pertains to each dignitary is not clearly determined. It is, in most cases, dependent on his own personality. The 'well-born' children of large-scale pig-owners enjoy as a birthright a definite advantage. On the other hand, the rates for the acquisition of grades in such cases are set at double those imposed on the poorer classes. Thus custom offsets social inequality by maintaining as a factor of prestige the obligation to distribute one's wealth when one has the privilege of power.

There are other possibilities inherent in the concept of titles acquired in the course of a lifetime. In the south-central region of the New Hebrides archipelago, between the south of Epi and Efate, we find an apparent desire to exploit to the full the logical possibilities of another type of organization, which in fact derives from certain trifling local variations. The small island of Tongariki is the place where, even today, an apparently aristocratic system operates most effectively.

In addition to his individual personal name, each adult male can subsequently receive another title, which gives him the right to use certain parcels of land throughout the island without regard to the territorial limits of the four villages. If he does not obtain a title, an islander has no claim to lands, except on a precarious and revocable tenure, a situation which holds true for only one of the island's inhabitants at the present day.

Groups of titles are placed under the authority of the holder of a title which is traditionally considered to be higher within the same village. Each village consists of a number of these groups or *varea* whose material existence used to be marked by the construction of a communal men's house, also called *varea*. The chief of each *varea* receives an offering of the first-fruits of the yam harvest and in some cases a pig from each title-holder who owes him allegiance. In return he has to officiate at the ceremony of laying-on of hands for the installation of each title-holder. The chief of each *varea* depends, in his turn, upon the holder of a higher title who is then living in one of two villages which have higher status than the two others, inhabited by persons of lower rank. Local society is therefore divided into parallel hierarchies which do not correspond in any way to territorial divisions. It would seem that the parcelling out and haphazard division of scattered pieces of land is the outcome of a determination to avoid disputes regarding property between territorial groups and thus to prevent outbreaks of internecine wars. The principal chiefs depend in turn on a suzerain who resides in one of the other islands of the Shepherd's group, especially in Emae. These chiefs, however, can have a number of title-holders living outside Tongariki who owe them allegiance.

The methods of succession to titles appear to be the most operative element in this system. They could be hereditary but in fact are nothing of the kind. The holder of a title is chosen by the principal title-holders of the hierarchy upon which he depends. The oldest members of his *varea* play some part in this election. There have been instances, though they are rare, when men holding a title of inferior grade have been promoted to a higher one; in so doing they abandoned their original scattered estate for another one, just as scattered. Conversely, men who have been away from the island for too long or who are considered not to have carried out adequately the duties of their rank have been put back to the foot of the ladder, their titles and their lands being withdrawn.

The reason for the persistence of this formalized society with its hierarchical series of nomenclatures and groups, where men are differentiated in terms of an elective procedure, is to be found in the mechanism of land tenure. Land-holding and membership of local groups, *varea*, are independent of the patrilineal kinship structure, which prevails in the south of the archipelago and is structurally very close to the kinship prevailing in central Polynesia (Tonga).

In the Samoan Islands we find a system of traditional ¦chieftainships still in favour with this Polynesian people. Their *matai* system is not very different in principle from that described for the Shepherd Islands. A *matai* is a man who has been chosen to receive a title belonging to his local group. This title-holder can be chosen from inside or outside the group, in the absence of a valid heir in the male line. The choice is made by all the members of the extended family, *ainga* (a local patrilinear, exogamic group), whether by descent or by adoption. Less frequently the right of nomination is assigned to a man of high rank or to the descendant of a man, even a foreigner, who has rendered some signal service in times past and has received as a reward the *pule*, the power to nominate the new title-holder.

The importance of these titles derives from the fact that they give the holder authority over the members of the *ainga* and the landed property which belongs to the group. This property control, also called *pule*, is the power to administer in some measure the goods of the group to the general profit, but without owning them and without possessing the power of the *matai* to dispose of parcels of land belonging to some members for the profit of others. He is unable to refuse the application for a building-site for a hut, but he has the choice of the plot to be allotted to his kinsman who makes such a request. In order to finance a community project or the preparation of a feast he is permitted to forbid, *pro tempore*, the private harvesting of scattered plots, so that the yield therefrom can be assigned to the collective undertaking. The *matai* can have his fields cultivated by the adults of his group, provided he divides the produce fairly among them. The members of the group owe him help and assistance, on request, and regular gifts of food.

The holder of a title can, in the last resort, be a woman and there are many instances of this. In principle, the qualities and personality of the candidate are the main criteria of selection intended to assure peace and harmony within the group. It is not enough to be the son or brother of the previous holder, except in the case of a title of high rank. In this case closeness of blood-relationship is a preponderant consideration. A title can be withdrawn, by general consent, if the holder does not fulfil the duties of his rank. His selection has necessarily depended on his attitude towards his predecessor, but his continuance depends upon his subsequent conduct towards the group as a whole. At once formalized and ceremonial in appearance, but easy-going, almost democratic in reality, the institution has survived in a dynamic form and is still basic to the modern Samoan State.

The appearance of democracy in a group property-holding system is enhanced by the institutions called *fono*: village, district or regional councils which control public affairs. The order of seating and speaking, as it applies to each of the *matai* (the only participants) is pre-ordained by a mnemonic device known as *fa'alupenga*. At the level of the village *fono* we find the classical distinction between the highest title-holder, *ali'i*, and the orator, *tulafale*, whose function is linked with a precise title and whose authority may, in fact, be more important than that of the chief to whom in principle he owes allegiance. The kingdom, an independent political entity governed by a chief with the title of *Tui*, testifies to a delicate and unstable equilibrium. For each of the local hierarchies of *matai* has private alliances, vis-à-vis the principal *ali'i* sometimes separately, sometimes concurrently with an *ali'i* of another region. Certain groups assure a minimal internal cohesion for the whole, while others maintain external contacts.

This multiplicity of intersecting allegiances allowed an anarchic system to flourish, with the result that, in contrast to the Tongan situation, a unitary state could never be maintained in Samoa before the European period. The unity of a district or of a region was symbolized by the *tuinga*, the elaborate coiffure worn by the *taupou*, the virgin daughter of the *ali'i*, or his son, the *manaia*, both of whom played an important part in the ceremonial cycle which called into play all the heraldic lore of the orators of several districts or regions.

Hereditary chieftainships

As soon as authority becomes hereditary, the function of a title of nobility changes to some extent, being no longer at the mercy of the choice of all the interested parties. But the principle always remains that allegiance to the chief is a measure of the extent to which he respects the rights of those subordinate to him; they can leave him if they have serious cause for complaint. Sometimes the court of a chief may even include a dignitary whose task is to remonstrate with him or even to punish him physically. Elsewhere, a group of other dignitaries can decide collectively to depose the holder of a chieftainship. This in no way inhibits a profound respect for the person of a chief. It is a classic convention that he must sit at a higher level, his head, by its sacred character, being above those of all others present.

Even without the presence of the Samoan orator who possesses the traditional lore, decides points of etiquette and holds, by virtue of his office, the tables of allegiances and land tenure, no hereditary chief is, in fact, an autocrat. The term chieftainship, which is, in the last resort, unsatisfactory if we take it literally, implies here an equilibrium or a set of delicate equilibria whose relative instability is a factor in the dynamism of society. The study of the history of these chieftainships over the past two centuries shows a succession of authorities imposing themselves one after another, of groupings and schisms, all generally culminating in more complex structures.

In New Caledonia the chief confines himself to a political role at least vis-à-vis other groups: he initiates peaceful ceremonial relations, or decides for a war, in which he does not take command. He is the figurehead representing the group as a whole. In his shadow there lives an unobtrusive man whose word may carry more weight than his own: he is called 'master of the land' because, in contrast to the chief, his business is to know all that concerns the soil and the tenure of land. He arbitrates in all disputes relating to them and is in permanent contact with the invisible powers on whom the fertility of the soil depends.

The chief does not normally possess either magical power or religious prerogative, even within his own clan. With regard to the group, on the other hand, he is considered to be responsible for the good order of things, as if his personal conduct had cosmological implications. If there is a failure of the harvest, his misconduct will have been the cause, and he will find against him at this moment both the master of the soil and the master of agrarian rites. Each region has a master of yams who will eat the first yam of the new harvest and pronounce, at this time, the auguries for the harvest.

This official, in his religious function, determines the commencement of the ceremonial

41

27. New Guinea, Kalabu. *Men's ceremonial great house.*
28. New Guinea, Lake Chambuli. *Orator's stool.*

period, and this for a district which may embrace several chieftainships. No chief would wish to make an enemy of him.

A similar situation is to be found in northern Malekula, New Hebrides, where the clan master of the first-fruits extends his authority over several chieftainships grouped in pairs, to which the myths attribute a common origin. The two men act together both in war and in ceremonial, and take it in turn to offer one another enormous slaughterings of pigs. In New Caledonia we find a more complicated modality of this dualism: the chieftainships of the great part of the island are grouped into two fratries which are also partners in ceremony and in war.

A still greater complexity obtains in the Isle of Pines, the Loyalty Islands and the Fijian archipelago, where the composition of the chief's court is particularly elaborate.

Each clan provides a dignitary for the court, usually the chief, unless the latter prefers to name a deputy to carry out his duties. Each dignitary has a specific role to fulfil, a privilege which gives him a portion of authority within the chieftainship, if not, as is sometimes the case, over the chief himself. The duties are of all sorts: those of spokesman, priest,

diviner, war-magician, guardian for each of the directions, messenger for communications with the exterior along specific routes, craftsman for the construction of canoes or huts, maker of maces, fisherman, pounder of a special type of yam or other foodstuff with a symbolic value employed in an annual rite, councillor, food-taster, a personal servant who alone may touch what remains of the chief's food or his leavings, and sleep in the same hut, where his body may serve as a pillow for the principal wife while she has intercourse with the chief. Each of these duties is undertaken as circumstances require: at occasional ceremonial events in the course of the year, or on a more or less permanent and continuing basis. The principal officers used more often to control the chief than to serve him and could in all cases, within the framework of their privileges, take initiatives without waiting for orders. One of them at council meetings, used to sum up the discussion which it was his duty to close by announcing the decision, in which the chief himself often took little part.

In addition to this courtly organisation, there were differences within the chieftainship's sphere of influence. Within the district limits, where the chief's authority was theoretically accepted by the population, he had his true subjects, descendants of the cadet branches of his clan, who owed him unquestioning allegiance. Besides these people, who represented between a quarter and a third of the whole population, there were other, more or less autonomous groups, who accepted the presence of the chief, provided it did not weigh too heavily upon them.

There are the descendants of the oldest inhabitants of the land whose allegiance to the chieftainship is purely nominal since its existence is a function of their goodwill. They are the arbitrators in all questions of real property. Considered as dangerous—in the magical sense— because of their permanent relationship with the invisible powers who are lords of the soil and its fertility, they can be represented at the principal chiefdom by chiefs of lesser importance, but of great repute, because of the power with which they are invested by the intermediary of their subjects, 'the men of the soil.' To them we must add other secondary chieftainships which have preserved their own organisation and their own subjects. These represent the old, scattered political authorities of the country before the development of a more unitary structure established a contrived equilibrium between these different elements.

Group celebrations

Life in Oceania presents two aspects. On the one hand are the homes, either grouped together or dispersed: small, simply fitted huts where the women and children live, and where the men do not feel quite at home. On the other is the area organised for ceremonies and dances: an area of earth carefully stripped of plants (Melanesia in general), a wide path flanked by side paths and covered with closely-cropped sward (New Caledonia; Polynesia sward only). In both cases, coconut trees, erythrinas and banyans provide shade for the inhabitants, who avoid being exposed to sunlight whenever possible. Nearby stands a large, sometimes gigantic hut built to a round or a rectangular ground plan with a conical or ridge roof; this is sometimes horizontal and sometimes turned up at the front in the form of a pointed arch. The building in some cases has thick walls to protect against the cold, at others it is

29. New Guinea, Sepik. *Anthropomorphic decoration on a great house.*

open to allow free passage to the breeze. It is raised on piles or on a platform of stones and earth. It is here that the men meet sleep, deal with the affairs of the community, drink *kava* or give themselves up at times, in a very few regions, to the pleasures of organized homosexuality.

In front of the communal house the great space is open on the days of ceremonies and the nights of dances to the women and the children. As the setting for collective rituals, and for aesthetic manifestations. In Polynesia (Tahiti) and the Hawaiian Islands, the emergence of a priestly caste and of somewhat esoteric theological systems has given rise to the construction of earth platforms, stone monuments and enclosures reserved for religious rituals. Secular festivities take place elsewhere, sometimes in a less spectacular setting.

The public rituals assume the form of stage plays, with, as actors, local men, partners in ceremonials who must be invited, and, as audience, the local women and children, neighbouring groups and men belonging to groups which have come purely out of curiosity. The programme is often rounded off with women's dances. In the arena, in front of at least one immense hut and against a background of leaves or bluish peaks, the ceremonial develops along a predetermined pattern and rhythm. Nightfall is the most auspicious time for vigorous group activities even if the dance place has been planted with araucarias and ancient banyans to shade a great part of it from the sun. At these times the natives of Oceania flee the heat of the sun which would otherwise compel them to moderate these displays or set back their time of celebration.

Bodies gleam with perfumed coconut oil. The lines of each man's face are picked out in different colours; in his hair are flowers, combs and feathers. The muscles of his legs are striped with white shells and red or white bands. Extraordinary costumes make their appearance, in which all the resources of modelling and collage are employed, and every kind of vegetable product incorporated. Their value stems from the long months of effort, journeyings, and negotiations to obtain, by traditional routes, from neighbours near the coast, components from the sea: shells, and discs of tridachna in crescent or bar shape. But other elements may be used in combination or by themselves which are of local origin and many of which are most surprising:—spider-webs, bronzed beetles arranged in rows, coloured plaster-work in mud, or plaster to be coloured subsequently, and complex patterns of leaves in all hues from trees like the dragon-tree and many others.

For an observer watching this group-play from a tree-top, the festivities in progress are seen to trace motifs on the soil: longitudinal, transverse, circular, oval, spiral, devised with a careful eye to a central point or an axis. Sometimes we seem to detect a symbolism directly related to the myths of life and death or some locally accepted cosmogony. The gyrations of the dancers correspond to the undersea or underground dance of the gods, just as to the deeds of living men correspond the inverted acts of dwellers in the lands of the dead, where men feed on things repugnant to the living.

30. Australia, Arnhem Land. *Body painting marking the lifting of an embargo.*

THE RELIGIOUS ASPECT
OF SOCIAL LIFE

Nowhere in Oceania does the idea of death involve that of annihilation. It is rather another kind of life. The living lean upon the dead who surround them perpetually and who, in certain cases, take the visible form of trees or animals. It is their good- or ill-will which rules the destinies of their children or grand-children.

The cult of the ancestors, found everywhere, even in Christianized regions at the present day, makes itself felt, unobtrusively, on the everyday level by means of murmured prayers and minute offerings placed in secret places. It is the guarantee of a certain stability in an evolving world where the isolated man feels dazed and 'lost'; a balancing factor to which the men of Oceania still cling. Its lack of formalism has permitted it to survive. But even if it always remains beneath the surface, its semi-clandestine nature rarely allows it to serve as a source of aesthetic inspiration.

On the other hand it may form a solid foundation, even a dynamic factor, in the messianic movements, Cargo Cults, which have flourished in Melanesia in the past decades after appearing for the first time in Polynesia at the beginning of the last century (Mamaia in Tahiti, Siovili in Samoa, Tuka in Fiji). Such movements often include elements from Christianity. An old myth already explained the difference in material standards between Europeans and Oceanians as the result of a violation of a tabu by the Oceanian's ancestor which led to the departure of one of two brothers with the material wealth which then belonged to the Whites, while the other preserved the 'real' foodstuffs. In another version the hero who brings civilization leaves, promising a messianic return.

The easy acceptance of white settlers was often linked with these myths and their hope of better things to come. The general disillusion was usually rationalized in terms of the theft of the Cargo by the Whites who changed over the labels on the goods in the holds and thus got possession of the objects which the dead were sending to their black descendants. As a result attempts were made to arrange for the goods to be sent direct, for the return of the ancestors with all their power, and by means of a cataclysm to bring about a reversal of social values so that Blacks lord it over Whites and the sources of all wealth are installed on the territory of the former.

Thus the outbursts, which are sometimes violent and always passionate and which frequently develop into anti-European affairs, at least in their later phases, are one of the indications of the exceptional importance of ancestor-cults in the complicated religious structure of Oceania.

In former times, it was thought proper, outside the place of cult where an invisible presence was addressed, to erect a memorial to the memory of the ancestor. Of these the New Zealand

31. New Guinea, Sepik. *Basketry mask.*

sculptures are the most elaborate. They represent, by way of conventional themes, persons endowed with a recognized historicity. Elsewhere the same role is filled by figurines surmounted by a skull with modelled features. These are found in the New Hebrides (the *rambaramb* of South Malekula) and New Guinea and the resemblance to a real face is often very striking.

The same need to raise a memorial to the ancestor is the basis of the complicated aesthetics of the *malanggan* of New Ireland and the neighbouring small islands. As in the case of the sculptures of the New Caledonian 'big house,' the *malanggan* consists of a group of pieces of

carved wood, specially made and erected on the occasion of a commemorative feast given in honour of one or more dead persons, each of whom is represented by a carved figure. The group of figures, and their arrangement on a decorated platform, is the property of a clan which can cede the right of carving them to another clan: in which case it will itself have to acquire another carved and painted group from a neighbouring community.

The ancestors thus honoured are usually those of the uterine kin. The ritual, which consists of representing their image in association with numerous decorative and mythical themes, is in

32. New Guinea, Asmat. *Mask for the jipae funerary rite*.
33. New Hebrides, Tomman Island, Malekula. *Overmodelled skulls*.

no way intended to affect their standing in the other world or even to gratify the dead. It seems that there was inherent in this practice, in a materially disinterested manner, a desire for prestige, even an obligation imposed on the responsible clan, with the possible penalty of considerable loss of face in public opinion. Thus homage to the dead is paralleled by homage to the living, and the death of a clansman many years before serves as a pretext for a collective ceremony aimed at the glorification of the group. True ancestor-worship runs on different lines.

The making of a *malanggan* seems also to have had as its object the re-establishment of equilibrium in the local cosmos, since its prolonged absence could react unfavourably on the harvests and life of the men who failed to make it. This seems to hold good at least as regards the immovable articles in wood—the attitude to masks, or anyhow to certain masks, being apparently different. Thus, in most cases, making images of the dead is an act far removed from filial piety as we understand it. The *malanggan* is one of the elements of group cohesion vis-à-vis the outside world. And it is this which counts, especially in New Ireland, where the members of a matrilineal clan are scattered through several hamlets, for in it they find one of the rare means of becoming a corporate entity in a positive sense.

To sum up, the cult of the ancestors was often not a public matter, until relatively recently, among groups in revolt against Christianity, whose effects have disappointed them. Collective ancestor worship, publicly practised, has become the driving force of the native Cargo Cults, the most recent form of that messianism which has flourished to some extent everywhere under the influence of European contacts and the new religious ideas these have imported. It is

34. Australia, Arnhem Land. *Funerary posts*.

not surprising, therefore, that the cult of the dead has led to so few plastic interpretations.

Is this also true of Totemism? This classic term covers a variety of institutions even in Oceania. Many authors have tended to include within it all usages of plant and animal symbolism or natural phenomena. Such symbolism is extremely common especially in relation to persons of high rank who are customarily identified with certain birds, such as the owl, the eagle, the *notou*, or the frigate-bird. This analogy leads by a natural transition to speaking of such-and-such a bird in such-and-such a place. In Hualu valley, New Caledonia, a reference to the owl of Neburu for example is tantamount to naming one of the chiefdoms of the valley. None of this corresponds to a ritual nor to any specific belief.

Certain great huts of the chiefly clan bear the figurative representation of a bird, or a fork of wood that symbolises it, on the roof crest. In the New Hebrides, the roof ridge figure represents an eagle with outspread wings, *nabal*, symbol of the clan's prestige: the man who reaches the summit of the hierarchy of grades will himself be identified with this bird. Elsewhere it will be the shark. It is a case of a descriptive symbolism giving rise to plastic imagery.

52

35. New Ireland. *Detail of* 36.
36. New Ireland. *Malanggan mast.* Basle.

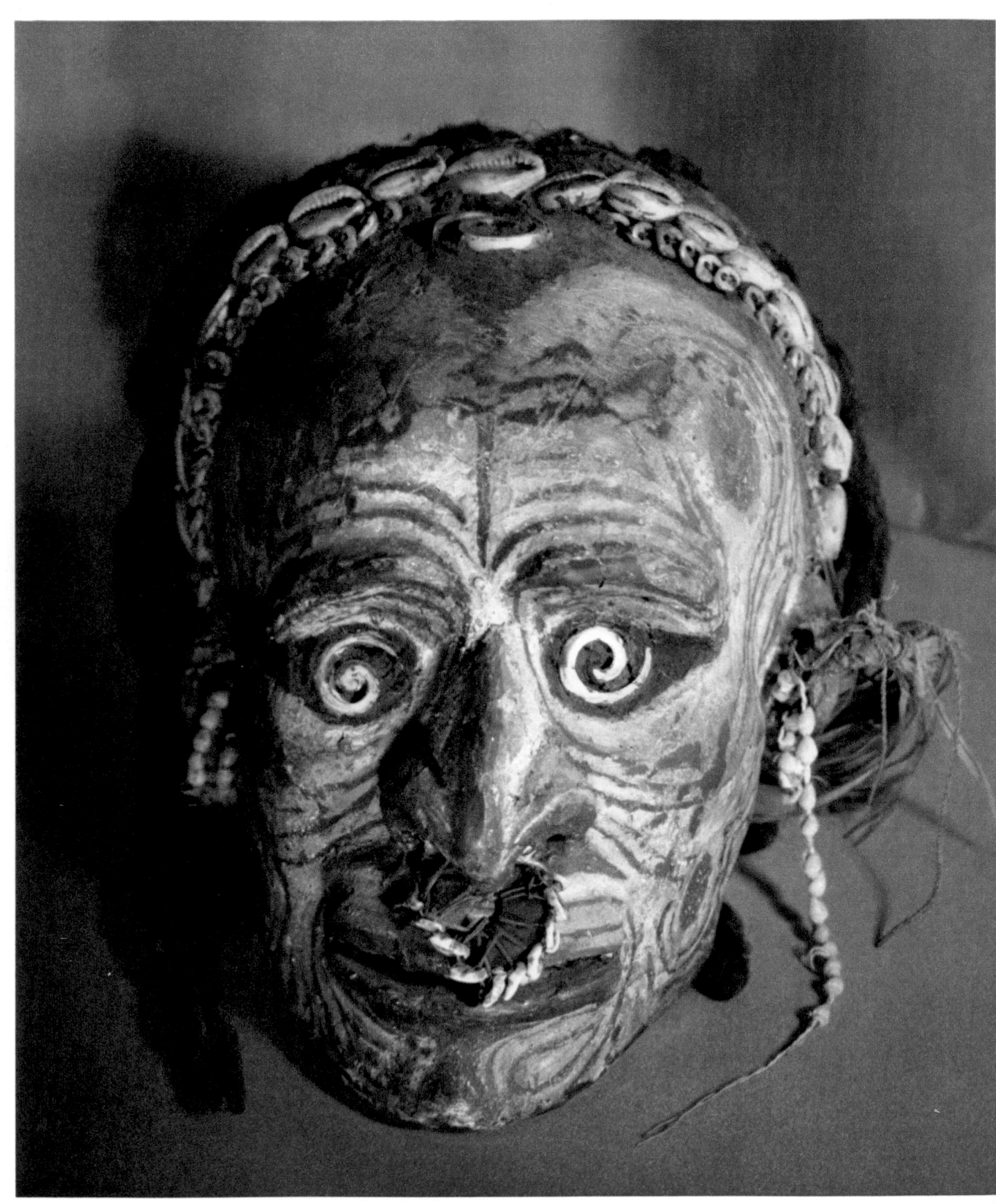

37. New Guinea, Sepik. *Overmodelled skull.*

Another system of thought leads to the classification of the universe, and particularly of the useful parts of the universe, into categories, each of which is allotted to a human group. This group has at its command the magic rites which enable constant multiplication of animal and plant species and the beneficent or maleficent intervention of the atmospheric forces which are attributed to it, in virtue of a sort of contract. This applies to Australian totemism.

Such concepts may be more or less systematized. At Efate, New Hebrides, the totality of local patrilineal social groups is intersected by a number of matrilineal linkages, *naflak*,

38. New Ireland. *Malanggan openwork bas-relief*. Basle.

each of which bears the name of an animal, a plant or an object useful to man's nourishment. Marriage is confined to those who do not come under the same symbol. This institution served another purpose. The compulsory solidarity between members of the same *naflak* provided them with one or more allies in each village. This ensured an advance warning of an impending attack or furnished a refuge in case of need. It was, in a warlike and divided society, a factor making for a certain stability, and preventing the destruction of whole groups. The introduction of fire-arms at the beginning of the nineteenth century cancelled out this advantage. Murderous internal wars, encouraged by the arms-dealers, added to the massacres perpetrated by pirates who roved these waters, and deaths from introduced diseases, would have eliminated the local population, if it were not for the timely establishment of a proper administration.

In New Caledonia each clan has one or more animals, plants or atmospheric elements serving as its symbol, by which it is referred to in speeches. There is no rite of multiplication.

Each of these totems plays an essential role in the agricultural life of the clan, as prayers are offered to it for the success of the harvests. The totem of the uterine clan is the most dreaded, and it is needful to propitiate it. If this were not done, it would take its revenge for such lack of respect by penetrating the offender's body and causing the particular illness which falls within its province. Offsetting this is the possibility of sending the totem into the body of an enemy, who will have to die unless a diviner can diagnose what totem has entered into the sick man and the priest of the responsible totem can be persuaded to intervene. It should be noted that, despite the terms of respect applied to the totem, which is called grandfather, there is no question of its being the group's ancestor. Indeed this whole notion of descent from a 'totem', which was so much stressed by earlier writers who had no opportunity to verify the values attributed to the collections of symbols since their informants, often missionaries, tended to give a religious connotation to everything of a pagan appearance.

Although some myths tell of men born of trees, fruit, or the union of a woman with a protean animal in human form, these myths are not closely linked with the New Caledonian totemic system. Elsewhere, especially in the New Hebrides, many groups subscribe to a myth according to which they are descended from a certain fruit or animal, without this symbolic ancestor being the object of a specific cult, or even in most cases, of a food tabu. Indeed, food tabus are often justified by reasons which seem to have no connection with the alleged totemism.

In Oceania as a whole we find, either separately or together among the different factors contributing to group cohesion, group food tabus, animal or plant symbols, myths relating to a miraculous origin, and agrarian magic, both beneficent and maleficent—for rain may be sent inopportunely to one's neighbours. These form the elements of social and ritual groupings whose forms and functions vary from one place to another.

Douglas Oliver has rightly noted in Siuai how the myths which deal with the animal origin of a clan and the way it came into being account for the system of land tenure prevailing in the local group. Such a function seems to explain the role of myths which have a definite link with specific place-names. Their recital seems to justify the presentation of a list of places which is in reality a claim to land.

It seems difficult under these circumstances to group these features under the term of totemism. In most cases, evidence is lacking to relate them, with absolute certainty, to the many animal representations found in Oceanian art.

The cycles of initiation often offer a greater possibility for aesthetic expression. It is, however, convenient to distinguish between initiations and the *rites de passage* which are organized for the youths either before or after puberty as circumstances warrant. In order to secure a sufficient number of candidates, youngsters of all ages are accepted. Basic to initiation is the surgical operation of slitting the prepuce. True circumcision is rare.

During the two-weeks period of convalescence the wounds are carefully washed and dressed daily with herbal products. This involves a phase of seclusion in order to ensure discipline, and in the course of this the adolescents are subjected to all kinds of insults and vexations in order to make them manly. At the end of this period, the youths who have thus won their entry into manhood are returned to their families wearing festive attire. The circumciser is paid, as are the men who have acted, whether or not as a result of precise kinship ties, as personal guardians of each of the adolescents during the period of seclusion.

This period also often serves as the pretext for a terrifying dramatic performance meant to impress the women, who are intended to believe that a monster has swallowed their children and then restored them to life. An assortment of instruments producing both shrill and muffled sounds are played, either within the enclosure of the initiates or in the forest nearby, in such a way as to give the women the impression that the monster is giving forth. The youths are then initiated into the secrets of the voice and are taught to play the bull-roarers and other wind instruments, under threat of dire penalties if they reveal the secret.

The monster theme lends itself to plastic representations, which serve both to scare the novices themselves, before teaching them how to construct the body of the creature, and to enable the women and the frightened children to catch a glimpse of the awesome creature from a safe distance. The making of these figures from vegetable plaques, stretched and glued on a light framework, calls for much ingenuity. This is an initiation of a limited type. It is distinguishable from the incision period and associated with a customary payment, in pigs needless to say, for integration into a restricted group whose members share the knowledge both of the employment of musical instruments and of the manufacture of hats, costumes and masks, or of a group of artifacts that will be shown, always from a distance, to the rest of the population.

Such 'secret societies' as they are wrongly called (since their membership is usually a matter of public knowledge), can be unique or multiple, permanent or temporary. Their religious character is a moot point. The beliefs imposed upon the uninitiated as to what goes on inside the enclosure, are connected with the alleged intervention of the dead, or of terrifying beings. Only the initiates know that no form of cult is required and that the secrets to be learned are of a purely material nature. Since it is extremely rare for any man not to be initiated into some secret of this ceremony, it is obvious that usually these masquerades, even though more or less genuine, have no authentic communal or religious significance.

But this is not always the case. In Fiji there were once secret rituals called *nangga*, practised within a rectangular enclosure marked out with standing stones. Private cult places were marked by stone pyramids and by a temple, *bure*, of small size, but carefully constructed. This enclosure was used in turn by members of two fratries from one year to another, neither of the two groups having an exact knowledge of the other's rituals.

By seeking communion with the dead, these rituals were intended to ensure the success of the harvests. They consisted of tests for novices and an initiation into the use of certain musical instruments. For the women, on a given day, the rite consisted in crawling along the ground and bringing the sexual organs into contact with freshly made piles of earth like those in the yam fields. Afterwards came a session of sexual promiscuity in which the normal kinship tabus were waived. During this ceremony invocations were addressed to the dead collectively.

The famous confraternity of the Arioi, in the Society Islands, seems to have been the most elaborate of these institutions. The male and female members of the group, which practised infanticide, went from district to district giving dramatic representations of the myths, interspersed with mock fights. The confraternity had branches on each of the principal islands and its headquarters at Raiatea.

A hierarchy of eight grades provided the Arioi with a strictly ordered internal organisation. They had a large following of servants who were not bound by the same obligations and whose presence saved them from material cares. The whole society travelled in a regular fleet of several dozen double canoes and enjoyed lavish hospitality everywhere. The Arioi were thought to be possessed by the gods: indeed, one of the conditions of admission to the confraternity was a demonstration of the fact of this divine possession.

Compulsory service in the lower grade of initiates, from which only a few individuals of high rank were exempt, enabled members to learn, over several years, the recitations, chants and traditional dances as well as to rehearse carefully the theatrical performances dealing with sacred and profane themes. The god of the confraternity was Oro, the god of war, in whose honour the Arioi practised special techniques of combat. For public presentation the recitations and chants, ranging from descriptions of the creation of the world to crude or comic details about the lives of the gods, had to be known by rote.

Australia, Arnhem Land. *Paintings on bark.*
39. Oenpelli. *Dignuk, the night fishing-spirit.*
40. Oenpelli. *The kangaroo spirit, Kandarik.*
41. Goulburn Island. *Underground tubers with their bines.*
42. Oenpelli. *The Namarakain spirits.*

The dances seem to have had as their theme the representation (as realistically as possible) of acts of love and procreation. These entertainments were reserved to the lower grade; Arioi of higher standing were content to enjoy the privileges of the confraternity without having to make any personal contribution. Indeed the masters of the Arioi were regarded as being a species of superman, earthly representatives of the gods, a status confirmed by their privileged existence, exempt from the ordinary rules of life.

The sexual promiscuity in which they indulged (so often described by writers of the period, from the French Consul Moerenhout to the missionary chroniclers) was confined to the lower orders; seen against the general background of their daily lives, it brings to mind the orgies of Greek and Roman antiquity. This was one of the reasons which, in early days, led to the view that the Polynesians had a civilization which Europeans could appreciate, a civilization almost worthy of being exalted to their level.

The existence of masks has already been noted. This class of artifact calls for special mention: are they theatrical accessories or rather an essential element of ritual and of religious drama?

In the islands of the Torres Straits the mask was worn in public but the name of the wearer had to remain secret. Masks representing human beings used to be worn at the time of the harvest feasts on Mabuiag. Dancers, wearing masks portraying a sword fish, took part in a ritual intended to ensure the coming of the rainy season. On Aurid a mask representing a human figure with skulls above it was the image of the god Kulka, to whom were offered the skulls of slain enemies. On Yam the hero-civilisers Sigai and Maiu, who according to the myth came from Australia, are associated with effigies and masks of tortoise-shell representing the hammerhead shark and the cayman. The disclosure of their true nature was part of the initiation of the young men: for this reason they were shown only within the sacred enclosure.

It is difficult to distinguish the masks from the head-dresses of the Banks Islands, which conceal the wearer under a cloak of leaves. These do not represent anything in particular, except an elaborately painted geometrical design which seems to derive from the features of the human face.

The local Men's Society is divided into a number of confraternities called *Tamate*. As the Rev. H.H. Codrington wrote: 'From time to time the members rouse themselves into activity to bring themselves into evidence, to attract recruits, to impress the people with a sense of their importance, and to enjoy a festival. Then they begin to make new masks and dresses within their lodge, and the solemn sound of the *linge tamate* warns all without that the mysteries have begun. The country is said to be closed, *o vanua we gona*, no one can venture along the paths without the risk of being beaten by the *tamate*. They assume the greatest licence in carrying off all they want, robbing gardens and stripping fruit-trees for their feast, and then any one will suffer who has spoken or acted without due respect to the society. The ghosts in disguise will rush into the villages, chasing the terrified women and children, and beating anyone they can catch... but there are some that do not terrify or beat, but come out to show their finery and dance.'

Further on he touched upon the social function of these groupings: '... in the early morning one day, in the island of Mota' a strange cry was heard repeated from every quarter, shrill,

43. New Guinea, Asmat. *So-called ancestor figure.* Brussels.

44. New Guinea, Sepik. *Wooden mask*. Museum of Primitive Art, New York.
45. New Guinea, Sepik, Tambanaman. *Mask being worn.*

prolonged and unmistakable. It was the cry of the *tamate*... Upon enquiry we were told that in the evening before a man in anger had taken up his bow. In accordance with the teaching of Bishop Patteson, and with the authority of the great man of the island, the society of the Great *Tamate* had forbidden the use of the bow and arrow in private quarrels under penalty of a fine to them. On this occasion the man who had been guilty of the offence hastened to atone for it with a pig, and all was quiet again.'

Here we have a formal aspect of social control, one of the possible techniques of managing public affairs.

In the New Hebrides, as in the Banks Islands, most of the masks are not explained by any myths. (Some notable exceptions are described below). Most of the masks bear names which are those of the specific ritual to which they pertain. They may consist only of animal representations. The principal ones bear the names of the gods (*temar=tamate=*death). But it is not usual to profess to recognize in them any definite person. It seems as if, in the absence of a word for mask in the language, the use of the term meaning death or god was more convenient.

46. Torres Strait. Mabuiag Island. *Tortoise-shell mask*. British Museum.

The bearer of the mask thus represents a group of men to whom the mask belongs, because each has paid the price for seeing it at close quarters and learning how to make it. The mask can be linked more particularly with a privilege, as in the south of Malekula. Those who have acquired, by payment, the right to make it, have at their disposal several minutes in the course of each ceremony, when they parade round the dance floor, the head partly concealed by what is a heavy head-dress covered with faces rather than a mask in the strict sense.

In New Caledonia we find once again a religious element in the mask. It is the only carved work which represents a specific mythological figure and not the anonymous horde of ancestors. It is the god, the selfsame god, with bright skin and body spangled with eyes, and bearing the name Pijeva, who leads the dance of the dead in their country beneath the waters. He can be seen weaving his way through the troubled waters of the estuaries in the form of a shark, or in the guise of a lizard, or as bubbles coming to the surface at the foot of a waterfall. Or he may appear as a person wearing a mask and tunic of net and plumes. Then he is called Gomawe, though he is recognized as being identical with Pijeva. And he also presides over the making and keeping of the pearl-shell coins which make up each clan's treasure, in which case he goes by the name of Urupwe.

In the northern part of the 'Mainland' of New Caledonia we find a great variety of masks corresponding to a family of gods whose forms are somewhat hazy and who may, in the last resort, be no more than doublets of Pijeva.

47. New Britain, Sulka. *Tall ceremonial head-dress*. Basle.

The wearer of a New Caledonian mask has special prerogatives and may strike the spectators or play tricks on them provided he does not overstep the accepted bounds.

Masked persons take part in certain funeral rites, *jipae*, among the Asmat in the southwest of New Guinea. The name is simply that of the tree whose bark supplies the basic material of their masks. The object is to drive from the country the dead victims of head-hunters, by forcing them to follow the cassowary of the sun on her daily voyage westward to the land of the dead. To avoid their return with the sun, on the morrow, the ceremony ends with an attack on the mask-wearers and with their simulated deaths. Each mask represents a specific dead person: the wearer of the mask acts ritually in the name of the dead man's family, who have to support him while the mask is being made.

Thus the religious function of plastic representations strikes us as elusive, sometimes indeed incomprehensible, since every element varies from place to place in its nature and its symbolism. The Polynesian region, however, famous for its theology, its divine hierarchies and its literary cosmogonies, might be expected to show more homogeneity and bring more comfort to the systematic spirit.

But here we must go warily. Complex divine hierarchies do not obtain everywhere in Polynesia. In the south of the New Hebrides, on Aniwa Island, where Polynesian is spoken, the great god Tangaroa has been reduced to an ophidian, a sea-serpent with a black-striped body which can be seen sleeping at low tide in crevices of the coral reef.

The extension of theologies centring on the cult of great gods, often rivals, is a corollary, in the Society Islands and the Hawaiian Archipelago, of the rise of a priestly caste who acquired an increasing importance in the body politic. In Hawaii the ambition of the priests finally provoked a brutal reaction by the royal house which publicly violated the tabus and had the statues and temples destroyed.

On Tonga the powers-that-be took care to hinder the development of a united priestly class capable of getting a hold on the people. The priests were confined to the modest role of seeing to the worship of local deities. The great gods belonged by right to the supreme personage, the Tui Tonga, master of a maritime empire governed through an aristocratic hierarchy, in which all authority and all functions derived directly from the semi-divine monarch.

'In the beginning was the boundless void.' Such could have been the beginning of a Polynesian cosmology. 'From the void was born first perfume, and then Dust, and then what can be seen and many other things. The intermarriage of these things engendered Tangaroa, the creator of men.' One might just as well reverse the order and say that Tangaroa was in existence at the beginning in the womb of nothingness, that he created things and, by coupling with them, engendered a lineage of which the gods and men are part. Tangaroa can be replaced by Tui or Taru, who precede him in some cosmogonies.

To the first act of creation were added other actions of the demiurge or his rivals: the raising of the sky, the ordering of the sun's course and of fishing in the Islands. Too many authors, even today, have been led astray by a desire to resolve the false problem of the authentic and apocryphal versions of the great Polynesian myths. It is assumed that the priests had come from Asia with the people, equipped with a ready-made theology which certain evil persons had perverted from its true form: the investigator's task is to re-establish the true image.

66

48. New Caledonia, Yedyeban Island. *Fragment of an old mask.* Leenhardt Collection.

As soon as they touch upon Polynesia, the most venerable scholars, the most critical minds, seem to become possessed by a romantic frenzy. The exegesis of Polynesian religion has, in Europe, its orthodox and its heretics, and excommunication, if not the actual loss of research grants, is the fate of those who dare to leave the beaten track.

Shall we ever know whether or not Kiho Tumu was the demiurge of an esoteric cosmogony in Tuamotu? If writers had decided to accept the authenticity of each local variant of mythological themes and their role in assuring the cohesion of groups, they would perhaps no longer make a major issue out of every unusual statement made by an informant, who may well have been a literary genius with a powerful imagination.

There were dozens of Polynesian deities. From one island to another the same name could cover widely differing situations and beliefs. The rise of certain deities in the hierarchy corresponded to the appearance of wider social units with a sounder structure and a concept of regional solidarity which Europeans thought fit to materialize in the form of 'Kingdoms.' The interested

67

members of the hierarchy lent themselves with a good will to activities in which they had everything to gain.

These well-ordered theologies were, in any case, full of contradictions. There were, above the earth, ten superimposed heavens, homes of the gods—so they assert on Rarotonga. At the end of an underwater journey, the dead went to live in the west, in the island of Bulotu. If certain gods divided the storied heavens between them, others lived at the four cardinal points, in the mountains, along the rivers or under the earth. Specialized divinities concerned with the skills of sea and soil, dwelt in the religious centre of the clan which celebrated their cult, or in the carved images which were made of them.

On Samoa three classes of gods are distinguished: the *atua*, original divinities in the guise of demiurges; the *tupua*, deified dead chiefs; the *aitu*, sons of the *atua*, who become tutelary deities. The *atua* and the *aitu* live at the same time at Bulotu and in the highest heavens without ever settling in a fixed habitat. The *tupuo* live at Bulotu or near the homes of men. After their death, they become *aitu*.

There is no system here, and the same incoherence prevailed in Melanesia, where Codrington was able to distinguish between gods who had been men, and those who had never lived, and where there was sometimes a conflict between the notions of various underground lands of the dead and of the heavens peopled with deities.

In the case of the Society Islands, Moerenhout introduced the distinction between the *atua*, national gods, objects of public worship, and the *oromatua*, domestic divinities. Only the former had temples, those terraced pyramids, the *marae* built of stone, whose harmonious architecture still commands our admiration, and on which spectacular rites and human sacrifices took place. Outside, a stone wall marked off an enclosure containing the priests' huts and those in which the clumsy images of the gods were housed.

Besides the myth of the Creation, the Polynesian imagination has invented sacred epics where the goddesses are married at the end of a series of tests: where Hina, daughter of Tangaroa, after a voyage which takes her as far as New Zealand, decides to settle in the moon so that no one will be vexed any longer by the noise of her bark-cloth beater; where the god Mauitikitiki, an aborted foetus that has survived, captures the sun with a cord made from the hair of his sister's pubis, then half kills it with the jaw-bone of his grandmother, who has starved to death. He seizes the sun's fire to give it to the world, lifts up the firmament so as to prevent it from crushing mankind and finally raises all the lands up out of the Ocean. But these epics have never been translated into visual terms. They survive only in the domain of oral literature.

49. New Guinea, Asmat. *Mask for the jipae funerary rite*. Amsterdam

ORAL LITERATURE

All writers have stressed the importance of Polynesian oral tradition and it has given rise to many European literary works, some of which are delightful in their way. But it still awaits a detailed study analysing its techniques and methods.

In other parts of Oceania also there exists an oral tradition which, far from being devoid of interest, is as varied and rich as that of Polynesia. The oral texts fall into several categories. Prose: fables, stories, legendary tales with a semi-historical content, fully developed myths with a religious subject-matter, cosmogonies, ceremonial discourses. Poetry: dirges, love songs, improvised songs, religious songs, magic formulae. There can be no question here of giving more than a general impression of this complicated and copious body of work.

Images and symbols are basic to Oceanian poetry. Two general tendencies are observable in this connection, but it is almost impossible to differentiate between the Polynesian and non-Polynesian. One explains and expatiates on each image in one or two verses, the other concentrates its effects in a single word acting as a signal, or a single phrase suggesting a whole series of visual and aural images.

Here is a verse of a *wahayhay*, sung in Melanesian (Hura Yay), from Uvea, Loyalty Islands.

Behold the wind on the sea,
Wind favourable to the land,
I come from the opposite shore,
Behind Hüjonem,

(*A place in Heo, the island where the underground entrance to the country of the dead is situated*)

To the home of Walewe and Hida.

(*A mythological couple living in the land of the dead*)

I see in the mangroves,
walking in the brush,
I see my beloved there.
I see the *mamaday* bird.

(*a sea bird*)

I turn again,
Sinengalu turns away,
And the daughters of Unec will have
none of me.

This text plays on a contrast between the evocation of the land of the dead—the *wahayhay* is a threnody—the allusion to an amorous adventure—the dead man who speaks regretting this phase of his past—and the rapid description in the last couplet of the dance itself, a dance of women who in turn, almost without moving from their places, look at the spectators as if inviting them, and then turn away. (The words are spoken by a dancer.)

Another poem in the Polynesian language, from the same island and without mythological allusions (which is rare), evokes a dead man and shows how the images can follow one another and reinforce each other.

> I come from under the earth;
> I part the bamboo leaves before me,
> I look to the heights,
> I face two red clouds;
> They make me weep,
> If they were nearer
> That would be the colour of my song.

Next we have a song from Northern Malekula, New Hebrides, which is sung by men who have successfully dragged a fresh corpse from an ambush and proceed to hang it by the feet to the top of a wooden drum with a carved head:

> The dead water sleeps at Natar;
> He does not cross before it,
> Raptamb does not cross before it.
> The dead water bursts forth,
> It devours the sacred eagle,
> And the group of his subjects behind him.

This is a true story of the rivalry between a chief and a celebrated warrior, a rivalry in which the chief met his end. The image of the dead water corresponds to the belief in the malevolent power of stagnant water. The eagle, a small local species, is the usual symbol of a chief.

Another verse would seem obscure to us without a commentary:

Vano Bwitarovar noti melok ani ae	Tenmaru, gloomy place,
noti melok ani ae	gloomy place
Nekhabat a mweleun vèsi nail	Nekhabat, powerful chief.
nadap tar bangenaran a (twice)	Earth remains clouds,
noti melok ani ae	gloomy place

The deserted village of Tenmaru, whose poetic name is Bwitarovar, is overgrown by brush —hence the idea of obscurity; the chief is extolled by a double comparison with the earth and the clouds since this makes him indestructible in the same way as they are, and in contrast to the ancient dwelling-place which has been destroyed.

On Ambrim the stanzas of the songs of the *pata* dance are the only ones in the local language; the other songs and dances have been brought from outside the island, as have the texts in the original language. These songs describe both sad and happy events as, for instance, the lamentations of a man abandoned by his wife. Each stanza is a self-contained verse—the words drawn out and phonetically transformed—separated from the other verses by a refrain. Putting the verses together and omitting the refrain, we get a text which is easier to understand, consisting of short phrases and simple, undeveloped images.

Refrain : I have come to a stop;
I have placed myself under a ban
On account of my marriage which has come to a standstill.
I think deeply,
I am sad to have my wife no more
To beautify my house.

She used to sweep,
She used to sweep clean,
Cleaner than clean;
Her eyes were beautiful,
Her eyes were bright,
Lilon was the first,
The sacred wife of Melwe.
She is in the jungle
Under which tree?
Look for that tree,
Look in the plantations.
I do not find,
I seek at Fanla
I seek and I find;
I break off a branch,
I play with it
At planting it in the earth.
I say to this branch of *lire*
Lire tree, fire pig,
Who runs at Fufuteng
Who makes a noise at Fufuteng
From Fufuteng to Linbul.

I have come to a stop...

Those whose duty it is to invent texts, or even new tunes for a dance, form an honoured class in many places, and their services bring them material advantages, in pigs; also a degree of prestige that allows them to remain, if all goes well, outside the normal *cursus honorum*.

The love charms collected in the Trobriands, near New Guinea, by Bronislaw Malinowski, contain passages both of detailed eroticism and of lyricism.

> Thou goest my way, crying for me,
> Thou enterest my house, smiling at me.
> The house is shaken with joy, as thou treadest my floor.
> Tease and tear out my hair,
> Drink my blood so that I feel joyful.

And again :

> My flashing decoration, my white skin :
> I shall take the faces of my companions and rivals
> I shall arrange for them to be rejected.
> I shall take my face, the face of me (proper name)
> And I shall get a flattery-bond for it
> For my beautiful full-moon face.

It will have been noted how the poets of Oceania like to make their images more precise by the use of proper names, either of people or of places. Each of these names gives rise either to a succession of images or to reminiscences of mythological themes, and enriches the texture of a verse. This tendency is particularly marked in Polynesia where verses like these, without proper names, are rare. This example is quoted by Katharine Luomala.

> 'Awake, O rain, O sun, O night,
> O mists creeping inland,
> O mists creeping seaward,
> O masculine sea, feminine sea, mad sea,
>> Delirious sea, surrounding sea of Iku,
>> The islands are surrounded by the sea,
> The frothy sea of small billows, of low-lying billows,
> Of up-rearing billows that come hither from Kahiki.'

In Polynesia the most elaborate ceremonial was constructed around the public display of the fruits of poetical inspiration. Poets engaged in contests, in which the spectators or chiefs of high rank were judges, and where the lot of the loser was far from enviable. And while the practices of the Airoi of Tahiti were the most complicated from this point of view, everywhere the poet was an honoured person, protected by the great and fêted by the people as a whole. His noblest role, the one which gave him a sacred character, consisted in hymning the great gods, those who were living at the time of the creation, and their many sons, homonyms and doublets:

Behold the gods of Hawaii, the birthplace of lands!
        of Hawaii, the birthplace of gods!
        of Hawaii, the birthplace of people!
Gods internal, gods external,
gods above, gods below,
gods of the ocean, gods of the land,
gods incarnate, gods unincarnate,
gods of retribution, gods to pardon sin,
man-devouring gods, gods slaying warriors,
man-saving gods,
gods of darkness, gods of light,
        gods of the ten skies.
Can all the gods be numbered?
Nay the gods are beyond numbering!

Inevitably these translations fail to give an idea of the metrical techniques employed: the rhythms, rhymes, and alliteration. Certain Polynesian languages also may well include variants which indicate tonality and Polynesian prosody has not yet been subjected to detailed linguistic analysis.

Oceanian prose perpetuated by the oral tradition has been collected by numerous researchers: there can be no question of giving many examples here since the texts are generally long ones.

Traditional texts may take the form of fables and amusing or cautionary tales for children, or of myths where regional themes include variants, each of which is the work of a specific community, justifying in its own eyes its claim to a specific social status, and often assigning a lower one to neighbouring groups. Some of these texts, and not only in Polynesia, are very long, indeed full-length novels, with episodes and exciting incidents. Others are quite short, and have a content whose symbolism and emotion are all the stronger for being concentrated.

This prose is sometimes rhythmic, in which case it is in the style of the ceremonial discourses which are one of the high points of gatherings, the moment when homage is paid to the guests by giving each his due, recalling the deeds of his ancestors and embellishing the truth (though the facts are known to all) so that no-one's susceptibilities may be offended. A language rich in images is employed and proper names are often replaced by animal symbols and names of places belonging to the clan, spaced out along a mythical route and assigning a poetic designation to each group. Moreover, in the best examples, we find lyrical descriptions of the force and cohesion of the host group (which is likened to a canoe), or of the fratry to which it belongs, preluding the dance of the crowd at the orator's feet:

I, liana, enormous phallus which grows and crushes
I, liana *cocaytyo*, that covers the country
I, liana, with the milky sap, ornament of the house which sucks it, upright on the thunder mountain

I shall chant a song, I shall strike the bamboo, I shall kick the *mangi* and *doea* trees
I shall find in the air the body of the land breeze and the body of the *bé* grass
I shall kick the sleepers and the cowards into wakefulness
I shall set up the plumes of the egrets
I shall cause the gods to dance in the whirlwind
And set in motion here the dance which will last till day-break...
... I tap with my foot the house foundation
I touch the paddle, rudder of the dwelling and of the land
I steer to the heart of the vast, root-stock
and I seize the forest standing on the mountain-side,
I plunge inside the roots of the tree of the god Gomawe
I tack to the rock which blocks the river
and standing there I stay to listen to the song of the water...

This traditional eloquence, often accredited solely to the Polynesians, is a factor of authority and prestige throughout Oceania, whether it is exercised directly or whether usage ranking requires the use of a spokesman, a professional orator. This technique of good speaking, a decisive element in group relations, was essential for the psychological conditioning of warriors. It is still indispensable for rousing the enthusiasm needed for communal labour.

Under the stress of the violent changes brought about by seizures of land and the colonialist mentality, the orator's eloquence was sometimes directed to airing the grievances of the community, as in a text the author obtained at Ponerihuen in the Hebrides, entitled '*Oration against the Whites who have seized the land of the Blacks.*'

TECHNIQUES

There is one basic material lacking among those used by Oceanian artists and craftsmen: metal. However, they practise the arts of netting, basketry and modelling as well as carving stone and wood.

Stone has the merit of durability. Although today few craftsmen are capable of working it, accidental finds and planned research have brought to light buried pieces, often of great beauty, whose origins are something of a mystery. Fortunately, archaeological work is beginning to give us more exact knowledge of the life of this region in the remote past. And it seems that the finest pieces are almost always the oldest: those which exhibit the best craftsmanship were not made within living memory. A stone sculpture, if it was portable, was exchanged and passed from hand to hand, and may have originated far away—both in time and space.

It is not, however, true to say that work in stone is less skilled than that in wood. Before making such a judgment the relative hardness of the material should be assessed, for coral limestone may be as hard as stone of volcanic origin. It is right to admire the precision with which some stones are worked despite the inherent difficulties. Such precision is not without a degree of softness, however, a feature which distinguishes pieces of recent workmanship, since modern craftsmen do not bother to conceal the file-marks.

Volcanic tuffs are easy to work, but have the disadvantage of fragility. The hardest stones, including basalt and serpentine, were also used.

Nowadays the triangular rasp is the common tool: the ancient technique was hammer-dressing which demanded constant patience and great delicacy of touch. The hammer was a stone of equal or greater hardness. The bowdrill supplemented the hammer work. It has been reported that rats' teeth were used for fine work where hammering was impracticable.

Polishing was done on boulders, and the marks of it can still be seen. Abrasive river sands, without shells, were also employed.

Wood-workers had a large number of tools at their disposal as well as the classic adze, with elbowed shaft and a blade of stone or tridachna shell. They also used stone flakes, shells with a worked cutting edge, teeth of sharks, rats and marsupials (New Guinea), and, especially, wild boars' tusks whose inner convex edge is remarkably sharp. Polishing was done with pumice stone which is very common on beaches owing to the number of submarine volcanoes existing in the Pacific. In contrast to the technique used in hollowing out canoes and the great drums, fire was employed but little in sculpture since it too drastically destroyed the contours.

The final polish was effected by hanging the object for a long time over a fire, hand-polishing it from time to time with coconut oil. Many wooden objects had an incised decoration made with the same tools as were used for the carving. Throughout New Guinea it was the general practice to fill the incisions with chalk or colours which contrasted with the artificially darkened wood. Similarly the lines cut in bamboo (which was never burnt in), were rubbed with black substances so as to stand out against the light ground.

The lower parts of tree fern trunks were used as well as wood. These consist of a mass of fibres, half-buried in the soil, which are hard, proof against rot and bristling with spikes (these were sometimes used as spear-tips and as teeth for combs or for animal masks). A well-sharpened adze was needed to shape the trunk. When a smooth surface was desired (this was not always the case), the surface exposed was given a coat of moist earth or sand, which then was 'fixed' with a vegetable varnish such as breadfruit-tree sap.

The technique of modelling might be thought to derive from the manufacture of pottery; but this is true only in a small number of cases. Skulls from New Guinea with overmodelling were worked in clay, but in New Britain and the New Hebrides vegetable paste was used. In the New Hebrides certain creepers with friable wood and pith are grated and the resulting paste is bound with coconut milk and breadfruit tree sap. Similar pastes are bound with crushed fruits, especially the flesh of over-ripe breadfruit.

The history of Oceanian ceramics is wrapped in mystery. Pottery had entirely disappeared from Polynesia when the Europeans arrived, except for imported pieces on Tonga which originally came from Fiji where the technique persists in a small number of places. But pottery is found in archaeological levels on the Marquesas, Samoa and Tonga. The same is true of the New Hebrides, where although only the inhabitants of two villages, Wusi and Nogugu on the west coast of Espiritu Santo, still make pottery, archaeological remains have been found in plenty throughout the archipelago.

Pottery, like mats and tapa, is woman's work and is governed by a number of tabus. Two techniques exist side by side in Melanesia: in one, the object is hollowed out from a lump of clay, using the flexed knee, for example, as a matrix; in the other 'sausages' of clay are rolled into spirals, then worked on the inside with a round stone or a piece of shell, and on the outside with a wooden beater.

Nothing of the nature of a potter's wheel is used; only a circular rest built up with leaves. Some very large pottery from New Caledonia and New Guinea presents oval and spherical forms of a remarkable regularity. The need for a tempering material is understood. After several days of drying, the pots are carefully placed upon solid stone supports and covered with sticks and brushwood which are set alight. The fire is replenished until the firing is considered complete.

In Fiji the pottery is promptly 'glazed' by rubbing the hot surface with koari pine resin. A concoction of mangrove-tree bark may be mixed with the melted gum, producing fine colours, ranging from dark red to gold and green. In the New Hebrides a certain brick-red earth is fetched from a distance and used to make a slip which retains its colour after firing. In New Guinea the basic decoration is sometimes in champlevé, enhanced with colours.

Basketry, flexible or rigid according to the nature of the raw material used, is not confined to the classic range of baskets. Both flat strips of leaf and round withies may be employed. In the first case the strips are made of varnished pandanus leaves, dried in the sun and sliced

with a pointed tool, then made flexible with a knife and preserved in tight rolls. Sometimes, too, they are boiled in sea-water before being cut into thin ribbons, which are plaited to form mats and baskets.

The basket-workers also use long strands, sometimes quite thick, which may be rigid or more or less flexible, for making the heavy cloaks worn by wearers of the Asmat mask, the corselets of Micronesia, the bird or cayman-headed head-dresses of the Sepik region, the light masks of New Britain (Sulka), the long bell-handles of the New Hebridean maskers, and the framework which supports the feather-head-dresses or the feather-decked images of gods in the Hawaiian Islands. We should note the great knowledge which the peoples of Oceania have of lianas and forest creepers with their qualities of flexibility, strength and durability. In the absence of osier, reeds are little used for basketry, except in south-western New Caledonia.

The finest examples of geometric decoration are to be found not so much on carved wooden surfaces, as in the close-woven mats. For the more slender the pandanus strips, the more flexible is the mat and the nearer it approaches to a textile. The best mats are used for clothing; in Polynesia for skirts or ceremonial belts, and in Melanesia for cache-sexes, penis sheaths and women's headcloths. They are then of an even finer texture than those of Polynesia, and are adorned with open-work patterns of an exceptionally high quality.

This technical perfection gives rise to active commercial dealings between islands or districts; there are villages or islands specializing in a particular type of mat. In the New Hebrides, for example, the penis sheaths of Ambrim are manufactured by the women of small islands to the north-east of Malekula, Vao in particular. In the north of Malekula itself each village has exclusive rights in a special motif which the women apply to the penis-sheaths. This 'trade-mark' indicates not the village of the man who wears it, but that of the worker from whom he has obtained it. This 'trade-mark' is a recent innovation.

Tapa is a name incorrectly applied to the vegetable material which the Polynesians call *siapo*. Basic to the production of barkcloth is the cultivation of the mulberry *(Broussonetia papyrifera)*. The manufacture of the tapa from mulberry bark is women's work and forbidden to men, who, in theory at least, ought not even to watch the process.

The worker uses the trunks of young mulberry trees which have been selected for their straightness. The trunk is cut off at ground level and the bark stripped with extreme care. The worker's hands are used to lift the bark, and her teeth to cut or pull it. With equal care the outer bark is stripped from the *liber*, the material of which tapa is made. This inner bark is rolled into bundles which are temporarily laid aside until the kneading process begins. In some places the bark is soaked in water until fermentation sets in. In all cases it has to be thoroughly moistened before work on it can be resumed.

The bark is worked on a log of hard wood, which is laid on two logs placed at right angles. The upper side of the log has been fined down to a flat surface. The tool employed is a beater with a round handle and a body, square in section, having at least two of its faces longitudinally grooved, or else given a criss-cross grooving of a varying degree of fineness. The fineness of the grooving on the beater increases as the work progresses. In New Caledonia, when the bark from aerial roots of the banyan is also used as raw material, the beater is cylindrical for all its length.

50. New Guinea, Papua. *Carved stone pestle.* British Museum.

51. Huon Gulf. *Top of a stone pestle.* Nat. Hist. Mus., Chicago.

52. Polynesia, Tahiti. *Sculpture in volcanic stone. Mother and child.* ▶

The worker seats herself before the anvil, places a length of bark on the flat surface and beats it slowly and to a particular rhythm. As a result of the beating the bark gradually spreads until it reaches as much as twice its original width. When the bark has been soaked in water for a considerable time this beating produces the 'felt' texture characteristic of East Polynesian tapas.

When enough of these widened strips have been made, the next task is to fill in the gaps by adding strips that are securely held in place with a glue made from the flesh of an over-ripe breadfruit, from starch derived from the root of *Taccaceae* (arrowroot) or from the sap of a special kind of liana.

A similar operation, but on a larger scale, consists in joining a number of strips into a big piece whose thickness varies according to the purpose for which it is intended (clothing, bedclothes, personal adornment, napery, display, etc.). This stage of the work is carried out on the curved side of an old canoe hull. The technique used in arranging the various strips

80

53. New Hebrides, Ambrim. *Grade symbol carved in tree-fern*. Musée de l'Homme, Paris.

54. New Hebrides, South Malekula. *Heavy head-dress in overmodelled tree-fern*. Malraux Collection.

55. New Guinea, Sepik, Kararau. *Incised pottery touched up in colour.* Nat. Hist. Mus., Chicago.

one on another and achieving an even, unbroken thickness in the end product (often consisting of three layers), is rather like the solution of a problem in solid geometry.

The same technique was used for beating out a plain piece of tapa and then affixing it to a coloured one (so that the resultant length of barkcloth was, so to say, double-sided), and for inserting bands of different colours (Hawaii). The final beating made it possible for a geometrical motif to be imprinted, even at this late stage, on the texture of the cloth to give a mottled effect.

The pigments and colours used are natural in origin, and few in number. Yellow and red ochre come from deposits which, although worked on a very limited scale, give rise to a barter trade between islands and villages. The mineral pigments, greens, blues and black (manganese), are even scarcer and still more sought after. Black is often obtained from powdered charcoal or, more commonly, from roasted siccative nuts whose oil is mixed with charcoal. White is always obtained from quicklime whose manufacture is common knowledge, both for this purpose

84

56. New Guinea, Sepik, Amuim Klinjam. *Pottery (detail)*. Nat. Hist. Mus., Chicago.

and for bleaching the hair. The raw material is calcined shell. The pigments are dissolved in water or in a binding medium of vegetable origin stored in shells or in wooden containers which are carved on their underside (Sepik).

The colouring of textiles (mats and tapas) is much more complicated. In the case of mats, the vegetable dyes are cooked with pandanus strips prepared in advance. Then natural-coloured strips can be interwoven with red and black ones.

Another method, closely resembling that of the Indonesian *batik*, uses a 'reserve' technique calling for highly skilled craftsmanship. It consists of plunging the mat into a dye so that the whole is impregnated, except for the 'reserved' areas in geometric motifs. For this purpose, the mat is wound round a smooth log whose circumference equals the width of the material. The mat is held in place by slender lianas wound tightly round it, each coil clamping to the mat tiny fragments cut from the stem of a banana tree, whose forms placed side by side make up the pattern to be reproduced.

85

A long, deep trough is constructed with lengths of supple bark from certain trees. This container is filled with water to which have been added pieces of the various kinds of bark used for dyeing, and set on the fire. The prepared mat is placed in it and the contents of the trough are made to simmer for several hours. Then the mat is taken out, and set to dry before being unrolled: the motifs show up in yellow on a red ground. This technique is commonly used for such small mats as penis-sheaths, and also for the large ones made as shrouds (Aoba).

Tapas are also given 'printed' and painted decorations. The fraying of the end of a twig or a piece of a branch provides a brush capable of applying both broad and narrow stripes of colour.

57. Polynesia, Wallis Islands. *Young woman beating tapa* — 58. New Guinea, Sepik, North Maprik, Ulupu. *Artists at work* — 59. Polynesia, Wallis Islands. *Incised wood stamp for impressing designs on tapa (detail)*. Musée de l'Homme, Paris.

The method of 'printing' (which can be used in conjunction with the 'reserve' technique) is employed to cover the tapa with a ground pattern upon which certain details are subsequently picked out with the brush. It is also used for impressing in great detail strips of geometrical motifs, separated by strips without any decoration or with only occasional motifs. The simplest form of this technique was employed in Tahiti by the direct application of fern leaves whose outline and ribs had been rubbed with pigment. Another technique is to stretch a string rubbed with colour above the tapa, to lift it by its middle and then to let it go, so that it strikes the material, imprinting a straight line in which the twisted pattern of the string can be seen.

In Central Oceania (Cook Islands, Samoa, Tonga, Futuma, Fiji) a vegetable sheet, made

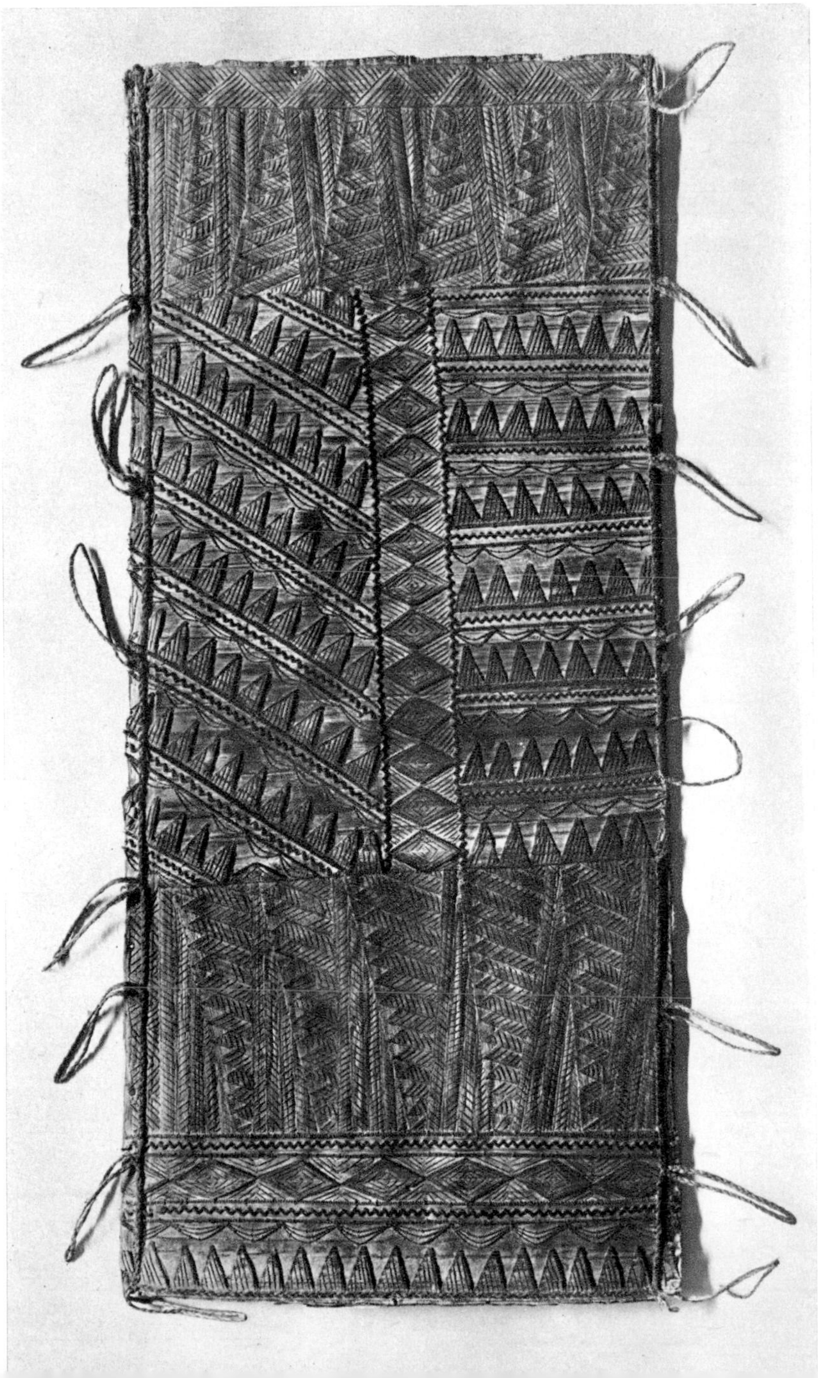

60. Polynesia, Wallis Islands. *Vegetable stamp for tapa.* Musée de l'Homme, Paris — 61. New Guinea, Sepik, North Maprik, Ulupu. *Sculptor at work.*

from the broad leaves of a species of *pandanus*, some overlapping and some out of alignment and stitched together, is edged with a hem made of coconut-husk fibre. On one surface there is a running pattern made from a similar fibre stitching or pieces of coconut-palm rib also secured with stitches. This matrix is usually placed under the tapa which is rubbed with a tapa tampon impregnated with brown paint. Only those portions which rest on the underlying motifs in relief receive a rather blurred design, and themselves acquire a slight relief.

Leaf and stitchwork matrices are sometimes replaced by a wooden matrix (Tonga, Wallis Islands, Samoa, Cook Islands). In the Cook Islands this was used to stamp on the design.

In Hawaii thin strips of bamboo, with geometric designs in relief, were dipped in the colour container and then wiped on its edge. By means of these it was possible to print directly on the tapa, the material being lashed with the strips, a motif whose regular repetition produced wide bands of decoration at intervals. The contrast between decorated and plain bands formed the basic element of the design, and to this an entirely new aesthetic dimension was added by the use of petals or the pollen of scented plants to produce perfumed tapas.

The dyes employed in the decoration of tapas, as in that of mats, are of vegetable origin: a greasy soot derived from a nut of the *aleurites* genus; a red pigment from the seeds of a bush, *abrus precatorius*, grown for this specific purpose; saffron root; tinctorial leaves and barks. In Hawaii fifteen different methods of dyeing were known, certain plants yielding a different colour when a different part of the plant was employed. The bark of *aleurites moluccana* gave a red dye, as did that of *morinda citrifolia*, while its roots supplied a yellow tint.

Another form of coloured decoration was produced in the Hawaiian archipelago by fixing feathers on capes, mantles and helmets and also on images of the gods. The making of supple capes and mantles was basically simple: each of the knots in a net held the stem of a feather: bunches of feathers were sometimes fixed in two adjoining knots, one above the other. The same technique is used in the black woodpigeon-feather mantles which hang below New Caledonian masks. By varying the colours of the feathers, geometric motifs can be obtained. A similar technique was used for making the feather mantles of the Society Islands and New Zealand, though here a different netting technique was used.

Fixing the feathers to the rigid basketwork of helmets and divine effigies was another matter. Two methods were used. The first, deriving from the capes, consisted in making a close-meshed net covering the basket-work to which it was securely attached; each knot held one or more feathers. In the second, the craftsmen fixed the feathers in parallel rows along one side of a long ribbon which they then wound round and fastened to the basketwork, starting at the bottom, each coil lying above the preceding one and the whole being stitched to the underlying basketry framework at regular intervals.

62. Micronesia, Nitendi, Santa Cruz Islands. *Fine mat.* Basle.

FUNCTIONAL ANALYSIS

Before turning to questions of decoration and styles, it may be well to consider the *functions* of the pieces usually described as 'objets d'art.' What exactly do they mean to the craftsmen who make them, and to their possessors?

Art in everyday objects

The study of the geography of styles in later pages will show how many objects of daily use are given a painted or incised decoration, or adorned, at least in part, by carving. Our brief account of techniques has shown how the problem is solved in the case of mats and tapas, with flat surfaces and more or less rectangular outlines.

It is not easy, at least in Polynesia, to establish the exact origin of a mat, since the various types of mat and the ways of making them are common knowledge from one archipelago to the next. On the other hand, it is much easier to distinguish New Hebridean mats from those from the Solomons, which oftener than not serve as articles of clothing. Here, however, it is a question not so much of forms as of the manner of use. The delicacy of the design on the Micronesian mats, on the other hand, is unique in Oceania.

Mats are used for interior decoration as well as for clothing. New mats on a layer of old mats or woven coconut leaves provide a soft, resilient floor surface. An unrolled mat serves as a table for food. Mats laid out one above the other at night and rolled up during the day, are the universal form of bedding. A man may even roll himself in a mat to sleep, as he will be rolled in one when dead.

Other New Hebridean mats, narrow and extremely long, carry the same coloured motif at regular intervals, repeated as often as is needed to indicate the length and the value of the mat. For these mats serve as currency in minor business transactions (Malekula-Aoba). In Maewo some of them were hung inside a special hut from which they were not allowed to be removed. There a constantly burning fire covered them with a thick coat of soot hanging down in stalactites. This was a guarantee of the age and value of the mats, which changed hands without changing place. An assemblage of mats furnished a magnificent ceremonial costume in the Banks Islands.

Baskets may be either square or flat, the shape being determined by the technique used for setting up the framework and making the base of the receptacle. The range of possible variations in the decoration is much the same as that of the mats. However, the baskets are more pleasing to the eye because they have a great number of surfaces, which intersect and provide a third dimension.

For what purposes are these baskets used? Those with the finest texture are used to carry cooked food, personal possessions, packets containing magic objects or drugs, jewellery (bracelets, necklaces, pendants) tobacco, lime gourds and betel nuts, anything, in fact, which is highly valued and not too bulky. In New Caledonia the sacred basket holds the coins of mother-of-pearl and the carved head lying in a model canoe whose presence ensures the renewal of the hoard despite constant bartering. In the Loyalty Islands, big flat baskets, carried on the back, form part of the men's costume, like the net pouches decorated with painted motifs which are also carried on the back. Used by the women of New Guinea, the pouches are sometimes embellished with mother-of-pearl rings.

Tapas may be of considerable size, in Polynesia at least. They are used as tablecloths, blankets, as articles of clothing (cache-sexes, breast-cloths) or to decorate houses. They are kept rolled up until the time of a family feast when they are used for exchanges or as obligatory contributions.

In New Caledonia, tapa, made either from the bark of the mulberry tree or from that of the aerial root of the banyan, is used to wrap the penis or any other precious object. It also serves for a banner, fixed to a hardwood pole, and flourished as a symbol and gift of welcome. When knotted, it is sent as a message of alliance or of war. When money is offered it is placed on a piece of tapa and coins are wrapped in a roll of tapa cloth before being stowed away in a basket. It is referred to by orators as one of the minor symbols of life.

In Tanna, New Hebrides, tapa is used for belts consisting of a stiff band on which black and red motifs indicate the wearer's place in the social hierarchy. Elsewhere, it is wrapped on a light wooden frame to cover masks portraying mythical beings.

Happily the craft of tapa-making is not extinct, at least in the islands of central Polynesia (Samoa, Tonga, Rotuma, Futuna, Wallis) and in Fiji. It is still possible, despite the westernization of certain themes due to the use of compasses and rulers, to recognize the styles of each archipelago or each region.

In the Society Islands the place of tapa is taken by *tifaefae*, a species of large blanket made by sewing coloured patches on to a uniform ground. The motifs, however, are inspired by the textiles printed with the big floral designs of which the Polynesians are so inordinately fond; they have absolutely no connection with the autochthonous art of the past.

This dual purpose of mats and tapas is paralleled in the case of pottery. Large vessels are used for the braising of root vegetables; smaller containers are in daily use for cooking small quantities of freshwater shrimps, shellfish, fish, woodpigeon or pork so as to add a little salt and meat to relieve the monotony of eating nothing but starchy food twice a day. They are also used as water-pots, sometimes with lids of the same type as our water-coolers, and as bowls for the preparation of coconut milk and of kava. But there are also cauldrons used by sorcerers for making baneful brews and sacrificial vessels for cooking the first of the new season's yams; in the steam rising from them, dead ancestors and living gods can be addressed and prayed to. Finally, in New Guinea (Sepik) pottery is used to adorn the ridge-poles of the great men's-houses: these portray groups of mythical or symbolic beings (bird-men).

Pottery conforms to an intensive geographical specialization. Villages of potters (never very numerous) in Fiji, New Caledonia and the New Hebrides, the Solomons and New Guinea, used to live on the work done by the women. The objects they produced were subject to a system

64. New Hebrides, Banks Islands. *Ceremonial cape.* British Museum.

66. Solomon Islands. *Large wooden plate embellished with mother-of-pearl.* Honolulu.

of barter which was sometimes organised on almost scientific lines, the result being that the output, consumption and pricing of these necessaries of life become standardized. (*Kula Cycle* in eastern New Guinea, described by Malinowski.)

Thanks to its plasticity clay lends itself to an infinite variety of forms, all the more so since the absence of the wheel inhibits absolute symmetry. The usual form is spherical, or that of a sphere sliced either at the diameter or near the top. The top may be open or surrounded by a rim set at a more or less sharp angle to the line of the body. In both cases the decoration is confined to the upper part, out of reach of direct flames, and consists of incised motifs, lines or dots, sometimes so near each other as to give the impression of having been rouletted. In practice this effect can be obtained quite easily by means of light taps at regular and short intervals with straws held between the fingers. In New Guinea and New Caledonia we sometimes find a motif in relief symbolising a human face. In the New Hebrides and Fiji, incised or relief geometric motifs are picked out by scallopings in the body of the paste.

Mats, baskets, tapas and pottery are far from being the only artifacts of Oceania. The way of life of its inhabitants and its amenities are far more complex than might be supposed from the rather derogatory title of 'the men of polished stone' which is so often bestowed on them.

The accessories of sleep, footed head-rests of wood or bamboo, provide a classic example of the technology which prevails in all Oceanian cultures. The functional part is the upper section, flat or curved or sometimes a plain cylinder, since a round billet of wood provides all that is needed.

95

65. New Guinea, Sepik. *Incised double hook.* Philadelphia.

67. Admiralty Islands. *Large wooden plate*. Honolulu.

The supports are embellished with incised or carved decorations which, in the case of certain examples from New Guinea, have real beauty as works of art. This is particularly true of head-rests from the Sepik region and those from Huon Bay.

In the monumental beds of the Admiralty Islands we find a more advanced form of the arts connected with sleep: the carpentry is at once efficient and conventional, based on tenons dovetailed into slots in the legs (at the same height as those of our own beds), which hold together a carved and painted framework for the loose planks.

In a house with straw or leaf walls, whether resting on the ground or raised on a stone platform, rats are constant if unwelcome guests. One means of defence against their depredations on the owner's larder is to use a double food-hook hung from the roof by a thin liana (sometimes with a flat disc affixed to it so as to prevent the rodents from climbing down it); on the hook are hung quarters of meat, baskets of food and even enemy heads taken as trophies. The structure of this piece of household equipment lends itself to decoration. For example, human or animal figures can be fixed to its central axis or the hooks themselves given the shape of heads or distorted bodies. Here again we are dealing with a utilitarian object whose beauty is linked directly with its function and in which no element is superfluous.

A constant aesthetic urge in Oceania finds expression in colossal dishes: kava bowls in Polynesia, food dishes in Melanesia, and dishes for pulping taro and breadfruit throughout the Pacific. These are everyday objects but are used only when a visitor is present. Their value is ceremonial. Special restrictions may regulate the behaviour of those present while these dishes are in use, depending, for example, on whether or not the prepared food is sprinkled with coconut milk and whether the food is being served inside or outside the hut.

68. Trobriand Islands, Kiriwina. *Lime spatula*. Basle.
69. Eastern New Guinea, Rai. *Bamboo lime container*. Leningrad.

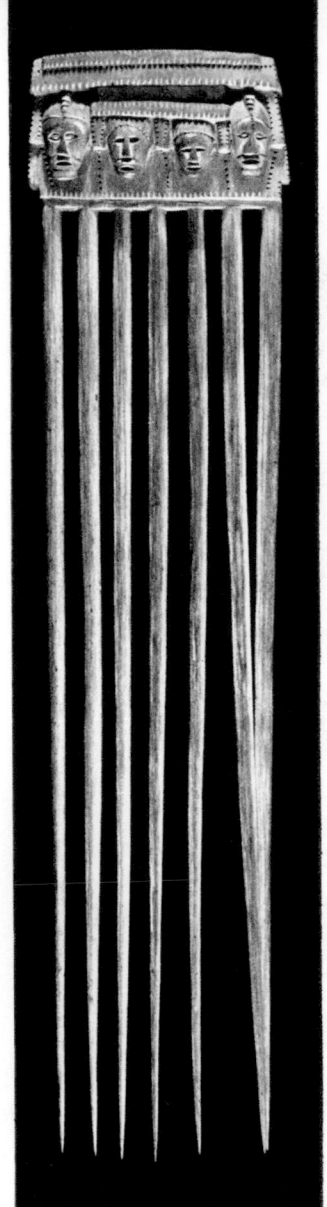

70. Admiralty Islands. *Carved wooden comb*. Honolulu. 71. New Guinea, Papua. *Incised bark belt*. Budapest.

The rites connected with the consumption of kava in eastern Melanesia and in Polynesia involve a highly intricate, schematized use of wooden bowls. The rites are performed daily, even when they are concerned with the ancestor cult. In this case a religious relationship is established between the kava root, the man who chews it and the ancestors to whom a few mouthfuls of kava, chewed up and spat out, are dedicated. Here, the bowl itself is of minor importance and plays the part of a container, nothing more.

The huge hollow bowls, such as those from the Solomon and Admiralty Islands, are designed for a specific cookery technique. The food is placed in the bottom and covered over with a pile of heated stones which are replaced as soon as they cool off. These bowls, carved in the shape of a bird, with their bands of geometric motifs in a mother-of-pearl inlay which pick out the

98

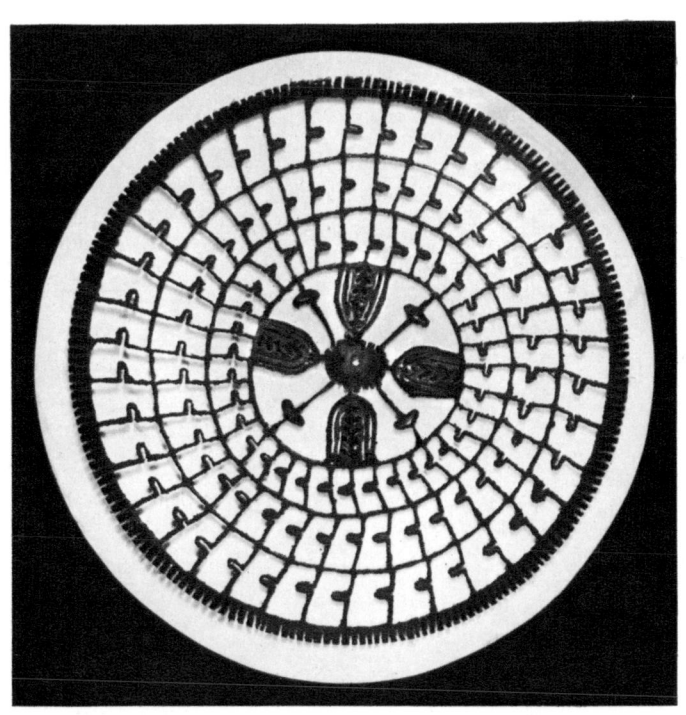

72. New Ireland (?).
*Tortoise-shell and shell
pendant*. Basle.

forms, are among the most beautiful pieces of all Oceanian art. To make such inlay work, soft wood is used, which is subsequently dyed with a vegetable liquid mixed with crushed wood charcoal.

The hardwood horizontal bowls of the New Hebrides are used for pulping taro and bread-fruit. Each household has a set of bowls of various shapes and sizes. When the dishes are truly monumental, as on Espiritu Santo, twelve men can crouch inside them and pound the roasted taro which the women have skinned. The rhythm of the pounding conforms to a well-established tradition and the sound carries for several miles. These dishes, placed over a trench and struck with a hardwood bar, are also used as makeshift drums.

The preparation of large quantities of vegetable food cooked for long periods, if not actually reduced to pulp, necessitates the use of spoons. These are usually made from the half-shell of a coconut fitted with a handle. Spoons of this type are found from the Solomons to New Guinea. Others, made of a single piece of wood with the handle and the beginning of the bowl carved with human faces, are very handsome pieces, remarkable for the functional simplicity of their form (Tami).

The scraper used for reducing the coconut kernel to a spongy mass from which the oil can be extracted is another standard utensil in the household equipment of Pacific islanders. A tool, a suitably grooved and scalloped piece of shell, has to be tied at a certain height, so that it can be used above the container. For this reason the scraper is fastened to a plank which is placed on a log and held in position by a man straddling it, or, better still, on a three- or four-legged stool which acts as a fixed support. The stools from Micronesia are the most elegantly constructed.

Closely related to cooking utensils are those which are concerned with the consumption of

99

betel: gourds, and especially, spatulas, pestles and mortars for lime. The forms of the spatulas are functionally related to the wooden knives of eastern Melanesia used for cutting yams, a foodstuff so highly prized that it must be neither cut nor broken without ritual precautions. Both these implements have carved openwork handles which are sometimes painted. The finest specimens come from the region of Massim—the south-easternmost tip of New Guinea and the neighbouring archipelagos.

Human figures are represented in every conceivable position, and these are supplemented by a whole bestiary of finely carved animals, forming composite scenes with precisely executed detail. These are the finest examples of sculpture found in a region where large-scale carving is rare or clumsily executed and where the general tendency is towards a combination of painting and incised, openwork decoration, of the kind that also figures on the bodies of the effigies on the tops of the spatulas.

In the Sepik region the lime containers made from the internodes of bamboos have a wooden stopper surmounted by a figure, usually a bird standing on what appears to be a cayman's head. The bird figures are enhanced with alternate white and red incised motifs.

The smooth surface of the bamboo lime container has an obvious appeal for the Oceanian artist who is often an engraver or chaser rather than a carver. The lines incised in the hard surface are blackened with soot, and the motifs stand out more clearly than on ordinary wood. This is especially true of the human face where the linework defines the contours of the various masses blocked out by the sculptor.

The mortars in which areca nuts are crushed before being mixed with lime and leaves of the betel-pepper are not always carved. Only a small, light receptacle is needed and a fragment of coconut shell suffices. Nonetheless, the mortars may be of wood with a carved surface. Sometimes the mortar is hollowed out in the lower part of a thick-set figure or has a band of openwork figures placed around it.

The essential elements of personal adornment are combs, ear-ornaments, pendants, bracelets and belts. To these we should add fibres or pieces of tapa which are tied round the forehead or the fleshy part of muscles, and which are sometimes used to hold a white shell in place on the dark skin. Lastly, there are tall head-dresses, plaited and adorned with feathers.

The combs and hairpins necessitated by these towering coiffures are, like the head-dresses themselves, tokens of male vanity. The men carefully wash and frequently delouse their hair. It is cut in fantastic patterns and partially bleached with lime. The combs are made of wood or bamboo: in either case they are given an incised design, sometimes in openwork, which, when placed at a becoming angle to the hair, adds to the general effect. Some combs from the New Hebrides and New Caledonia have teeth carved individually from tree-fern wood and attached to one another by a ligature which is either flexible (New Caledonia) or rigid (Pentecost). The incised motifs on both wooden and bamboo combs are either human faces or birds; today these are occasionally replaced by aeroplanes.

The bark belts are also incised, at least in Papua, with designs of a geometric type, the lines of which stand out in relief against a white ground. A careful study of the decorative themes current in this region shows that the lozenge-shaped motifs derive from the human face; indeed, their resemblance to it is often unmistakable.

73. New Guinea, Sepik, North Maprik, Yemal. *Maprik dancer in full dress.*

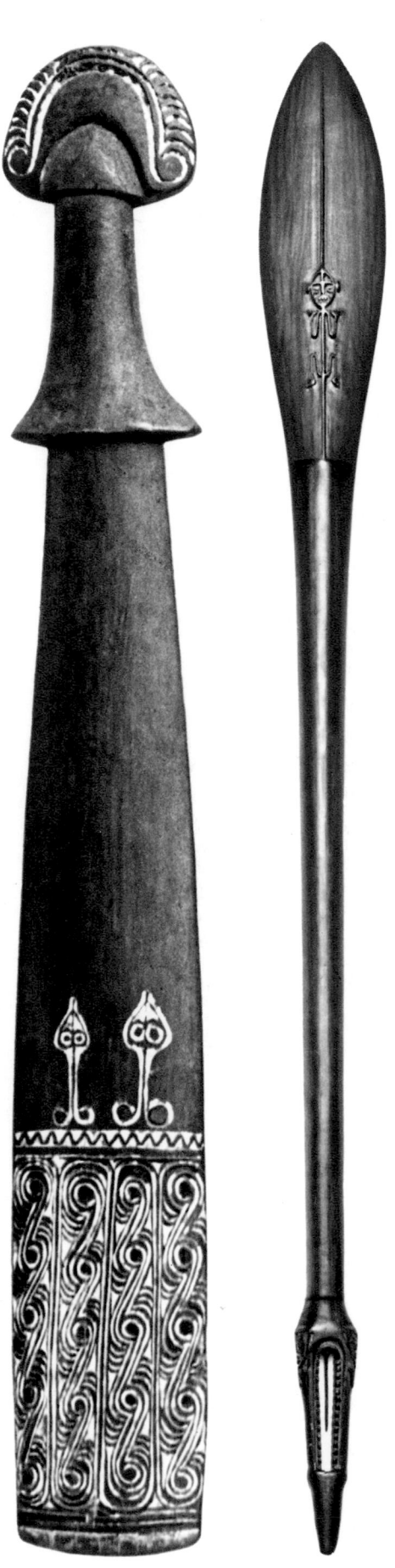

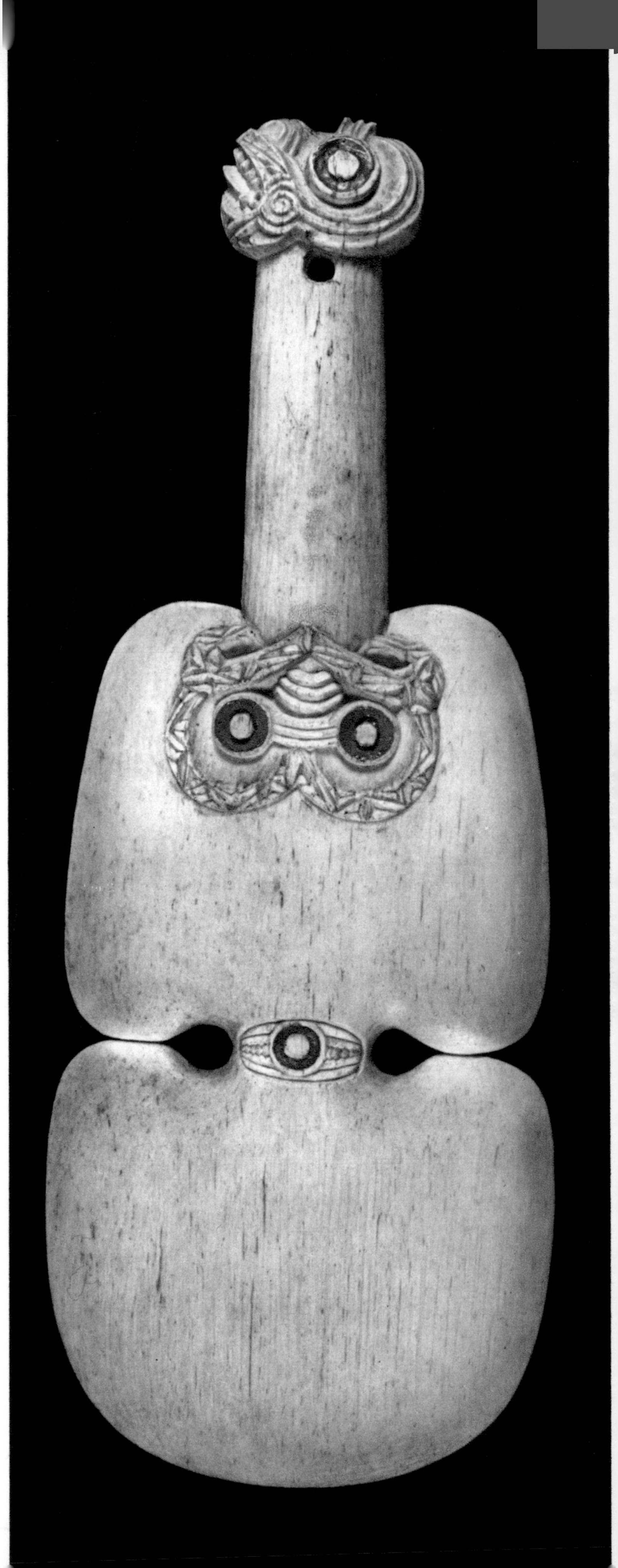

The use of brilliant white ornaments of shell, bone or ivory on a dark skin has a parallel in the black underclothes sometimes worn by women in Europe and America.

The teeth of various animals—sharks, dogs (canine teeth only), and sperm-whales—are also used for aesthetic purposes, strung in necklaces or inset in diadems. A highly polished sperm-whale tooth by itself makes an effective pendant when hung on the end of a finely plaited string.

The same kinds of teeth figure on similar ornaments in Melanesia, but there is a marked preference for the gracefully curved tusk of a boar whose upper canines have been broken off. A tusk is also used as a bracelet which indicates its owner's wealth in pigs. The double spiral formed by a pair of tusks fastened together at the base or along the sides makes a handsome pendant, often worn on the back.

Skilful use is made of shell. Shell beads are sewn on plaited strips, sometimes alternately with black coconut-shell beads, or linked in wreaths of various sizes which are draped round the neck or worn on the upper arm, if of sufficient diameter. A great variety of ornaments is obtained by using boar's tusks, mother-of-pearl rings and beads, and cowries sewn on bands of plaited fibre. These often end in the tips of pigs' tails, tokens of the of the wearer's past and present wealth. By rubbing down the helicoid part of certain shells small discs with a natural spiral pattern are made. These are stuck to the nostrils, or more often to the temples.

Shell disc pendants are added to necklaces of round beads made of shell or fish-bone and cylindrical ones made of coconut-shell or the long bones of flying foxes. In north-eastern Australia (Kimberley) we find cache-sexes engraved with a seemingly geometric motif which recalls, if remotely, the superimposed swastikas symbolizing the human body. On Santa Cruz and the Admiralty Islands similar plaques have a hole in the middle, in which is fitted a motif delicately cut in turtle-shell. In New Ireland the openwork patterns display a striking geometric regularity.

Hot-worked turtle-shell is used, not to manufacture the combs dear to our grandmothers, but ear-rings which are fixed either singly or in strings to the ear-lobes; also armbands and bracelets, the former being worn only by men.

Black or white plumes stuck in the hair, pig-tails passed through holes in the ear-lobes, reddish-brown scented leaves tucked into belts—all are regarded as indispensable elements of male finery. Similarly, at Ambrim, the woven penis-sheath with red and yellow motifs is carefully folded back at the top and fastened to a reddish-brown bark belt held together at its centre with an uncoloured bamboo clip.

What a man holds may, by virtue of its colour and decoration, add lustre to his personal appearance. The carved or painted dance paddles of Polynesia are notable examples; so are the ceremonial clubs, usually made of very heavy wood. They are sometimes given a polished stone head, and in this case the effect derives entirely from the beauty of the material employed. This also applies to certain ceremonial axes from the interior of New Guinea, whose beauty derives from the colour of the blade and its translucent edges, and also to the New Caledonian parade axe which has a green nephrite disc. Here the colour, symbolizing life, complements the shape and the delicacy of the craftsmanship.

Marquesan wooden clubs repeat on their two-sided heads the *tiki* that frequently figures

74. New Guinea, Massim. *Club*. Leningrad.
75. Solomon Islands. *Club*. Mus. of Primitive Art, New York.
76. New Zealand. *Short whale-bone club*. Honolulu.

on the tattooed bodies of the men that carry them, the result being a harmony between weapon and user, due to the repetition of the same theme as cicatrice and as carving.

The variety of forms we find in Oceanian clubs is quite prodigious. They are classified by the shape of the head: cylindrical, spherical, discoid, truncated cone, turtle-beak, phallic, paddle-shaped, and so forth. But a good number of them can only be described as geometric. The various shapes which they assume are specific to well-defined regions. By and large these consist of geometric forms or groups of forms in which (in Melanesia at least, with the exception of Fiji and Tonga) ornamentation plays no part. The purity of line would call for a more detailed study were it not that these pieces, largely owing to their shapes, do not readily lend themselves to illustration.

The long lances used for thrusting, (Espiritu Santo, Malekula, Micronesia, Polynesia) and the short spears meant for throwing, have little aesthetic interest, except for the barbs. These are carved in wood, and often have a certain beauty due to their regular arrangement. Sometimes they are made from the spines of sting ray, either pointing backwards to the haft (this is the most deadly type) or towards the tip of the spear. The spines are lashed in position with meticulous care.

A small carving is sometimes placed just below the point or at the place where the shaft is gripped. This often represents a face (New Caledonia, New Hebrides), an animal head (e.g. the jaws of a cayman), a human figure or an entire animal. The criss-cross multicoloured lashings sometimes produce an interesting ornamental effect; this is particularly true of the arrows. They fall into distinct regional groups (Santa Cruz, Astrolabe Bay, Geelvink Bay). In northern Australia and the Admiralty Islands, pointed flakes of stone are fastened to spears by thongs and a vegetable gum embellished with painted decorative motifs.

The bow is seldom decorated, since any incision might weaken it, but spear-throwers which serve to increase the projectile's impact are often decorated with local themes in Australia and the Sepik region. In Australia the geometric designs are carved directly in the wood, while in the Sepik region delicately carved naturalistic motifs in bamboo are fastened to the spear-thrower.

In regions where the shield exists—New Guinea, the Solomons and Australia—the large surface available lends itself admirably to decoration. The form of the shield, which tends to be massive, is never modified. The decorative motifs comprise the usual local themes and techniques: incised (Australia), painted (Sepik, Massim), partial coverings of pearl-shell inlay (Solomons).

In the Solomons a shield is found made entirely of interwoven reeds and creepers forming regular geometric patterns which are emphasized by coloured lines. On Karkar Island, off the north coast of New Guinea, a similar technique is employed for joining together and decorating three curved lengths of wood. In southern New Britain, plain rattan thongs are used to bind the shield together, and the exposed wooden surfaces carry an incised and painted decoration of concentric circles and parallel rows of notches. The shields of the Sulka, in the north of the same island, are painted with simple themes resembling those on the masks covered with tapa-cloth.

The Asmat shields, from the interior of south-western New Guinea, are decorated with

104

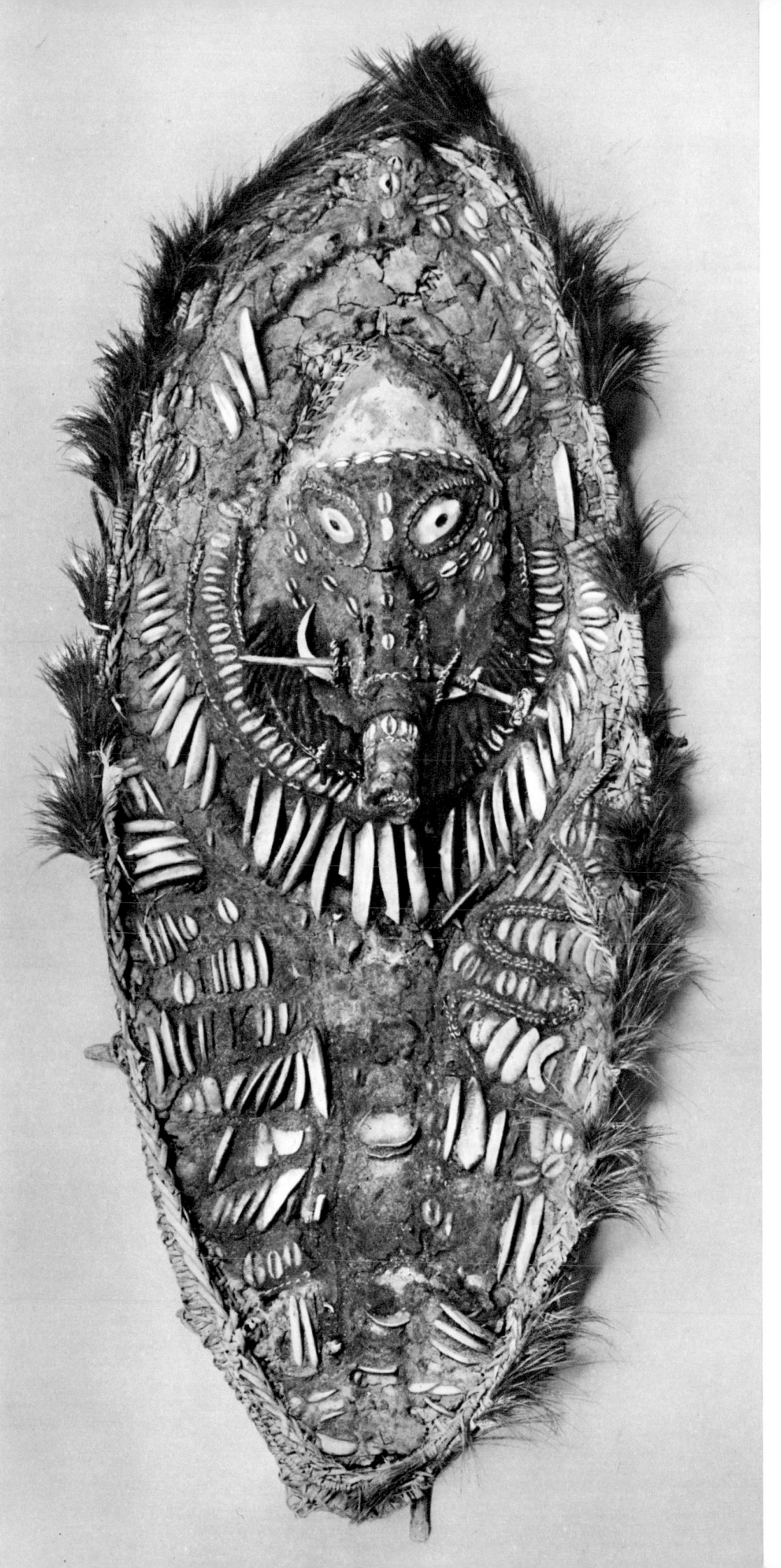

78. New Guinea, Asmat. *Manufacture and painting of shields*.
79. New Guinea, Asmat. *Shield*. Mus. of Primitive Art, New York.

representations, in relief, of groups of figures or motifs derived from large segments of the human body. They are enhanced with colour often used in an original way: the design in relief is given the same colour (usually white), as the ground, while the interior of the motif or figure, which is countersunk, stands out in red.

Of the agricultural implements there is little to be said from the aesthetic viewpoint. Among the rare exceptions are the carved ladders used for staking yams in New Guinea. These are cut out of a single tree-trunk and the steps have an incised decoration or are supported by figurines. To the same category belong the stilt foot-rests carved with *tiki* faces from the Marquesas. These however are playthings rather than useful tools.

Secular Art

In the New Hebrides the construction of grade monuments serves to commemorate a man's attainment of a certain rank in the social hierarchy. These monuments present certain purely aesthetic elements, since they involve the employment of sculpture, platforms, stones and flowers, which though symbolic are devoid of content. The symbolic sequence is interesting to study. In North Ambrim, we find a hierarchy of thirteen grades, called *mage*, of the following types:

1. *Fangtasum:* the attribute of this grade is a private cooking hearth, away from women and children.
2. *Mwel:* the attribute is a young cycas palm planted on the edge of the dance floor.
3. *Wer:* the monument is an upright flat stone painted black.
4. *Sagran:* the attribute is a low relief sculpture in tree-fern above which is a platform where the title-holders come to dance, one after the other, while the crowd pelts them with fruit and nuts.
5. *Liun:* accession to this grade is marked by the erection of a flat stone painted with patches of red surrounded by black circles.
6. *Gulgul:* (two variants):
   (a) *Gulgul wer:* a monument of flat stone, with red and black patches, set up on a mound.
   (b) *Gulgul bwerang:* tree-fern carving of a human face.
7. *Wurwur:* the attribute is a high relief sculpture with a human face above an animal, fish or lizard; on top is a dance platform.
8. *Simok:* the attribute is a flat stone, half black and half white, standing on end.
9. *Hiwir:* the monument is a large sculpture with a human face and arms crossed over a penis: this, too, is surmounted by a dance-platform.
10. *Wet ne mweleun:* a flat, upright stone, half black, half white, on a small mound.
11. *Mage linbul:* this grade is indicated by a ditch, covered with a single pitch roof, sheltering a pair of statues, male and female, having huge heads and exaggerated sexual organs.
12. *Loghbaro:* the attribute is a rectangular heap of stones with a large flat stone erected at one end.
13. *Mal:* the same block of stones surmounted by a roof set on carved posts with the carving of a falcon on the ridge-pole; the flat stone in this case represents, in miniature, the façade of the men's house.

80. New Hebrides, Ambrim. *Grade-symbol carving.* Basle.

81. New Hebrides, South-east Malekula. *Grade-symbol carving.* Musée de l'Homme, Paris.

82. New Hebrides, Ambrim. *Grade-symbol carving*. Basle.
83. New Hebrides, Ambrim. *Grade-symbol carving (detail)*. Basle.

Here we are dealing with a visual representation of a complex hierarchy where one can detect a progression based upon flat, upright stones, painted in various ways, and a parallel progression of tree-fern sculpture, beginning with a stylized human face, followed by a complete body, and culminating in the representation of a couple. No two of these hierarchies of grades are exactly the same, and nowhere do we find all the same attributes. In the New Hebrides and the Sepik region, there is a system of sale and purchase of ceremonial elements which permits the acquisition of a monument or a ritual to be added to one's own possessions or sold again to a neighbour. This permits the most unexpected hybrid structures in which the logical sequence seen at Ambrim often disappears. Material components shift from the secular cycle of the hierarchy of grades to esoteric cycles with a more obviously religious context, or vice versa, at the purchaser's whim.

The hollow wooden drums form a category of monumental work much more generalized in Oceania. In the New Hebrides they stand upright in the ground, but elsewhere they are used horizontally, set on logs. The Polynesian drum has a large opening and is turned on its

110

side so that it can be struck both on the outer surface of the upper lip and the inner surface of the lower. The value of this Polynesian drum is determined by its shape and the quality of the wood. Unlike skin drums, whose hollow body is covered with openwork decoration, it is seldom decorated.

The Melanesian drum has a narrow opening. If it is used upright it is usually beaten on its right side and has a cavity hollowed out in consequence. The horizontal drums tend to lose their cylindrical shape and, viewed from the side, show flattened faces terminating in a lip.

New Hebridean drums are not connected with the hierarchy of grades. On Ambrim there are special rituals for making and setting them up, but no specific symbolism is attributed to them. On Malekula the rituals of consecration form part of a vaguely correlated group of rituals called *nalawan*, a name which conveniently serves to cover both semi-secret ceremonies and those of a less secret nature.

Some have thought to see a phallic form in the shape of the New Hebridean drum, a view which seems to be supported by certain examples from South West Bay. The slit would then be the vulva, and we should have a case of a double sexual symbol. Native informants however, in no way confirm this suggestion. Although the drum in the Musée de l'Homme, brought back by the 'Korrigane' has a rounded top, with eyes and mouth countersunk and no other decoration, and gives the impression of a circumcised penis, others from the same region have a straight-cut top and nothing phallic in their appearance. Furthermore, the Melanesians never shrink from sexual symbols, and it hardly seems necessary to add to those which they spontaneously employ.

In New Hebridean drums the slit is the mouth of a person whose face is portrayed in relief above the body of the instrument. The personage is unspecified and has no name. The instrument is given human form, as is logical, because it has a voice, but it embodies no spirit and no cult is addressed to it. Tabus govern its manufacture and setting up, but subsequently the only restriction imposed is that it should not be played without sufficient reason, since this would, for one thing, tend to reduce its effectiveness as a transmitter of messages. There is nothing surprising in the respect paid to an instrument so costly to acquire and so useful to the community.

An early authority, Parkinson, states that in the Admiralty Islands the body of the drum stands for the belly of a person whose head and shoulders are represented by one carved end of the drum, and lower limbs by the other.

Whether the owner of the drum is an individual for whose benefit the sculptor has worked on commission, or a community for which the drum is an essential means of communication or merely a generator of rhythm, the playing of the drum is for the benefit of all. In Oceania, there is no drum 'language' of the African type; instead signals are sent by means of rolls of differing rhythms, each series of which has a precise significance. To designate an individual the drum roll indicating his father's village will be followed by that for his mother's village. If this combination is, by any chance, insufficient, there may be added the drum roll appropriate to the rank assigned to the man to be summoned.

An elaborate ritual goes with the inauguration of each new drum. Once its 'voice' has been established by means of a magic rite which procedes several hours of uninterrupted drum-

84. New Hebrides, Tomman Island, Malekula. *Monumental drum (detail)*

ing, the instrument takes its place beside its predecessors in the paraphernalia of everyday life : to pass messages as well as to provide, as part of a set of several drums of different sizes, the rhythmic accompaniment to dances and songs. The only qualification needed for its use is the competence of the player whose role is in no sense comparable with that of the priest of an idol.

The material culture of the New Hebridean archipelago provides us with another instance of secular art embracing social value: drawings in sand or dust, a tradition which existed in the central area of northern New Hebrides. In Ambrim these are called *tu*, a term which Christian translators were too quick to take as meaning writing. Elsewhere the same term is applied to string games, known to, but generally despised by, those who practise these drawings which are related to the universal, but particularly South Asian, theme of the labyrinth.

A suitable space in the black sand or the powdery, volcanic soil is cleared and smoothed with the palm of the hand. The draughtsman first sets out the main features of his design by means of isolated dots or parallel lines; or better, and most frequently, he makes a grid consisting of a double series of parallel lines intersecting at right angles. From this point, the technique seems similar to that of some western drawing games. The object is to achieve a continuous line without removing the finger from the ground and without crossing the grid except at its points of intersection and never in the same direction at the same point. Success in such a test implies a certain capacity for abstraction. These designs seem to be the fruit of a tradition in which neither privilege nor function plays a part; prestige accrues to the most skilful performer, no matter who he is. Starting from the grid, tresses and scrolls unfold themselves and sometimes lines are added to the edges of the design to make clear what is represented: bird's feet, the smoke of a steamer, etc. The finished designs give an impression of symmetry as regards one axis at least. They may include representations of plants: yams, taro fruit trees; or of sea creatures: fish, sharks, turtles; of birds or bats; or even of a hut, a canoe, or a European ship. Mythical subjects may be treated: the guardian of the land of the dead, or the garb of a marine monster which certain sorcerers are said to assume in order to drag their victim under water, to give the impression of accidental death. Or they may represent ritual objects (masks) in which case they must not be seen by everybody.

Except when performed for people who have already learnt to carry out the designs, the work needs to be accompanied by explanations. This usually takes the form of a game in which the oldest take the lead in order to instruct the adolescents. Even when a certain design cannot be executed in the presence of a non-initiate, a woman or a child, the ban has nothing to do with the technique; it applies only to the object portrayed.

The string games, which occur everywhere, contain a greater automatic element, since the position of the fingers, as regards the loops held or left free, necessarily determines the next figure. Each of the figures in a series, or the principal figure culminating a sequence, possesses a particular meaning which varies from island to island; the chanting of a couplet gives the explanation. Often, too, the symbolism dealing with birds, fish and flowers, is overtly sexual and the elders amuse themselves by explaining it to the youngsters.

Another type of design occurs on the engraved bamboos of New Caledonia. These

85. New Hebrides, Mendu, South-east Malekula. *Group of drums*.

pieces, today very rare and dispersed through various museums of Europe, are something of a mystery. Madame Lobsiger-Dellenbach, director of the Ethnographic Museum, Geneva, has published reproductions of most of them, with a learned commentary. Her interpretations, while not exhaustive, show with what skill and precision the Melanesian artists depicted, from one bamboo to another, agrarian and ceremonial rituals and also alluded to their contacts with Europeans.

Nothing suggests that this art lasted for any time. It disappeared quite soon without leaving trace and none of the museum pieces is recent. While it is true that incised decorations, often geometric, on bamboo internodes, are known throughout the archipelagos of Melanesia, and that the bamboo-flutes of Ambrim are decorated on the upper surface with masks and canoes, we never find such complete scenes, so precise a social or technical 'geography', as on these pieces. Technically very close in style to the engraved bamboos are certain spontaneous designs of Maurice Leenhardt's first pupil, Boesou Eurijisi, a Protestant pastor and one-time carver of masks.

In the case of the engraved bamboos the observer cannot fail to be struck by the fact that the European costumes are those of officers, soldiers and sailors of the Second Empire, that the European houses are of the pre-fabricated type manufactured at that time in Australia, that the

115

hut carvings are most frequently in the style of the Canala region where Napoleonville, the colony's chief military base, after Noumea, the capital, was located. This justifies us in thinking that this artistic flowering may have been the result of the meeting of two cultures ; also perhaps, of the amazement of the Melanesians at what seemed to them to be the magic power of writing and of drawing too since many naval officers of that period made a hobby of sketching and painting.

Magic Art

The term 'magic art' has acquired a wealth of meanings and its use in æsthetics has increased over the past decades; a recent example is André Breton's *l'Art magique*. If we disregard the realm of literature and the magic of words and confine ourselves to the results of a half century of research, we shall properly restrict the epithet 'magic' to those acts which the protagonists believe to be directly efficacious. If the intervention of an ancestor or of some mythical person who is invoked is necessary, the rite in question has no more than mediate efficacy and belongs to the realm of religion; the sign supplements or reinforces the verbal formula.

Art which is magical in this sense has a very restricted range. The ingredients and accessories normal to Oceanian sorcery are no more than packets of herbs, leaves, twigs and pebbles which

86, 87. New Hebrides, Ambrim. *Sand drawings.*

may be supplemented by material of human origin: hairs, nail parings, excrement, and the remains of food. In 'love magic', use may be made of the conjunction of more or less phallic stones and others which resemble the vulva, but these are no more than natural freaks. The magic stones used in fishing or agricultural rites may not be sufficiently recognizable and may be 'improved' to make them more obviously portray fish or tubers. But they are so crudely shaped that it is difficult to include them in the category of art, even under the rubric of magic.

The amuletic stones of the New Hebrides furnish a better example. These stones, of a compact, easily worked, volcanic tufa, shaped to a roughly ovoid outline, bear on one or on all sides, one or more human faces, either incised or in low relief. In some of these the line is strong and clear-cut, comparable with the style of the best drum heads inscribed within a crescent (Ambrim). This face is generally surrounded by a lozenge-shaped motif, symbolizing two pig's lower jaws, with spiral tusks.

On Pentecost the possession of such stones is thought to bring wealth to their owners in the form of finely worked mats or pigs. Rain-makers, in the islands to the north-east of Malekula, make use of them for a ritual in which the stones play the principal part; wrapped in symbolic leaves and fragments of bark, they are placed temporarily in a water-hole in the barrier reef.

On Ambrim these stones are always known as 'pig stones' *muyu ne bu*. Their owners use

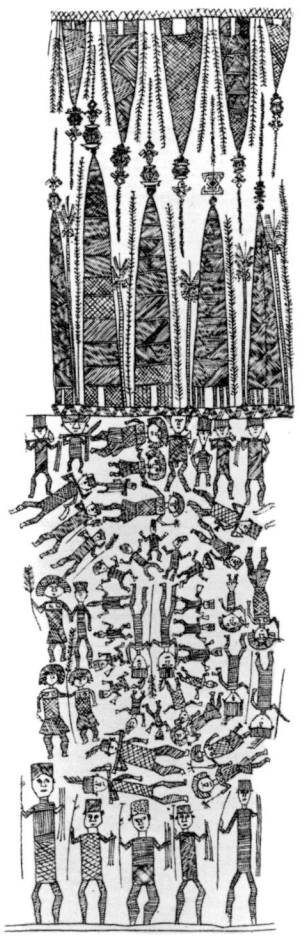

88. New Caledonia. *Incised bamboo tube.* Geneva.

89. Easter Island. *Male statue (detail)*. British Museum.

them in a rite intended to ensure the success of negotations for the purchase, sale or borrowing of valuable pigs on the most favourable terms. Success in these transactions is a necessary condition for 'making the grade' in the social hierarchy. If the terms for borrowing valuable animals were too onerous, repayment would be difficult and would impede any further social advancement by the borrower.

Three different techniques for employing these stones are in current use. The carved stone may be taken from its usual hiding-place and set at the entrance of the hut or village with its face (if there is only one), turned in the direction in which the owner intends to go to do business. Another method is to leave the stone called 'mother stone,' permanently in contact with smaller translucent stones called its 'children.' One of these secondary stones is then slipped into the belt to ensure the success of forthcoming discussions. A third method consists of scraping the surface of the stone on one side, collecting the powder thus obtained and rubbing the body with it.

Whatever the method employed, myth has no place in these techniques: in each case the user is performing a 'sympathetic' rite whose efficacy is thought to be both automatic and certain.

At Ulawa in the Solomons the father paints a frigate bird motif in chalk on the arm of his adolescent son at the moment of initiation, as a protection against those who might wish him ill.

118

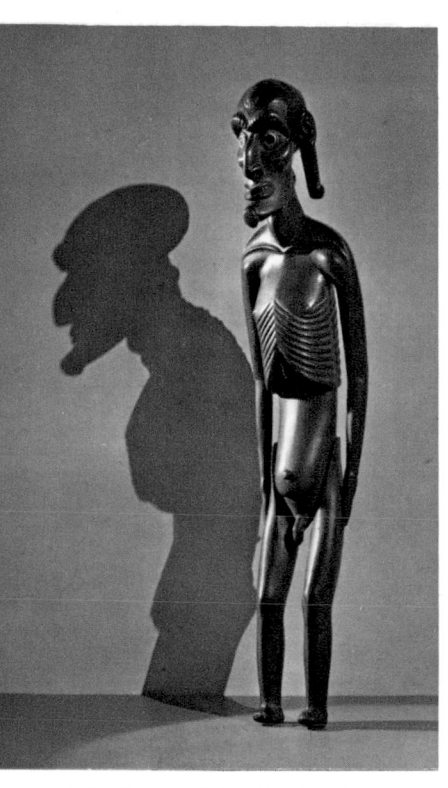

90. Easter Island. *Male statue*.
Philadelphia.
91. New Guinea, Papua. *Votive plaque*. Leningrad.

In their love magic, certain aboriginals of Arnhem Land, North Australia, make use of small carved objects portraying a bird with an insect in its beak, a fish or a rat, or made in the form of the anchor of a Malay *prau*. Placed in front of or upon the girl being wooed, and manipulated from a distance by a piece of string, the object represents both the desire experienced by the lover and the love which is to grip the woman and draw her to her waiting suitor. No aesthetic intention lies behind the naturalistic device. The wax figure whose heart is pierced with a needle has never been regarded as a work of art, any more than have the anatomical diagrams or the bronze figures which indicate the crucial points for acupuncture.

On the other hand when we turn to bodily adornments of a temporary kind, we should be careful that our judgments are not too dogmatic. The practices of facial painting, of temporary tattooing by means of mildly blistering juices, of wearing feathers, flowers and ornamental or perfumed leaves, serve at once a personal aesthetic ambition and a desire to make a favourable impression on the beholders, male and female, or upon one particular individual among them. During festivals, the decoration of the body is accompanied by magic rites designed to ensure its efficacy. The dancer should be irresistible, not only for the prestige which his group gains thereby, but also to ensure success in his love affairs. In this case the work of art is the person himself, but we are here in a domain in which the aesthetic element has always been considered to be marginal, despite its undoubted social dynamism.

Ritual Art

Certain aesthetic acts are the object of groups of rites and detailed prohibitions, in contrast to the acts concerned with the manufacture of drums and monumental sculpture, which even when they form part of ritual equipment, are made by paid specialists. But the fact that rites centre about a work of art does not mean necessarily that it has a religious content. Hence the distinction which we are trying to set up between secular, religious and ritual art.

Where tattooing fulfils an essential social function, (for it always includes some elements of this), it is the result of a rite whose performance is itself an act of aesthetic creation. Polynesia is its *locus classicus*.

The technique of this type of bodily decoration is based on two procedures: the making of lines or bands of dark colour, by inserting under the skin an oily soot derived from nuts or, in New Zealand, from pine resin. The implement was a sort of bone or ivory comb with sharp teeth, fixed almost at right angles to a haft, rather like an adze. This tool, after being dipped in pigment, was placed on a selected point on the body and driven in by a sharp blow with a piece of wood used as a mallet; tapa cloth tampons were applied to staunch the blood. The use of closely packed points ensured a satisfactory surface effect.

Both in New Zealand and in the Marquesas the tattoo design exhibits the same themes and motifs as those on wood carvings. In New Zealand the implement sometimes had a cutting edge instead of points so that the skin was cut instead of being perforated. This gave a cicatrized effect, the lines of the design appearing hollow. This operation caused a swelling of the lips and was so painful, that carved funnels were used to enable the patient to take food. He was not, in any case, allowed to touch the food with his hands.

120

The motifs had no local significance, at least for the man who wore them. Famous tattooists were called in from a distance. They reproduced their own designs upon the faces of their patients. On the other hand, complete facial tattooing was a mark of high birth for reasons of prestige and the cost of the operation. The heads of chiefs were carefully emptied after death, heated in an oven and then smoke-dried. Many museums possess specimens of these.

Each curvilinear motif received a different name, corresponding to its location on the face but the shape of the motif, a rudimentary or garbled spiral, does not seem to have been described by this name.

The Marquesan tattooist's art was more complex and ambitious since it aimed at covering the whole body. It was believed that its success depended upon rigorous sexual abstinence which had to be observed by the artist, his assistants and the patient before and during the operation. The artists were members of the highly esteemed class called *tuhuna*, experts in incised decoration on stone, wood and human skin; they were enrolled in this class by virtue of their experience after a long apprenticeship. The path to the place of tattooing, a new hut which was burnt when the operation was finished, was forbidden to women.

Virtuosity was the desideratum. By twos and threes in the same hut, the 'masters' competed in tracing, with the maximum intricacy, the basic design, in setting up records of dexterity and speed and of endurance on the part of their clients.

As Mrs. Willowdean C. Handy has pointed out, tattooing was available to everyone. But the area of body covered depended on the remuneration paid to the artist and consequently indicated the rank and relative wealth of those concerned, though no rules governed this aspect of the operation. Boys and girls were equally eligible for tattooing. No motif indicated either rank or office. At most, at the end of the work when the body was almost wholly covered, a final motif might distinguish one island from another or denote a mark of a local school.

It might be supposed that the basic tattoo theme, the schematic portrayal of the human body in the form called *tiki*, was the representation of a god. A cycle of myths relates to a god called *Tiki*, but the word *tiki* by itself by no means always has an exclusively religious connotation. *Tiki* is simply the name given to a stylized image of the human body and was consequently a favourite motif for incised decoration. It has no divine connotation, except in certain specific ceremonies which are directed to a definite end, when the powers invoked, vouched for by myths, play a mediatory role.

On the southern fringe of Malekula in the New Hebrides we still find fully modelled portrayals of the human body. These consist of figures made of vegetable matter. The limbs are made from rolls of banana leaf, reduced to their ribs by fermentation. The trunk consists of a flat piece cut from a tree-fern base; the whole is covered with a vegetable plaster which holds the parts together and enables paint to be applied to the surfaces and to the modelling indicating shoulders and knees.

A dried skull with a spider's web wig and a modelled face is used for the figure's head. The skull is that of a dead man, and an attempt is made to reproduce his features, once it has been cleaned by ants. The proportions of this figure are based on the measurements of the long bones. An attempt is made as far as possible to reproduce the dead man's characteristics, both of appearance and of social status, as indicated by the painting of his body, his ornaments, armlets and leg bands. Other indications are the small effigies on the limb-joints, in the hair or piled one above the other on vertical extensions rising from the shoulders. Each of them indicates a rank or a private ceremonial privilege.

This figure plays a leading part, six months after the man's death, in the last funerary ceremony which marks the end of mourning and of the compulsory seclusion of the widow. The latter, seated at its feet, takes part in the ceremony, weeping and caressing the image of her husband. The myth describing the circumstances of the manufacture of the first of these *rambaramb* speaks of them as 'dumb images.'

After the ceremony the figure is placed in the man's house. When it has disintegrated, the modelled skull is attached to the rafters. In no case are these images objects of worship, or even of fear or reverence. Those concerned with them have no compunction about selling them, although nothing would induce them to approach the communal ossuary where all the bones, except the skull, of the clan's dead are deposited.

Another feature of social life which also has a certain aesthetic quality is what, for want of a better term, we have to describe as coins. 'Traditional treasure' would be more accurate, for these objects are basic to skilfully controlled transactions between contracting parties on the occasion of births, marriages, deaths and the installation of a chief. The shell money of New Caledonia is one of the finest examples, technically speaking, and the most familiar from the sociological angle.

Certain clans have the privilege of fishing for the shells which form the raw material; they regulate the quantity and the rate of increase of the shells, both by magic and by hoarding them in a secret, shallow cache on the reef.

The flat face of the shell is ground down until a hole appears corresponding to the starting-point of the central internal canal. Then the cone of the shell is broken in such a way as to leave only the lower disc which is then reduced to the condition of a rudimentary bead. A large number of these beads are threaded together and worked over at the same time, by rubbing them down on a piece of flat schist, water being constantly poured on them while this is being done. Thus by dint of long, assiduous labour, evenly-shaped beads are produced, and these are assembled when there are enough of them.

Next the 'head' of the coin has to be constructed, for the whole piece symbolises the human body. The extremity is formed by a vegetable cord, on to each strand of which is fixed flying-fox fur, dyed brick-red. Between this and the string of beads, two rows of small cylinders, cut from the long bones of flying-fox or from the vertebra of fish, enclose a rectangle of finely woven coconut husk fibre edged with beads on each side. Fish-shaped pearl-shell pendants on each side represent the two arms of the body.

Each piece of money is carefully wrapped in a roll of vegetable cloth embroidered in fine thread known as 'flying-fox fur.' This purse is closed by a drawstring which must never end in a knot. An assemblage of several of these purses form the sacred money-bag of the clan. It always includes a model of a canoe hull, covered with grass cloth and flying-fox fur, a container in which is placed, according to the region in question, a miniature human head representing the god Urupwe or a figurine entirely in grass-work, made in a technique which, despite the difference in scale, is very close to the woven divine figures of the Society Islands.

122

Here we touch on the ambivalence in function of these shell coins, for the money itself has a symbolic value, although its use is secular. The hoard of money with the figure lying in a canoe constitutes, per se, one of the essential elements of local group cohesion, a feature which persists to this day. The image of the god must not be handled, nor must the 'basket' as a whole (a series of wrappings in the form of a packet) be touched without undergoing rituals in which creepers of a symbolic value are involved (*meamoru*). These plants avert the dangerous power emanating from the basket. All these elements: shell, flying-fox bone and fur, coconut fibre, the absence of knots, link up with the symbolic representation of life, and consequently with the continuity of the group: that is why exchange must be the rule, while the treasure itself can always remain intact.

Religious Art

The representation of divine beings is, in general, considered either as a religious act or as serving in some manner to complement religious acts.

We shall first consider rock paintings, called *wondjina*, from Kimberley district, north-western Australia. They are of two types, of which one portrays figures with vertical stripes on the body, as if floating in a robe. In this type the face has no mouth and is outlined by a red horseshoe-shaped band which may represent a forehead band, the halo with short rays being the hair. Against the white face the eyes stand out in black, sometimes ringed with white from which black eyelashes spring. The single nostril is joined to the eyes by a double line. There is a white belt round the body; the hands are sketched in roughly and feet, indicated by an imprint of the soles, complete the figure. Many examples are known, and its unexpected appearance in Australia has given rise to a number of hypotheses.

Other images, beside occasional drawings of animals and fruits, portray giant serpents, sometimes with *wondjina* figures and with drawings of men in a different style. This is the rainbow serpent, a classical figure of Australian mythology.

At the beginning of the appropriate season there takes place a ritual renovation of the colours of the paintings. The *wondjina* and the rainbow serpent represent the powers which control the atmospheric elements. In the Australian desert rain is a precious commodity. The parallel stripes on the body of the *wondjina* represent rain drops. Repainting the faces should ensure frequent downpours, though their form alters a little with each repainting. If animals and plants are depicted nearby, the ritual will ensure the multiplication of these species sufficiently to meet human needs. When the *wondjina* are female, the rite will ensure numerous children for the wives of the tribesmen. We see here a certain belief in the efficacy of the painting by the evocation of the power of the god *wondjina*, lord of the rain. This act of painting is not, therefore, to be considered solely as a magic rite. We have here a type of silent prayer, such as also occurs in social relations where a symbolic gesture suffices to indicate formally the suppliant's need.

The ancestor carvings of New Caledonia are more akin to bas-relief than to work in the round. They are found in various places and on the threshold of the great men's houses of the clan, as well as on the summit of the roof where the figures often have two faces. Their purpose is to give an impression of power and sometimes, as in New Zealand, by means of the motif of a protruding tongue, to symbolize force and wisdom. These carved pieces serve as memorials, to affirm the presence of the ancestral group whose unseen life continues. There is no question here of portraiture, not even of a schematic type. At the funerary feasts in honour of dead chiefs, the uterine kin of the dead take home the new images they have just inaugurated. As a result these images seldom remain where they were carved. But when the sacrifice takes place nearby, and prayers are offered in the steam that rises from the pot in which the votive yams are cooking, they are addressed to the effigy of the ancestor. His presence is thus a pledge given to the dead to leave the living in peace. At the end of the period of mourning, the dead man is addressed as follows:

Go back now to your maternal kin in the forest. Leave us.
We have loved you: we have made your portrait.

Polynesian statuary, where it exists, comes nearer to our idea of religious art, stemming as it does from elaborate cosmogonies. The statues or rough images of the divine being serve as permanent lodgings for the divinity which the priests alone can see.

In Tahiti, Oro, the god of War, was represented by a sort of woven packet. Carved human figures were used only as instruments of black magic.

In the Cook Islands the deity was a cane whose upper part carried a frieze of schematic figures, alternately full face and in profile: the smooth lower part was embedded in a roll of tapa cloth. The symbolism of these representations responds to the esoteric theologies of the priestly caste. The less exalted deities, clan divinities and those with specialized functions, fishing for instance, were more easily visualized, and given a more realistic appearance.

This abstract formalism is also found in the Marquesas where the representation of the divine ancestor was a cylindrical pole thrust in the ground and decorated with incised geometric motifs which recall more or less exactly the *tiki* theme. The stone statues surrounding the cult places were no more than spectacular adornments.

In New Zealand a carved fork, the only sacred object, was intended to serve as a perch for the spirit invoked, at the time when it was thought to be listening to the prayers and receiving the offerings. The human figures in bas-relief which cover the walls of the great houses portray the ancestors of the group but have no role in the cult. Each figure had its own name and commemorated a dead hero.

In the Hawaiian Islands, the principal gods were portrayed by a roll of tapa cloth decorated with feathers, which only the priests were allowed to see. The classical grimacing figures of Hawaii were deities of local groups or of workers' guilds. Less important figures made of basket-work covered with feathers, were carried by the priests into battle where their deliberately terrible appearance added weight to the curses hurled at the enemy.

The Easter Island sculptures pose an analogous problem. The small male and female ancestor images, *moai kavakava, moai paepae* were regarded as cult objects although their role was never precisely defined. They were carefully wrapped in tapa and exhibited at the time of

the festival of first-fruits and, usually, attached to the bodies of the dancers. Special hymns were chanted whenever they were taken out from their wrappings.

The large carvings in tufa were intended to be installed on the stone mausoleums, *ahu*, some of which had room for several of them. The oldest informants have always insisted that they were not cult objects but were put there merely to decorate the burial places. There is no reason to disbelieve them.

The votive plaques of Papua have the shape of an elongated oval with a kind of handle at each end. They are carved and painted with motifs portraying a human face, schematically depicted and set on a summarily indicated body. These plaques were carefully preserved in the men's houses (*eravo*). They are said to represent or serve to house certain water spirits which exercise magic powers and whose secrets are known only to their owners. For this reason they were sometimes placed near enemy skulls to protect the living from the invisible presence of the hostile dead. Some served as bull-roarers which were swung round to emit sounds which represented the voice of mythical beings or of the dead. Throughout Oceania, there is nothing more dangerous than the ghost of a man who has been murdered and whose funeral rites have not been carried out. Similarly, in Polynesia, the maleficent power of the spirits of still-born children is feared. The god Tiki is the interpretation of this concept in mythological terms.

Art as the Interpretation of Myth

In this section we propose to consider those images which represent not a single divine being but groups which are not yet, strictly speaking, cult objects.

In most of Central Australia, each clan preserves in a secret cult centre carved plaques of wood or schist called *tjurunga* which are periodically rubbed with red ochre and fat while the meanings of the motifs are explained to the newly initiated. This explanation takes the form of a narrative sung while the singer's finger follows the successive elements of the incised design, each of which suggests an incident in the myth. The classical accounts of these objects given by Spencer and Gillan enable us to detect a systematic symbolism based upon themes which, at first sight, seem purely geometric.

Two figures given by these authors show the two sides of an Arunta *tjurunga* belonging to a man of the Frog totem. On one side there are three groups of concentric circles representing three famous gum trees which grow side by side on the bank of the Hugh River at Imanda, the local cult centre of the Frog totem. Around the smallest circles are frogs born from these trees: the parallel lines joining these small circles represent the legs of the frogs. In fact, in the hollow parts of these trees there is found a species of frog whose croaking predicts the coming of rain.

On the other side of the *tjurunga* the gum trees, represented in the same manner, are linked by wide bands of parallel lines—their roots. Here and there are several smaller concentric circles from which sprout short strips of parallel lines representing small gum trees with their roots. Spots mark the tracks of frogs which are jumping on the river's sandy bed.

The artist has found it necessary not only to depict the solid masses of the objects, but also to emphasize the reality of their existence by showing everything that links them with the ground: tree roots, limbs and tracks of the frogs.

93. New Hebrides, South Malekula. *Heavy head-dress of tree-fern.* M.A.A.O., Paris.

There is no need to give here a description of each of the *tjurunga* for which we have adequate documentation. On comparing them, it is evident that no explicit language is involved; but the symbolism of the motifs presents a number of analogies a brief account of which may help in the understanding of this type of art.

The concentric circles represent living forms (men, animals, totem plants, eggs) or a part of such a form (eye, intestines, ovaries) or topographical settings mentioned in cycles of myths. The motifs seem to correspond to a feeling that certain elements are of special importance. Hence the primacy assigned to certain organs: the eye as the instrument of sight; the ovary which contains the life-creating power of the feminine element; the intestines which house the emotions and intelligence. As soon as a place is described in a myth, it acquires a specific 'personality' which the concentric circles represent in the same manner as they represent the body or its parts.

The bands of parallel lines linking the concentric circles stand for limbs of animals, the roots of plants, everything which binds them to the soil and reveals to the eyes of the experienced hunter, the existence of an animal, by revealing its tracks. Taken singly these lines represent such essentially linear elements as human tracks, paths, threads, or decorative marks on the body.

The spots also stand for the tracks of humans or animals. When placed around concentric circles they evoke a men's dance around a tree. In this case there is no need to represent the roots of the tree, since the footprints merge with them and combine to fix the trunk in the ground.

Interlocked hoops symbolize seated or, by extension, standing figures. They can also represent anatomical points: joints, or ribs. A similar analogy of forms can convert them into boomerangs.

Sinuous lines allow of a variety of interpretations wholly deriving, it would seem, from similarities of appearance: snakes, worms, lizard tails.

This is an almost unique instance of an art in which the symbolism of motifs has been studied in detail and in situ by ethnologists.

Another instance of the plastic interpretation of myth is to be found in the ground drawings of northern Central Australia (Warramunga). The best, from the aesthetic point of view, are those which relate to the snake Wollunqua, a giant serpent whose head, when it stands erect, is lost in the clouds. He lives in a water-hole in a lonely valley of the Murchison Mountains, and it is always feared that he may emerge and wreak destruction. His name, Wollunqua, is kept secret and may not be uttered but he is addressed as *urkulu napaurina*; otherwise men would wholly lose control of his deeds, and he would end up by devouring them all.

The rituals centring on Wollunqua are intended to propitiate him and at the same time to reaffirm the control which the group, claiming kinship with him, exercises over him. Thus there is no question here of the classical rites ensuring the multiplication of material totems whose existence is necessary for human survival. These rituals re-enacted the journeys of Wollunqua who made waterholes and left the seed of human beings wherever he halted. These 'Spirit-children,' to use the local terminology, used to wait there until a woman passed by; then they would enter into her body and cause her to conceive.

First, a sinuous line of red down on a white down ground was traced round a mound

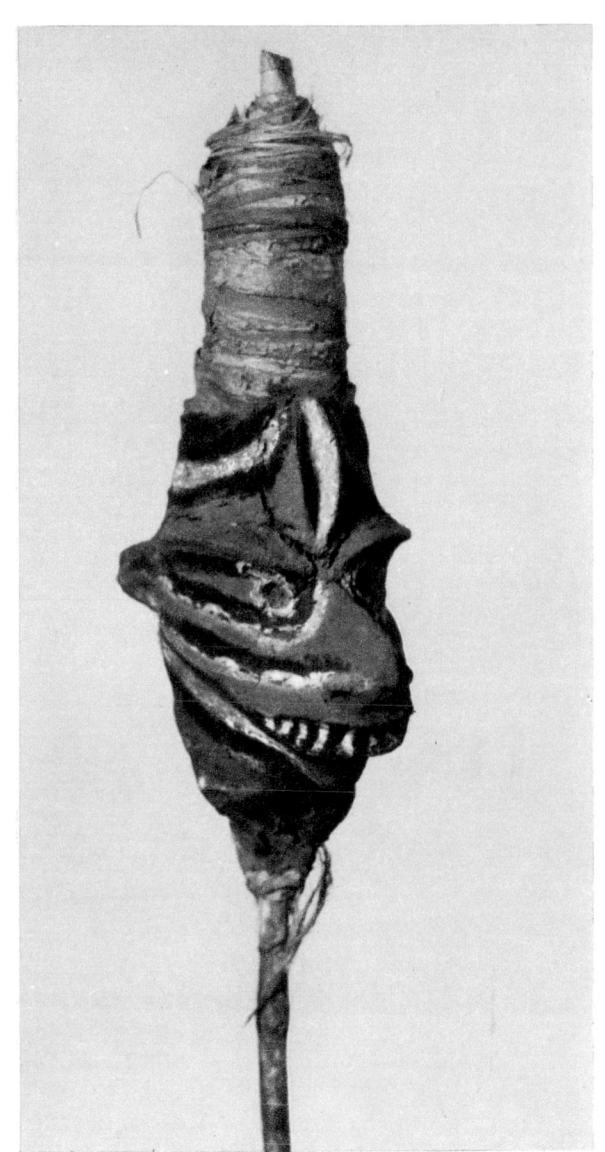

94, 95. New Hebrides, South Malekula. *Temes nevinbür figures*. Musée de l'Homme, Paris.

of earth shaped like the hull of a boat. The serpent thus depicted was accorded every honour and was even stroked at certain moments. It was destroyed at dawn by spear thrusts and blows from clubs before the rites associated with the paintings began.

Next came a sequence of paintings invoking the chief events in the life of the serpent. After a space on the ground had been carefully cleared and flattened, water was poured on it and the surface was rubbed until quite smooth. When the water had evaporated, the ground had a hard crust to which was applied the first coat of red and yellow ochre. Then, using a finger dipped in red ochre or powdered charcoal mixed with animal fat, depending upon the colour of the background, an elder traced the principal motif: serpentine lines or circles. Next, the younger men covered the ochre ground with a mass of white spots. The pigment was kaolin, mixed with saliva in the mouth, then spat into a container and diluted with water. This colour was applied to the ground with a brush made by chewing the end of a stick to fray it. All these operations were accompanied by songs telling of the journey of the serpent

129

97. New Guinea, Sepik, Kaminimbit. *Canoe shield.* Basle.

Wollunqua. Each day the previous day's painting was obliterated and a fresh one made.

The first of these paintings represented Tikoneri, the place where Wollunqua, starting out from his home in a water-hole, tried to bore through the earth but found it too hard and gave up the attempt. Concentric circles represented the water-hole; two curved lines at the bottom, the neck of the serpent turning from side to side; three lines curved at the top representing sloughs of little serpents; and other concentric circles representing trees where the Wollunqua had left a large number of 'Spirit-children.'

Another drawing, of exceptional size, was rather less conventional. At the place called Ununtumura Wollunqua ceased his wanderings, dug down into the earth and returned home underground. A long sinuous line indicates the serpent: its head is marked by a swelling just beside the concentric circles which show the place where the serpent is in the process of entering into the ground. Further concentric circles figure at various other points: the biggest represent trees, the smaller the bushes where the spirit children were left. Human tracks near the serpent

131

96. New Guinea, Sepik, Iatmül. *Ridge-board of a house.* Mus. of Primitive Art, New York.

recall that a man accompanied Wollunqua in his wanderings with the intention of trying to make him return. When they reached Ununtumura, the man struck the serpent with all his might in the hope of making him go down: two curved bands represent the man's arms in the act of striking. Wollunqua coiled himself around the man, drew himself up and plunged straight into the ground. So it was that he returned with his companion to Thapauerlu.

The most characteristic element in the regional culture of Papua is, perhaps, the communal house, a huge edifice with a roof whose long axis curves upwards giving it the form of a hull. In this enormous building, known locally as *ravi* or *eravo*, take place all the major rituals. It may measure more than a hundred yards in length, and has an open verandah with a widely jutting roof which thrusts upwards like a monster's gaping jaws.

The communal house is divided into two 'sides', to accommodate two intermarrying groups having reciprocal ceremonial functions. Within this basic division, the interior of the house is divided on each side into as many compartments as there are patrilineal groups in the community. Masks and cult objects belonging to each lineage are stored there. At the end of the house there is a room, cut off by a wall, access to which is permitted only to the leading men of the tribe. Stored there are the huge basketwork figures which the women must never see. For this reason, whenever they are transferred from an old to a new house, this is done under the cover of night. Each figure is conceived of as being at once the property and the tutelary spirit of the lineage. Offerings are made to it; auguries may be had from it. A myth links it simultaneously with a branch of the Purari river and with a fish which embodies it in the waters.

In addition to the votive plaques discussed above, whose motifs are specific to each clan and are vouched for by reference to a definite myth, tapa masks are stretched on a framework of reed, and decorated with a human face in red and black treated in the style of the votive plaques. The edges of the painted motifs are emphasized by thin reed strips fixed to the tapa cloth; these delimit the area of each colour before the actual painting. This is not carried out until just before the feast at which these masks will be displayed. They are worn, over a long leaf-cloak reaching the ground, at the feasts at the end of the initiation rites for youths, when women and children are allowed to watch. The end of such feasts used to be marked by the despatch of a human victim, an outsider, whose blood splashed the masks.

As many as a hundred masks might be displayed at these feasts, each bearing the name of the mythical personage it purported to represent. These masks were of great size and did not, in practice, differ greatly from each other. The coloured motifs which surrounded each face were peculiar to a specific lineage. Smaller masks, of more originality, represented totems: insects, birds, fish, plants or even quite imaginary forms, sometimes mounted on a conical support. In contrast to the first category, these were not considered sacred and did not possess any esoteric symbolism known exclusively to initiates. After use, they were left to rot away. The large masks on the other hand had to be burned ritually, while the spirits they represented were thanked for attending the feast and were assured that they would be invited again.

In Cape York peninsula, in the far north of Australia, which has contacts with the Torres Strait and the Papuan world, there is a cycle of myths involving initiation and the use of masks.

This occurs among the Hibu Kokoyao tribe. Ihway, the salt water cayman is the the *tjilbo*, 'old one', the chief of the ancestors, for whom all toil. Inventor of the drum, he is the moving spirit of the initiation ceremonies which recount his life and tell of the opening of the vagina which permits the union of men and women.

Various masked figures take part in the *Okainta*, an initiation ceremony which is linked with the Ihway myth. Masks of human faces, called *olko*, are used in the first part of the rites. These are made of palm leaf, fitted with a beeswax nose and with transverse bands painted in black and red. The other masks are of two kinds: first a plain open gullet, set horizontally, its jaws furnished with sharp teeth; second, a cylindrical head-dress which acts as a pedestal for an elongated, thinner figure with two open jaws. Either of these objects may represent Ihway but the second type may also portray Nyiwall the saw-fish; Ihway is recalled by a pair of toothed, open jaws springing from the pedestal itself. All these masks carry wands decorated with white feathers, each mask having a fixed number of wands.

The masked figures dance to the sound of a small drum, a cylinder of hollow wood, one end covered with a yam skin, the other end terminating in a cayman head. Totemic animals are depicted on the sides in poker-work. This drum, unlike the masks, may be used in the presence of women and of the uninitiated. The initiatory rites, of the Ihway cycle however, take place within a sort of rectangular courtyard, fenced with interwoven branches.

In the south of Malekula, New Hebrides, we find a series not so much of masks as of head-dresses of varying weight which are covered with, or made from, a vegetable paste. In the latter case the structure is reinforced with strips of bamboo. The light framework is often joined to a heavier object made from a piece of tree-fern stump. This composite structure is difficult to wear for more than a few minutes on account of its weight. It consists of a sort of head-dress which serves as a pedestal for a complete figure, shown seated with arms and legs crossed.

One of these beings, known as *temes malaw*, is believed to live under a stone on the island of Nour Tombui (Ten Sticks Island), south of South West Bay. Now and then he arises from the earth and comes to take part in dances held in distant villages. He can be recognised by his refusal to eat the pork which is offered to him. Another mask represents the ogress Nevinbimbaau: a small figure at her side is either her son, Sasndaliep, or her husband, Ambat Malondr. A myth tells how Nevinbimbaau caught her victims by making them fall into a pit whose opening had been carefully concealed. The god Ambat and his four brothers, who have names resembling those of the five fingers, were captured in this way, one after the other, but they escaped by following a banyan root which led to the village of Iumorau on the island of Tommau. Ambat is the god who brought civilisation to south-western Malekula.

Nevinbimbaau presides over another institution, called *Nevinbür*. In this ceremony, figurines consisting of a modelled head fixed to a stick or to a piece of bamboo are displayed behind a high fence. Sometimes arms are added to the head. The puppets are thought to be the children of three manikins, *rambaramb*, who are placed on seats in front of the barrier, under the shelter of a roof. These represent Masip and his two wives, whose mother is Nevinbimbaau.

The Nevinbimbaau play, in three scenes, is given for the benefit of women and children and the uninitiated. In the first scene four initiates dance inside the enclosure near the barrier. Each holds in his hand one of the figures, a *temes nevinbür*, so that it appears to be dancing above the barrier. An old man emerges from the enclosure, club in hand, and, appearing before the barrier, crushes the heads one after another with a blow.

After this rite the initiates set about making hundreds of new figures, a task which may occupy the whole of a year. A new dance is then staged, with the dancers carrying new *temes nevinbür*; the dancers stamp their feet on planks set over a ditch, to make a dull sound which is the voice of the *temes*. After this dance, comes a new scene in which the actors are two marionettes with arms, named Awus Nambangk and Ambwir Mbuas. Someone in front of the barrier offers a taro cake to them which they take and put into their mouths.

Next, an old man comes out of the enclosure and picks a quarrel with Mansip, who answers from inside the enclosure through buried bamboo pipes. The reply is in the dialect of the Wilemb district, which lies north of Seniang where the ritual takes place. After a brief dialogue the old man thrusts his lance through Mansip and his two wives. At this moment a red vegetable fluid to simulate the blood of the victims is poured from inside the barrier and heartrending cries come from the bamboos. Finally the barrier and the three mannikins are set on fire.

Some masks from New Ireland, with large openwork appendages on the sides, are called *murua*. They are worn so that the arms are left bare, the body being covered with leaves from the armpits downwards. William Groves (1936), described the ritual observed in connection with them:

'*Six large figures, appropriately decorated, the* murua *themselves, emerged from the crema- tion ground where they had been secretly prepared. They made their way in file, with slow, heavy tread, up from the beach to the open space in the village, where hundreds and hundreds of local natives and visitors had gathered round. With each heavy step the figures took, a bustle-like bunch of* Cordyline terminalis *leaves bobbed up and down on the rump ; shell rattles attached to wrists and ankles provided appropriate music to the solemn, stately, forward movement. After each deliberate step the figures paused, to turn their great ungainly* murua *heads slowly from side to side, as if peering uncertainly into the unfamiliar world of mortal man. One old woman, unable to control her emotional outburst, rushed forward and placed her hands on the body of one of the figures, wailing and calling upon it by the name of someone dead in her time. Other women followed, until each of the figures was surrounded by a number of older women, all wailing piteously and calling them by names of deceased kinsmen. In the assembled throng, children, cowered in fear at their squatting mothers' feet, and even the modern sophisticated youths of the village appeared impressed to the point of silence.*

'*As the spirit figures (for that is what they were), their peculiar dance performance ended, made their slow way back towards the cremation enclosure, the old women walked beside them talking appealingly, saying amongst other things: "Wait for me ; soon I too will come".*'

This is clearly a case of what Marcel Mauss called *expression obligatoire des sentiments*, but it also evidences a belief shared by both actors and spectators in the real presence of the dead within the masks.

In Central Australia ceremonial adornments are made with bird's down, which may be white or dyed red, and are stuck to the skin with human blood. The whole body is covered with sinuous lines which continue upwards to a high head-dress. The man thus concealed in a fantastic garment of red and white represents the ancestor whose exploits he mimes in public. Once he is thus attired he assumes the ancestor's personality; his consciousness of his own existence is completely absorbed by the myth so that he comes to believe that on his present role depends the future fertility of the crops from which he and his kin derive their subsistence.

All these examples give an impression of myths being in a sense lived out. It is doubtful whether the recital of a myth without being possessed by it is normally possible. Only occasionally have Polynesians tried to represent a myth by engraving it on a durable and solid substance. Apart from the upper registers of the carved poles which, in the Cook Islands, represent the families of deities, one of the only instances is that of the ear ornaments from the Marquesas. In each case we find a series of figures displayed in different situations. However a complete myth can be related in this manner:

'We see chief Akani with his two slingers and the two bird-women on their high swing; At the chief's order, the slingers aim at the bird-women; The bird-women are brought down.'

The rock-carved and engraved images of the god Makemake of Easter Island fall in the same category except in cases where they are the objects of a ritual cult. The bird-man with an egg in his hand symbolized the yearly rite at the end of which the notable, whose servant had discovered on the isle of Mohunni the first egg laid by the sea-swallow, became for the period of a year the personification of a bird-man.

A similar motif, of a man and a bird, is found in the sculpture of New Guinea, especially on the prows of canoes. While in some areas their presence is deemed necessary for the success of voyages, others attribute to them a merely ornamental function and the prestige which accrues to the owners of the canoe who have paid the sculptor's fees. Codrington illustrates a carved head attached to the prow of a canoe from Florida which is extended to the keel by a piece of flat wood fastened by vegetable thongs: the head's sway is believed to have the power to calm the waves. Bamboo tubes are attached above the head: these tubes are wrapped in red tresses, and filled with relics of the dead and with leaves possessing magic power. This shows how little efficacy is attributed to the sculpture itself.

That ancient myths are still a source of inspiration under certain circumstances is proved by the very interesting results each time an investigator, usually a missionary, places paper and pencil in the hands of either young or old folk. Father O'Reilly has collected and published a series of drawings illustrating the folklore of the Solomons (Bougainville). Others had done the same before him, from Codrington, Fox and Ivens in the Solomons to Maurice Leenhardt in New Caledonia. These drawings are worth studying.

Codrington, Fox and Ivens, all Anglican missionaries, (Melanesian Mission), reproduced in their works closely comparable drawings, spread over several generations, which came from the south-east of the Solomons. They portray the sea creatures, known as *adaro* in San Cristobal and dreaded by the fishermen. Each is shown in the form of a schematically presented human body with fish in place of head and feet, and other fish stuck to the body, especially on the joints. In neighbouring islands it is said that these creatures originate in San Cristobal. Formerly the carvings decorating the shelters on the big canoes represented the *adaro* in the same manner. There were other figures whose bodies were adorned with frigate birds.

The drawings of Boesou Eurijisi, sculptor of masks and one of the first Melanesian pastors in the Grande Terre Island illustrate quite admirably certain passages in Maurice Leenhardt's *Notes d'Ethnologie.*

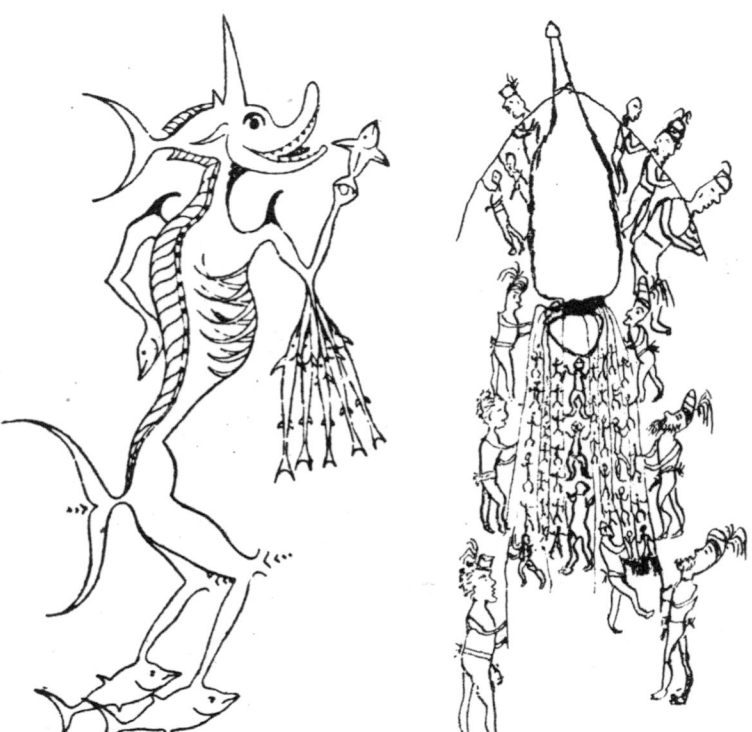

98. Solomon Islands. *Marine deity.* — 99. New Caledonia. *Building a house.* — 100. Solomon Islands, Buka. *Seeking the soul after death.*

Father O'Reilly has published drawings enhanced with colour by Somuk and others, documentary drawings and illustrations of stories. Somuk is a man from Buka in the north Solomons. His manner of rendering the human body is very close to the style of the statuary produced in the same region, at least when he confines himself to the representation of specific scenes. The drawing by the old man from Bekut about the origin of trees and cultivated plants show them emerging symmetrically—those destined for the uterine kin to the left, those for the paternal to the right—from the forehead, the neck, the joints and the genitalia. Here the technique resembles that used in portraying the *adaro* fish and frigate birds.

136

More recently Ward H. Goodenough has published some paintings by a student from Kiwai, near the mouth of the Fly river (Papua), in which the artist explains in his own way the origin of the totemic and magic rituals pertaining to his father's lineage. These show how the men of his clan descend from sculptures brought to life by his ancestor Spila and how Nugi, the first of these men carved out of a tree-trunk, had to consent to carry the world on his shoulders in exchange for which he receives offerings of the heads of slain pigs and a species of snake. The cosmological implications of the work seem to have made Mealdei, the artist in question, feel a need for symmetry. The same need was felt by one of the artists from Buka in similar circumstances.

101. Solomon Islands, Buka. *Funeral dance before a body laid on a platform.*

AUSTRALIA

The Australian sub-continent has always attracted the attention of those who are interested in 'primitive' forms of society. It took two generations of scholars to discover to what a degree of complexity and abstraction the 'aborigines' had developed their institutions. But their art fails to show the same progress in technique. Work in the round is practically unknown, except in regions in contact with New Guinea, especially the north tip of Cape York peninsula where wooden masks are found, representing the heads of cayman and saw-fish, and others, in lighter material, which portray human heads. Here we are dealing with cultural elements brought from the island of the Torres Straits and adapted to the illustration of cycles of specifically Australian myths.

This is not the only case of an apparent influence from New Guinea. The art of Arnhem Land, also, may well be result of a hybridization which has given rise to wholly original forms. Attempts to work in the round can also be seen in the quadrangular posts carved to resemble a human figure. The most realistic portray foreigners: Dutchmen and Indonesians. The flat bodies (only the head has any modelling) are enhanced with white, black and ochre lines in different shades arranged geometrically; the effect depends upon the minute complexity with which the bands are arranged. On the ritual posts, whose core or end is hollowed out, the painted decoration more often consists of non-geometrical themes which sometimes include the human face.

The paintings on eucalyptus bark are the most remarkable and indeed the best known objects from this region. Technically the decoration is the same, but the designs have more scope for free development on the larger surfaces, and exactly rendered natural forms contrast with a background of bands of varied hatching. We find not only totemic animals and mythical persons, sometimes in an appropriate landscape, but also pictures of Malay sailing prahus, hunting scenes and funeral ceremonies. One of the characteristics of these works is the meticulous representation of the viscera within the body, a practice which is also to be found in the rock paintings. The artist shows not only the details that he can see but also those which, from his experience as a hunter, he knows to exist.

In the same region the skulls of the dead are given coloured designs in white, black and red ochre, arranged in cross-hatched or stippled panels.

When considering the use of colour we should note how often this aesthetic adjunct is applied to a surface from which it will soon disappear: the ground or the human body. The ground drawings of central Australia consist of concentric circles, volutes and braids from which naturalistic themes sometimes emerge : snakes or birds. The soil is prepared by being sprinkled with water, or even human blood, as a dressing, and the drawings are in black, red and white.

More than two colours are seldom used, the red or black design contrasting with a dotted white ground.

In another technique blood is used to stick alternating bands of white and red-dyed down on to the body with a high head-dress to give an effect of extra height. The motifs may be simple longitudinal lines intended to accentuate the length of the body or may seek to achieve an effect of symmetry or asymmetry by means of parallel stripes running in different directions and concentric circles. Sacred objects both light (*waninga*) and heavy (*tjurunga*) are decorated in the same way.

The walls of caves and rock-shelters may be covered with paintings, or rather with outlines enhanced with colour. This is so at least in the north and the north-east. Further to the south, scenes of everyday life, dances, warfare and hunting, are depicted with great skill. In the centre and south-east there are numerous engravings on rock-surfaces, both flat and vertical which are often comparable in the quality of the drawing, with the wall-paintings of the northern edge of central Australia.

Engraved design is the most frequent, if not the most spectacular, expression of Australian art. It is used to decorate various weapons: boomerangs, spear-throwers, spears, clubs and different types of shields; sacred objects: æolian harps, *tjurunga* and drums; ornaments, and shell pendants. Generally the decoration is geometric and the motifs fall into two categories: (1) hatchings, broken lines, and concentric squares; (2) serpentine lines, concentric circles, spirals and tapers. It is possible to analyse their distribution regionally. In the centre, curvilinear designs; angular, in the east and west, where the geometric decoration serves as a background for figures of men and animals in line or low relief.

It would be difficult to determine the affinities of Australian art without undertaking a detailed study of a large number of pieces. As far as the north and centre are concerned, we find an art of curves and volutes which recalls, though less complex, certain art forms from New Guinea. In Arnhem Land which was historically the meeting-place of influences (Indonesia, New Guinea) we find original developments, though the techniques are close to those of New Guinea. Elsewhere, the analysis of various elements of Australian material culture reveals constant contacts between Australia and New Guinea, and especially the Sepik region.

102, 103, 104. Australia, Arnhem Land. *Rock painting.*

105. Australia. Cape Steward. *Fish (clan symbol)*.
106. Australia, Victoria. *Incised wooden panel*.
107. Torres Strait. *Portable drum*. Mus. of Primitive Art, New York.

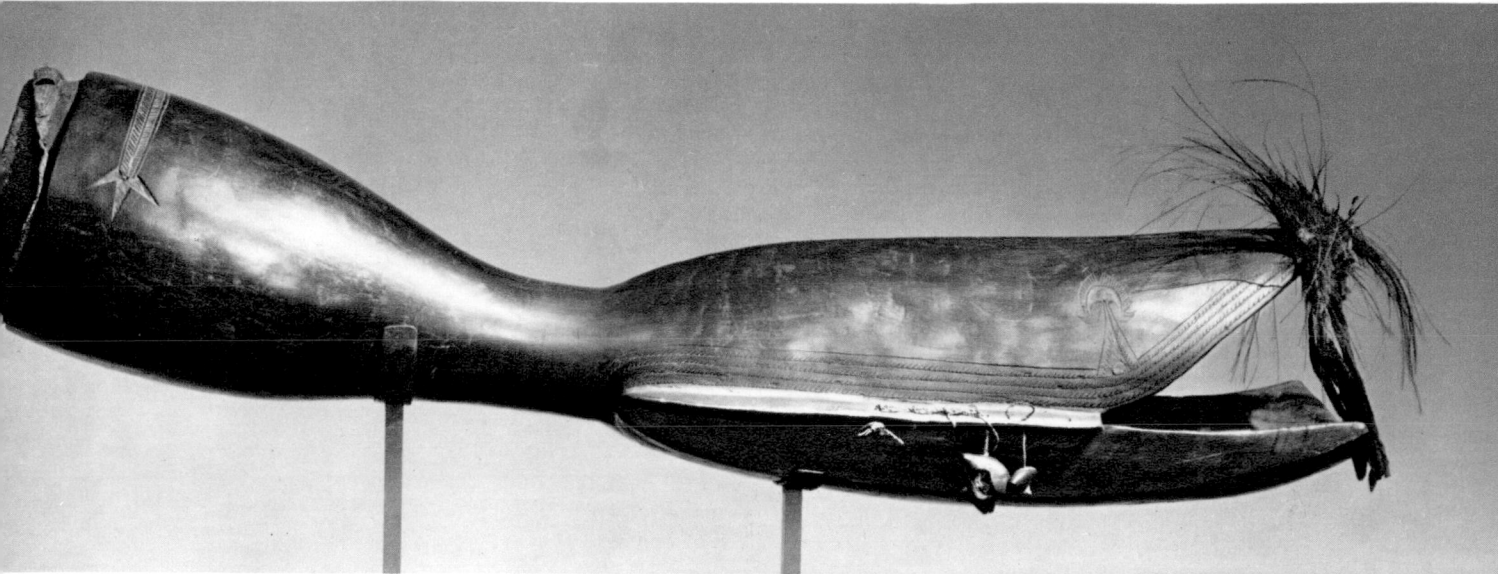

TORRES STRAITS

The art of the Torres Straits is now extinct and preserved only in museums and private collections.

The objects consist essentially of masks and tortoise-shell head-dresses. The shell pieces were sewn or stuck together by heat, a technique which made it possible to give them a certain relief. By means of this unusual technique the human face could be depicted surmounted by a crest and adorned with a variety of lateral additions in the same material, usually executed in very fine openwork. The subjects were animal figures: fishes, sharks, crocodiles. They were treated in angular lines and adapted to the texture of the material in which they were carried out. Some of these pieces, though very fragile, were of great size and consisted of composite constructions of superimposed human and animal forms. Human face masks in wood also existed in the western islands.

Other objects, especially drums, had finely incised decorations on the edges. The original open-throated, hourglass form of the small portable drums suggests the form they would have if they were made in shell.

Just behind the points of the wooden arrow-heads there was an incised and stylized cayman with long, gaping jaws. Elsewhere, we find figures with realistic heads, the body being replaced by a geometric design.

143

108. Torres Strait. *Tortoise-shell mask*. Private collection, New York.
109. Torres Strait. *Tortoise-shell mask*. Lecorneur-Roudillon Collection.

144

GULF OF PAPUA

The Gulf of Papua provides the instance of an art which has become extinct because it was deliberately suppressed by its creators. Without any outside pressures hundreds of irreplaceable pieces were destroyed on the spot by men who wished to free themselves completely from their past and to construct a new society based upon an almost mystic craving for economic development and progress.

Since sculpture is almost non-existent there, we might be led to believe that the insalubrious and marshy deltas of the Purari and Fly rivers were unfavourable to the development of work in the round. But this would be to overstress the effect of the material environment, for we find that the forms and motifs do not change as we move from the marshes to the hills. All the objects from this region, where coloured zones and bands are outlined by incisions, give an impression of great uniformity. Their ritual and social functions do, however, differ from west to east.

The craftsmen seem to have aimed at providing a support for the colour which is regarded as the essential factor of suggestion. Hence the numerous painted plaques believed to act as repositories for the spirit of an ancestor. Certain wooden objects of this type were worn in the manner of masks above a fibre cloak.

The decorative theme is almost always the human body or, at least, the face. Irregular curves, tooth-patterns, and chevrons conceal to some degree the rigorous symmetry about the long axis, sometimes indicated by a ridge in low relief representing the nose. The face is almost always topped by a dark head-dress, contrasting with the white ground against which the slotted and toothed mouth stands out. The round eyes are set each in the middle of a comma motif, the tail of which circles the bottom of the face, usually without touching it.

Below this, the body is unskilfully portrayed, with splayed arms and legs and a clearly indicated sexual organ, whose symbolic form is less apparent when associated with geometric motifs in which stylized limbs can sometimes be recognized. The rest of the piece is adorned with essentially decorative motifs which sometimes stress the tendency of the whole to fit into a somewhat irregular diamond-shaped pattern. Shields, æolian harps and flat double hooks are decorated in the same manner, as are the fine belts in incised and painted bark. The bases of small drums, cut to resemble heads, carry the same design of a human face in champlevé and painted.

The masks made of tapa stuck on a light wicker frame are sometimes of considerable size. They are considered to be sacred and are ritually burned after use. Smaller ones are found in considerable numbers in museums, since, having no religious significance, they escaped destruction.

These masks, often provided with large ears and a prominent nose, resemble somewhat the faces on the wooden painted plaques: the design is executed by fixing pieces cut from dark tapa on the light tapa which forms the main covering. The same technique is used for making figures with a body half-human, half-animal in aspect, on the big masks.

146

111. **New Guinea, Papua.**
Votive plaque. Budapest.

110. **New Guinea, Papua.** *Votive tablet.*
Nat. Hist. Mus., Chicago.

147

112. New Guinea, Papua. *Painted votive plaque (detail)*. Pierre Vérité Collection.

113. *Detail of* 114.

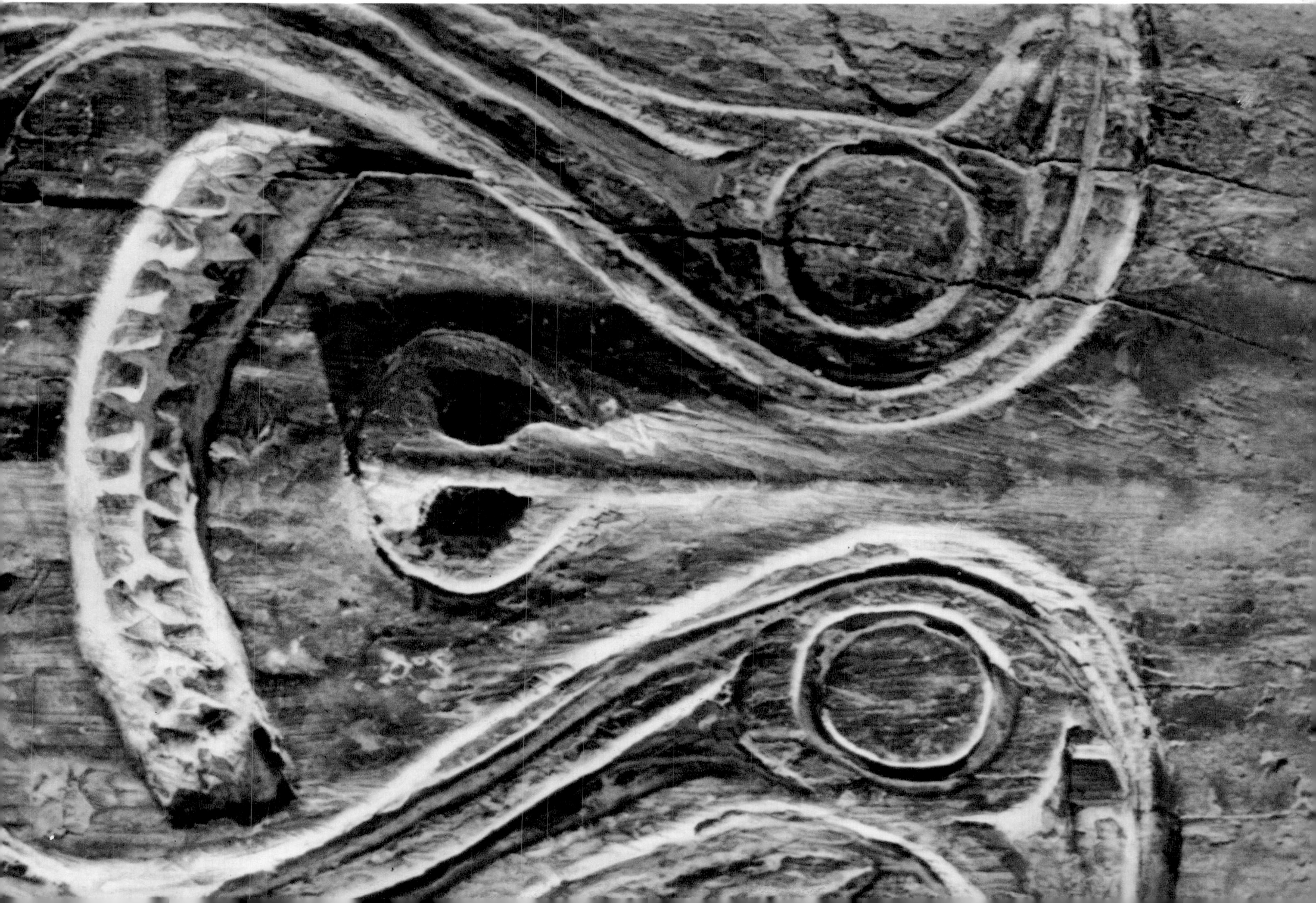

114. New Guinea, Papua. *Full-length figure.*
Mus. of Primitive Art, New York.

150

115. *Detail* and 116. New Guinea,
Papua. *Painted bark belt*. Budapest.

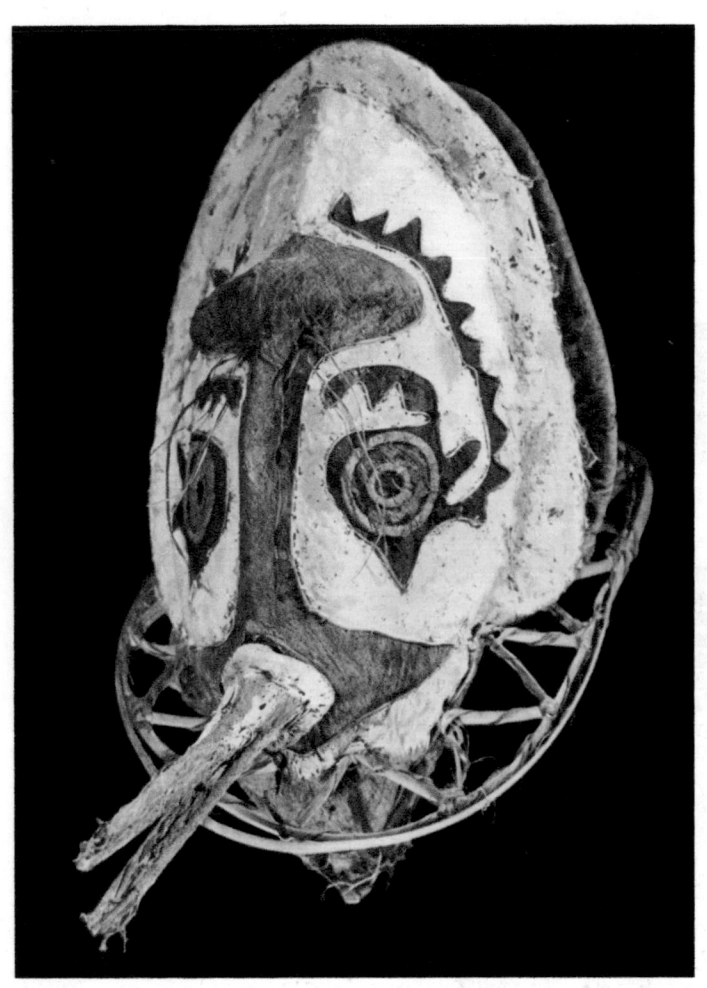

117. New Guinea, Papua. *Tapa mask*. Budapest.
118. New Guinea, Papua. *Tapa mask*. Mus. of Primitive Art, New York.

SOUTH-WEST NEW GUINEA

Little is known about the south-west part of Western New Guinea. The art of this region, which continues to flourish, has features common with that of Lake Sentani and with the *korovar* technique.

From this region came the ancestor figures made by the so-called Asmat people. These figures, which seem to play a part in funerary rituals, represent a crouching or kneeling figure with its chin on its fists. Being at once squat and elongated, they give an effect of emaciation owing to the fact that on the outer surface of the limbs the muscles are shown in counter-relief. The face looks bloated because it is carved to resemble the mummified face of a corpse. When one has seen the effect of natural mummification of bodies in certain conditions of humidity, the skill of the portrayal is most striking.

The carved prows of canoes furnish a second group of interesting pieces. An openwork interlace of curves of various shapes and sizes binds together human and animal figures, either complete or with their head alone emerging from the delicate filigree. A sequence of volutes with short braids in wider bands, and enhanced with colour, sometimes sets the whole in order. In a piece in the Basle Museum the scene depicted dominates the arabesques: two figures with interlaced limbs can be seen, one with a prominent phallus. It is impossible to say, however, whether this is an erotic scene or one of cannibalism. The faces of the figures, which are strongly stylized, seem to be all mouth, and the mouths resemble lower jaws. Spear-heads of a wide, flat type have an openwork decoration of the same type.

To another well-known class of objects from this region belong the wooden shields where only the outline of the design is raised; the motif itself, coloured red, is countersunk. The ground of the shield is white. The red border sometimes has simple incised motifs, though the human head may be portrayed in relief. The general effect is attractive, even gay.

The stylized motifs derive from man, fish and bird. As regards the last, one can trace from one shield to another how the bird turns into a widespread V with the tips of its arms curving outwards. This raises the question whether the motifs apparently disposed at random, (except that the smallest motifs are systematically grouped around the largest), do not relate to different elements in a narrative which they are intended to recall symbolically, and episodes which they purport to illustrate. Other shields however, bear a purely stylised decoration.

The bird theme found so often in New Guinea recurs in the big Asmat masks with cassowary heads. These masks are used in the ceremony of ritual expulsion of certain categories of the dead: those who are victims of murder. A cassowary head with a wide curved beak protrudes from each of two great discs fixed to the netting worn by the mask-bearers. Holes bored in the discs enable them to see out. Here we have not so much sculpture as flat pieces cut out and incised.

119. New Guinea, Asmat. *Carved canoe prow.* Basle.

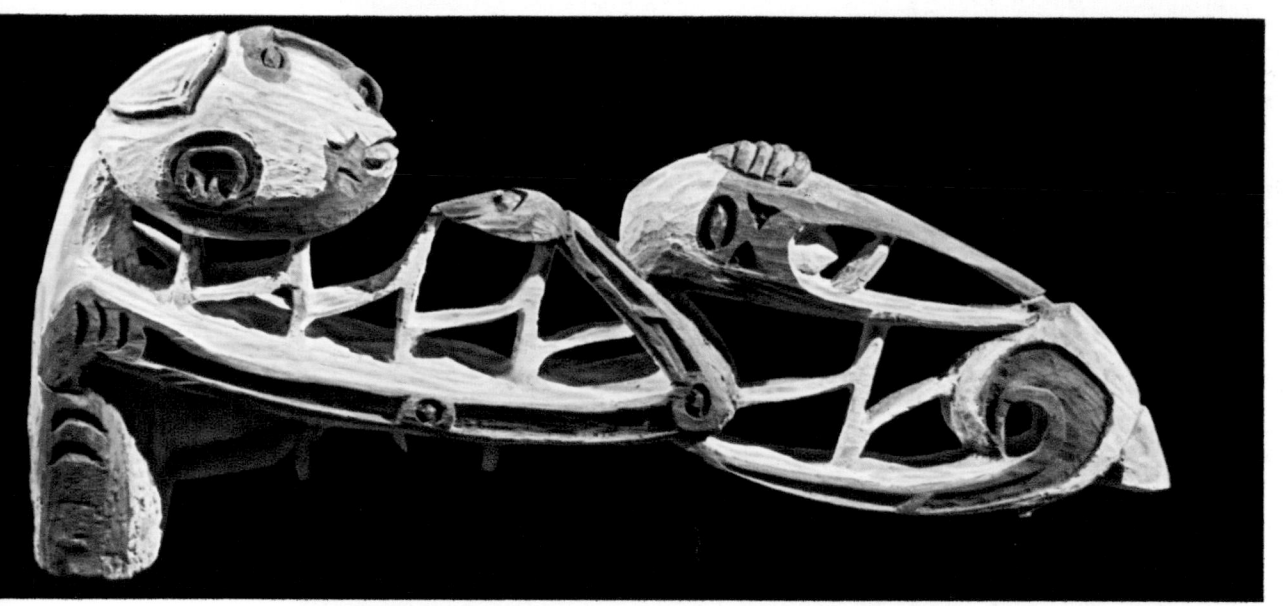

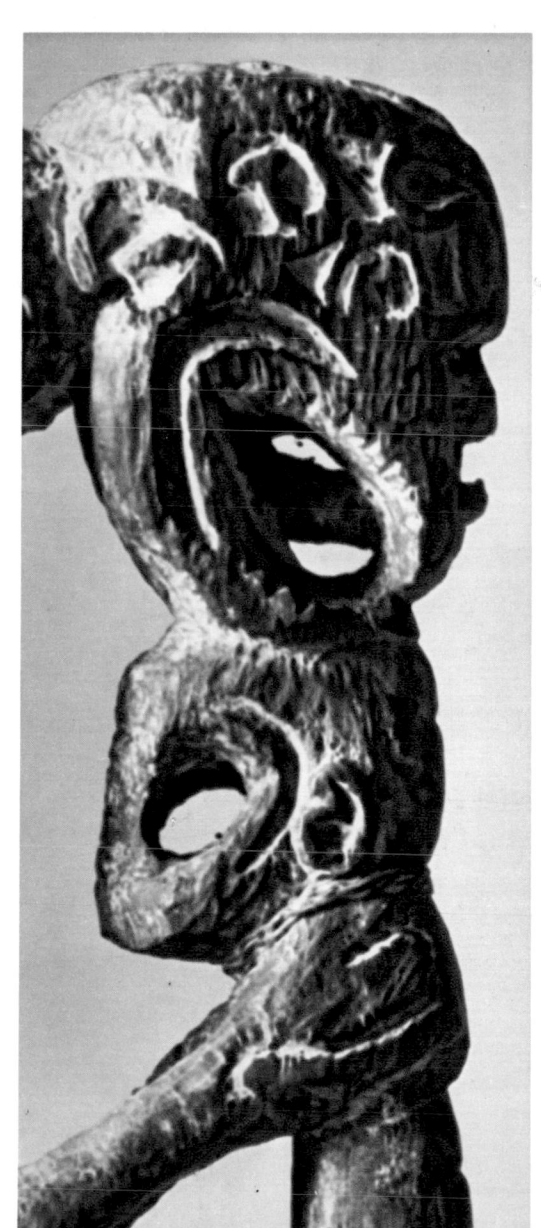

120. New Guinea, Asmat. *Canoe prow*. Basle. — 121. New Guinea, Asmat. *Canoe prow*. Budapest. — 122. *Detail of* 120.

123. *Detail of 121.* — 124. New Guinea, Asmat. *Shield.* Budapest. — 125. New Guinea, Asmat. *Shield.* Mus. of Primitive Art, New York.

LAKE SENTANI

The art of the region of Lake Sentani and of Humboldt Bay has recently been the subject of a masterly analysis by Professor Kooijman, Keeper at the Rijksmuseum voor Volkenkunde, Leiden, published by the Museum of Primitive Art, New York. Comprehensive stylistic studies in this field are so rare that special mention is called for when they are to be found.

Lake Sentani waters a region of particular interest since traces of ancient contacts with the Bronze Age of South East Asia (Dong-son) have been found there. In many cases the blades of bronze axes have been transmitted, until the present day, from generation to generation; others have been found in the course of excavations. The incised decoration on these pieces is intricate but systematic and has structural affinities with the present local style. A myth tells of the coming by sea of these historic relics from the west, the point of disembarkation and diffusion being the Sepik.

Another interesting feature of the material culture is the use of a very hard stone, chloromelanite, for the manufacture of adze blades. With these it is possible to work ironwood, whose resistance to decay makes it indispensable for the building of the great men's houses on piles. These technical considerations seem to lie behind the treatment of the incised ornamentation on the top of the T-shaped posts, each with the base turned upwards. The broad curves, consisting of registers in relief, as regular as possible, serve as a ground for the forms of openwork lizards, either flat or in strong relief, which sometimes seem to collide with each other. The upright part of the post may be given the form of an efflorescence of curvilinear motifs or carry a human figure which, because of the nature of the support, has to be stylized.

These pieces are of crude workmanship despite a certain effort to render anatomical detail, in the modelling of the limbs for instance. Some attempt is also made to treat the face in more than one plane but this is not wholly successful. An incised hole indicates the navel or the eye: a double line the mouth. The sexual organs are clearly shown but without emphasis, except in the case of the female clitoris.

Both inside and outside the great house, free-standing sculpture adorns the floor and is devoted to the initiation rites of the male members of the community. Those who take part in these are under the personal control of the chief, *odoforo*, who decides on the ritual to be followed. These carvings, less restricted to the vertical, are usually curved themselves, or fitted into a series of sweeping curves. Limbs are rounded, faces long, noses narrow, eyes barely indicated, mouths conventionalized and chins protruding. The neck has usually disappeared. The whole produces an effect of remarkable serenity, a fact which S. Kooijman would have us see as a cultural feature of the local social system.

Other sculptures seem less formalised, more naturalistic. The theme of mother and child occurs frequently. In this case the muscular formations are usually shown, and also such ornaments as armlets.

In the carvings on the ridge-poles we find an extension of the style (but in stronger relief) of the openwork edges of the great posts. The human and animal figures on the brackets are elongated as if intended to convey the motion of strain and effort.

The ends of head-rests exhibit the same tendency. Here craftsmanship and skill compensate for the disproportion of certain elements such as hands and the relatively greater volume given to the head.

But the characteristic feature of the local style is found in the incised, remarkably regular, volute decorations found, for example, on the bottom of the shallow oval plates. We have here an art aiming at a simple or a complex symmetry, which it achieves, though not without difficulty. The effect produced is all the more striking because the hollow parts are subsequently whitened. The point of departure for the volutes, which are always elongated on the inner side of a band or a circumscribed sector, is usually an S, more or less broken or folded back on itself. These motifs may form the body of a stylized animal, of a fish with a tapering tail, or, more usually, a frog. This proliferation of curves often yields place to angular sequences of equal symmetry and regularity in relation to the two axes of the plate. Sometimes the decoration is limited to a double band along the edge—as though any asymmetrical ornament were unthinkable.

The same ornamentation is found on the central part, or on the covering of the body, of hour-glass drums. The single or multiple handles may be surmounted by a human body, or rather a bust.

The same is true of the hooks which are essential elements of New Guinea furniture. When these are flat, an incised decoration emphasized with white is the most frequent. When the hook is quadrangular, a wealth of small figures, sometimes fixed to it by their feet, crouch above the suspension hole.

Incised decoration also occurs on the rounded adze-heads, on lime-holders, and, even more symmetrically treated, on the tobacco-holders made from bamboo internodes.

The handles of sago spoons and pounders also carry an incised decoration, which is often very scanty. The same is true of daggers made from human bone.

Discs with a central hole represent the sun and have a design in the same style composed in terms of a double symmetry.

The tapas show a curious jumble of birds, lizards, fish, snakes, plants and stylized, painted stars. Here and there, the frog or the bird motif can be seen to split up, to give rise to a proliferation of bodies and heads which furnish an occasion for a further efflorescence of volutes. When the motifs are taken in isolation the stylized animals curiously resemble the half-human, half-animal designs of the Solomons. The outline of the body is accentuated by a wavy line resembling a fish bone or the spinal column (which is always shown). Animals rendered in a similar manner sometimes occur in relief on the plates.

126. New Guinea, Lake Sentani. *Carved central house-post*. Amsterdam. — 127. *Detail of 129*. — 128. New Guinea, Lake Sentani. *Carved ridge-board*. Amsterdam.

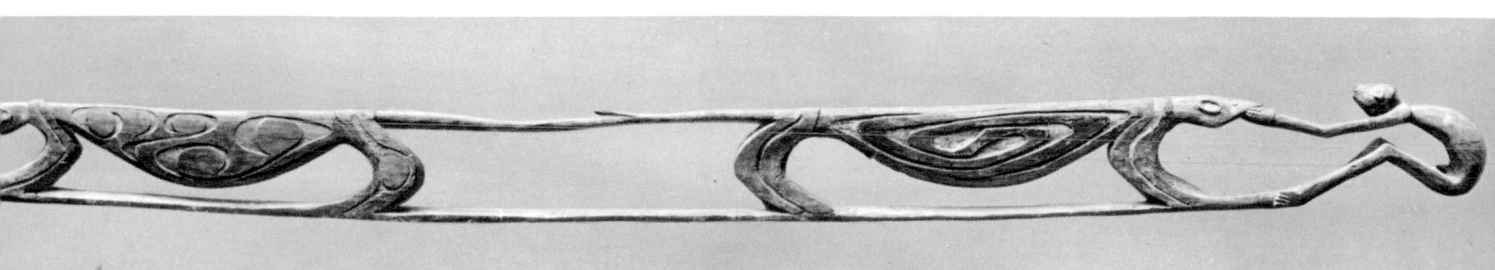

129. New Guinea, Lake Sentani. Kabiterau. *Motherhood*. Basle.
130. New Guinea, Lake Sentani. *Carved ridge-board*. Basle.

131. New Guinea, Lake Sentani. *Dish with carved base.* Amsterdam.
132. New Guinea, Lake Sentani. *Dish with carved base.* Basle.
133. New Guinea, Lake Sentani. *Carved portable drum.* Basle.

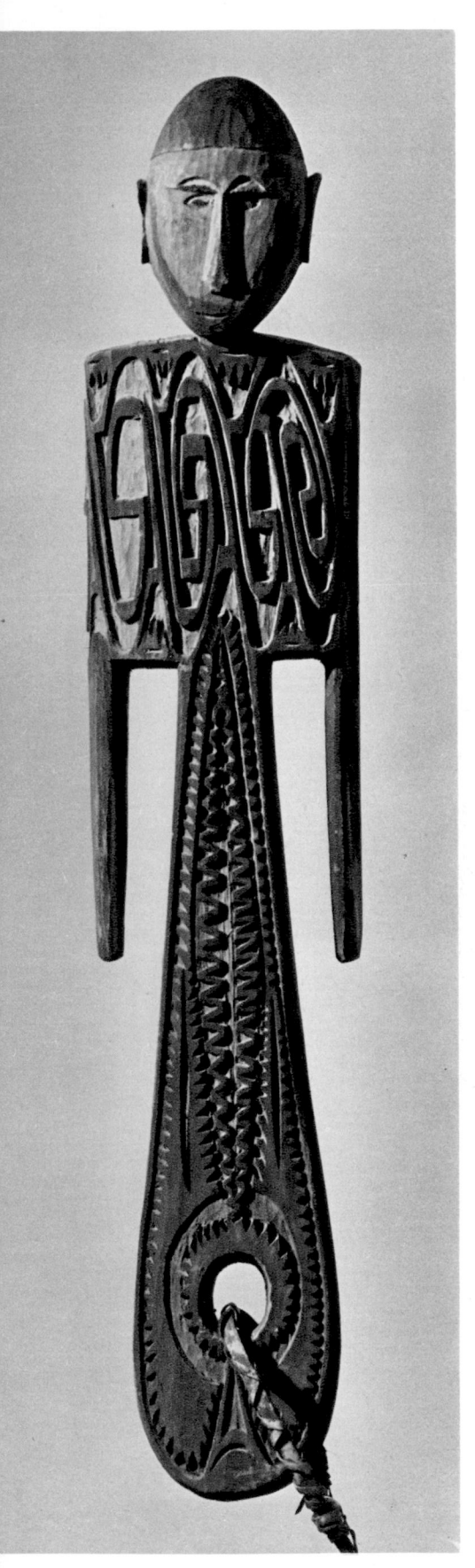

134. New Guinea, Lake Sentani. *Double hook*. Basle. — 135. New Guinea, Lake Sentani, Ajafo. *Gable decoration : solar disc.* Basle. — 136. New Guinea, Lake Sentani, Saboiboi. *Piece of ritual tapa.* Basle.

168

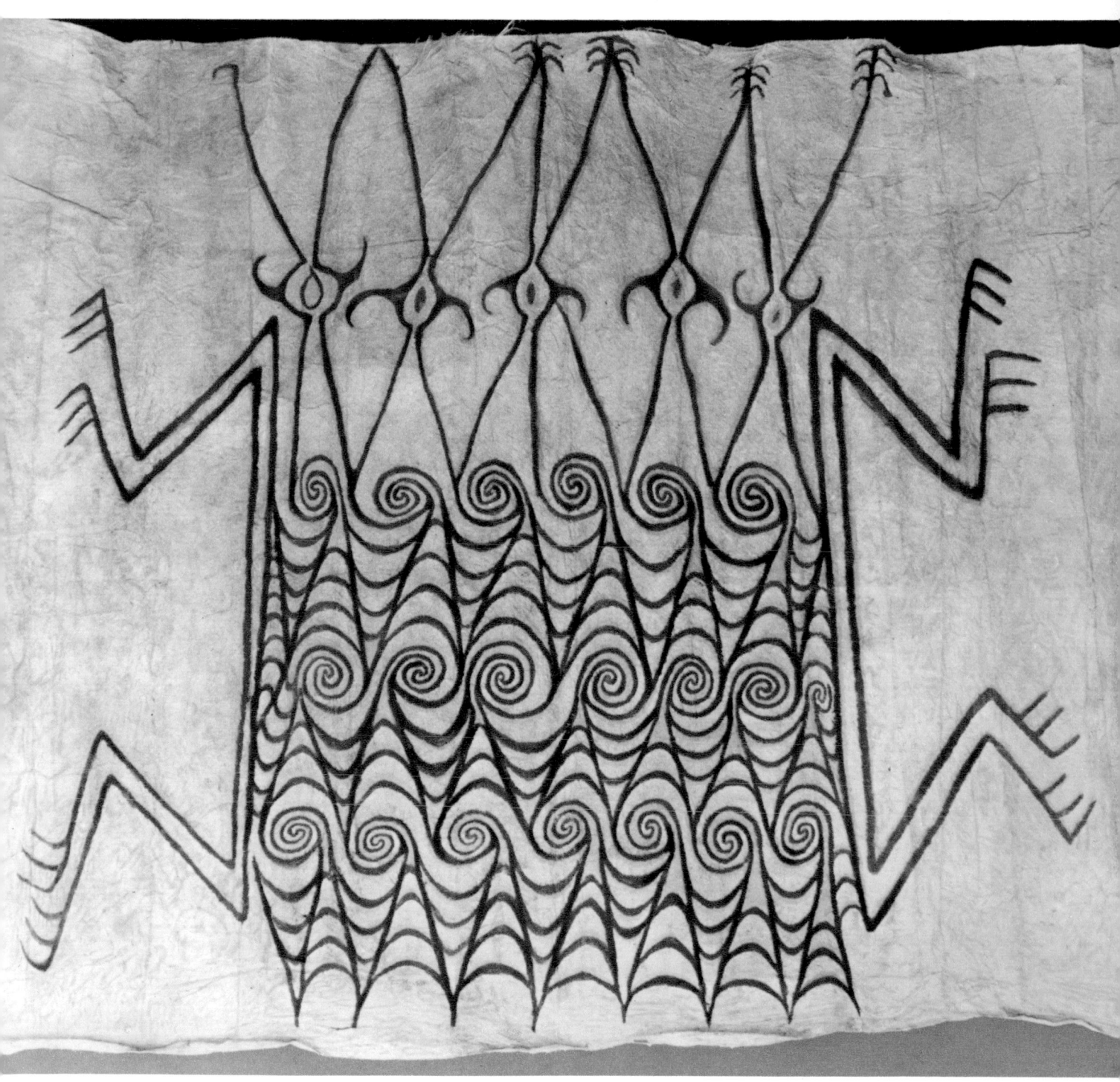

II

THE SEPIK RIVER REGION

Sepik is one of the great names in the art of Oceania. So many pieces in museums, outstanding for their boldness and great variety of forms, are labelled Sepik, that one is tempted to read into them a unity underlying this heterogeneity. The objects are exchanged, bought and sold locally so that the collector, who has travelled along the river or the coast, may know where he has obtained each piece but has no guarantee that this is its place of origin. Only those few anthropologists who have paid prolonged visits to the area are able to provide precise data on the localities where the themes originated. But it has now become clear that the art of the Sepik is multiform and cannot be reduced to a single category. We shall try here to distinguish the local styles as far as our present knowledge allows, despite the inadequate documentation arising from the uncertain provenance of so many museum pieces.

Washkuk

The people of this name live in the upstream region of the bend of the middle Sepik, below Ambunti. Thanks to Dr. Bühler, Director of the Basle Museum, an integral collection of interesting paintings and sculptures from this district is available. The paintings are done on the opened-out sheath from the base of the leaves of the forest palm. The human face, whether round, oval or fitted into a rounded 'lozenge', is depicted schematically with round eyes, an oval or quadrangular nose, a crudely bow-shaped mouth. Decorative effect is obtained by underlining each of the scant elements of the design with double bands of confronted red and white indentation, and with white, dotted lines or groups of dots. Empty spaces are charged with spirals. The general effect much resembles that of the painted decoration on the tree-fern carvings of Ambrim, in north central New Hebrides. The carvings on posts and beams of the great houses, which belong with the paintings, show the effects of this relationship. They have soft forms with limbs whose joints are turned towards the inner surface, and derive from a linear technique having affinities with the art of the New Hebrides, where it acts chiefly as a support for patches of colour.

The pottery has the same human face motif incised on the sides.

Maprik.

The Maprik region (Prince Alexander Mountains) is the home of the Abelam tribe. Here, too, the paintings and carvings on the large houses are interrelated.

Paintings, always executed on the same palm-leaf material, also decorate the underside of the roofs of the large clubhouses where the men meet to perform their special rites. Here a contrast is struck between flat colours (red and yellow ochres) and zones finely hatched in white. The human body constitutes the leading theme. Sometimes the face is only faintly indicated; in such cases it is encircled by an aureole of white and ochre strokes, broken lines, conventional circular hatchings, and large hatched plaques are added on either side. The head is treated broadly with the hair built up into a cone set off by a halo placed above the red line of the hair; the brow is divided in two by a triangle. A T-motif frames the tiny eyes and indicates the nose; the latter is prolonged by a vertical line defining two huge sub-orbital areas whose lower curves enclose a minute mouth with a row of pointed teeth along the edges. The diamond-shaped body is outlined by a double hatched band. The ochre chest is set off by a necklace and a white pendant. A red triangle, lower down, may represent the pubis.

The carvings seem to have served as a model for the paintings, except that the head, while treated in exactly the same manner, is usually topped by a bird whose beak dips down towards the human face and this is given a curved profile in which the line of the nose runs parallel to the beak of the upper motif. The oval trunk is framed by two thin, curving members, the arms. The legs are sausage-shaped, the knees being marked by circles. Double hooks are decorated with similar human effigies. Sometimes friezes are built up with a long series of human faces and birds (the latter being shown both full-face and in side-view). Here the human body gives place to a diamond motif enclosed by two thin, smoothly rounded members representing arms crooked at the elbow. These figures, both male and female, are aligned in rows, each with a white shell hung on its belly.

In the northern part of the region, the paintings are placed high up on the front of the house and sheltered by a projection of the roof. A row of carved heads meets the eye lower down. Here the way in which faces are painted resembles the Washkuk style, with this difference: a single or triple plait motif figures on the forehead. The triangular surfaces beneath the eyes are extended down the cheeks by a curving red plaque edged with white parallel lines rising above the mouth. The general effect is richer and more colourful, the contrasts are better balanced than is the case in the south of the region.

The wicker masks of this region are rather puzzling works. The central theme consists of two circular eyes separated by a sort of crest. The general effect is that of a bird's head. Protuberances on the side may repeat the central theme, which in some cases also figures on the openwork decoration of the crest.

Tchambuli.

This tribe lives on the shores of the lake of the same name, whose waters flow into the Sepik river. Its art is much the same as that discussed above; in particular the treatment of the human face shows no essential difference. Little can be said, however, about the paintings since we have virtually no examples which certainly derive from this particular area.

It is hard to distinguish the actual work in relief from the white lines which serve to emphasize its elements. Everything having a curved form, in space or in the design—eyes, nostrils, mouth—is covered with a proliferation of concentric curves which tends to cancel out the visual impact of the actual modelling and to replace it with a vague, imaginary relief. Here we find no more hatching or broken lines. The seeming hugeness of the eyes is due to the painting, which makes them fill the whole suborbital depression, ending with the gaping mouth. The curved nose is built up of broadly treated masses and the mouth is given a prolongation which runs downwards and curves back at the same time. Sometimes this extension may end in another, miniature head. This may be a tongue, as in certain masks of the region and the great carved wooden plaques of the Iatmül.

A mask in the Musée de l'Homme, recently brought back by Françoise Girard, may give an interesting clue to the solution of this problem. Above the human face, complete with nose, the forehead is prolonged by an independent vertical bar which joins up with the lower part of the mask. This bar is incised with notches in the same direction as those found on part of the length of the beaks of carved birds. It may be that this is a remnant of the motif of the bird with a downward-curving beak which crowns the human head. This hypothesis would account for the various types of nose-beak and nose-trunk characteristic of other districts of the Sepik region.

This style is found not only in the wooden masks and the larger, similarly constructed heads which are fixed to the gables of the great houses, but also in the full-length statues, in the wooden double hooks surmounted by a figure and in the offering-stools fixed to an erect human figure, where the stool stands for the body, and the lower part of the face has the classical prolongation.

In the pottery we find the beginnings of relief modelling with the appearance of protruding human faces.

The *Iatmül*, described by Gregory Bateson, link up, as far as their art is concerned, with the Tchambuli. They inhabit the downstream reach of the Sepik bend near the confluence of the river and the outflow of the lake. The masks *mwai* are partly coated with a clay and lime paste inlaid with fine shellwork. The nasal appendage is covered with it, except for the nostrils which are left free, as is the whole area beneath the eyes. The almond-shaped eyes and the bridge of the nose are painted red; the outer corners of the eyes taper to the rear. A cowrie or a piece of polished shell lends vivacity to the eye. Under the nose a curved boar's tusk is set on either side. The figure on the double hooks may be embellished in a similar manner, as are the figures holding the stool beside which the orators stand.

The skulls of the dead, once cleaned and dried, are in some cases worked over and covered with a clay representation of the dead man's face, this being made as lifelike as possible. If a male face is being portrayed, ornaments may be added to it: double boar's tusks below the nose, and the prolongation of it by a tress covered with shells, a series of shell pendants, with feathers and fibres above, below and on the sides. Thus adorned, the heads are placed on top of poles behind a barrier and, known by the name of *mbwatnggowi*, provide the women with a display of life-sized marionettes having a ritual fertility role. Other portraits, of both men and women, are also modelled on skulls and set up on top of a doll decked with ornaments on the occasion of funerary ceremonies.

Of the tribes we are discussing, the Iatmül are the only ones to make use of monumental drums, which rest on the ground. The ends are carved with a number of human faces of different sizes enclosed within an overall design consisting of the same face with its whole length covered over by a projection in the form of a beak springing from the forehead. We often find an ornamental motif consisting of semi-oval, slightly overlapping lozenges around the face or on the prolongation of the upper lip. A house post illustrated by Bateson is paralleled, curiously enough, by one in a photograph which Speiser took in central New Hebrides (Ambrim).

Among the Iatmül we begin to find the beautiful crocodile-head canoe prows which belong specifically to Sepik art. The double hooks are treated on similar lines: above a semi-human face is a repeat motif of the eyes and a pattern of sunken lozenges crossed by a beak.

A remarkable piece found by Dr. Wirz consists of two parts. One is an openwork board representing a male body, almost without relief, built up round a hole in the centre. Through this opening runs an object set diagonally in unstable equilibrium. This second carving, of remarkably fine workmanship, is adorned with feather pendants and has a female figure at one end and, at the other, a cayman's head surmounted by a bird. These two animals and the woman's head are inlaid with cowries. This elaborate technique in which one form merges into another is employed on a larger scale on the great carved posts of the long houses, where human figures are again represented; also on the stoppers, carved with graceful animal forms, of lime containers, and on cayman-headed canoe prows.

The Carlebach Collection in New York contained in 1960 two large painted wooden plaques (from the Tshuosh) with openwork carving on the lower part. The main body of these pieces is patterned with schematized human faces sometimes twisted into amoeba-like shapes. On the top, in the middle of a large white patch, a human face, either broad or contracted, is outlined in red, ochre and white curves; the eyes are round, the nose plaited. Only the mouth differs from the usual type by the addition of spirals at the junction of the lips.

Kambringi.

We come now to a lower reach of the central bend of the Sepik river. The local style resembles that of the Kambriman through whose territory the 'Korrigane' expedition passed.

Here, too, wicker masks whose theme recalls the cowrie masks of the Iatmül have been found. The circular eyes in red, the widely gaping mouth and the bridge of the nose, prolonged by a flexible appendage which curves down into the mouth, stand out against two large patches of white paint on the wicker-work. These masks always have the same appearance: a human face combined with the head of a bird.

The familiar motif of a man with a bird above his head, carried out in terracotta, figures on the tiled roof-ridges of the men's clubhouses. The rolls of clay which go to form the body and limbs of the figures and the bird produce by the simplest means an astonishingly lively impression.

Cayman-head canoe prows are also to be found here, and the same theme is repeated on head-rests.

As far as masks and carved gable-end heads are concerned, our present knowledge of them is still too limited to allow of any generalizations. There seems, however, to be a tendency to emphasize the nostrils, treated first in relief, then flattened out on the sides. A mask made from bits of fibre sewn together achieves a similar effect by adding semi-circular shell discs to a thin plaited nose (Paul Wirz Collection, Koninklijk Museum voor de Tropen, Amsterdam).

The orator's stool is another ceremonial object peculiar to this region; we have already noted it among the Iatmül. Despite the four legs, the vertical extension of this stool, which is more of an altar than a seat, supports a head in relief in a style similar to that of the masks.

Middle Sepik.

Under this rather indefinite name it is customary to group the tribes in the neighbourhood of Tambanum and those known as the Kanigara, who dwell around, and dowstream from, the confluence of the Sepik and the Yuat rivers. The Basle Museum contains the largest collection of pieces from this region; it forms the subject of an excellent monograph by Dr. Paul Wirz: *Kunstwerke vom Sepik*.

Pottery is as much in favour here as in the region described above. Large jars have on their necks a stylized human face in which the nose emerges from the junction of two groups of concentric circles. Also to be noted is a cone-shaped vessel in the Basle Museum whose surface is covered with incised spirals running in the same direction and scarcely leaving room (at the ends of the same diameter) for two stylized human faces on which vestigial ears can be seen. The incised grooves are filled with lime. A terracotta roof ornament carries the motif of a human face with a nose prolonged by a curved appendage, dotted with cupules of various colours; above it is a cock with open wings, reduced, however, to mere stumps.

Wooden masks, placed above or in the middle of a framework over which sago-palm sheathing has been stretched, are found as far as Lake Tchambuli. Everywhere they show local characteristics in the treatment of the face. These masks are said to be for use on canoes and shields—perhaps because they are too light to affect the balance. Except for the mask itself, it is doubtful whether the surface as a whole could provide any effective protection.

The wide-open mouth from which a pointed tongue hangs down; the bridge of the nose running up to the top of the forehead; the nostrils rolled over on each side; the eyes marked by cowries and surrounded by a red line which curves back towards the top of the ear; a round, red spot on the cheek, with the ochre outline cutting across the white ground—none of these would justify any claim to local originality. Nor would the small masks which were fastened to the hair; here parallel serpentine lines, springing from a spiral design, follow the curves of the face from the root of each ear, then separate following the contours of the nostrils. This is a variant on the use of concentric circles. On other, larger, full-length pieces, everted nostrils —rare in the Sepik area—can be seen. The lack of technical skill, exemplified by a head inserted in an almost closed crescent (Budapest Museum), does not seem to be a purely local phenomenon.

The figures joined to the orators-stools provide interesting variants, since they do not form an integral part of the stool but are shown seated on the edge of it. Rows of chevrons run along the shoulders, arms and thighs, while faces are treated as described above. In other stools, the seat itself is supported by the shoulders of the figure. Some of the stools have a secondary female figure and several effigies of animals in high and low relief.

The double hooks, surmounted by a small human figure, furnish better illustrations of the great variety of local sculptural style. (This does not apply to the faces, which all have a family likeness and are painted in the same way). As in the case of the seated figures of the stools, the sculptors exaggerate buttocks and shoulders, a disproportion characteristic of these carvings. The figures are both male and female. In one case a woman suckling a child has small breasts superimposed on a male chest.

Mention should also be made of various museum specimens vaguely labelled 'Middle Sepik' without any specific details. These include large, slightly convex shields (known from the middle and lower Sepik Valley) with a human head carved at the top and the body covered with symmetrical patterns of 'hairy' spirals. Another piece from this region is a wooden plaque carved in low relief and representing a woman with outspread legs. Two small fish are nibbling her genitalia—a familiar symbolic theme.

From both Lake Tchambuli and the Middle Sepik a type of roof-crest is reported which consists of a complete figure, placed on the elongated frustum of a cone, with its face carved in the style of the local masks. Above the figure is a bird with its head thrown back and outspread wings rising vertically: according to Bateson this is a fish eagle.

Some large incised wooden plaques with openwork carving recall the linear designs of Massim art in the way the scrollwork winds round a double motif of birds' beaks. At the top is a circle, consisting of a flat human face along whose vertical axis runs a tapering bar resting on the middle of the face and hanging down far below it. A human face is carved at the top of the bar; its vertical movement is emphasized on either side by the figure of a bird, carved in relief with its wings folded close to the body. On the rest of the plaque the bodies of two birds can easily be identified. They are shown in side view and set spirally against a profusion of motifs based on birds' heads, beaks, tails and wings.

Paintings on areca palm sheaths have similar themes, forcefully treated and portraying in various ways either the usual motif, of a human face surmounted and surrounded by birds, or birds only, back to back. There is an obvious striving for symmetry, but the nature of the support makes it difficult to avoid irregularities. The bird represented is always the same, the local type of hornbill with a large curving beak and a hard protuberance on the top of its head. The human face has one characteristic feature: the mouth is overlapped and reduced to insignificance by the great size of the nostrils, which take the form of two confronted rudimentary spirals. A motif of double strands runs from the root of the nose to the ears. The forehead is covered with a sort of head-dress with braids on either side, while the face is encircled by a white ring dotted with a series of ovals; above and on the sides are birds. In some cases the birds are omitted and the face stands out on a ground of coiled leaves.

Mundugumor.

This tribe, inhabiting the valley of the Yuat, a tributary of the Sepik, has been studied by Margaret Mead. Its special interest for us lies in the carved stoppers which protect the embouchures of the sacred flutes. These wooden fittings always represent a standing figure, upon whose head rests a basketry framework which supports a crest of black cassowary plumes. The body is thin and set on thick legs which part at the level of the knees. The back of the head is supported by the body but the face is detached and placed well forward, in front of the shoulders and chest, leaving visible the extremities of the dangling arms and a penis which hangs down to the knees.

The face is almost as large as the whole of the rest of the body. Its striking appearance is due to the double eyebrow ridge, a massive hooked nose, eyes whose sockets may be inlaid with cowry, prominent cheek-bones, a mother-of-pearl crescent running through the nasal septum, a string of tortoise-shell rings, progressively increasing in size, fastened to the ears and a basketry frame attached to the chin to carry a beard made of human hair. Miniature human heads are sometimes carved on the back of the figure. These works, only about 20 inches high, are one of the outstanding creations of Sepik art.

The aesthetic and technical qualities of Mundugumor art can also be seen in other objects, such as the head-rests in the form of a dog or a pig. The expert use of carving and painting combined goes to produce work which is both expressive and stylized, while the limbs of the animals, folded crosswise on each side, ensure the stability of the openwork ensemble.

Other striking examples of this somewhat contorted style may be cited: a lizard, for example, clinging to a branch, whose body ends not in a tail but a pair of crossed arms beneath a human head adorned with a wig of real hair. The face, with a prominent nose, is designed in the style described above. To the same category of human representations belongs a face made of cowries and spiral fragments of shell set in vegetable gum on a woven framework. Here we have one of the finest examples of this peculiar technique, which is practised all along the north coast of New Guinea and in New Britain. Often the gum does not impair the suppleness of the flexible framework. It is furnished with a peg which the warrior holds in his mouth to enable him to hide his face behind another of his own devising.

The wickerwork masks of the Mundugumor are among the most remarkable of the Sepik region. One of these, representing an entire cayman seven feet long and worn on the head (now in the Auckland War Memorial Museum), is strikingly lifelike. The wickerwork lends itself to the representation of the cayman's hide, while the use of the beast's own teeth makes the object even more convincing.

Lower Sepik.

The marked cultural degeneration of the tribes of this region makes it difficult to decide with any certainty which elements of their art actually originated here. The problem can only be solved by detailed field studies and iconographic analyses supplemented by an examination of the traditions handed down among the natives, assuming that this is still possible. It is known that a flourishing art once existed here, but to describe it without reliable data about its origin is difficult. Apparently stylization was prevalent, as well as the practice of covering even the smallest surfaces of carved forms with an incised decoration of irregular curves and spirals.

Small ancestor statues exist, both male and female, but have no distinctive characteristics, except that the man wears a face mask, the woman a skull. From the river mouth comes a female statuette with shoulders and bust decorated with spirals; the breasts are, for once, shown naturally and not superimposed on a male chest.

The faces on the double hooks from this region are much like those described above. Limbs are omitted wholly or in part, and the body is lozenge-shaped. The mouth is wide open with a tongue curving downwards, the nose broad and flattened, sometimes with everted nostrils, while the eyes tend to bulge.

The close relationship between the art of the delta and that of the middle Sepik Valley is well demonstrated by a piece in the Museum of Primitive Art, New York. A painted panel shows two female figures facing away from each other, one light in tone, the other dark, against a background of birds' heads. Between them is a central figure, that of a man. Here one feature recalls the style of Arnhem Land, in northern Australia: in the case of the man, the viscera are shown within the body; one of the two women (the black one) appears to have a fœtus in her womb, while the other (the white one) has a symmetrical design on her body which is more difficult to interpret. The figures are surrounded by birds' heads.

A bas-relief from the same region is a more complex composition. In the last analysis the theme is a human one, but it is based on bird and lizard, the two most favoured companions of man in Oceania. Only the two flat legs, adorned with a painted decoration, the knees marked by a broken line in relief, together with the oval face of a realistic type with a calm expression, are definitely human. The body is that of a lizard whose tail takes the place of the penis. On either side of the lizard's head are two flat birds with openwork contours like those of the lizard's body, treated in a technique recalling that of the T-posts of Lake Sentani. Under the figure's head is a large flat crescent whose outlines are also in openwork. Above is a second crouching figure with a crudely rendered face, the arms and legs splayed out on a flat body which mingles with that of a bird whose head, in relief, springs from the belly and whose beak stands for the penis. Here we have one of the most characteristic demonstrations of the range of Sepik art, whose intermingling of human and animal symbolism gives rise to works having a well-balanced harmonious rhythm.

The Coastal Region around the Sepik Delta.

Several ancient, well authenticated specimens exist originating from that part of the north coast of New Guinea which lies to the east of the estuaries of the Sepik and of the Ramu, and at Potsdamhafen. They enable us to define the style of this region, all too often confused with that of the Sepik valley proper. The masks are its most characteristic feature, for it is from this region, it seems, that the very beautiful masks with a special type of nose originate. In these, the ridge joins up with the wings of the nose which are so elongated that they give the impression of a sort of curved bird's beak. Occasionally it forms a real beak.

On the Ramu river the oval eye-socket is surrounded by a ridged border whose lower edge sometimes merges into the nose. Another mask seems to suggest a different facial type with everted nostrils, until we realize that this double spiral inserted in the nostrils represents a shell ornament worn in the usual manner. In this mask the mouth is treated more realistically. In both the small mouth juts out slightly, while the orbit of the eye is clearly separated from the flat or hollow cheeks.

The statuettes (they are common in museums and private collections), are the best known of the complete human figures. They are of two kinds distinguished by the treatment of the nose, which is either very prominent, though of normal proportions—the only realistic element in the whole composition (Ramu Valley)—or else prolonged by a curved appendage which may dangle loosely or curve back to the belly and even to the penis, which then forms a further prolongation of it (Potsdamhafen). The eyes are merely sketched in, like those of a mask, or else are so protuberant that they occupy all the space in the face which the nasal appendage leaves free.

On the ends of the big drums which stand on the ground we find the same figures, coupled with ill-defined animal forms which possibly represent ant-thrushes. On the body of the drum an incised decoration, composed of lines and white surfaces, is filled with lime. Here the technique closely resembles that of the Sepik paintings. Again two styles are distinguishable. At Potsdamhafen the figure has a long beak-shaped nose curving in towards the belly; the decorative design then represents two symmetrical faces. In the Ramu Valley, the face and body of the figure are more compact, while the decoration is geometric, generally hour-glass shaped and built up around themes recalling motifs derived from the lizard.

Further east, from Potsdamhafen and Adalberthafen, there come elongated convex shields bearing an incised human face with a nose in relief, the sole projection in an otherwise wholly incised decoration with lime rubbed into the grooves. The motifs above and below the face form a symmetrical arrangement of flattened spirals. The valley of the river Ramu yields wooden plaques carved in very low relief and painted with designs representing a human face surrounded by decorative elements. The whole is treated rather in the manner of Papuan bark plaques. The lizard motif can still be detected in the axis of the face, forming an upward extension of it.

Objects in exactly the same style come from the Mushu, Bertrand, Guilbert and d'Urville islands to the west of the mouth of the Sepik River. The head-rests alone, supported by one or several figures, show minor differences.

The Aitape region, midway between the mouth of the Sepik and the frontier of West Irian, provides specimens which are not sufficiently differentiated from those of the mouth of the Ramu to form a separate stylistic group. A statuette in the Budapest Museum is of interest, not so much on account of the rudimentary face, as for the head-dress, with two birds (ant-thrushes) rising above the ears, and also the full curve of the buttocks. A head-rest in the same museum, with a number of human heads carved at each end, shows faces hardly less schematized, with their noses adorned with a shell pendant.

A local theme is that of figures bent double, the head enclosed in a sort of lunar crescent running perpendicular to the body. The Berne Museum possesses a vertical frieze of such figures superimposed and linked to each other by fish.

137. New Guinea, Washkuk. *Painted vegetable plaques.* Basle.

138. New Guinea, Abelam. *Ridge ornament.* Am. Mus. Nat. Hist., New York.
139. New Guinea, Tambanum. *Back of an orator's stool (detail).*

140. New Guinea, South Maprik. *Painted plaques*. Basle.
141. New Guinea, Kalabu, Maprik. *Frieze of the fronton of a great house (detail)*.

183

142. New Guinea, Kalabu, Maprik. *Lower part of the fronton of the great house (detail).*
143. New Guinea, Bogmuken, South Maprik. *Carvings inside a men's great house.* Basle.

184

144. New Guinea, Abelam (Bogmuken). *Carved figure*. Basle.
145. New Guinea, Mouth of the Sepik. *Beaked mask*. Brussels.

187

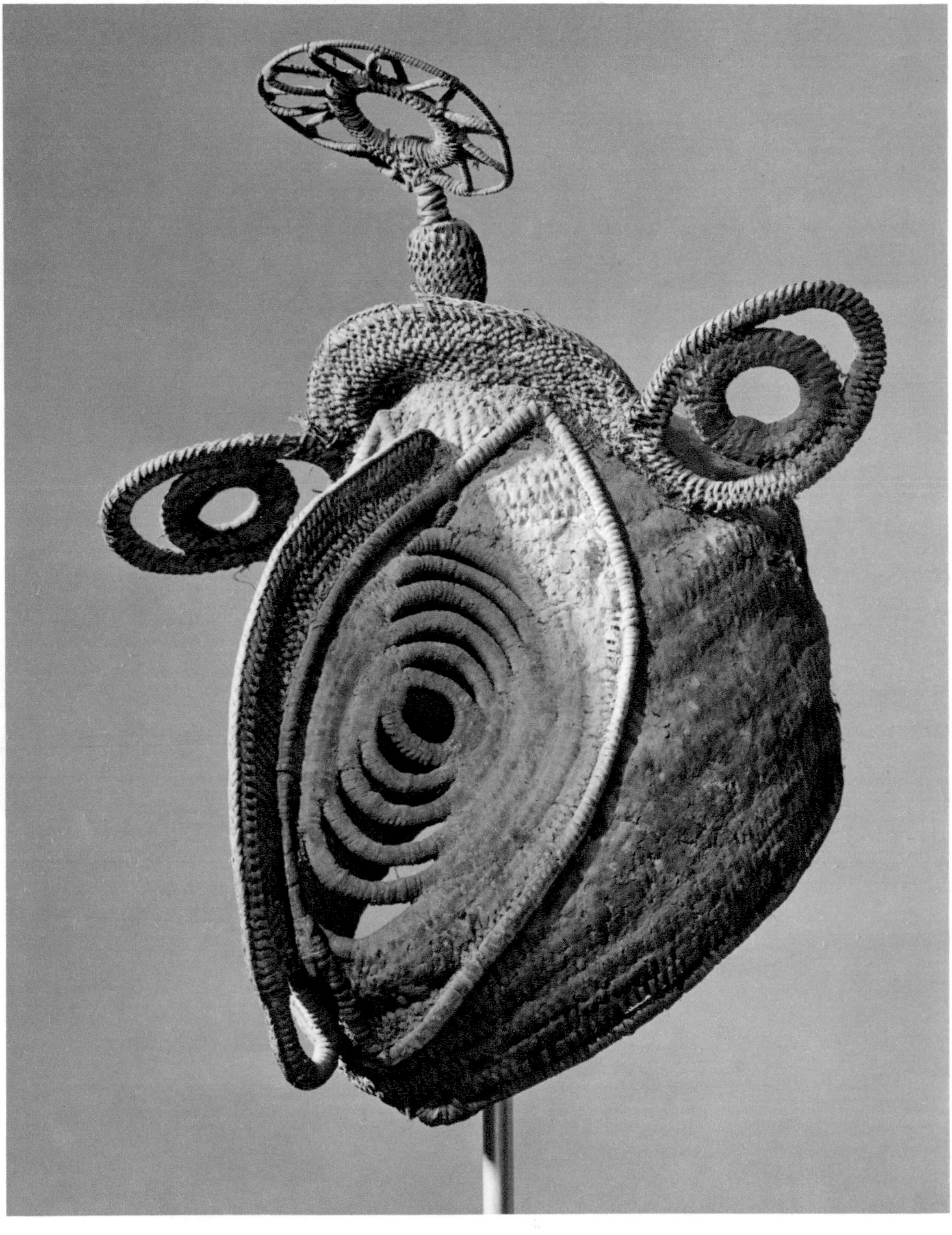

146. New Guinea, Maprik. *Basketry mask.* Mus. of Primitive Art, New York. — 147. New Guinea, North Maprik. *Lower part of a fronton of a great house.* Mus. of Primitive Art., New York. — 148. New Guinea, Uambong, Lake Chambuli. *Gable end.* Musée de l'Homme, Paris. — 149. New Guinea, Sepik. *Gable end.* Mus. of Primitive Art, New York.

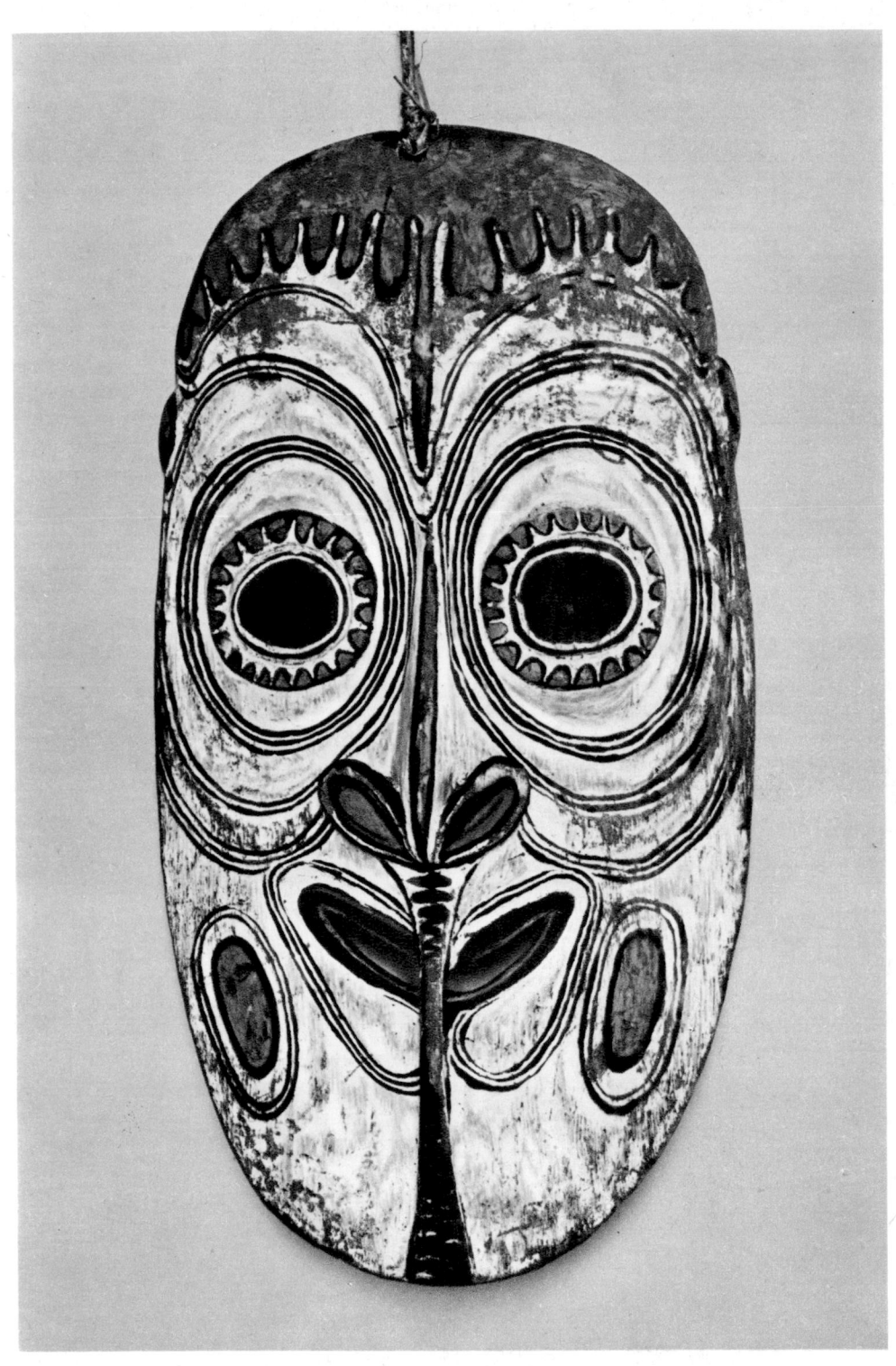

150. New Guinea, Kararu, Middle Sepik. *Gable end.* Nat. Hist. Mus., Chicago.
151. New Guinea, Sepik. *Polychrome carved wooden plaque.* Mus. of Primitive Art, New York.

190

152. New Guinea, Lake Chambuli. *Pottery with human face*. Basle. — 153. New Guinea, Sepik. *Sculpture with human symbolism*. Budapest.

154. New Guinea, Iatmül, Middle Sepik. *Painted overmodelled skull.* Mus. of Primitive Art, New York.
155. New Guinea, Iatmül, Middle Sepik. *Canoe prow.* Mus. of Primitive Art, New York.

193

156. New Guinea, Iatmül, Middle Sepik. *Hook*. Mus. of Primitive Art, New York.
157. New Guinea, Sepik. *Basketry mask*. Philadelphia.

158. New Guinea, Sepik, Kabriman. *Gable end.* Basle.
159. New Guinea, Sepik, Karawari River. *Orator's stool.* Mus. of Primitive Art, New York.

196

160. *Detail of 159.*

161. New Guinea, Middle Sepik. *Pottery*. Basle.

162. **New Guinea, Middle Sepik.** *Ridge tile*. Basle.
163. **New Guinea, Sepik, Töpfer River.** *Shield*. Steyl Museum.

164. New Guinea, Middle Sepik. *Ridge tile*. Basle.
165. New Guinea, Tambanum, Middle Sepik. *Mask*. Basle.
166. New Guinea, Kaminimbit, Middle Sepik. *Full-length sculpture*. Basle.

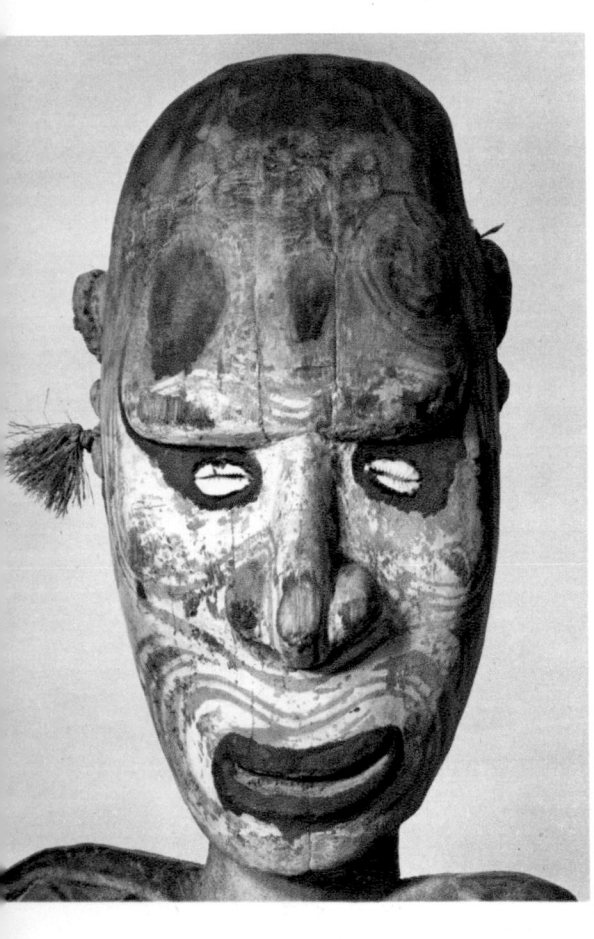

167. *Detail of* 168. — 168. New Guinea, Mandanan, Middle Sepik. *Orator's stool.* Basle. — 169. *Detail of* 166.

204

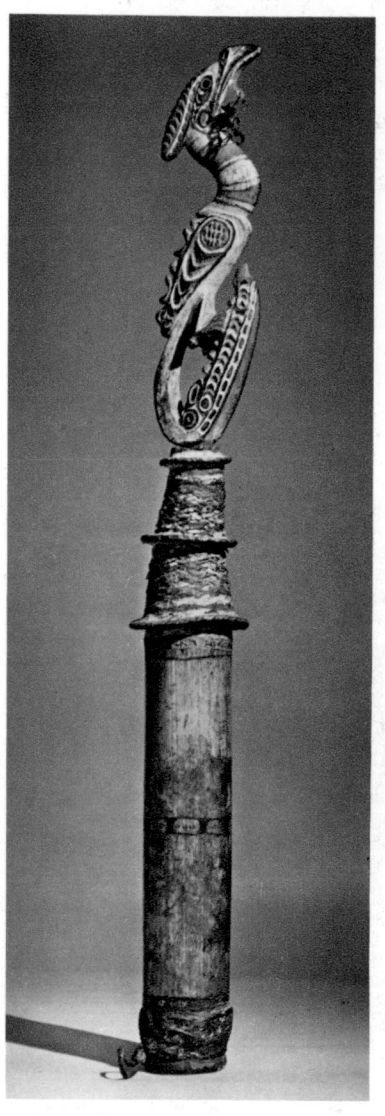

170. New Guinea, Sepik. *Shield of lime gourd.* Honolulu. — 171. New Guinea, Sepik. *Lime gourd.* Mus. of Primitive Art, New York. 172. New Guinea, Mimika, Avea. *Canoe prow.* Mus. of Primitive Art, New York.

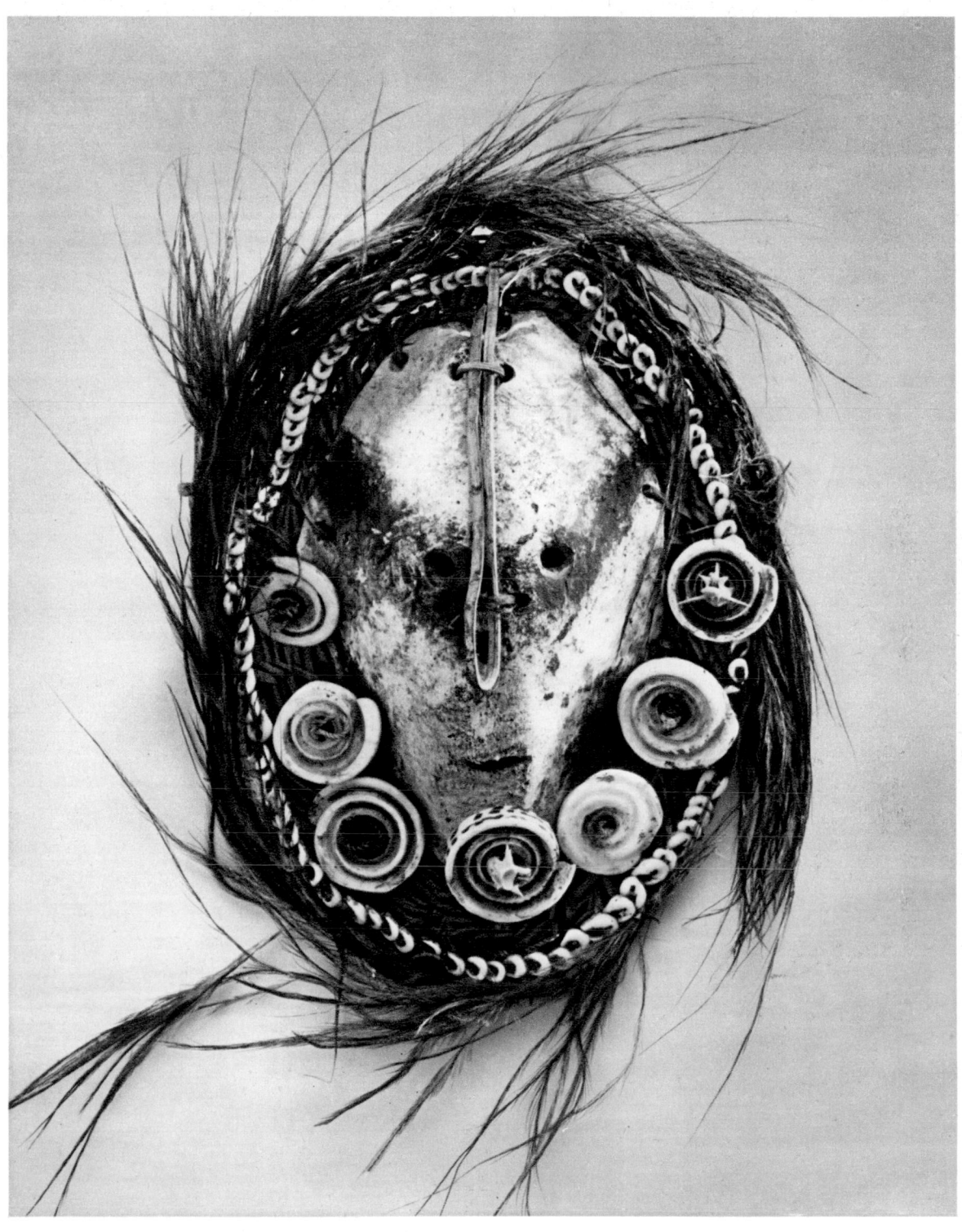

173. New Guinea, Kebiang, Middle Sepik. *Carved ridge-board.* Mus. of Primitive Art, New York.
174. New Guinea, Sepik, Poropolo. *Mask.* Mus. of Primitive Art, New York.

 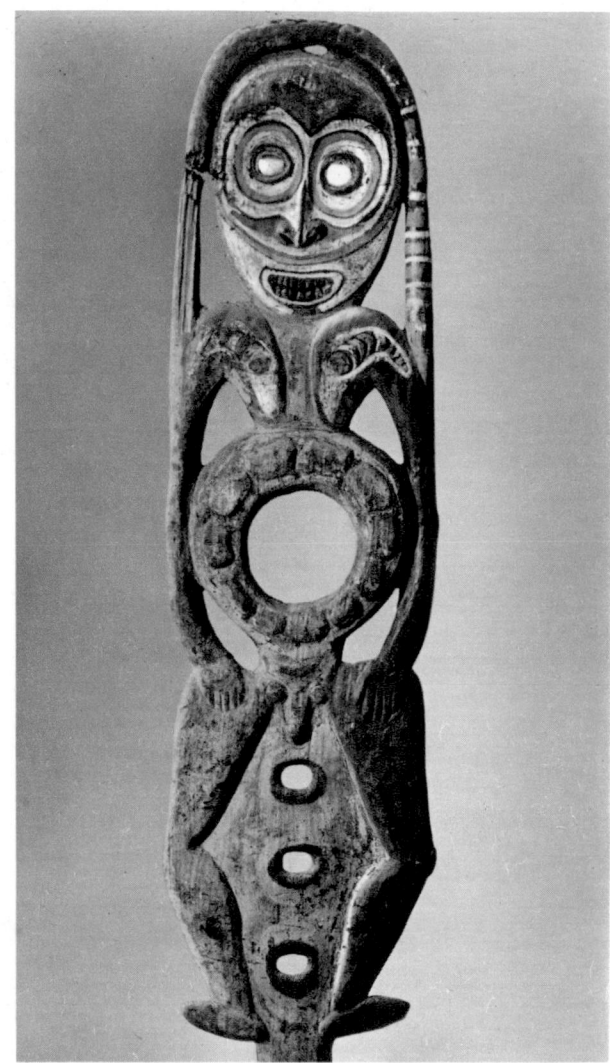

175. New Guinea, Middle Sepik. *Bas-relief*. Amsterdam.
176. New Guinea, Mindimbit, Middle Sepik. *Representation of a myth*. Amsterdam.
177. New Guinea, Middle Sepik. *Openwork incised plaque*. Mus. of Primitive Art, New York.

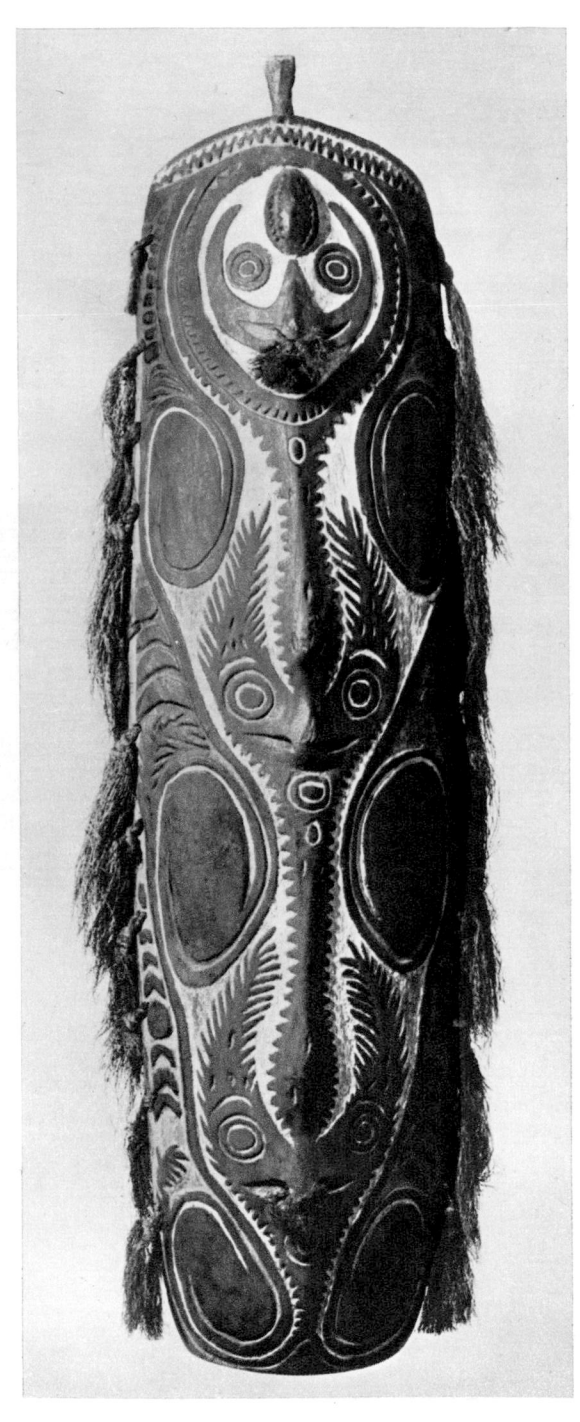

178. New Guinea, Kanduonum, Lower Sepik.
Shield. Mus. of Primitive Art, New York.

179. New Guinea, Kambrambo, Middle Sepik. *Painted vegetable panel.* Basle.
180. New Guinea, Kambrambo, Middle Sepik. *Painted vegetable panel.* Basle.

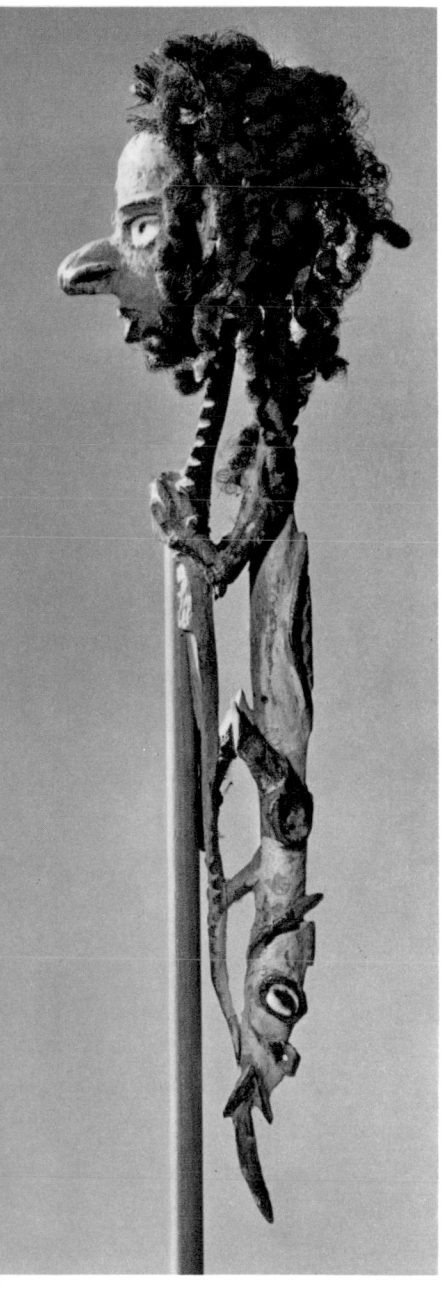

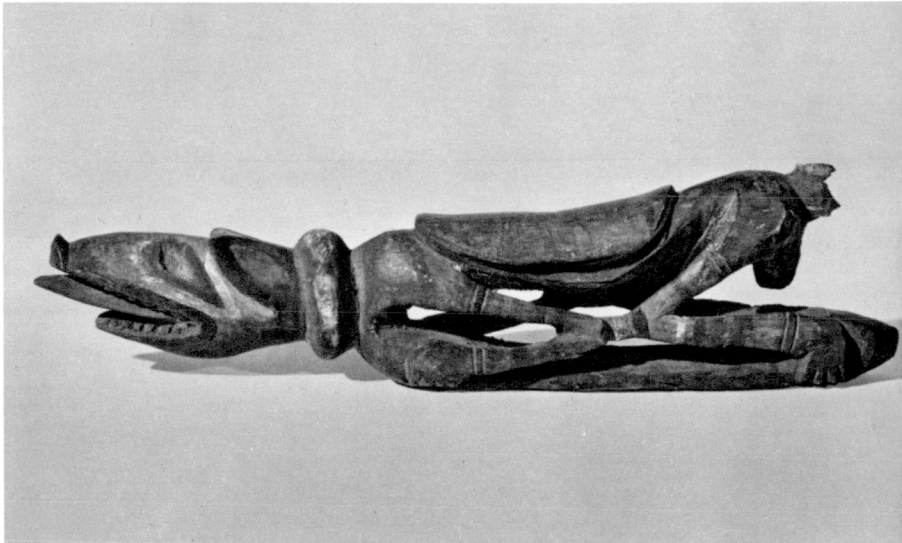

181. New Guinea, Yuat River. *Flute mouthpiece*. Basle. — 182. New Guinea, Yuat River. *Head-rest*. Mus. of Nat. Hist., New York. — 183. New Guinea, Yuat River. *Protean figure*. Mus. of Primitive Art, New York. — 184. New Guinea, Yuat River. *Head-rest*. Mus. of Primitive Art, New York.

185. New Guinea, Yuat River. *Representation of a human face*. Mus. of Primitive Art, New York. —
186. *Detail of* 187.

187. New Guinea, Mundugumor, Yuat River. *Carved squatting figure*. Mus. of Primitive Art, New York. — 188. New Guinea, Seleo Island. *Vertical frieze*. Bremen Museum.

189. New Guinea, Lower Sepik. *Carved wood panel.* Mus. of Primitive Art, New York.
190. New Guinea, Sepik. *Wooden mask with trunk.* Budapest.
191. New Guinea, Sepik, Postdamhafen. *Beaked wooden mask.* Budapest.
192. New Guinea, Sepik, Potsdamhafen. *Wooden mask.* Budapest.

221

193. New Guinea, Sepik. *Water drum.* Basle. — 194. New Guinea, Valley of the Ramu. *Full-length statuette.* Leningrad.

195. New Guinea, Sepik. *Full-length statuette (detail)*. Vérité Collection, Paris.

196. New Guinea, Sepik, Potsdamhafen. *Shield.* Budapest. —
197. New Guinea, Valley of the Ramu. *Monumental drum.*
Mus. of Primitive Art, New York. — 198. New Guinea, Valley
of the Ramu. *Wooden panel.* Mus. of Primitive Art, New York.

224

199. Eastern New Guinea, Manam Island. *Head-rest*. Mus. of Primitive Art, New York.
200. Eastern New Guinea, Tavaraj Island. *Head-rest*. Budapest.
201, 202, 203. Eastern New Guinea, Aitape. *Statuettes*. Budapest.

NEW HEBRIDES

The central and northern portion of the New Hebridean archipelago is (after New Guinea) one of the richest in plastic forms. The arts of the southern part link up with central Polynesia: here we find only curiously shaped clubs, kava cups in the form of canoe hulls, and double figurines carved from coral, these last originating from the small island of Futuna off Tanna.

Except in the case of a few rare and original pieces in stone, such as the kava dish from Malo in the Basle Museum, or the carved heads from the south of Pentecost Island and from Ambrim, the sculptors used wood or the lower part of tree-fern trunks as their raw material. The tree-fern trunk, consisting as it does of a mass of hard, interlocking spikes, will not take incised details and has to be covered with a smooth paste if colours are to be applied to it. In this area there is little stylistic difference between carvings in wood and those in tree-fern.

Portrayal of the human form is the most usual theme, though animal figures (birds, lizards, fish) are also found. The bird is especially found on the prows of canoes from the islands to the north east of Malekula: Vao, Atchin, Wala, Rano. Three styles can be distinguished. In the Banks Islands, in the north of the archipelago, and the northern part of Malekula the carvings are mainly in tree-fern: a semi-geometric stylization of a human face is set in a circle or a jagged oval. The nose is ridged, the mouth and small eyes protrude sharply. The body is non-existent or only faintly indicated, except for the genitalia. The long sinuous arms meet on the belly or are folded behind the head. The legs are straight or joined at the knees.

In most of Malekula, except for the south-eastern tip of the island, we find fewer sculptures in the strict sense than posts, both short and long, deeply carved depicting one or more human figures, one above the other, along with fish or tortoises. Because of the nature of the medium the limbs adhere to the body; the arms are bent upwards; the face is indicated only by the lines of the eyebrows, round or elongated eyes, a broad triangular nose, and a rounded chin in relief, having intersecting curves which may be meant to indicate the lips, and perhaps the tongue as well.

The most striking specimens from the New Hebrides are the great upright drums from the area around the south-western bay of Malekula. In these the single motif of a face, standing out in isolation at the top of the column of wood above the slit, achieves a spectacular effect with a minimum of means.

A blue statue from Malo Island is the only work that shows a skilful handling of the plastic elements of the body, but the arms are out of proportion and the head is in the style of those from the Admiralty Islands, though the face is not set so far forward. The nose is thin and straight. A small mouth cuts across, above the pointed chin, which overhangs the body. The head is prolonged by a bar carved with a series of pigs' lower jaws one above the other.

The style of Ambrim and of the south-eastern tip of Malekula seems to have certain features in common with that of the upper Sepik region. The tree-fern is hollowed out to represent the whole of the face below the eyebrow ridge. In the centre is an enormous nose whose wings sometimes turn up as far as the eyes. These are almond shaped and drawn back, or widened out, or even completely omitted. The treatment of the body differs little from that found in the Banks Islands or Malekula, except that there is slightly more relief.

229

204. New Guinea, Lower Sepik. *Vegetable panel*. Mus. of Primitive Art, New York.

The best pieces are undoubtedly the monumental drums of Ambrim. There are two distinct types. In the west and south of the island the drums stand several yards high, decorated with a series of superimposed faces set in successive ovals. These in turn are surrounded by three or four indented outlines enclosing a smooth double band whose inside line ends at the bottom with a hand. The lower part of each oval contains the button eyes and a nose with bulging nostrils projecting over a curved surface on which the mouth is not always indicated.

The carving of the single head on the North Ambrim drums ranks as one of the major achievements of Oceanian art. The head is not merely indicated on the rounded surface of the trunk, but carved into a crescent and set upon the drum as on a body. In the treatment of the features we find two variants. Either the strongly aquiline nose, swelling at the base, presents everted nostrils opening widely on the sides while the two eyes are reduced to a curve; or else narrow nostrils, tapering as they recede, leave the space necessary for the huge round eyes. Under the projecting eyebrows and the nose, the lower part of the crescent contains a large oval surface corresponding to the cheeks and upper lip. On either side hatched bands represent hair and beard. The lower ends of some of these bands curl round the body of the drum. These faces give an impression of serenity and composure which says much for the skill of the professional sculptors who made them.

In the pole-axes for killing pigs, hafted like adzes, we have another category of ritually important objects. Whether they are carved or not depends on the rank of the owner. They often have abstract motifs such as the crests of several cocks, or one or more faces treated in the local style. The same is true of the adzes with tridacna-shell blades which, in south Ambrim, are given a more angular shape.

The wooden dishes used for the preparation of pounded foods made from roasted taro or breadfruit are, in some regions (Espiritu Santo), the only known examples of local art. In the Shepherds Islands they are given a form roughly like that of a tortoise or, sometimes, that of a bird. Underneath, a figure can occasionally be seen or, as in Ambrim, an abstract motif, apparently a stylized human face. The small groups of clubs from South Pentecost has a similar but more explicit, stylized motif. They go, however, by the name of 'falcon's heads.'

Modelling is another characteristic form of New Hebrides art, which recalls, in some respects, that of New Guinea (Sepik and New Britain).

The skulls modelled over with a vegetable paste to resemble faces of dead men are intended to be placed on a manikin (*rambaramb*), coated with the same paste, to which are affixed all the insignia of rank accorded the dead man during his lifetime. When no space is available for them on other joints, these insignia may take the form of modelled heads attached to projections running out from the shoulders.

Modelling is done not only on skulls and on rolls of leaves, but also on coconuts and other fruit and on pieces of soft wood which serve as a support for a human head. The figures thus obtained can be used as marionettes exhibited behind a fence (*temes nevinbür*), as decorative elements for a frail structure erected on the occasion of mounting a guard (*namangi*), or as grotesque dolls *(naluan)* which only initiates are allowed to see.

The making of masks and ceremonial headdresses in light or heavy material, always of vegetable origin, gives another occasion for modelling. On a tree-fern base a face in heavy relief

205. New Hebrides, Aoba. *Stone dish*. Basle.

is built up and crowned, by way of head-dress, with graceful, delicately wrought mythological figures. Few of these fragile pieces arrive undamaged in museums. Light head-dresses are known in the Banks Islands, and some were illustrated by Codrington in their original undamaged condition. Equally fragile masks, whose standard form is a face set in a lozenge, come from Aoba, Ambrim and south-east Malekula. They have triangular motifs above and below the eye-sockets, and a stylized nose which tends to curl back on itself.

Modelling is also applied to the small masks fixed to the thick spider-webbing worn as a hair ornament by dignitaries.

In south Pentecost and the small islands to the north-east of Malekula, we find, as well as light masks, carved masks having a handle, with globular eyes and prominent noses perforated at the base.

Finally, pottery is still being made in the west of Santo with relief ornamentation (exclusively geometric), on the bowls and pots.

231

206. New Hebrides, Metamli, Ambrim. *Carved head*. M.A.A.O., Paris. — 207. New Hebrides, Gaua, Banks Islands. *Grade sculpture*. Basle. — 208. *Detail of 207.*

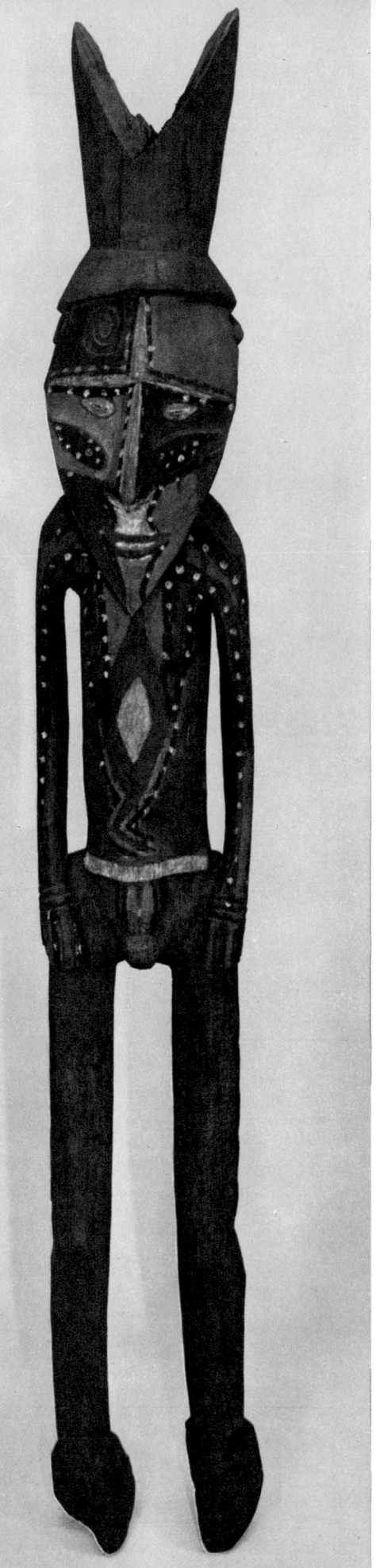

209. New Hebrides, Malekula. *Grade sculpture.*
Geneva. — 210. New Hebrides, Pao, West Malekula.
Carved post. Basle. — 211. New Hebrides, *Full-length*
sculpture (detail). Musée de l'Homme, Paris.

212. New Hebrides, Gaua, Banks Islands. *Carving in tree-fern*. Musée de l'Homme, Paris.
213. New Hebrides, Fanu, Ambrim. *Monumental drum : detail of the head*. Musée de l'Homme, Paris.

214. *Back of the head in 213.*

238

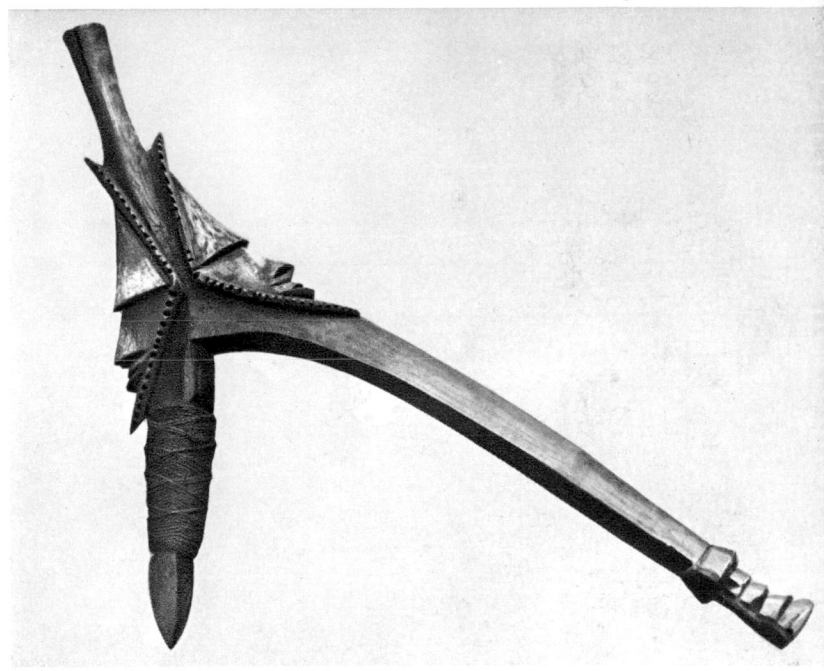

215. New Hebrides, West Ambrim. *Monumental drum*. Basle.
216. New Hebrides, Atchin. *Canoe with prow carved in the form of a frigate-bird*.
217. New Hebrides, Ambrim. *Weapon for the ritual slaughter of pigs*. Basle.
218. New Hebrides. *Adze*. Honolulu.

219. New Hebrides, Espiritu Santo. *Carved wooden dish*. Musée de l'Homme, Paris. — 220. New Hebrides, West Ambrim. *Underside of dish*. Mus. of Primitive Art, New York. — 221. New Hebrides, South Malekula. *Funerary figure: rambaramb*. Musée de l'Homme, Paris.

240

222. New Hebrides, South Malekula. *Funerary figure: rambaramb*. M.A.A.O., Paris.
223. New Hebrides, Aoba. *Mask*. Musée de l'Homme, Paris.

224. New Hebrides, South Malekula. *Temes nevinbür figurine*. Musée de l'Homme, Paris.
225. New Hebrides, South-east Malekula (?). *Diamond-shaped mask*. Musée de l'Homme, Paris.

226. New Hebrides, South Malekula. *Tree-fern mask*. Basle.
227. New Hebrides, South Malekula. *Tree-fern mask*. M.A.A.O., Paris.
228. *Detail of 227.*

229. New Hebrides, North Malekula. *Human face motif on the end of a spear*. Musée de l'Homme, Paris.
230. New Hebrides, Ambrim. *Light mask*. Musée de l'Homme, Paris.

231. New Hebrides, Malekula. *Mask*. Musée de l'Homme, Paris. — 232. New Hebrides, Pentecost. *Mask*. Musée de l'Homme, Paris.

233. New Hebrides, South Malekula.
Ceremonial head-dress. M.A.A.O., Paris.
— 234. New Hebrides, Banks Islands.
Ritual head-dress. British Museum.

251

NEW CALEDONIA

The art of New Caledonia counterbalances the impression we have when we set eyes on the arid, vividly coloured soil of the island. It is an art which has nothing of the broken, contorted relief of the island itself, dotted with high conical huts decorated with carvings; but an art in which the regularized treatment of themes gives a touch of monotony to an element of majesty.

Most of the carvings are executed in low relief, recording in durable material the abiding presence of the ancestors on the threshold of the house. The pieces composing the carved group round the door are, when complete, seven in number: the threshold mascaron (*katara*), the door-jambs (*jovo*), a carved frieze above them (*pweretu*) and a head fixed on a central post facing the door, horizontal sculptured beams (*boedu*) and, lastly, the ring of posts carved on the inner side with bearded human faces.

The greater part of the door-jambs is covered with parallel broken or curving lines carved in ridges combining to form cross and star motifs. Above them is a thick bulge cut short by a sharply defined horizontal line which marks the chin. Next comes the mouth, a narrow slot from which a splayed-out tongue sometimes protrudes. The nose, very broad at the base, in strong relief with spreading nostrils and a central portion which is sometimes shaped like a bird's beak. This nose is the only feature of the face in high relief. In the best examples, from the north of the island, the nostrils are faintly indicated by long, narrow slits. Sometimes they open widely to the front, encroaching on the body of the nose which then appears to be awkwardly hollowed out on either side. Above the cheeks, which have the form of a rounded, sometimes protuberant surface, the eyes are almondshaped under overhanging brows. Sometimes the artist places the eyes on the tip of a short peg. Finally the surface of the forehead is cut transversely by a double series of confronted chevrons representing the cord of a sling. Local variations can be detected: the star motif changes into squares, lozenges or ovals as one moves southwards. The door-jambs in the Paty language region are narrower and higher than the rather low and wide ones of the north.

The roof spires of the great houses are certainly one of the clearest examples of intellectual realism that we know of in the South Pacific, as is proved by the explanation given by the sculptor to Maurice Leenhardt.

Above and below a human face, a series of motifs occur successively along a vertical axis. 'At the bottom a flat oval represents the stomach and thorax. The latter carries, like a scarf, a small basket containing magic herbs. Above this comes the neck, then the chin depicted by a bow with upturned ends; the face with the opening of the nostrils in front view and the ears pierced and projecting horizontally; the forehead stylized into two points; the hair divided into two stylized parts jutting out on each side; the sling-string, which in life the man wore rolled round the hair; another oval representing the nape of the neck (which would be invisible on the living model).'

Thus in order to represent the whole of the ancestor's head, without omitting anything, the sculptor has unrolled its salient features on to a single plane extending from the chin to the back of the head. In the north of the island, the upper oval was replaced by the motif of a toothed comb pointing to the sky. Further south the spire had a face on each side. At Canala, the roof-spires are differently treated, the large ovals being omitted and emphasis laid on other representative elements: the ears pointing upwards in two widely opening V-shaped appendages, with the lobes pierced; the body depicted by a lozenge on whose edges are fitted, on either side, a series of arms reduced to independent truncated lines, beginning at the chin which merges into the shoulder. At the lower extremity of the arms, a bar cuts across them to mark the wrists. In the same region, and as far as the extreme south, there are also roof-spires composed of superimposed triangles and lozenges, sometimes of confronted crescents, tip to tip; this symbolism presumably related to the bird, conventional emblem of a chief. Attempts to combine the ancient symbolism with a more realistic vision are beginning to appear.

The plank called *boedu*, a derivative of the roof-ridge, which is placed horizontally inside the house at a certain height, calls for mention here. With other planks it serves to mark off an enclosure reserved for divinatory sleep. The illustrated figure has a lizard on its chest.

Sometimes the posts set in a ring near the doorways of the houses are carved with bearded faces turned inward, each with different features. Responsibility for the making and setting up of each post falls to one of the clans that support, or are subject to, the chieftain.

In the masks, or at least in the best examples of them, we find definite attempts at work in the round. In the centre of the island, faces are flat and treated in the same manner as those on door-jambs. But in the north the features curve in strong relief which almost seems to erupt from the face. The characteristics are: low foreheads, jutting eyebrow ridges, parrot-beak noses with sweeping curves, nostrils turned sideways with wide openings at different angles, mouths with raised corners and rounded projecting lips allowing a full set of teeth to be seen. The wooden mask is fastened to a plaited frame and embellished with a dome of hair and a handsome beard made of tresses of human hair. Beneath it is a net cloak, to each knot of which are fixed two or three black feathers of the *notu*, a jungle bird. An opening on each side allows the arms to be inserted, to carry clubs and bundles of spears.

Besides these classical examples we also find figurines which are made to be set up in the earth like stakes. Their area of distribution on the island corresponds exactly to that of the masks. The figurine often represents a person clad in a striped cloak, the garment of the mask-wearers. In the northernmost part of New Caledonia, very fine male and female figures have been collected; their limbs have the modelling found only in the best Oceanian pieces. The face is foreshortened, in much the same way as the faces in the other carvings. Representations of very young children have also been found: they are shown in the cradle of vegetable matter which the women carried on their backs.

Incised human faces occur on the shafts of spears, yam knives and coins. From time to time present-day sculptors try to revive this form of art, sometimes with a fair degree of success.

On the old-style earthenware pots there figured the design in relief of a beaked nose, with eyes above it on each side, or the representation of a lizard. Only seldom do we find more complex scenes, as on the magnificent specimen in the possession of the Mission Catholique de La Conception. Birds were also depicted in relief on objects with a hole in the middle, the bird in question being the *notu*, symbol of the chiefly clans in the north of the island.

We must not overlook in this context the engraved bamboos of New Caledonia, which we have discussed elsewhere, nor that finest, most typical example of New Caledonian art, the parade axe. This may be regarded as the end-product of an evolution which began with the primitive stone club. Polynesian tradition ascribes divine powers to the *toki*, the adze with a tridacna-shell or polished stone blade. In the aesthetic quality of serpentine, a veined stone, and the symbolic connotations of its hues of blue or green, the craftsmen found a welcome challenge to their patience and ingenuity. After its extraction from the quarries on Uen Island, the stone was worked until it was reduced to a flat disc with translucent cutting edges. Two holes drilled just below the centre enabled it to be lashed to a wooden handle, which rested on the top of half a coconut shell. The whole, handle and half-shell, was wrapped in tapa-cloth secured with dark red plaited thongs made of vegetable fibres and dyed flying-fox fur. The diagonal lashings on the handle met on the lower rounded portion of the implement to form a pattern of concentric squares. The object as a whole symbolized the human body, the stone, on account of its colour, being the symbol of life, as were the shell pendants added to it.

235. New Caledonia, North Zone (Gomen-Uebia). *Carved group from the doorway of a great house.* Musée de l'Homme, Paris. — 236. New Caledonia, Yambe (Ubatche). *Carved door-frame*. Basle. — 237. New Caledonia, Isle of Pines (Vao). *Carved door-frame*.

238. New Caledonia, Huailu-Burail Zone. *Carved door-frame*. Musée de l'Homme, Paris.
239, 240, 241. New Caledonia. *Roof terminals*. Basle.

257

242. New Caledonia, Warai (Huailu). *Carved beam.* Basle. —
243. New Caledonia, Cape Colnett. *House Post.* Basle. —
244. New Caledonia, Canala-Thio Region. *Roof terminal.* Mus.
of Primitive Art, New York.

245. New Caledonia, North of the Grande Terre. *Representation of a child in a traditional cradle.* Noumea.
246. New Caledonia, North of the Grande Terre. *Pwemwe mask.* Musée de l'Homme, Paris.

247. New Caledonia, East Coast. *Spe[...]* *(detail)*. M.A.A.O., Paris. — 248. Ne[...] Caledonia. *Parade axe*. Leenhardt Co[...] lection.

III

ASTROLABE BAY

A recent study by Tibor Bodrogi, Director of the Ethnographic Museum, Budapest, gives an excellent account of the various styles prevailing in this region, whose homogeneity had rarely been recognised before.

As is so often the case elsewhere in New Guinea, the form of art which demonstrates this best and most clearly is not the large-scale sculptures. These large works, given the name of *telum*, which have the form of posts and serve to decorate the precincts of the men's house, represent hieratic figures with sexual attributes, the hands resting on the hips. The face is flat; marked eyebrow ridges separate the plane of the forehead from that of the lower face; the protuberant eyes are rounded or almond-shaped, their outer ends merging with the line of the eyebrows. The straight nose, in low relief, has a pierced septum. The lightly indicated mouth is prolonged by a linear motif, sometimes with a serrated edge. It is difficult to tell whether this represents a tongue or a beard. Sometimes the motif runs downwards and joins up with the penis, which is clearly marked and always vertical. Trunk and arms are cylindrical. Arms are separated from the trunk, and placed in front of it. The lay-out conforms to the shape of the tree-trunks used for these carvings.

The smaller carvings, whose function is something of a problem, have the same general composition but ornamental themes are more in evidence. We find a disproportion between trunk and limbs; protuberances at the joints; the motif of a prominent ear-pendant joining up with the shoulder, and bi-frontal heads. The elaborate head-dress which figures on some of the *telum* is not found in the statuettes, above whose heads we find the classic motif of a bird burying its beak in the man's skull. Acording to early observers the *telum* were sometimes given an animal head (shark, crocodile) and were occasionally touched up with black and red.

It has been pointed out by several authorities that these carvings played no part in daily life. They seem to be effigies of ancestors, but only the Russian traveller Miklucho-Maclay went so far as to give individual names to these figures. In actual fact, however, there is no knowing what persons they represent. It seems that a feast was held, perhaps annually, at which they either received offerings of meat, or such offerings were eaten in their presence and, presumably, in their honour.

The masks, made of a single piece of wood, have handles. The style of the carving resembles that of the other sculptures, but the mouth is better defined and the nose is given considerable prominence. The ear-pendant motif, meticulously executed, counterbalances the nose. The whole has a compelling power not found in the other carvings.

The masks are called heads of Asa, *asa kate*, this being the name of the ritual initiating young men into the men's society. A special mask—we do not know whom it represents—is worn by a man who, by dealing blows to the young men, announces that their ordeal is over and the incisions have healed. The other masks are exhibited in processions and can be seen by everyone, albeit from a respectful distance.

Among other carvings we may mention certain crudely fashioned animal figures, such as fish or birds in flight. The straight or curved handles of cattle-bells are carved to resemble birds' beaks or a human face, whose volumes have a symmetrical, ornamental aspect rather like that of the yam knives of New Caledonia.

In other works produced in this region the art is almost exclusively ornamental. Examples are the bull-roarers, whose incised and painted decorations are always geometric. Lime is rubbed into indentations in the wood which sometimes forms short, straight lines or Greek key motifs, and sometimes irregular patterns. The human head is rarely represented, but the word 'head' is used, it seems, to designate the handles of the large flat incised and painted clubs.

The round or elongated wooden containers, shaped like canoe hulls, have on their sides a band of decorative motifs of one type or another. The motifs on shell armlets are the best executed, since this material calls for more accurate and finer work. Bamboo boxes are decorated with bands of similar motifs on a smaller scale. Irregular geometric motifs are found on the tapas; these are brushed in with broad strokes or in lines joining at their centres and ending in spirals.

This ornamental art is seen at its best in the interplay of contrasting colours and very simple motifs in relief, which characterise both the round wooden shields of Astrolabe Bay and the wooden drums, ritual components of the Asa. Their hour-glass shape is stressed by a single or double band of incised motifs round the waist of the drum. On one side of this band there is a plain handle and on the other an intricate openwork ornamental pattern comprised of curves and motifs forming a long series of lips or having the shape of birds' heads.

The motifs on decorated tapa cloth are quite simple: lines, indentations, concentric crosses.

249. New Guinea, Astrolabe Bay. *Full-length statuette*. Budapest.
250. New Guinea, Astrolabe Bay. *Telum statue*. Budapest.
251. New Guinea, Astrolabe Bay. *Telum statue with bird*. Budapest.

252. New Guinea, Astrolabe Bay. *Tortoise-shell armlet*. Budapest.
253. New Guinea, Astrolabe Bay. *Shield*. Basle.
254. New Guinea, Astrolabe Bay. *Wooden mask*. Budapest.

255. New Guinea, Astrolabe Bay. *Wooden mask*. Budapest.

256. New Guinea, Astrolabe Bay. *Tapa coverlet*. Budapest.

HUON GULF

Cut off by great mountain barriers, the Huon Gulf area does not seem to have been influenced in the least by the artistic flowering that took place in the Sepik region. Nor does Tami Island, whence come some of the best pieces in this group. If affinities are to be traced, these may best be found in the korovar style and that of New Britain. The stereotyped treatment of human and animal themes has been interpreted by Linton and Wingert as the expression of a static social order, linked with an elaborate system of ancient duties and rights. It would, perhaps, be better to begin by defining the nature of a 'static' society and ascertaining whether such a society actually exists. Local complexes of rights and privileges occur everywhere: it would seem that the decorative motifs, or at least their minor variants, are connected with these systems and cannot be transmitted from one group to another as easily as in the Sepik region. In these circumstances the local art, lacking a flexible repertory of themes allowing frequent fusions and renewals, could have taken on a static appearance—which, however, is far from being peculiar to the art of the Huon region.

The masks named *tago*, worked in bark on a light framework, are found, it seems, only on Tami Island; some believe, however, that the original idea came from New Britain through the intermediary of matrimonial relationships. The carved and painted wooden masks on the other hand, are remarkable for the regularity of their ornamentation: flat white faces, where only the nose-ridge appears in light relief, as do the wings of the nose, which are either curved or stylised into an extended M, with an occasional hint of realism. The eyes and toothed mouth are incised in the wood and drawn in white lines around strips of red. A double-triangle motif framing each eye recurs persistently in the wood carvings of this region. The faintly indicated ears are sometimes replaced by stylized birds with short beaks disposed around the face. These masks are provided with handles with which to hold them in place: the handle is sometimes carved to represent a tiny human body.

Full-length ancestor figures are treated in the same manner: red incised eyes, nose and nails on a white kaolin ground. The head is sunk into the body, with the result that the shoulders start level with the eyes and the ears disappear altogether.

Above the face rises a tall head-dress, incised on the sides with wing-like lines. A specimen in the Bernice P. Bishop Museum, Honolulu, on which the paint is in a excellent state of preservation, has a serrated motif in the form of a crescent with upturned points. A piece in the Budapest Museum gives a clue to the interpretation of this type of head-dress; it represents a bird with its claws resting on the figure's shoulders. In other words these incised motifs are yet another variant of the familiar bird theme.

The massive, flat body is partly hidden by the head, and ends in a penis outlined by incision or treated in relief. In one case a dangling penis is confronted by a snake's head. The arms are separated from the body and the hands rest on the hips. The legs are usually folded under the body, sometimes at an angle which is the reverse of any normal posture. Shoulders and knee joints are always indicated by an incised circle. Finally, a lizard in relief is sometimes placed on the figure's back.

The head-rests provide the finest examples of this style of sculpture. A kneeling figure holds on his head the upper part, which serves as a pillow: the elbows are linked to the pedestal by a motif of half-closed curves one above the other, repeating that of the open hands on the sides. This arrangement is sometimes reversed; the hands rest on the pedestal, and the same motif is repeated between the shoulders and the top of the structure. A very fine specimen in Budapest Museum, when seen from the side, shows the same figure; from in front, the body is seen to curve backwards so that the 'pillow' rests on the head and feet, while the belly and hands touch the pedestal.

Single or double food bowls of small dimensions are also characteristic of this region. Little true relief exists even in the handles, though they often depict birds' heads with short beaks, schematized into the form of an incompletely closed ring. On a double bowl we find highly stylized human motifs: triangular eyes from which the shoulders jut forth and short legs with circles at the joints; but more commonly the ornamentation takes the form of stylized lizards, snakes and birds carved in relief or incised.

The upper part of the bird is carved in low relief and the wings are outspread, while the body below is shown in front view and rendered by incised lines. Another winged creature swallowing a snake is viewed from above and seems to be leaping out of the wall where a double incised motif depicts its body. The frog is another favourite motif.

Large wooden food ladles are adorned at different points on their handles with human faces. Here the triangular motifs emphasizing eyes and nose-wings may account for the lateral projections unless these represent ears. The portable hour glass-shaped drums carry lavish incised ornamentation on either side of the waist; when a bird's head in incised relief is the leading motif it occupies a position exactly opposite the single handle.

272

257. New Guinea, Huon Gulf, Tami Island. *Tapa mask.* Budapest

258. New Guinea, Huon Gulf. *Wooden mask*. Honolulu.
259. New Guinea, Huon Gulf, Apo. *Wooden mask*. Nat. Hist. Mus., Chicago.
260. New Guinea, Huon Gulf. *Bas-relief*. Honolulu.

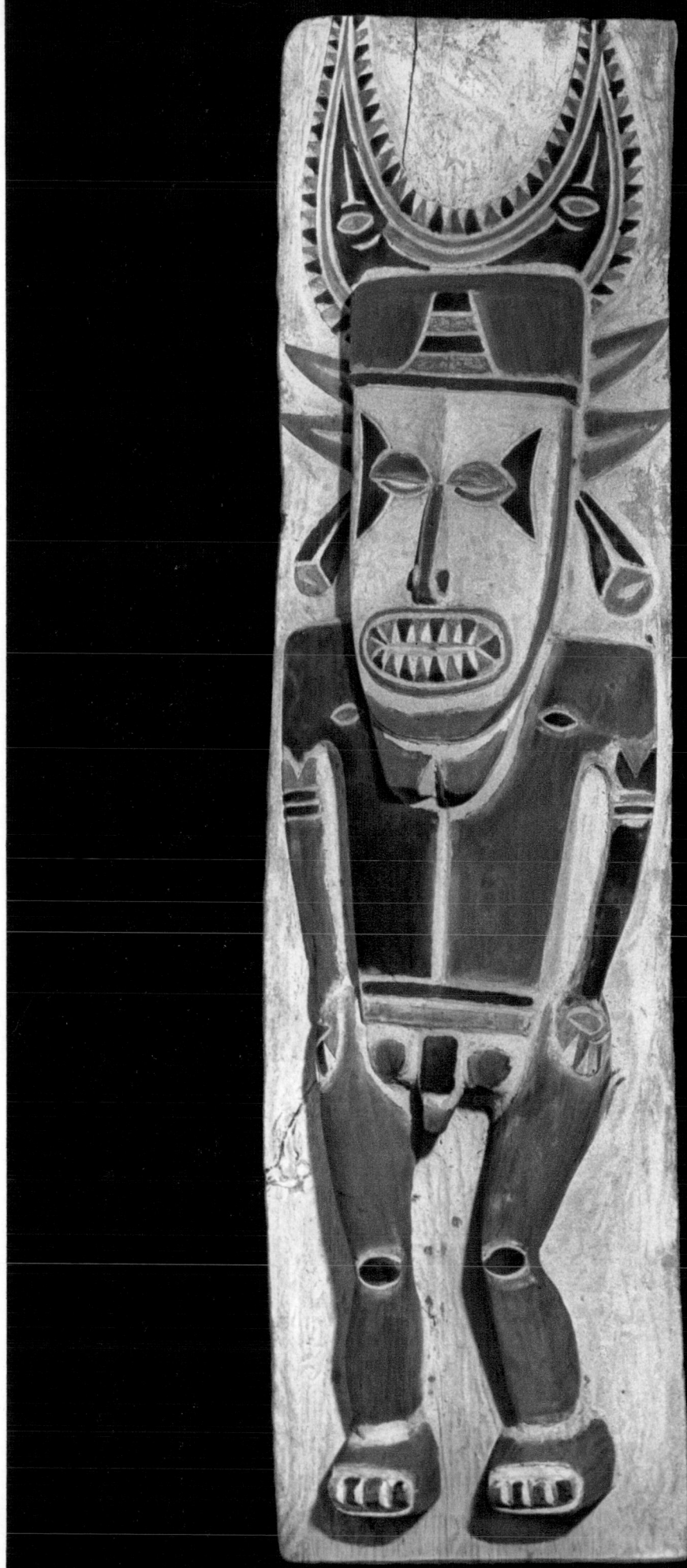

261. New Guinea, Huon Gulf, *Full-length statue*. Basle.
262. New Guinea, Huon Gulf, Molu. *Polychrome full-length statue*. Budapest.

263 and 264. New Guinea, Huon Gulf.
Head-rest. Budapest.
265. *Detail of 264*.

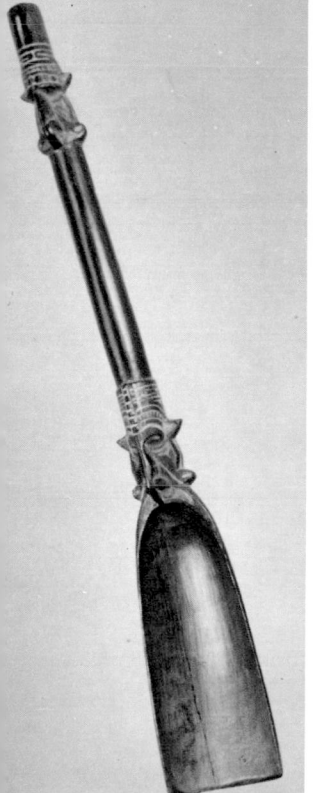

266. New Guinea, Huon Gulf, Tami Island. *Portable drum.* Budapest.
267. New Guinea, Huon Gulf, Tami Island. *Ornament of a wooden dish (detail).* M.A.A.O., Paris.
268. New Guinea, Huon Gulf, Tami Island. *Food paddle.* M.A.A.O., Paris.
269. New Guinea, Huon Gulf, Tami Island. *Carved double bowl.* M.A.A.O., Paris.

NEW BRITAIN

We may consider New Britain and the neighbouring islands as a transitional zone. For the most part it recalls Papua in the delicacy of its constructed objects, Sepik in its modelled skulls, and the nearby coast of New Guinea in its carvings. But this is far from saying that the art of New Britain is lacking in originality.

The best-known part of the island lies to the north and is called Gazelle Peninsula. Collections have been made of objects coming from two peoples in this region, the Sulka and the Baining.

From the Sulka come few specimens, notably the two fine canoe prows in the Budapest Museum. One portrays an animal, probably a dog, seated on a cone, its tail prolonged upwards by a broad flat appendage on which a stylized human body has been painted in fine lines. The limbs and a cylindrical object held between the animal's paws, have a decoration consisting exclusively of fine-spun lines: hatchings, spirals, ribbed axial lines enclosed in lozenges. Another similar piece has on its lower part a human figure with raised arms. The face of indefinite style, with an open mouth, is flanked by two flat appendages, round at the top and beaked at the bottom, either a reminiscence of the bird motif or a suggestion of ears. The painted ornamentation consists of white bands, underlined in red, surrounding the face and symbolizing, in the lower half, legs that have been forced to the sides to make room for a mortice hole.

But the Sulka are best known to us by their masks made of a lattice-work of narrow bands of pith interwoven with stiff fibres. This variant of the normal basketry technique enables the construction of light objects of considerable size. The bottom of the face consists of a truncated cone or a cylinder to which are added similarly made protuberances representing eyes on stalks, a long nose and ears. A big collarette figures either above or below the face, and the whole is painted in glowing colours. Fixed to the cone of some of these masks is a large disc, with painted star motifs, under which are isolated protuberances, suggestive of eyes. Whether the masks are wholly or only partly in wood, the style remains the same.

Oval shields, sometimes with a central boss, have a painted decoration in broad double lines, red and white, the edges between the two colours being serrated. The theme appears to be a double motif of faces symmetrically disposed about a transverse axis.

The Baining, who are neighbours of the Sulka, differ from the latter in the way in which they construct their tapa masks. These seem to be of two kinds. The first has at its centre a sort of tall narrow bonnet: at the back a slight extension counterbalances a small bamboo proboscis covered in tapa. This is painted in alternate light and dark triangles; the high cap with a face motif inscribed in a lozenge. Here the technique recalls that of the lozenge with a face enclosed that we find in the New Hebrides. The second type of mask consists of sheets of tapa stretched on sticks: under two large, round eyes painted in two-coloured concentric circles, is a sort of beak from which protrudes, but underneath it, what looks like an enormous tongue. The spaces above and below the eyes are painted with triangles, curves and red rings studded with white spots.

The Baining use the facial bones alone, instead of whole skulls, as the base for modelling a slightly stylized human face in vegetable paste: this is enhanced by lines painted round the

270. *Detail of the head of* 271.

eyesockets and mouth. Characteristic of the style is the elongation of the face by the addition under the chin of a beard rendered in white lines.

Crescent-shaped canoe prows from the Gazelle Peninsula have a painted decoration which appears to symbolise a bird with outspread wings terminating in spirals. The broad lines of the composition stand out on a ground of hatchings running in various directions. The whole produces an harmonious effect, reminding us of the 'classic' painted decorations of New Ireland. Similarly an enormous mask in the Chicago Museum, collected in central New Britain, recalls, with its powerful modelling and crested headdress, a detached and enlarged *Uli* head.

From the French, or Witu, archipelago, to the west of the island, come tapa masks technically similar to those of Papua, but with a painted decoration emphasizing two different-sized triangles round the eyes. Other masks, made in wood, have a flat face from which only the nose emerges in relief. The forehead is decorated with a Greek key band, and the face is treated in a manner reminiscent of the faces on arrows from the Torres Straits Islands. Elongated rectangular shields, known as dance shields, have an intricate incised motif of remarkable regularity in which can be recognized, thanks to the presence of an eye, the bird motif or that of a figure with outspread limbs.

The incised lime spatulas seem to belong to the art tradition of Massim on the east of New Guinea.

283

271 and 272. New Britain, Sulka. *Canoe prows*. Budapest.
273. New Britain, Witu Islands. *Tapa mask*. Budapest.

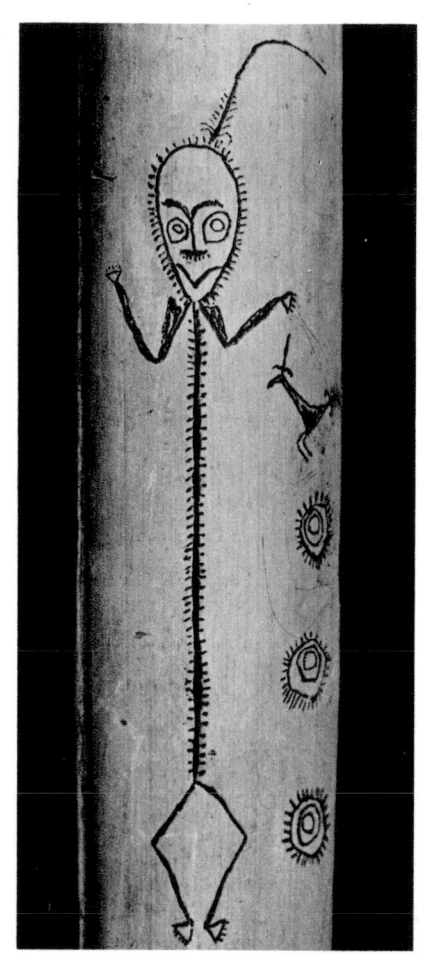

276. New Britain, Baining. *Tapa mask*. Hamburg Museum. — 277. New Britain. *Motif incised on a bamboo stick*. Budapest. — 278. New Britain, Baining. *'Blow-pipe' mask*. Basle.

279. New Britain, Sulka. *Shield*. Mus. of Primitive Art, New York. — 280. New Britain, Baining. *Over-modelled skull*. Budapest. — 281. New Britain, South coast. *Wooden mask*. Nat. Hist. Mus., Chicago. — 282. New Britain, French Islands. *Mask*. Budapest.

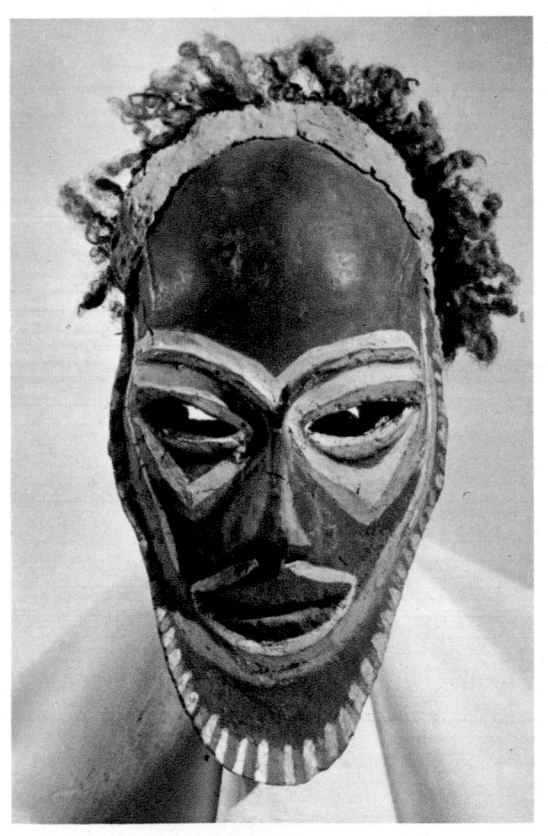

NEW IRELAND

This narrow island, one of the two largest in the Bismarck Archipelago, is the home of one of the most unexpected forms of art the world has ever seen—an art combining imaginative powers of the highest order with a well-nigh incredible technical virtuosity. In New Ireland, incised and painted decorations are combined with carving and the resulting synthesis seems practically to have eliminated all other forms of local art.

We do best to begin with an attempt to reduce the bewildering medley of forms to some sort of order. Almost all the sculptures are designated by the term *malanggan*, this being the name given to the ritual cycles with which they are associated. These *malanggan* fall into distinct categories: masts, *totok*, *kata*, *walix*, masks and *uli*.

The masts and *totok*, made to be stuck in the ground, are constructed on similar lines. Around a figure, or a series of superimposed figures and animals (pigs and cocks) carved in the round, is grouped an assortment of accessory motifs, human figures and animals (snakes, fish, lizards and birds), and interlaced decorative motifs which sometimes, owing to the play of shadows, tend to conceal what seems to be the essential theme. Even in the most intricate examples we can discern certain unwritten principles which guide the local artists: contrasts between the massive interior carving and the fragile grace of the tracery in front and on the sides; contrasts between the flat colours of the exterior tracery and the delicate brush-strokes and hatchings of the painted decorations of the main elements; and again, contrasts between the coherent interior theme and the bewildering plethora of themes around it. This combination of a stable axis and a spider's-web surround testifies to a virtuosity in the handling of forms almost unparalleled elsewhere in Oceania and combining sculpture in the round, painting and openwork decoration in three-dimensional form.

Not all the pieces, however, are so difficult to interpret. The least elaborate are precisely those in which artists' mastery of their means strikes us most. While the masts and *totok* produce an impression of an incomprehensible jumble of forms, the other types of sculpture produce an equal impression of artifice but seem better balanced, by our standards. This is partly due to the fact that we find here bas-reliefs and friezes where a certain symmetry to the vertical axis, gives a semblance of order to the proliferating themes, and allows more space for the main design to assert itself.

The bird is the commonest motif in the bas-reliefs. It is sometimes shown in profile, but also, fairly frequently, full face, the wings spread wide and a snake gripped in its beak. The beaks and even the bodies of the birds may be multiplied at the expense of the snake which is then shown in pieces. The flat colours of the snake strike a contrast with the detailed decoration of the bird. Human figures may be added to the wings.

The friezes link figures, always of the same type, with symbols or portrayals of birds and fish on either side of a central circular aperture, either left empty or decorated with a disc or a motif resembling an eye.

Other types of bas-reliefs and friezes carry in the centre a figure and, on either side, a network representing birds and snakes or large painted solar motifs.

A remarkable specimen in Basle Museum represents a giant fish preceded by a figure,

283. New Ireland. *Mask*. Musée de l'Homme, Paris.

with two others on its back and tail. The forms of birds and fish are painted in small brush strokes, admirably suggestive of scales and feathers. But it would seem that the artist seeks to achieve realism more in details than in the general effect.

Human beings are given somewhat thick-set bodies, treated in masses, with the details painted on the surface. Attitudes are not always as stereotyped as in the case of the upright pieces. There are two methods of rendering the face. One, relatively realistic, includes a curved nose, sometimes a beard, and an ornament passing through the nasal septum. The ears widely extended on the sides, have a hole pierced in the lower lobe. The body is often shown with the head enveloped in one of the regional masks.

The masks, as numerous and elaborate as the other carvings, fall into several categories, though all are alike in having the usual adjuncts of openwork decorations of various kinds and painted prolongations, on the sides and top at least.

In some masks the face is treated realistically, especially the nose and eyes, in which case they recall the technique of modelled faces found in New Britain. But it is extremely rare for the artist to fail to cover the face with a painted decoration contrasting delicate linear patterns and monochrome passages. A classic type of mask is fitted with a crest-like mop of hair, having on each side a large all-white volute—an allusion to the practice of shaving the sides of the skull and leaving only a single longitudinal band of hair in the centre. The thick-set face, on the other hand, is covered with a filigree of lines; it consists of three elements placed one above the other, with no transitional passages, and is treated in the manner of a caricature; with a low forehead, a short nose and a protruding, half-open mouth.

A third type is a miniature form of *totok*. Everything is there: the pig's snout with a stylized human face above it, and, covering them, a tracery of birds, snakes and fish.

Other masks consist simply of panels covered with painted decorations, sometimes incised as well. In these the nose is replaced by an openwork bird motif, and the mouth may be treated in the same way.

The appendages of all these masks are constructed on the same lines as the bas-reliefs, and carry the same imagery: birds, snakes and fish, and occasionally small human figures. Sometimes, too, as in the case of other carved pieces, a bird is fixed to the top of the mask head, with its beak coming down upon the face.

Finally, we find a type of mask in which wooden elements are partially or wholly eliminated and replaced by pieces of tapa stretched on a supple framework. They have affinities with the masks made wholly of cork, found on the islands of Nissan and Tanga off the coast of New Ireland. Those of Nissan are reinforced by the application of a vegetable paste like that employed for the overmodelling of skulls. Here, too, we find two themes: the semi-realistic portrayal of a face and a schematic grouping of circular elements according to a formula which recalls the technique of the Baining tribe of New Britain.

All these forms of art are found in the northern coastal fringe of New Ireland. The art of the rest of the island is less well known, except for the ancestor figures usually called *malanggan uli*. These are carvings of a kind peculiar to the mountainous region in the centre of the island. Differing in this respect from the *malanggan* so far studied, the *uli* must not be seen by women. The *uli* figure is hermaphrodite, with a phallus and prominent female breasts. The lower limbs

284. New Ireland. *Bas-relief.* Basle.

are short. The arms are either raised with the thumb pressing the head, or lowered with the hands placed on the hips or brought together in front of the body. In the latter case they are prolonged downwards, except when they are attached to the ridge adorned with painted triangles which links the chin to the belt. This reminds us of the procedure followed in the north of the island, all the more so since we sometimes find smaller figures perched on the shoulders of the principal one.

The bearded face has symmetrical proportions, the mouth is spanned by a large array of teeth, the nose triangular and the eyes emphasized by a circle of dark paint prolonged by a line running all around the chin. The head-dress bears a characteristic crest. The head itself is brightly coloured and the shoulders, breasts and genitalia are painted red, while the rest of the body is white, except for red spots placed laterally on the flanks, thighs and legs.

Certain masks, probably from the south of the island, in solid wood and without extensions, are akin both to the *uli* and to the carved heads of New Britain: they vary among themselves, the only common characteristic being a protuberant mouth extending the full width of the mask. From the same part of the island, as from the region of New Britain facing it, come figures carved in chalk having globular faces without much relief.

Some curious drums with solid multiple tongues have a surprising simplicity of form and decoration; the human theme is indicated quite summarily, by way of a crest and an eye drawn on the side.

Mention must also be made of the *kapkap,* breast ornaments consisting of a disc of turtle-shell cut in a dainty openwork pattern and fixed to a polished disc of plain white shell.

285. New Ireland, Lonan. *Totok sculpture*. Budapest.

286. New Ireland, Fatmilak. *Muligan bas-relief.* Basle.
287. New Ireland, Lesu. *Muligan bas-relief.* Basle.
288. New Ireland, Medina. *Muligan carving.* Basle.

289. New Ireland, North. *Wooden mask*. Budapest. — 290. New Ireland. *Wooden mask*. Basle.

291. New Ireland. *Wooden mask*. Basle.
292. Northern New Ireland. *Wooden mask*. Budapest.

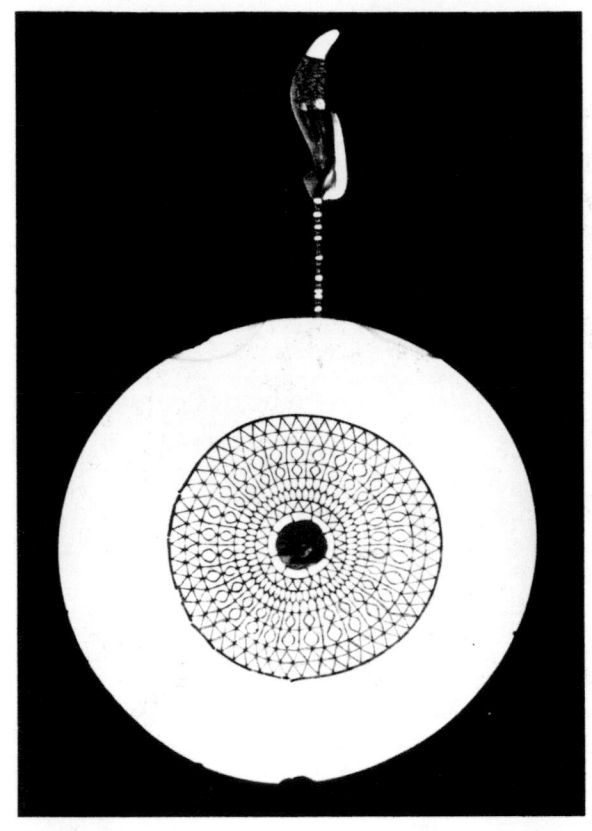

293. New Ireland. *Pendant*. Basle.

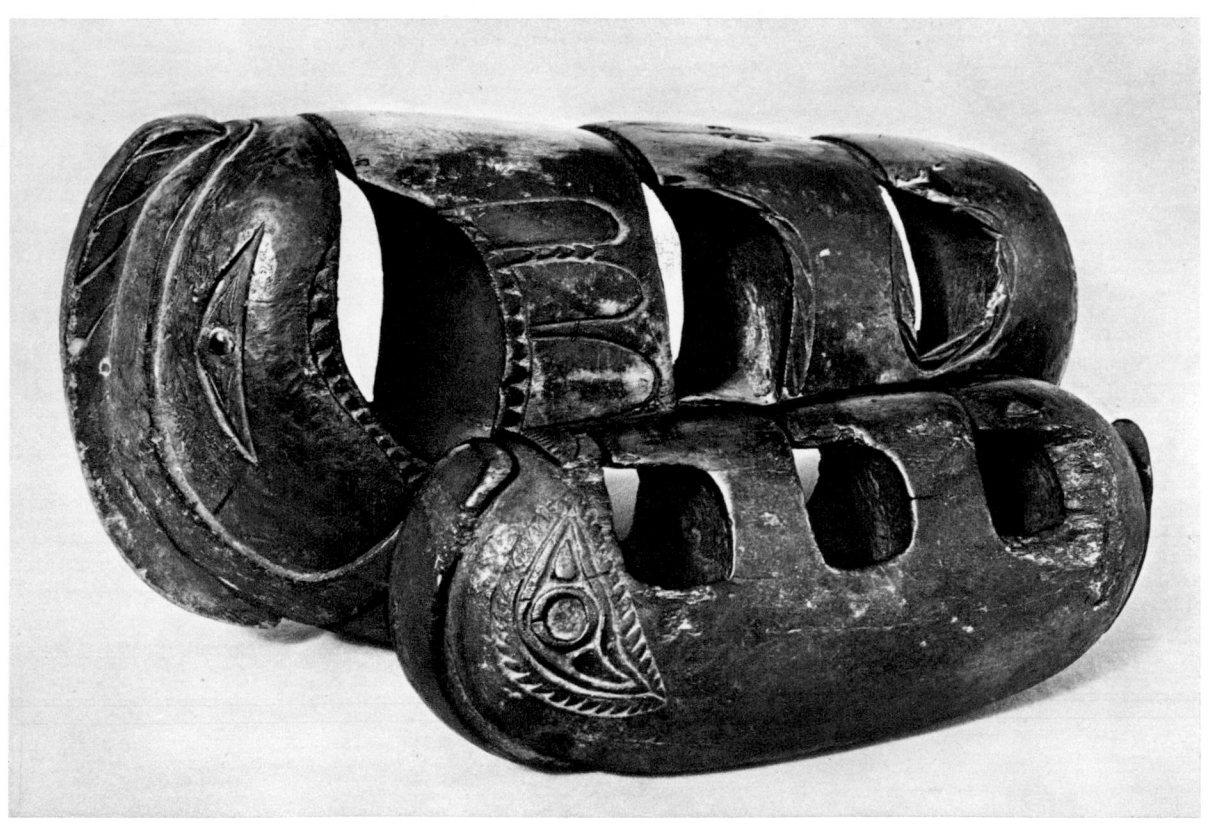

294. New Ireland. *Set of drums*. Basle. 295. New Ireland. *Full-length uli statue*. Basle. ▶

296. *Detail of* 295.
297. Northern New Ireland. *Tapa mask*. Budapest.

IV

NORTH-WEST NEW GUINEA
(Korovar Style)

The ancestor figures called *korovar* are probably the best known works from the western part of New Guinea. Each consists of a small figure standing or seated on a pedestal. The body is squat, the head disproportionately large and almost cuboid. In some of these figures the body is reduced to a geometric support on which was placed the skull of the dead man to whom the piece is dedicated. The practice was to make it during the lifetime of the man concerned so that, on his death, one of his two spirits (the one which has to remain on earth) could enter it and live there. We also find *korovar* figures in which the dead man's skull is wedged between two strips of wood and a carved face, stitched to the wooden side-pieces, has been placed in front of it.

The thick-set body tends to convey an impression of power. This is especially true of a specimen in the National Museum, Copenhagen, where a long-haired standing figure seems to be seizing or restraining another smaller figure, seated on the edge of the base. This is one of the finest pieces known, the movement of the body having all the rugged power of certain Polynesian figures.

Of particular interest are two distinctive elements of these pieces: the treatment of the face and the sort of openwork shield or escutcheon held by many of the figures. Usually, but not always, stylized, the face is remarkable for the prominence both of the nose, which forms a vertical extension of the brow, and of the thick, outspread nostrils which overshadow the cheekbones and deep-set eyes. The heavy ridge of the brow, prolonged on both sides, joins up with the ears. The mouth, however, is often a mere slit above an unaccentuated but markedly prognathous chin. In the more highly stylized examples, the nose, with its projecting nostrils, has almost exactly the shape of an anchor.

The escutcheon is something of a puzzle; we have ventured to give it this name owing to the presence of a fleur-de-lys carved at the top. The hieratic, semi-floral elements of the symmetrical arabesques composing the openwork design, as well as the style of the face, call to mind certain pieces from Indonesia, especially Borneo. A human figure in low relief is sometimes carved on the escutcheon, the hands fitting into and forming part of the stylized motifs. The question therefore arises whether these Oceanian 'escutcheons' may not have originated as a symbolic interpretation of the human figure. No answer is possible in the present state of our knowledge, since the evidence from transitional forms is so far insufficient.

The *korovar* style, and in particular, the motif of the escutcheon, is also found on some canoe prows, one of which is in the Peabody Museum, Cambridge, Mass. In this piece an appearance of extreme regularity is combined with a curious symmetrical displacement of the lateral elements; the superimposed panels, with openwork designs, rise along a slanting axis, producing an effect of aerial lightness. The same motif is repeated *ad infinitum:* either a single S-curve shown in various positions, or two such curves confronted. These prows adorned the canoes of the bold, adventurous seamen who, though obliged to pay a tribute of women and birds of paradise to the Sultan of Tidor, ventured on occasion to raid the coasts of the Moluccas in organised piratical bands.

On the coast itself of Geelvink Bay, the *korovar* disappear but similar figures occur, carved in the flat and with the characteristic head, on the pubic shields of the young girls and on sago-pounders.

Other canoe ornaments from the north coast of western New Guinea between Geelvink and Humboldt Bay are of a quite different type. On the prow the most frequent theme is the bird *mani*, either single or in groups, perched on a cross-piece whose terminals are grimacing human heads, to which fish are sometimes added. Sometimes, too, the body of the bird is placed above an openwork geometric design whose meaning is made clear by the addition of clearly defined feet. According to Mme M. Laroche, who has made a study of them, these figurations are intended to represent human beings: but one is also reminded of the 'frog motif' which occurs on the carved plates of nearby Lake Sentani. Other ornamental volutes, sometimes repeated again and again, seem undoubtedly to derive from the motif of a frigate-bird's beak.

Human faces, sometimes several together (but always single on the pieces known as *fafore*), figure on the sterns of canoes; they are carved with great attention to detail, and also characterized by extremely large nostrils splaying out at the base of the nose. Sometimes a diminutive seated figure almost reminds us of the Marquesan *tiki*. When shown squatting and reduced to the smallest possible size, the human body, it would seem, can only be portrayed in a limited number of ways. The fish motif recurs now and again on works of both types. All are painted in several colours. Certain pieces of pottery from the same region have designs painted in white, representing, for example, a lizard with star-shaped feet, recalling the Lake Sentani style.

From Gulf Maccluer at the western end of New Guinea, come objects ranging over a great variety of styles. Thus we find a mask with regular features executed in almost the western manner; only the painted motifs of the face recall the arabesques of New Guinea. Two carvings in the Leningrad Museum of Ethnography and Anthropology represent a short squat figure. Here the face is less angular than that of *korovar* figures, but resembles them nonetheless in the curved, anchor-shaped nose and the way the supra-orbital ridge is lengthened and widened so as to demarcate the puckered edges of the ears.

298. North-west New Guinea.
Korovar figure with a child. Copenhagen.

299. North-west New Guinea.
Korovar statuette. Leningrad.

New Guinea, Geelvink Bay.
e prow. Brussels.

301. New Guinea, Geelvink Bay. *Korovar statuette.* Frankfort.
302. New Guinea, Geelvink Bay. *Canoe prow.* Peabody Museum, Cambridge, Mass.

303. *Detail of the head of* 304.

304, 305, 306. North-west New Guinea, Merat Island. *Canoe ornaments.* Musée de l'Homme, Paris.

312

313

307. New Guinea. *Carved figure*. Leningrad. —
308. New Guinea, Maccluer Gulf. *Mask (?)*.
Budapest. — 309. New Guinea, Humboldt Bay.
Pottery. Nat. Hist. Mus., Chicago.

314

THE MASSIM AREA

This term is generally applied to the south-eastern tip of New Guinea and the three archipelagos that lie off it: d'Entrecasteaux, Louisiade and the Trobriands. It is a region where the social organization is more hierarchical and has disintegrated less than elsewhere in New Guinea. The practice of inter-island barter has been systematized as a result of local specialization and the same objects are in general use throughout the Massim area. Sculpture is a technique confined to specialist craftsmen whose products are much sought after. All this tends to produce æsthetic unity. Furthermore, Massim art is strictly ornamental, including neither ancestor figures nor masks in wood or in vegetable matter.

The decorated pieces are either objects of practical utility: nut-crackers, lime spatulas, paddles, shields, clubs, adzes, head-rests; or objects for display or ceremonial use, such as the canoe prows and the so-called dance shields, *kaydiba*, made in two parts joined by a thin piece of wood which also serves as a handle. The decoration is applied in the form of wide incised bands with openwork sections of varying sizes. The two halves match each other and the theme is once again the bird, given an almost purely abstract form: the body consists of a volute in which a plain central motif contrasts with a patterned edge of incised circles and the beginnings of interlocking spirals. Here and there, faint intimations of the human face or the bird's beak motif can be perceived. The projecting beak of the principal bird rests on a crosspiece whose decoration suggests a fish's or a snake's head. Lime is rubbed into the incised lines to make them stand out more clearly.

Canoe prows are made in two parts: one, flat and laid crosswise, supports a longitudinal piece pointing forward. The interior motifs have the form of completely flattened spirals; these look like elongated S's and are linked together. The whole structure of the decoration implies that the central part is a stylized human body, and this is repeated in miniature on the top. The lateral motifs are a series of birds' beaks. The longitudinal piece shows a development of the bird form, repeated again and again in white, or left unpainted in the natural colour of the wood.

Some carvings represent pigs or birds. A piece in Leningrad has a pig's snout, while its tail resembles a bird's beak. Other figures, male and female, are doll-like, sometimes dressed in fibre-cloth, and the treatment may be either realistic or stylized.

Lime spatulas are the most favoured medium for representing human figures. These are sometimes built up in S-curves, and their stylization brings to mind the *korovar*. The more realistic pieces (realistic so far as the face is concerned) recall the Admiralty Islands figures and also those of the Solomons in their renderings of the mouth and prognathic chin, the axis of the head being tilted forward and downward and no longer running vertically, as is customary in New Guinea.

Free fancy is given full play in these figurines and no spatula handle resembles another. The artists make much of contrasts between one part of the body represented realistically and the rest of it treated in an abstract manner, and the wide variety of human figures, sometimes composite and in all kinds of positions, is nothing short of prodigious. The technique employed, however, in rendering animals, birds, pigs, caymans, dogs is always the same. The decoration may become almost wholly abstract, but there is almost always some thematic connection

315

between the motifs, as witness the snake's head at the bottom and the bird's beak at the top of a spatula in Budapest Museum.

The betel mortars from the Trobriands have smooth sides decorated with an incised design: above (or below, when they are being used) is a stylized human face whose nose, with its pierced septum, is the only part in relief. A curved bar links the chin of the figure to the side of the mortar itself. On the back hollowed-out protuberances serve as handles.

Mention should also be made of the Trobriand shields, whose decoration is confined to painted designs, with no broad areas of colour, but with delicate linework which recalls pen drawings. Here the themes of the human face and the bird are treated with great simplicity. An effect of stippling is obtained by the repetition of a three-pronged motif (of unknown origin) in the form of a rake.

The axes from the Trobriand Islands, like most of the beautiful ones from New Caledonia, tend to be purely ceremonial objects, by virtue of the beauty of the stone and the fineness of the bird ornamentation.

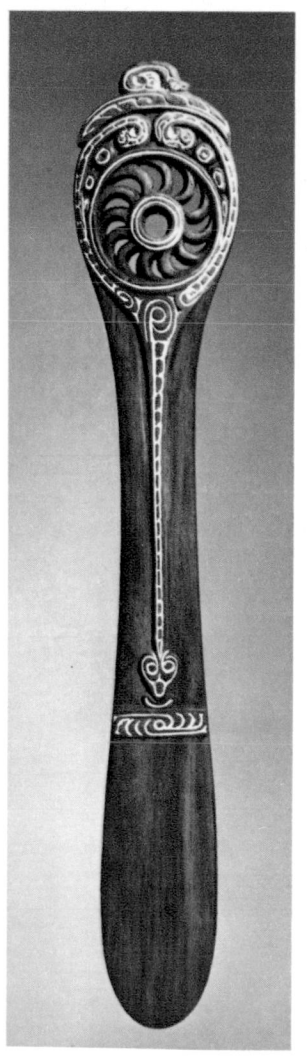

310. Trobriand Islands (?). *Canoe prow*. Musée de l'Homme, Paris.
311. Trobriand Islands. *Dance shield*. Leningrad.
312. D'Entrecasteaux Islands. *Lime spatula*. Leningrad.
313. Trobriand Islands. *Figure of a pig*. Budapest.

317

314. Trobriand Islands. *Lime spatula*. Budapest. — 315. Trobriand Islands. *Lime spatula*. Basle. — 316. Eastern New Guinea. *Lime spatula*. Honolulu. —317. Trobriand Islands. *Lime spatula (detail)*. Budapest. — 318. Trobriand Islands. *Stone axe-blade*. Museum of Primitive Art, New York. — 319. Eastern New Guinea. *Mortar for betel*. Leningrad.

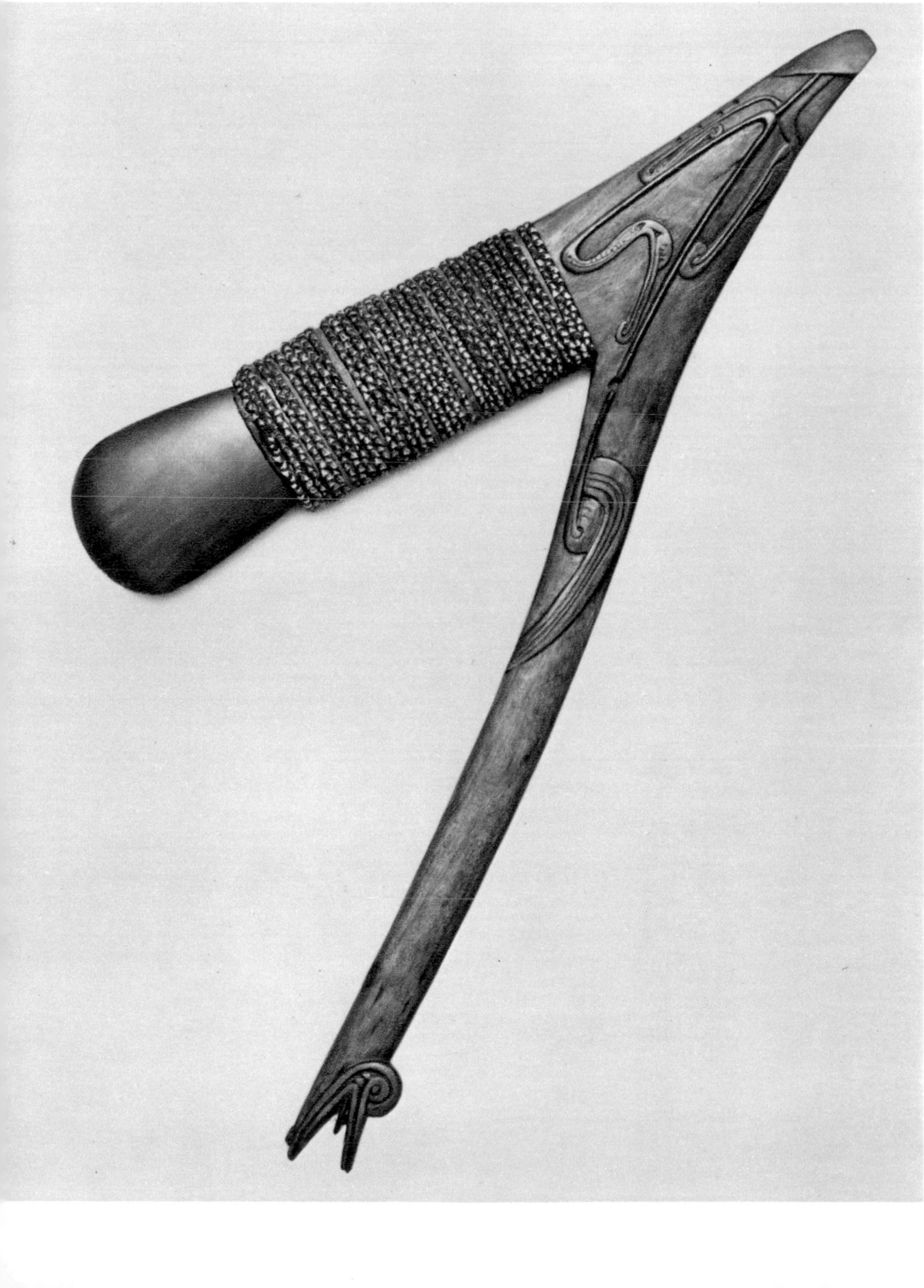

V

THE ADMIRALTY ISLANDS

Although they lie to the west of the Bismarck Islands, the style of the Admiralty Islands seems closer to that of the Solomons than to that of New Guinea. As with Massim art, the stylistic unity prevailing throughout this archipelago appears to be due to the existence of certain specialized groups of craftsmen supplying the entire demand for sculptures throughout the islands, in exchange for agricultural produce and articles of daily use.

The human body is the most frequent subject in these works. The head is portrayed not as a prolongation of the body but as overhanging it; the lower jaw, strongly emphasized, ends in a small, carefully executed mouth. Modelling of the lips takes the place of the usual array of teeth. The straight nose, with no very marked indication of nostrils, forms, with the lips, one of the few elements of the face to be carved in relief. The eye sockets are, in fact, but faintly indicated and the eyes themselves are no more than painted ovals. A zigzag motif in slight relief on a white ground may serve to emphasize the ridge of the brow and run diagonally across the cheeks. The general form of the face is elongated, the lower part being contracted and producing an impression of high cheek-bones. The ears are represented by a segment of a circle and extended by a gentle curve which represents the distended lower lobe.

Seen from the side, the body presents the characteristic outline of limbs in which the muscular masses are indicated by rounded protuberances in place of buttocks and calves. Broken lines emphasize the bony or smooth fleshy parts of the body and limbs. The genitals are indicated but the breasts are never protuberant. The posture is upright, the legs slightly bent. A distinctive feature in many figures is a high head-dress ending in a rounded topknot above a short cylinder.

Such figures were carved in all sizes, set up on house-posts and as free-standing life-size statues, or reduced to figurines a few inches high in the decoration of lime pestles and mortars, on the handles of daggers, on obsidian-bladed spears, the handles of spoons and spatulas, and the heads of war-charms. Together with representations of crocodiles and incised geometric motifs, they appear in more or less pronounced relief on canoe prows and on the raised wooden beds which are so characteristic of the archipelago.

Vegetable paste is used to smooth out the modelling and to stick together small, complex objects. The colours are simple: black, red and white; there is nothing here which compares with the greatly varied polychromy of some New Ireland pieces.

Other specific objects are the circular plates and bowls, both single and double, with four feet. Some of these are of great size and display an astonishing formal perfection. They are fitted with mortised handles in which a single spiral acts as a ground for openwork decoration. Sometimes these handles are given the form of a stylized human figure.

Other plates are carved out of a single block of wood in such a way that one handle represents the head and wings, the other the tail, of a frigate bird, of which the dish itself forms the body.

The underside of the plates may carry a decoration of bands in low relief, which, too, are incised with simple geometric motifs: parallel lines, and rectangles with their diagonals.

The disc-shaped pendants called *kapkap* have an openwork decoration in tortoise-shell which is sometimes less finely cut than in New Ireland.

To the south-west, Hermit Island specializes in the manufacture of spatulae with an expanded handle having an open-work carved motif in the form of a heart with double spirals on the top. The combination of this motif with an oval results in the schematized design of a tortoise.

320. Admiralty Islands. *Scoop fashioned from a coconut shell.* Budapest.

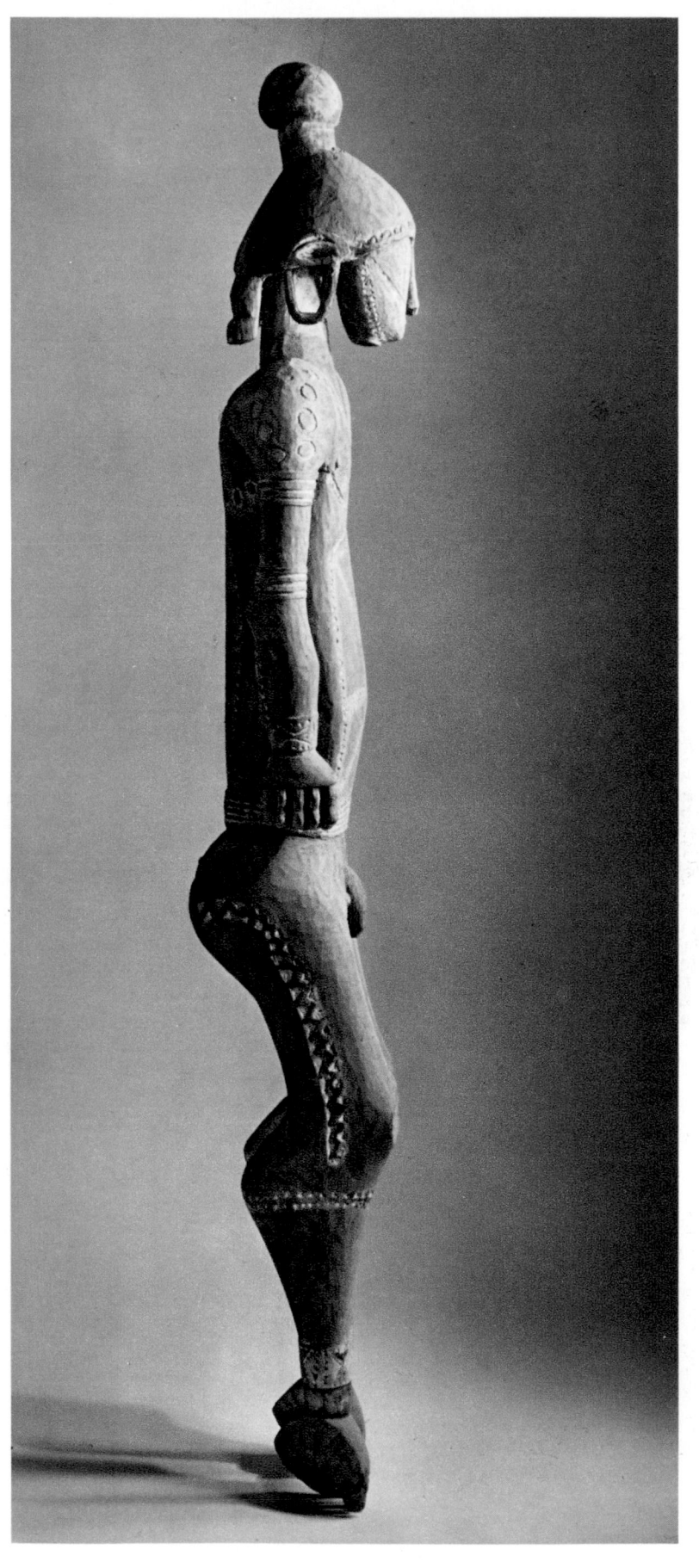

321. Admiralty Islands. *Full-length carving*
Bremen Museum.

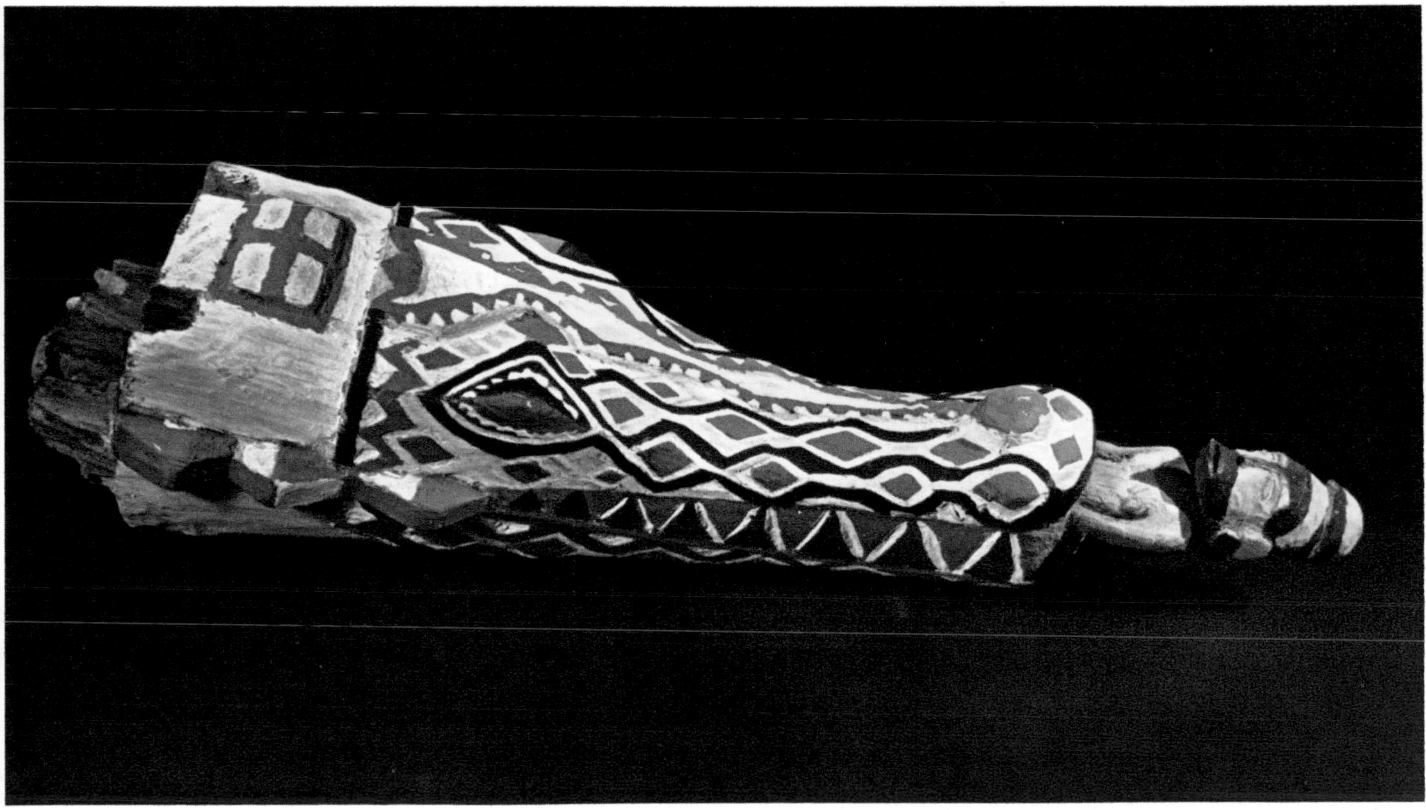

322. Admiralty Islands. *Spear point*. Budapest.   323. Admiralty Islands. *Canoe prow*. Budapest.

324. Hermite Islands. *Wooden spatula*. Leningrad.
325. Iru, Manus Island. *Commemorative plate*. Mus. of Primitive Art, New York.
326. Admiralty Islands. *Dish*. Korrigane Collection.

THE SOLOMON ISLANDS

The Isles of King Solomon—what visions of exotic splendour are conjured up by such a name! Discovered in 1567 by the Spanish navigator Alvaro Mendaña de Neira, they were among the first of the Pacific Islands to be visited by white men; after which they were neglected and not re-discovered for two centuries. Carvings from the Solomons are among the finest works of Oceanian art, but they now are hard to come by and poorly represented in museums. Presumably quite a number, inherited from voyagers of bygone days, exist in private hands, but remain unknown because their owners do not realize their value.

These pieces have scarcely been noticed by students or collectors, while many museum specimens remain unpublished. Perhaps they are considered, unconsciously, as examples of a minor art which offers nothing of the riches of the Sepik. It may also be that there are no masks, which are an essential element in our traditional view of primitive art.

Sobriety is the chief characteristic of Solomon Islands art. Stained and polished black, the sculptures are discreetly enhanced by narrow bands of shell inlay. The classic examples are the canoe prows from the central islands of the archipelago which represent a human head whose heavy, projecting chin rests on the thumbs of the clasped hands; the hands may also hold a second, smaller human head. Occasionally we find a complete figure in which the curves of the forehead, cheekbones, chin, eye-sockets, and the lobes of the ears are picked out with shell inlays.

From most of the islands of the archipelago come full-length carved figures which, were it not for the frequent use of black as the basic colour, would recall the sculptures of the Admiralty Islands with the rounded topknot of their head-dress above a prognathic face. Shell inlays are here replaced by white-filled incised lines. The posture is either crouching or erect. Several figures are sometimes grouped together and an attempt is made to depict a scene, as on a spear-stand illustrated by Codrington. The heavy ear-pendants and other body ornaments are carefully portrayed. This art has survived to the present day and some interesting attempts have been made to christianize it, as Father Patrick O'Reilly has shown.

On Gizo Island, among others, we find heads modelled over skulls and inlaid with mother-of-pearl, while the ears are adorned with huge, wheel-shaped ornaments.

Animal representations are of either fish or birds. In the south-eastern islands the shark in particular plays the part of a tutelary spirit of the sea. In the British Museum is a very fine sculpture representing a shark, inlaid with mother-of-pearl and remarkable for its purity of form and wealth of ornamentation. Other examples of animal carving are the great wooden bowls from the same region with the body carved to suggest the shape of a bird; one end tapers down to a flat protuberance adorned with pearl-shell, while the other stops short and carries the head of a frigate-bird whose beak is plunged into the curved body of a fish with the head facing forward. In other plates the tail of the bird is replaced by another fish set on the rim.

The same animals by themselves adorn the tops of net-floats. Dishes in the form of a pig, its body hollowed out, are also known. Here the carving is less stylized than that of the pigs from the Massim area, and here, too, we find bands of shell inlay.

The rarest and most beautiful objects, which are also, because of their size, the most difficult to reproduce, are the great single canoes, richly ornamented with shell inlays, which were used for head-hunting raids in the south-east of the Archipelago. The symbolism of the representations figuring on the canoes has been the subject of a detailed study by Ivens.

The portrayals of fish and birds seem elsewhere to be more crude, especially in the drawings made during the past century by informants working for anthropologists (who were usually missionaries). Codrington published the first examples showing human-bodied sea-gods with a whole fish coiled round their necks while more fish are joined to other parts of the body and replace the figure's feet.

The frigate-bird appears, equally elegantly rendered, on several types of shell work: on ornaments delicately cut from mother-of-pearl, with a series of symmetrical heads shown in profile, and again in the form of tortoise-shell motifs, with the figure of the bird recurring again and again. These pieces of tortoise-shell are fitted to a shell disc worn on the breast, like the *kapkap* of New Ireland.

On Choiseul the human figure appears in stylized forms on the open-work plaques carved in tridacna shell; a frieze of bending figures on their knees and holding hands is the basic element of the decoration.

Very beautiful shields of an elongated oval shape, which narrows slightly at the top, are coated with a red and black paste which holds in place bands of square incrustations in parallel lines set round a figure extending over the whole length of the shield. The dance shields from south-eastern Bougainville (Terei), made of two half-circles joined at the top, are similar in shape to those of the Trobriands; the incised decoration consists of cross and wheel motifs within circles, of scalloped designs and concentric squares in tiers.

In the extreme north-west of the archipelago the inhabitants of Buka decorate canoe paddles with designs whose grooved outlines are filled with lime. These represent a seated figure with thin spindly limbs drawn up close to the body; the thighs and buttocks, though prominent, are dwarfed by the head which occupies the whole width of the paddle. An enormous head-dress corresponding to the rounded head-dress worn in certain rituals, large round eyes, a triangular nose and a mouth with a jagged row of teeth, complete the figure. Its striking effect is largely due to the contrast between the ground and the white areas of the face, and the red and black pattern of the body.

The war clubs are actually ceremonial objects rather than weapons, whether covered or not with finely structured incised designs; some of them are also inlaid in places with mother-of-pearl. The elegance of their form and decoration gives them a somewhat Polynesian appearance. The shape of the curved clubs may well be intended to recall the theme, so frequent in this region, of a fish leaping from the water. Some have handles carved with seated human figures, the head resembling that of a fish whose tail joins up with a protuberance prolonging the figure's thighs at the back. Another specimen from the north-west of the archipelago and now in the British Museum shows in relief, on a miniature scale, the head of the figure painted on the paddles from Buka.

326

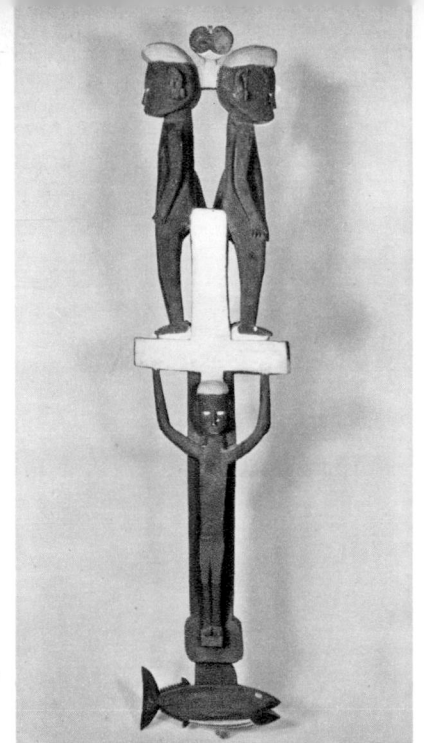

329. Solomon Islands, San Cristobal. *Crucifixion.*
Mission des Iles, Paris.

330. Solomon Islands, Rubiana. *Canoe prow.* Budapest.

331. Solomon Islands. *Full-length statue.* Budapest.

332. Solomon Islands, New Georgia.
Canoe prow. Basle.

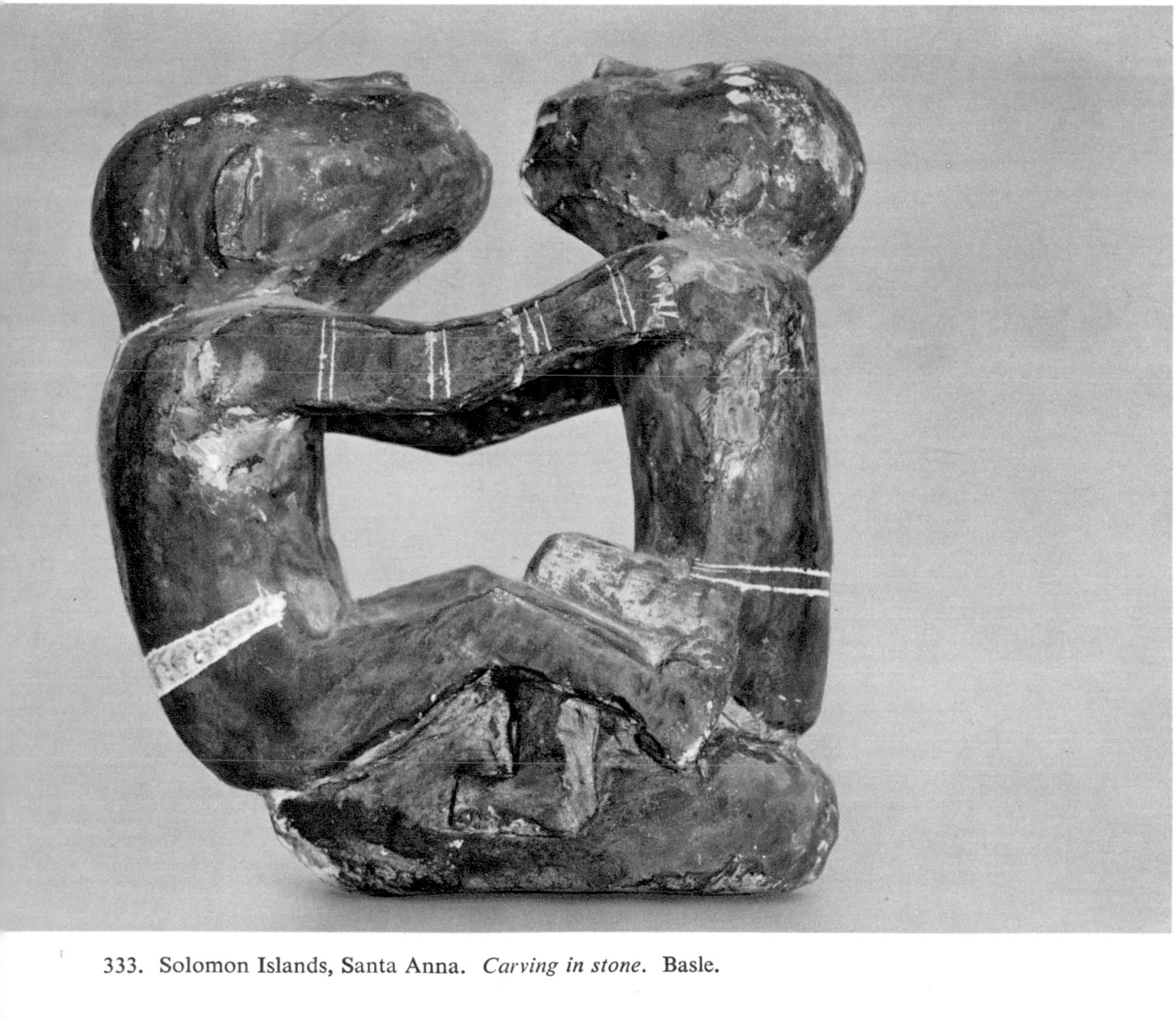

333. Solomon Islands, Santa Anna. *Carving in stone*. Basle.

334. Solomon Islands, San Cristobal. *Wooden dish*. Basle.

335. Solomon Islands, San Cristobal. *Wooden dish*. Basle.
336. Solomon Islands. *Club*. British Museum.

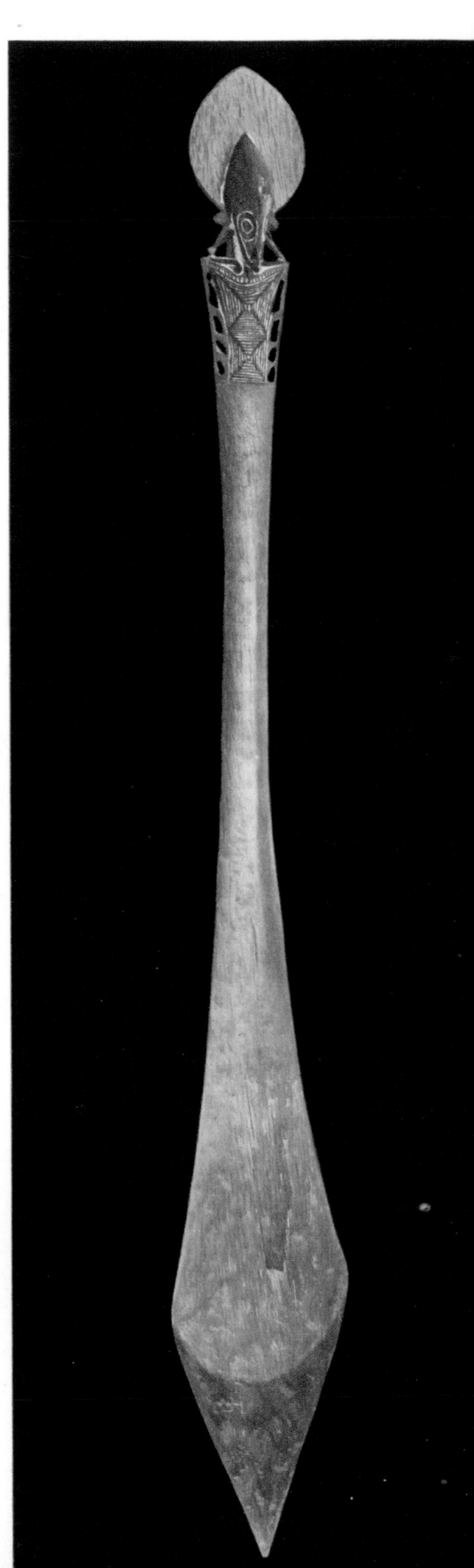

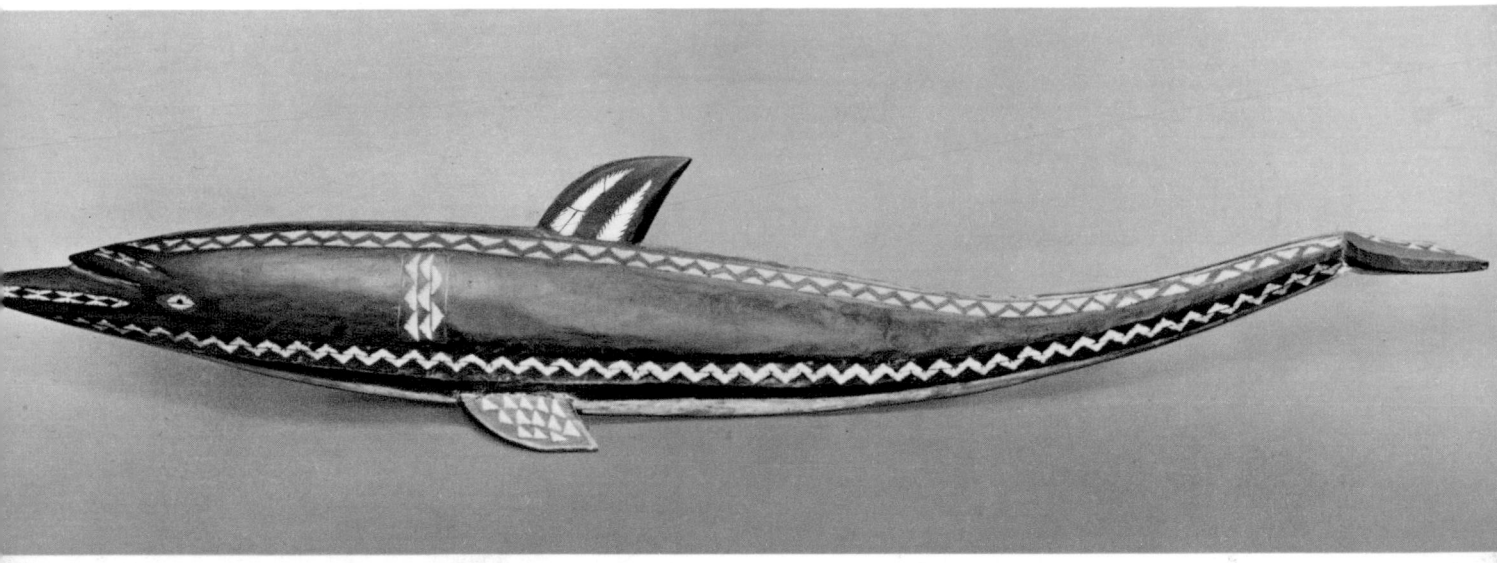

337. Solomon Islands, Ulawa. *Carving of a shark*. British Museum.
338. Solomon Islands, Ulawa. *The god Ngorieru*.

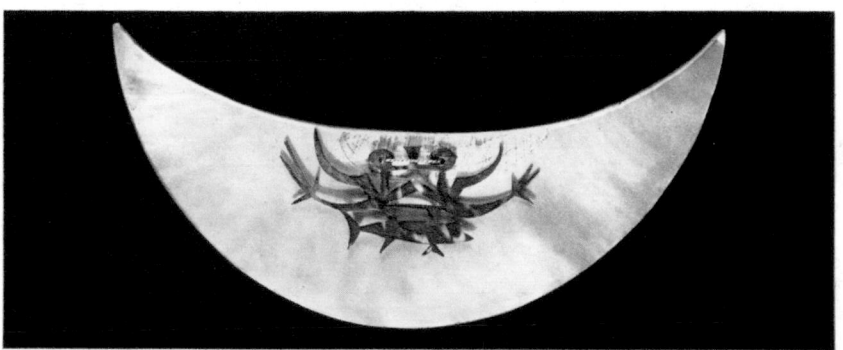

339. Solomon Islands, San Cristobal. *Pendant*. Basle.   340. Solomon Islands, Choiseul. *Openwork plaque of tridachna shell*. Ba

341. Solomon Islands. *Shield.* Mus. of Primitive Art, New York.

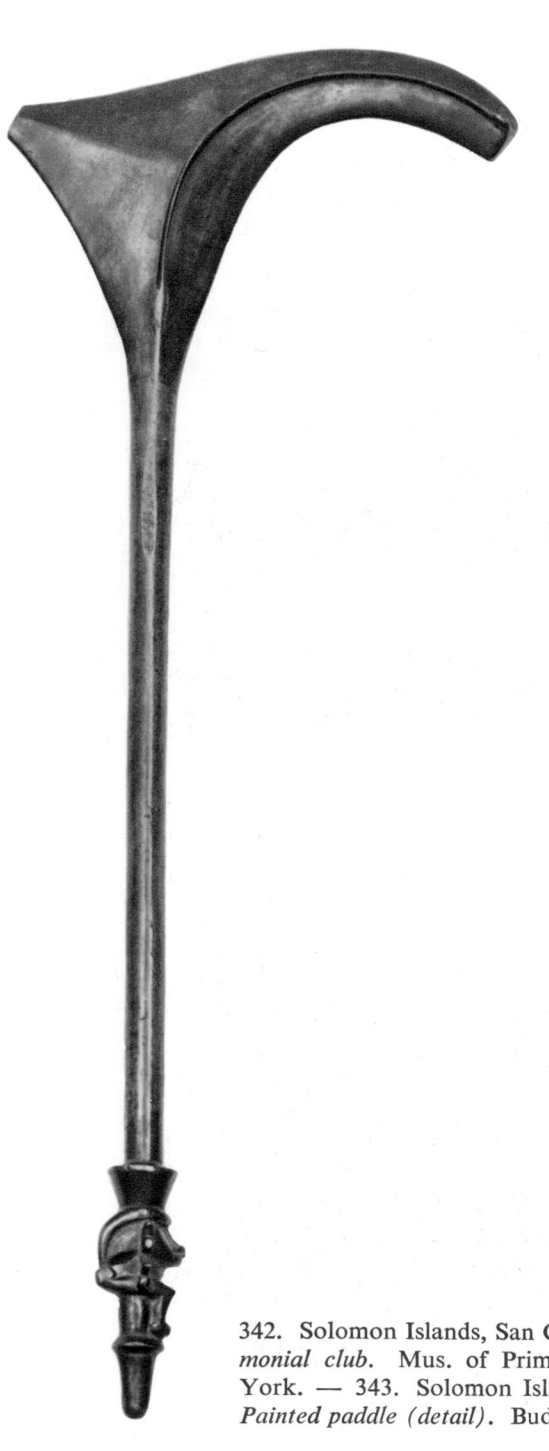

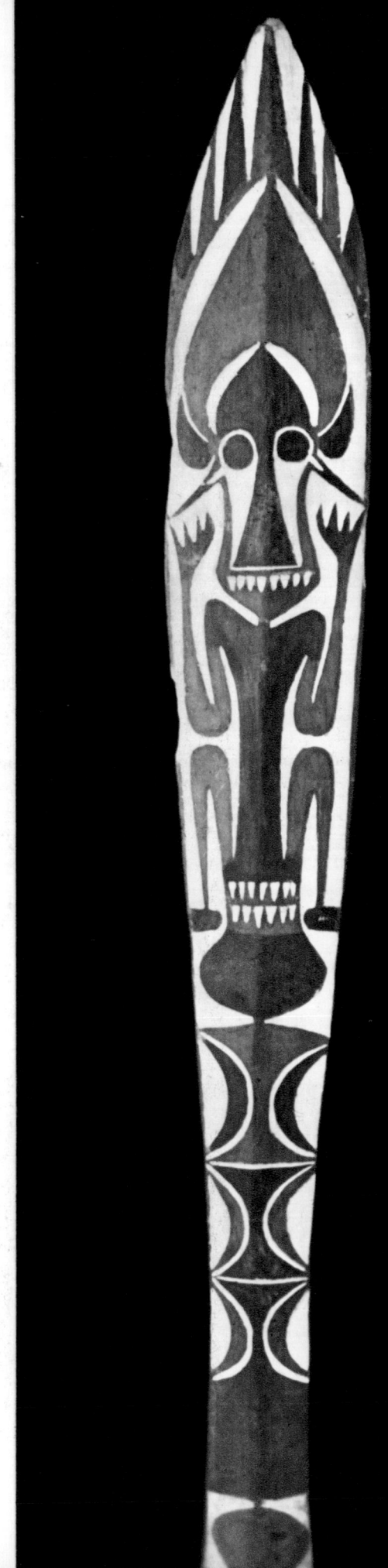

342. Solomon Islands, San Cristobal. *Ceremonial club*. Mus. of Primitive Art, New York. — 343. Solomon Islands, Buka (?). *Painted paddle (detail)*. Budapest.

344. Solomon Islands, Bougainville. *Dance shield*. Budapest.

FIJI' CENTRAL AND WESTERN POLYNESIA

While in New Guinea there are marked changes of style from one part of the island to another, central Oceania, though including many widely scattered islands, may perhaps be treated as a single stylistic zone.

Fiji to the west, and the Cook and Austral Islands to the east represent the two poles of an area which, generally speaking, forms a unified whole round a central point—Samoa, an island which, despite its size, is remarkably poor in works of plastic art. In fact, except for Easter Island which remains a case apart, Polynesian art shows very few variations throughout the area considered as a whole. There are no fundamental differences between Hawaii, the Marquesas, the Cook Islands and New Zealand. However, at the northern and southern ends of this area, forms and ornamentations manifest variations which may be explained by their remoteness from the centre. It is essentially their complexity that obliges us to study Marquesan and New Zealand art under separate heads.

It should be noted that we are dealing with complex, aristocratic societies with rigid hierarchies. Where forms of social and religious organisations were most subtle and sophisticated —as in Tonga, Samoa and Tahiti—we find that plastic art is almost non-existent. It would be tempting to infer a general rule from this correlation, attested in three areas, were it not that Hawaii with its caste society has produced wonderful sculpture.

Polynesian art is an art of seafarers who pay particular attention to the lines and technical perfection of their vessels: single and double canoes. Its two distinctive trends are revealed in the simplicity of forms which tend to become functional and in the constant urge to cover surfaces with decorative designs in which colour plays only a minor part.

The use of wood and, to some extent, of stone, is predominant. Having learnt how to join lengths of tapa together to make pieces which were sometimes of great length, the Polynesian employed it primarily as a textile and seldom tried to stretch it on a framework in imitation of sculpture in the round.

An archipelago, or even a particular island, is usually characterised by the design of its tapa-cloth; the motifs employed provide an accurate indication of origin. Broad lines on a printed ground are typical of Tonga and Wallis, though the work of the two islands can easily be distinguished from each other. Fiji has painted motifs in which a star figures frequently. Characteristic of Futuna are fine lines as if drawn with a pen.

Pottery used to be produced (as archaeologists have now shown) in the Marquesas, Samoa and Tonga. It was still to be found in Fiji when the Europeans arrived. There were certainly cooking pots, both tall and squat, whose roundness was a tribute to the potters' skill. The glazed vessels for carrying water are notable for their wide variety of forms including gourds, tortoises, single and double canoes, whale tooth, coconuts joined together and held in a string net, and finger bowls. The geometric decoration is in incised relief.

While dealing with vessels we should note the wooden vases, generally cup-shaped, and often with a foot, intended for the preparation of coconut milk (for the priests) or of kava. Both are obtained by means of grating and soaking, the liquid being extracted by hand pressure (coconut milk) or by squeezing in a fibre packet (kava). The reason for the foot, unless the

336

bowl is so heavy as to run no risk of tipping over, is that the hand of the servant who keeps it steady ought to be lower than that of the officiating priest or dignitary.

The shape of Fijian oil cups, often very shallow, recalls in some degree the plates of the Solomons. They, too, are decorated with tortoises, or with birds (sometimes in a highly abstract manner assuming the form of an arrowhead), or with a figure with arms widespread (a posture imposed by the shape of the vessel), the head alone being in relief. The feet are bent or straight and joined underneath to an outer ring or (seemingly a result of twisting), join the solid base to the upper bowl by a four-fold spiral. In the Cook and Austral Islands the bowls often resemble in general shape a canoe hull.

The kava bowls have the same form throughout the region. They are circular, and stand on four (Tonga) eight (Fiji) or even sixteen (Samoa) short vertical legs. The deep hollow makes them well suited for preparing large quantities of liquid.

The human body, needless to say, appears in other forms than as the design for a bowl. From Fiji and Tonga come statuettes in wood or whale ivory, divine images which are usually wrapped in bark-cloth and displayed only at ceremonies. Many of the statuettes are of women. The head is round; except for well marked ears, the features are only roughly indicated and the figure ends in short and stubby legs. When seen from the side, the bust and the bulging curve of the belly stand out emphatically, and there is a certain exaggeration of the muscles of the buttocks and calves. Although the shoulders are broad, the arms tend to become tapering vertical appendages. These figures represent household deities.

The human figure is not found in Samoan art: it recurs, however, further east but in a stylized form, of which there are two types: isolated figures and friezes dominated by a face.

The statuettes of the Cook Islands, often fishing gods, were placed on the prows of fishermen's canoes. Only the ears of the enormous head are in relief; opposed segments of circles mark out the great eyes, and the design of the mouth covers the chin. The schematized arms join on a prominent bulbous belly, and a swollen phallus points vertically from the navel rendered in relief. The hunched-up haunches and legs are compacted together and spread out, leaving the genitals exposed.

Certain larger scale examples of these figures have a number of smaller schematised figures like gnomes carved in relief on the chest and other figures on the arms, in low relief, with their limbs spread out: they recall those which occur in incised ornamentation.

This theme reaches its peak in Rurutu in the Austral Islands with the celebrated statue of the demiurge, Tangaroa, portrayed at the moment when he is creating gods and men who are shown as figures in relief in various positions on his body, his limbs and his round flat face. They are employed either to delineate the divinity's features, or as separate figures lodged in his hollow back. In the Leeward Islands the human figure, when it occurs, is crudely executed save for the stylised examples on the handles of fly-whisks from Huahine. Here we find two crouching figures joined back to back in a single body having the shape of a truncated cone, with angular arms crossed in front of the chest and two heads fused into a crescent whose tips form the two chins. The face, merely hinted at, is crowned by two protuberances which may be eyes.

Images of the gods are often no less schematized. Certain regional deities of the Cook

Islands are shown with a flattened head and noseless face treated as in the figurines. Above this, arms ending in a curve and a fretted edge seem to lift an openwork frieze portraying figures superimposed along an axis perpendicular to that of the principal face. These small double-fronted figures, joined back to back or side to side, appear to be horned because the large ears stand erect on either side of the skull, at least in the case of those seen from the front. This is so for every other figure, as the alternate ones have the face and body in profile.

The uncarved piece of wood beneath this frieze of small figures was smoothly rounded and covered with a roll of tapa-cloth. The culmination of this tendency to schematize the body and, above all, the face, is to be found in the pieces carved with highly elaborate openwork designs in which the same motifs are represented on superimposed circular surfaces; these angular protuberances represent human figures, but so highly stylized as to be scarcely recognizable. Finally, in Tahiti, sculpture in the round was not favoured. The god of war, Oro, was represented by interlaced cords of coconut fibre on which the limbs and facial features were shown in relief.

Incised ornamentation prevails throughout the region. The Fijians and Tongans use it to cover the surfaces of flat, heavy clubs whose shapes are to some extent peculiar to each archipelago. In eastern Fiji (Lau), Tongan clubs of local manufacture are to be found. The incised motifs, which are sometimes enhanced with pearl shell inlays and wispy human figures in low relief, cover the whole or the greater part of the weapon with asymmetrical panels consisting of parallel lines, hatching in different directions, and chevron patterns; fillets or a series of transverse fillets may separate the panels. The curved Fijian clubs, which widen and flatten towards the top are sometimes enhanced with a projecting lip or a horn. Sometimes we find on them a motif which stands out from a checkerwork ground and gives a vague impression of a symbolically interpreted human form.

In Samoa the carved geometric designs on the clubs are solid and devoid of incised decoration.

In the Cook and Austral Islands, on the other hand, we find a riot of incised and cut-work motifs. This is especially true of the beautiful paddles from the Australs and the handles of ritual adzes from the Cook Islands. The adzes with quadrangular or octagonal handles, whether massive or relatively slender, partly solid and partly in open-work, are carved with a geometric ornamentation in panels much like that of Tongan clubs. The emphasis on certain motifs, ✳ and XX, suggests a more definite significance. We have to go to the Australs to see how the human figure is transformed into engraved symbols which are difficult to interpret without reference to a whole series of transitional forms.

In a classic study, H. Stolpe has described in detail how an apparently geometric symbolism developed out of human figures deriving from the friezes of gods, one of which, from the Cook Islands, has been described above. These schematic figures continued to appear on the handles of paddles and ladles in the Austral Islands. On the flat handles the incised human figure remains clear and unmistakable, by virtue of the design of the head, the arms raised to support a segment of a circle, the breasts thrust to the side and the outspread lower limbs in which the thighs curve in the opposite direction to the arms. On the round handles, above the more schematic incised design of the body and limbs, we see an overhanging head,

338

cut out in the wood, with a flat face dominated by two lozenges in relief. The wide part of the paddle is wholly covered with an incised design of flawless regularity, in which the motifs forming the figures in the handle recur both in isolation and as friezes: confronted chevrons, crescents and lozenges charged with stars and suns.

The lower part of the bodies of vertical drums from the Australs is not only incised but perforated, with geometric panels above circular friezes of figures or human faces enclosed in a large semicircle.

Each end of the horizontal drums from the Cook Islands is encircled by an incised band beyond which extends a row of carved heads running around the whole circumference of the drum.

The head-rests of this region are all of much the same type with two variants the 'pillow' being either flat or cylindrical. Their purity of form makes them objects of considerable beauty, especially when made of contrasting materials: for example when the feet are in dark wood and the top is in ivory.

345. Fiji Islands. *Water pot*. Musée de l'Homme, Paris.

346. Fiji Islands. *Ritual oil cup.* Mus. of Primitive Art, New York.

348. Fiji Islands. *Oil cup*. Budapest.

349. Austral Islands, Raivavae. *Incised cup*. Mus. of Primitive Art, New York.

347. Fiji Islands. *Water pot*. Musée de l'Homme, Paris.

350. Tonga. *Female statue in whale-bone*. Mus. of Primitive Art, New York.
351. Cook Islands. *Male figure*. British Museum.

352, 353. Cook Islands, Rarotonga. *The god Te Rongo and his three sons*. British Museum.
354. Austral Islands, Rurutu. *The god Tanaroa creating gods and men*. British Museum.

355. Austral Islands, Raivavae. *Female divinity*. New Zealand.
356. Cook Islands, Mangaia. *Ceremonial spoon (detail)*. Budapest.

357. *Detail of* 356.　358. Leeward Islands, Huahine. *Handle of fly-whisk*. Mus. of Modern Art, New York.

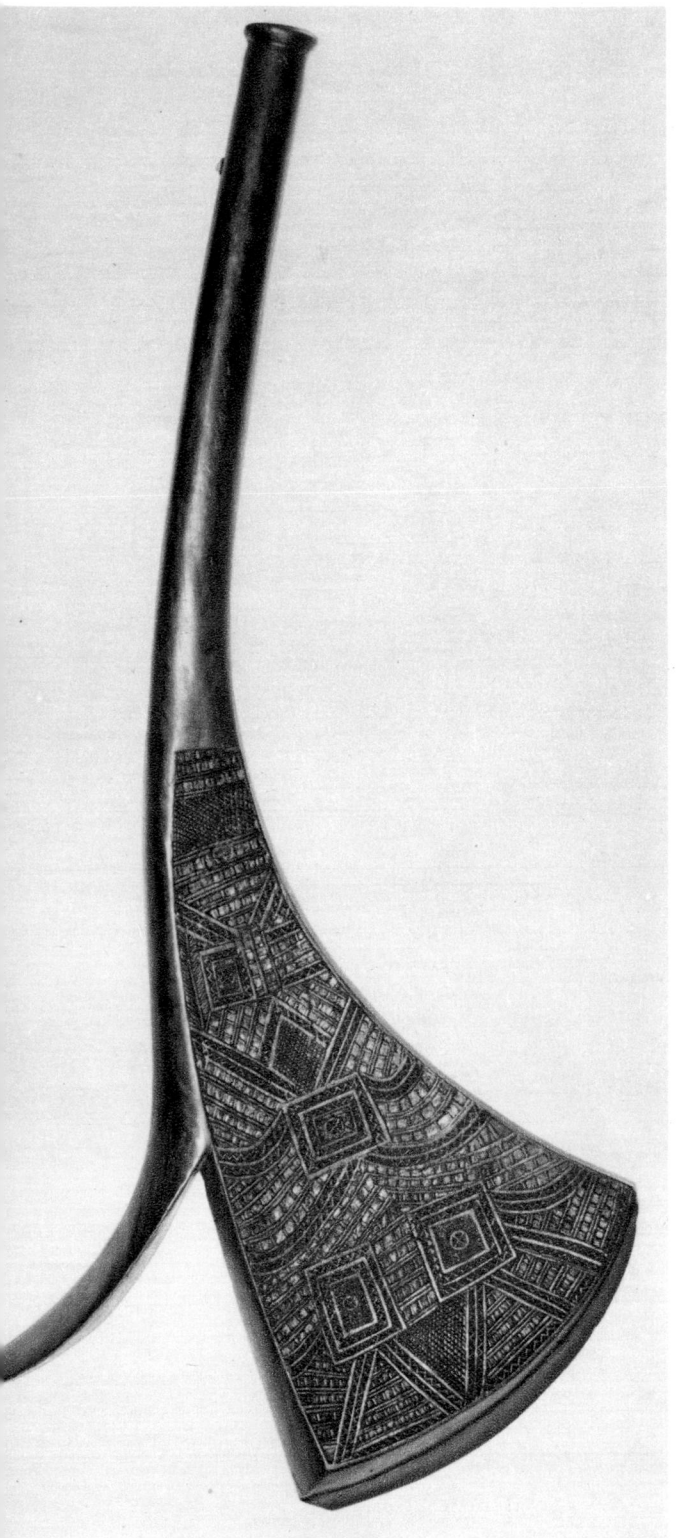

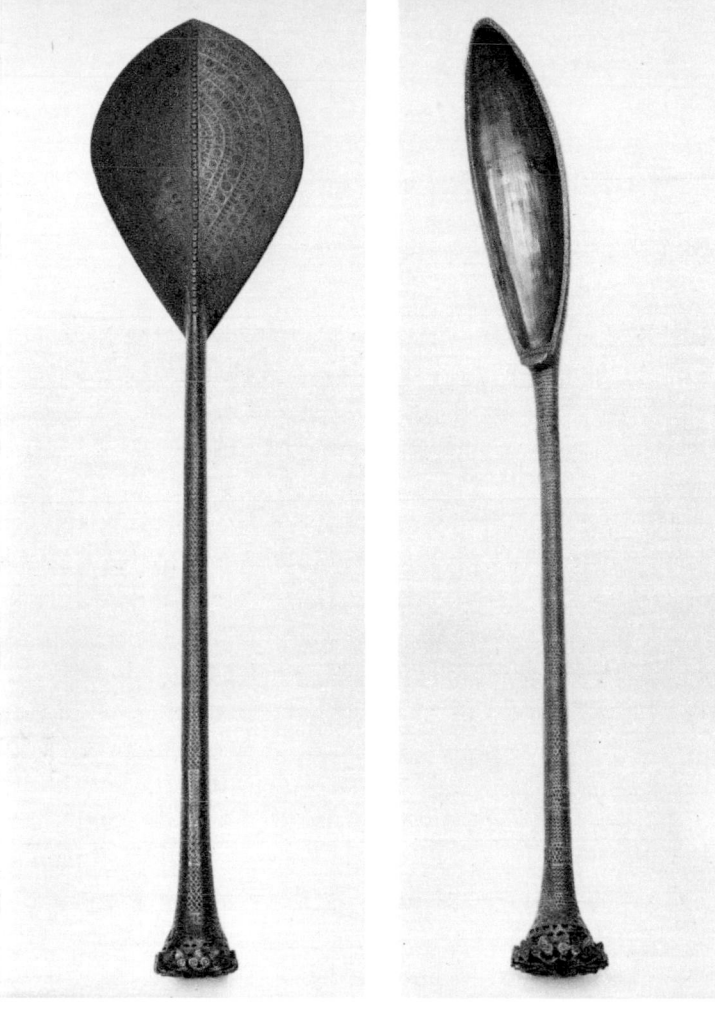
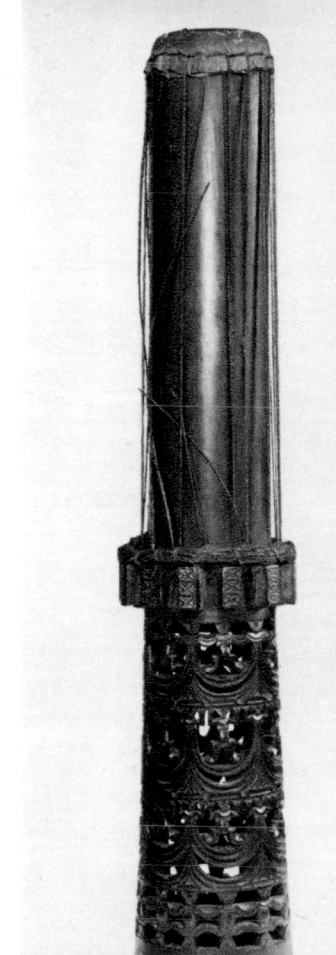

359. Cook Islands, Mangaia. *Ritual adze*. Leningrad. — 360. Fiji Islands. *Club*. Mus. of Primitive Art, New York. — 361. Austral Islands. *Ceremonial paddle*. Mus. of Primitive Art, New York. — 362. Austral Islands. *Ceremonial scoop*. Mus. of Primitive Art, New York. — 363. Austral Islands. *Upright drum*. Mus. of Primitive Art, New York. — 364. Tonga. *Head-rest*. Mus. of Primitive Art, New York.

OUTLYING ISLANDS

Four archipelagos and islands constitute this region: New Zealand, the Marquesas, Easter Island and Hawaii. The art of the first two is clearly related to that of the Cook and Austral Islands.

Maori Art.

There is no reason to challenge the historicity of the successive migrations which brought the Polynesians from the Cook, Austral and Society (Tahiti) Islands to New Zealand. In a new environment, with a colder climate, the Maoris developed a social structure and an art of a distinctive form.

Maori art is still very much alive today and has preserved its functional value in local Polynesian society. The number of well-attested works, of which museums, even in New Zealand itself, house only a small fraction, make it one of the richest of Oceanian arts. Thousands of carved objects still decorate the Maori *pa*, villages, or are privately owned, both by *maori* and by *pakeha*, white men, or by those who are proud to be of mixed descent. The museums of America are richer in specimens than those of Europe because Boston, Salem and Philadelphia possess collections of sculptures brought back by the crews of whalers which sailed from these ports.

Technical virtuosity is one of the characteristics of Maori art, which seems highly stereotyped precisely because of this very skill. Of first importance are the elaborate wood carvings used to decorate the dwelling-house, though similar motifs to those in the carvings are found on the underside of some of the wooden beams. Three categories of monumental sculpture are to be distinguished: full-length figures carved in the round; openwork friezes placed above or between the solid pieces; and the carved prow and stern pieces of the great canoes. In addition to human figures we find lizards, less frequently fish and sometimes the *Marakihau*, a marine divinity with a human head and arms, and a long, tubular forked tongue, who lured canoes and their crews to the bottom of the sea.

Full-length figures with a truly free-standing body are relatively rare: as a rule the body, treated in low relief forms the main theme of a rectangular panel. Usually it is schematized, with the hands outspread and flattened against the belly. In the most realistic works the face and thighs have an incised decoration which represents the usual tattooing.

In the bas-relief figures, carving in the round gradually gave way to a network of motifs deeply incised on the surface of the body: on the shoulders and hips, a double spiral whose direction differs according to the side; on the rest of the body, series of curves and hatched bands edged with thin, smooth lines.

From this portrayal of the human figure seen full face, we pass to a no less schematized figure which is slewed to show the head turned to one side. It is only a step from this to the representation, as in the Cook Islands, of a face in profile in which the grimacing mouth resembles a beak. Here we have a point on which the experts disagree. Is the so-called *manaia* motif, in which the face in profile seems to have a beak, a representation of a bird-man or not? No sculptor's testimony is available to support either view. The thesis put forward by Gilbert

Archey, Director of the Auckland War Memorial Museum, that the *manaia* motif derives from the representation of the human face seen in front view seems to us to be justified. A comparative series of motifs illustrates clearly the transitional forms and clearly shows how certain double spirals derive ultimately from the *manaia* motif.

It is interesting to note the existence of a series of male figures with tattooing on the face and buttocks, in which the body is treated in the manner of the Tonga and Cook Islands figures, and with the head covered with a wig of real hair, as in certain statues from Hawaii. It seems, furthermore, that these pieces, which are both ancient and rare, are the only ones which serve as cult objects in the true sense of the term. All the other carvings are commemorative or simply ornamental.

The openwork friezes, embodying the *manaia* theme and its derivatives, consist of faces seen from the front and arranged around the double spiral motif whose volutes are linked by short, striped bands. Some scenes with a number of figures, both full face and in profile, are difficult to interpret. Analysis allows us to distinguish local stylistic variants of which Archey has made a definitive study. The tongue which often projects from the mouth becomes an ornamental theme in itself and tends to take a spiral form.

The figureheads and stern-pieces of canoes with their intricately carved openwork are the finest pieces of Maori art, perhaps because they are not subject to the rectangular format which is imposed on works intended to figure in a house or on a monumental door.

The stern-piece is extended upwards by a wide openwork frieze whose vertical axis is slightly curved. At the foot of the curve is a crouching or recumbent figure which may be either stylized or realistic. His back rests against one of the two solid incised bars, set parallel, which support the openwork frieze of double spirals linked by *manaia* motifs. The prow consists of a wide frieze of only two spirals resting on a squatting, highly stylized human figure whose arched body leans forward with the arms swept backwards in the classic posture of a figurehead.

Many other objects are given similar decorations, either incised or carved in low relief, sometimes with openwork on the projecting parts. The boxes for preserving feather ornaments are a typical example. Mention should also be made of the chieftains' adzes, the wooden ceremonial clubs, the handles and bodies of fighting sticks, the wooden mouthpieces of conches, flutes, wooden horns, and food-funnels,—to introduce food into the mouth of a person in a state of taboo, *tapu,*—and the handles of shark-tooth knives, of ladles, etc.

The human figure, with the head, body, and limbs shown in grotesque distortion, also occurs in the *heitiki*, the jade pendant worn by women of high rank. It is also found on the blades of flat clubs made of wood, ivory or jade.

366. New Zealand. *Fragment of a door-post*. Philadelphia.
365. New Zealand. *Full-length figure*. Mus. of Primitive Art, New York.

367. New Zealand. *Bas-relief*. Washington.
368. New Zealand. *Bas-relief*. Leningrad.

369. New Zealand. *Derivations of the face theme and the manaia motif.*

370. New Zealand. *Manaia frieze.* Hamburg Museum.   371. New Zealand. *Realistic statue.* Glasgow. ▶

360

372. New Zealand. *Prow and stern of a war-canoe.* Honolulu.
373. New Zealand. *Box for plumes (rear view).* Mus. of Primitive Art, New York.
374. New Zealand. *Chief's adze with jade blade.* Mus. of Primitive Art, New York.

375. New Zealand, Taranaki. *Whale-bone club*. Honolulu.

376. New Zealand. *Nephrite pendant*. Pierre Vérité Collection. 363

Marquesan art achieves a high degree of technical perfection. It is the work of a class of skilled craftsmen who, while bound to follow traditional models, found personal satisfaction in the fineness of their line, their speed of execution and local specialization. The stone adzes come from the Island of Ei Ao, the pounders for taro porridge *poi* from Ua Huka, the tortoise-shell diadems from Hiva Oa, the ornaments in porpoise tooth from Ua Pu, the feather head-dresses from Nuku Hiva, and wooden carvings from Fahi Hiva.

True sculpture in the round is almost non-existent since the features of statues in stone are brought out by rubbing, a technique which precludes the possibility of marked relief. Similarly, in wooden figures, the form and features are no more than indicated in a cylindrical piece of timber so that the limbs are confined to hieratic poses. In fact, as Mrs. Willowdean C. Handy has noted, Marquesan art is essentially concerned with drawing. In the best examples the limbs carved free from the trunk recall, though more schematically treated, the classical Polynesian figure with the hands coming to rest on the curved belly, salient buttocks and legs slightly flexed. As in New Zealand art, the lizard also appears, as well as the fish or, once again, bird forms.

The Marquesan artist seldom resists the temptation to cover every open surface with incised designs. We may cite as evidence hemispherical bowls, tortoise-shell plaques for diadems, heads of war-clubs and ceremonial paddles. And this was even true of the human body which, in the course of a lifetime, was slowly covered with intricately designed tattooing.

Almost always, in Marquesan art, the human figure serves a purely decorative purpose. Among the rare exceptions are the small mythological scenes with figures, but we possess as yet no means of interpreting them.

Tattooing was a common practice and consisted of intricate ornamental designs in which parts of the body were combined with stylized objects of everyday use and a few animals and plants. More uniform as regards the themes employed, incised decoration was built up around single, double, and even multiple motifs deriving from the human face and different parts of the human body.

One is continually struck by the similarities between Marquesan art and the Maori art of New Zealand, with this difference, however, that in the Marquesas the vigorous curvilinear style of Maori art gives the impression of having been flattened out. The so-called *tiki* figure is the typical Marquesan theme. It closely resembles the representations of the human figure from the Cook Islands but the eyes are more rounded, almost circular, and the nose is given broad nostrils. Otherwise the relationship is very close. Similarly, the stylization of the figures arranged in rows on ear ornaments would resemble the friezes of deities of the Cook Islands, were it not that the small size of the pieces necessitated a greater simplicity.

The *tiki* figure recurs again and again in the decoration of canoes, on the rings made of dead men's bones, the heads of war-clubs, the carved footpieces of stilts, the wooden, bone or ivory handles of fans, and on the tortoise-shell parts of diadems. These last consist of alternating plaques of opaque and translucent shell. It is in the scenes incised on these shell plaques with their numerous figures, which are of sufficient scale to allow of some attention to detail, that we find Marquesan art at its most realistic.

377. Marquesas. *Net weights*. P. Vérité Collection.

378. Marquesas. Fatu-Hiva.
Statuette. — 379. Marquesas.
House-post. P. Vérité Collection.

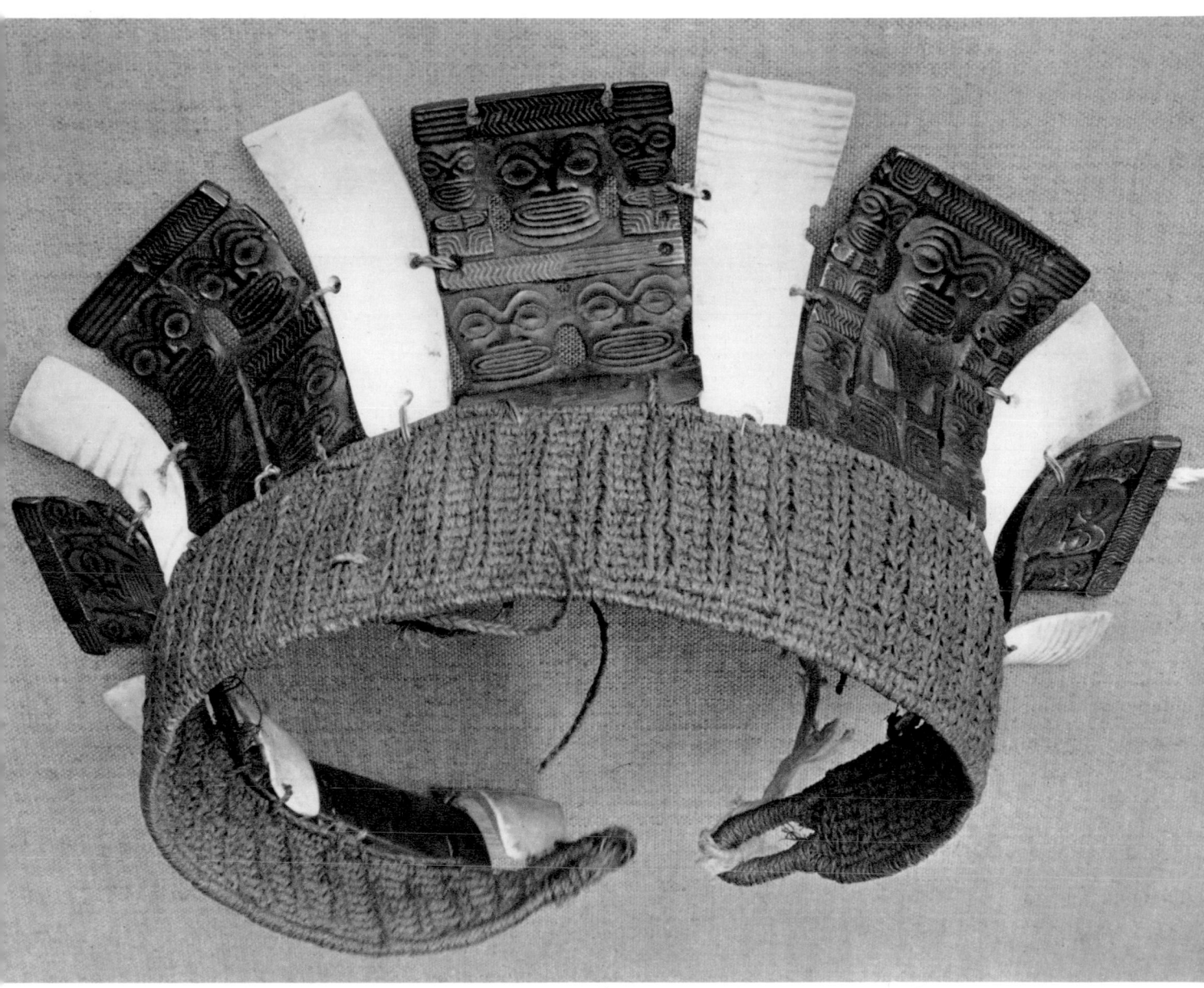

380. Marquesas. *Carved prow-piece for mooring a canoe.* Geneva.
381. Marquesas. *Woman's ear ornament.* Philadelphia.
382. Marquesas. *Fan-handle in bone.* Philadelphia.
383. Marquesas. *Diadem of tortoise-shell and shell.* Mus. of Primitive Art, New York.

Easter Island.

Easter Island is one of those exceptional places whose mysteries and romantic fascination have never ceased to intrigue both scientific investigators and imaginative amateurs. The results of the Franco-Belgian expedition of Métraux and Lavachery were insufficient to satisfy those whose apparent calling is to juggle with the more obscure elements of the past.

Apart from the monumental carvings and petroglyphs, old museum pieces and recent fakes are the only surviving evidence of an art which adapted itself to severe technical limitations and a precarious existence. Wood was so scarce that the artist had to adapt his work to the pieces that he could find.

Controversy may rage between medical writers, who seek to deduce from the carvings the deficiency diseases from which their subjects were suffering, and the anthropologists, who see in the *moai kavakava* statues, the image of an emaciated, half-decayed corpse. But to those who realize how hard life used to be on the Pacific islands, the arguments put forward by Dr. Stephen Chauvet are not without relevance, especially when we remember the state of emaciation of concentration-camp survivors. Most Oceanian societies experienced the horrors of famine to which each period of drought exposed them and such periods seemed to recur in regular cycles.

The bodies of the male statues, *moai kavakava*, are in fact remarkable for the emaciation of the trunk, that of the limbs being less pronounced. The lower ribs protrude and the pointed sternum, above the belly, curves back under the bottom ribs. The neck is marked by a goitre and an excrescence at the back. The face is equally gaunt, with a fringe of beard at the point of a bony chin, a strongly hooked nose, protruding cheek-bones and eyes inset with obsidian; the lower ear-lobes are deformed and adorned with cylindrical ornaments. On the top of the head the hair is sometimes replaced by a decorative human or bird motif. Limbs and trunk are slightly flexed, with none of the rigidity of a corpse. Certain figures have wigs of real hair. The genitalia are always clearly shown.

The female figures seem much more schematized, in the attitude of a coy Venus, with one hand on the belly, the other covering the genitalia. In contrast with the male figures these flat-bodied statues, *moai paepae*, are notable for the crudity with which the anatomical details are rendered. The most realistic heads are but poor copies of those of the male figures and Métraux considers them to be more recent work.

More curved pieces of wood were made to represent two types of figure: one with the head of a bird, *tangata manu*, the other with the head of a lizard. The first represents the bird god Makemake, personification of the sooty tern, *manitara*. To take the first egg laid by this sea-bird was a ritual exploit performed at the beginning of each nesting season by a different dignitary who thereby acquired for one year a kind of ceremonial pre-eminence. Although the beak is always present in these carvings, the degree of humanization of the head varies. The body is that of a man with projecting ribs, but the arms are replaced by wings which meet at the back.

The pieces portraying a lizard are also carved in bits of curved wood. The head of the lizard is clearly recognizable; the body recalls that of a man, treated in the local style but with its characteristics less emphasized.

Other examples of carving include:

1. Pendants, *reimiro*, in the shape of a crescent with a head in relief at each end. The head itself is crescent-shaped with the eyes set in sockets with projecting rims.
2. Staffs with an oval section whose handle is carved with a double human head treated in the same style as on the pendants.
3. Objects in the form of a double-bladed paddle, *rapa*, used for ritual purposes. In these the human face is suggested solely by a double U-motif representing the eye-sockets with two dots in relief. The rest of the face was apparently indicated by painting.
4. Globular objects, *tahonga*, carved to resemble a coconut and possibly bearing one or two human heads or bird heads. The Peabody Museum, Cambridge, Mass., possesses two unique specimens showing two squatting figures, the body covered with painted tapa-cloth; they may have served as models for tattooists. Less complicated carvings from the Marquesas are known to have served this purpose.

The monumental stone figures which were regarded as one of the mysteries of Easter Island have been studied in detail. The problem they present is more archaeological than stylistic and we must await the report of the recent excavations. These large figures are actually no more than busts, carved in volcanic tufa, which were apparently once coated with red ochre and white pigment. Intended, some of them at least, to be set up on stone platforms, *ahu*, they were all carved on the same model. The face, seen in profile, forms a quadrilateral whose upper side starts at the bridge of the nose, and whose base, on which the chin rests, is wider than the upper side formed by the forehead seen in section. This is a prognathic face, with thin lips, an angular chin, wide, raised nostrils, a concave nose and eyebrow ridges near the top of the head, above the deep sockets and the root of the nose. A long band in relief on the side denotes the ear and the deformed lower lobe.

These statues were topped by a cylinder of red tufa representing the hair. Recently sculptures have been found showing a seated figure. The question posed by the statues brought back a few years ago by Thor Heyerdahl is whether they are, wholly or partly, of recent manufacture; it seems that the answer is yes.

Finally we must mention the petroglyphs studied by Henry Lavachery: the characteristic theme is that of the man-bird. Another problem is that of the famous Easter Island 'writing', the mystery of which is gradually being solved. These pictographs are very close, stylistically, to the petroglyphs, though their size required a greater simplicity in design, which has probably ensured their accurate reproduction despite frequent repetitions. Their interpretation is likely to be the lifework of several specialists.

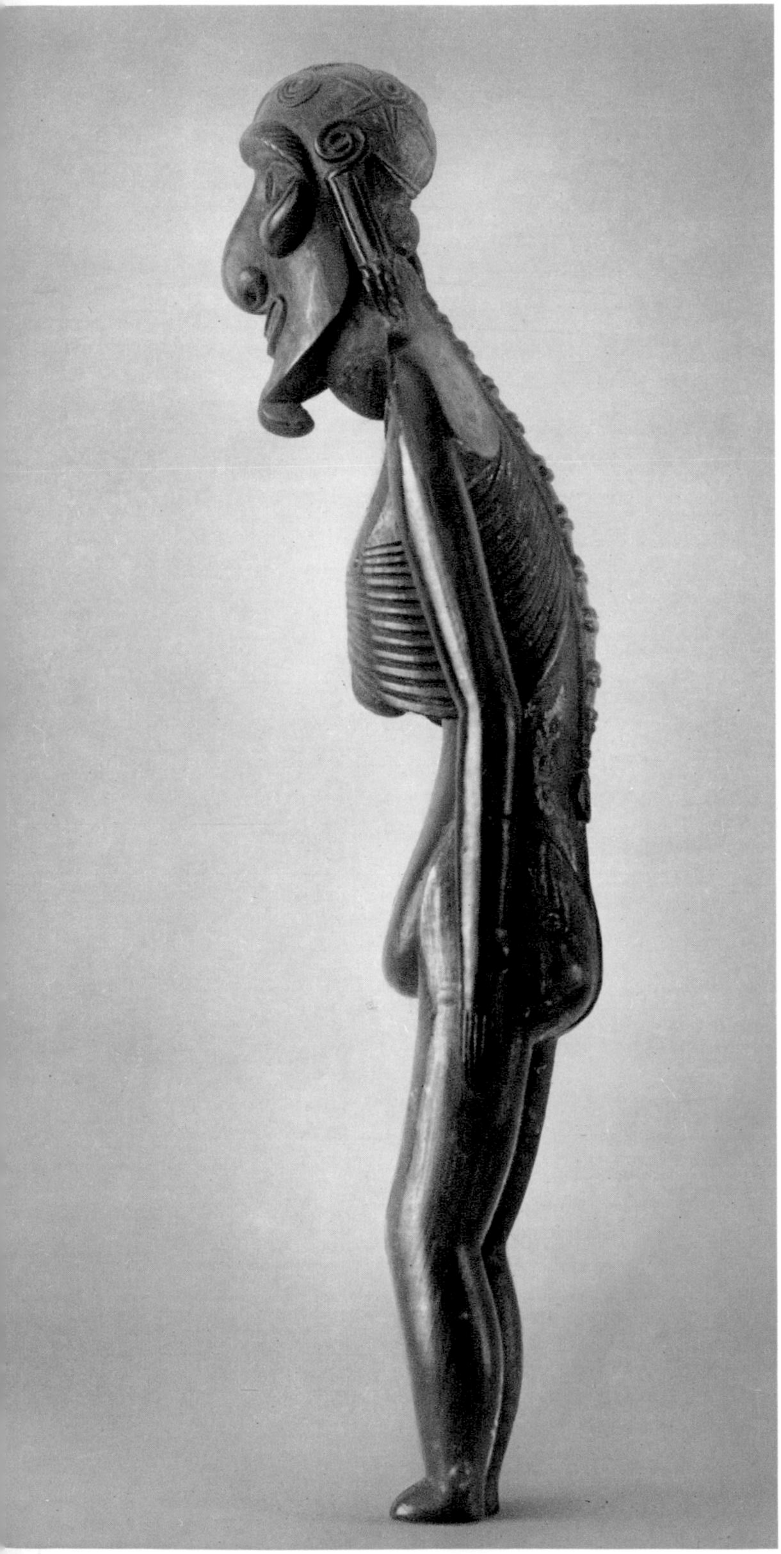

384. Easter Island. *Male figure*. Leningrad.

385. Easter Island. *Female figure*. Leningrad.

386. Easter Island. *Tangata manu (Man-bird)*. Leningrad.

387. Easter Island. *Human figure clad in tapa.* Peabody Mus., Harvard University, Cambridge. Mass.
388. Easter Island, Anakena Bay. *Monumental head.* Musée de l'Homme, Paris.

389. Easter Island. *Tapa head-dress*. Peabody Museum.

◀ 390. Easter Island, Orongo. *Stone carving*. British Museum.
391. Easter Island. *Petroglyphs*.

379

The Hawaiian Islands.

A quest for the spectacular tends to relate the art of Hawaii to that of New Zealand. It catered for a feudal society in which the priestly caste long played a leading part.

Hawaiian sculpture is of two kinds. In one, which recalls Maori carving in some respects, we find faces in which a huge grimacing mouth thrusts the eyes back beneath a head-dress with a complex serrated edge; the upturned nostrils, opening almost vertically, are all that remains of the nose. The body is in the usual Polynesian position, with the legs slightly bent, the arms dangling beside the body. In some statues the arms stretch out in front. The differences from one figure to another are mainly in the head-dresses. In one case the head-dress seems to merge into the head, the face being placed at a protruding extremity to appear like a reptile's head.

Other figures, found in caves, show a female body treated with remarkable realism, with only the shortening of the lower arm to cause surprise. The face, with inset eyes of pearl shell, shows no sign of stylization nor do the chest or the breasts. Another, apparently a male figure, has the lower part of the body wrapped in a stiff skirt of interwoven coconut fibre strands.

Other pieces of sculpture include drums adorned with a single or double frieze of carved figures. But these are rare: only three examples are known.

Some dishes are carved with seated or standing figures with the head thrown back. A remarkable example in the British Museum consists of two joined together by the arched body of a human figure, the joints and eyes being inlaid with pearl shell.

Others, again, are supported by three figures shown carrying the dish on their backs or their feet and walking on their hands.

Bracelets made of flat fragments of tortoise-shell, fixed to one another and cut with the concave surface uppermost, have small pieces of bone at regular intervals with a human head carved in relief at either end.

With the sculptures we should include human figures in wickerwork covered with coloured feathers. The only divine images to leave the sacred enclosures, they were carried into battle by the priests of the war god. These figures, with their vivid colours, consist only of a head which is covered with a crested head-dress or with human hair.

A similar technique is used for the helmets, which resemble those of ancient Greece, and have crests of various shapes topped with plumes. The splendid feather capes and cloaks, worn only by nobles of higher rank, fall into the same category.

Incised decoration is virtually non-existent, but designs stamped on tapa-cloth (not to be found in the Marquesas and New Zealand) served the same purpose. Tapa-cloth was used in the home and for clothing, and was adorned with a decoration unique in Polynesia for its delicate design and wide range of colours. A repetition of motifs set side by side formed long geometric bands alternating with undecorated zones.

392. Hawaiian Islands, Oahu. *Ku, the god of war.* British Museum

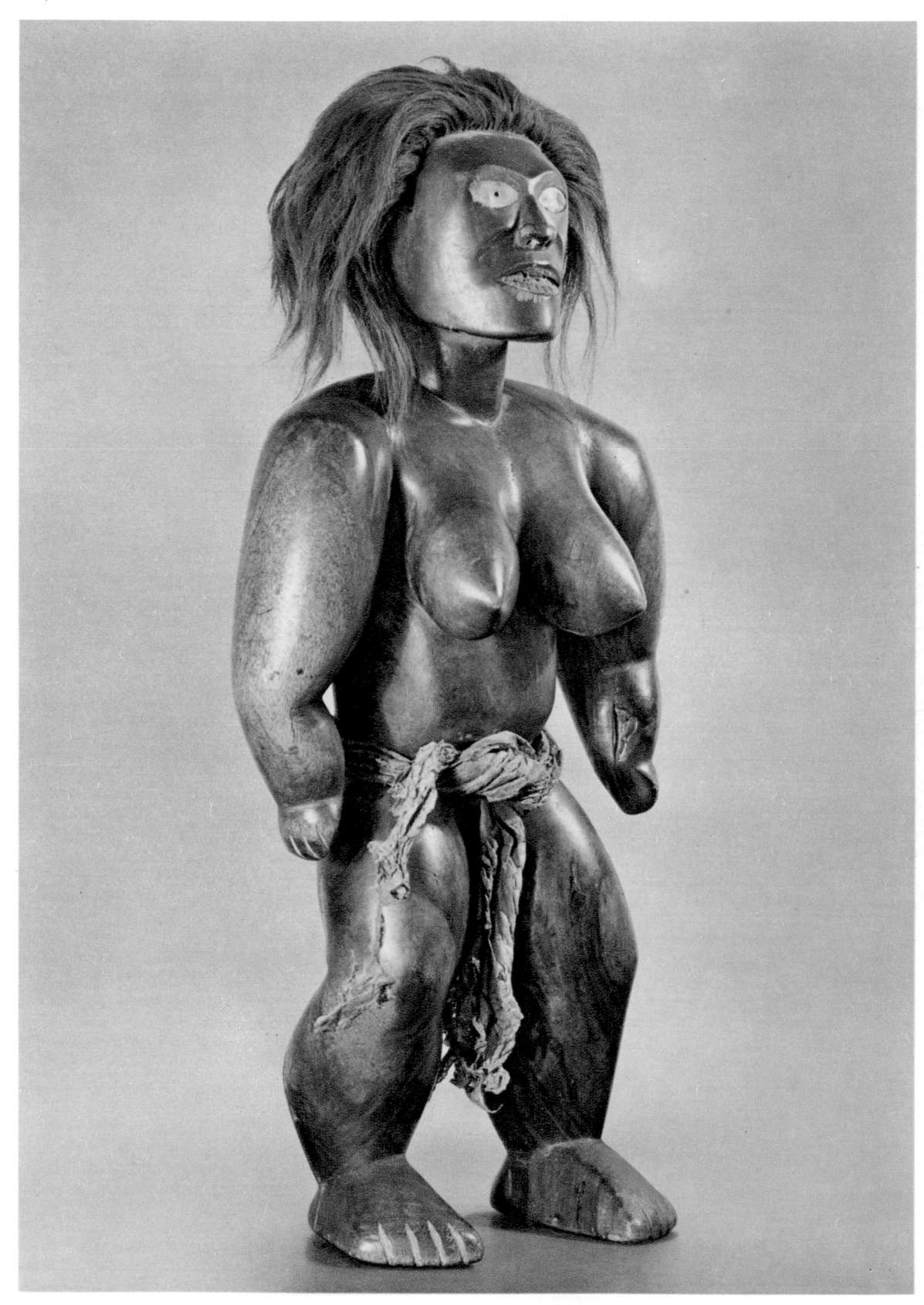

393. Hawaiian Islands, Kawaihae. *Statuette*. Honolulu.

394. Hawaiian Islands. *Statuette*. Honolulu.

383

395 and 396. Hawaiian Islands. *Cups*. British Museum.

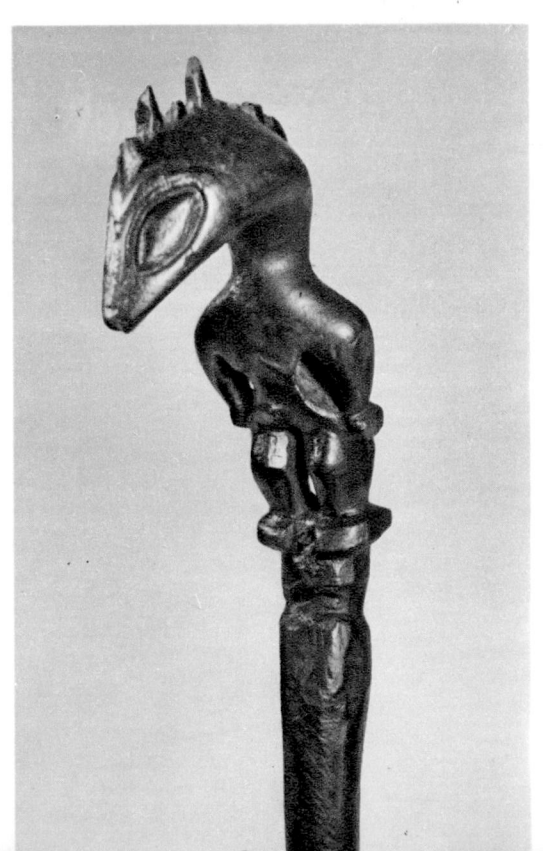

397. Hawaiian Islands. *Double dish*. British Museum.
398. Hawaiian Islands, Honaunau. *Full-length temple figure*. Honolulu.

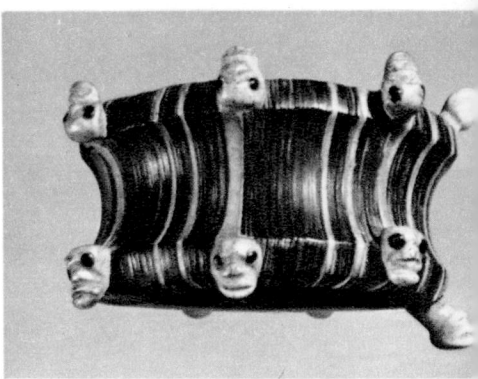

399. Hawaiian Islands. *Bracelet*. Honolulu

400. Hawaiian Islands. *The goddess Pele on a comb*. Musée de l'Homme, Paris.

401. Hawaiian Islands. *God of War*. Goettingen Museum.

402. Hawaiian Islands. *God of War*. Berlin Museum.

403. Hawaiian Islands. *Figure of a god.* Musée de l'Homme, Paris.

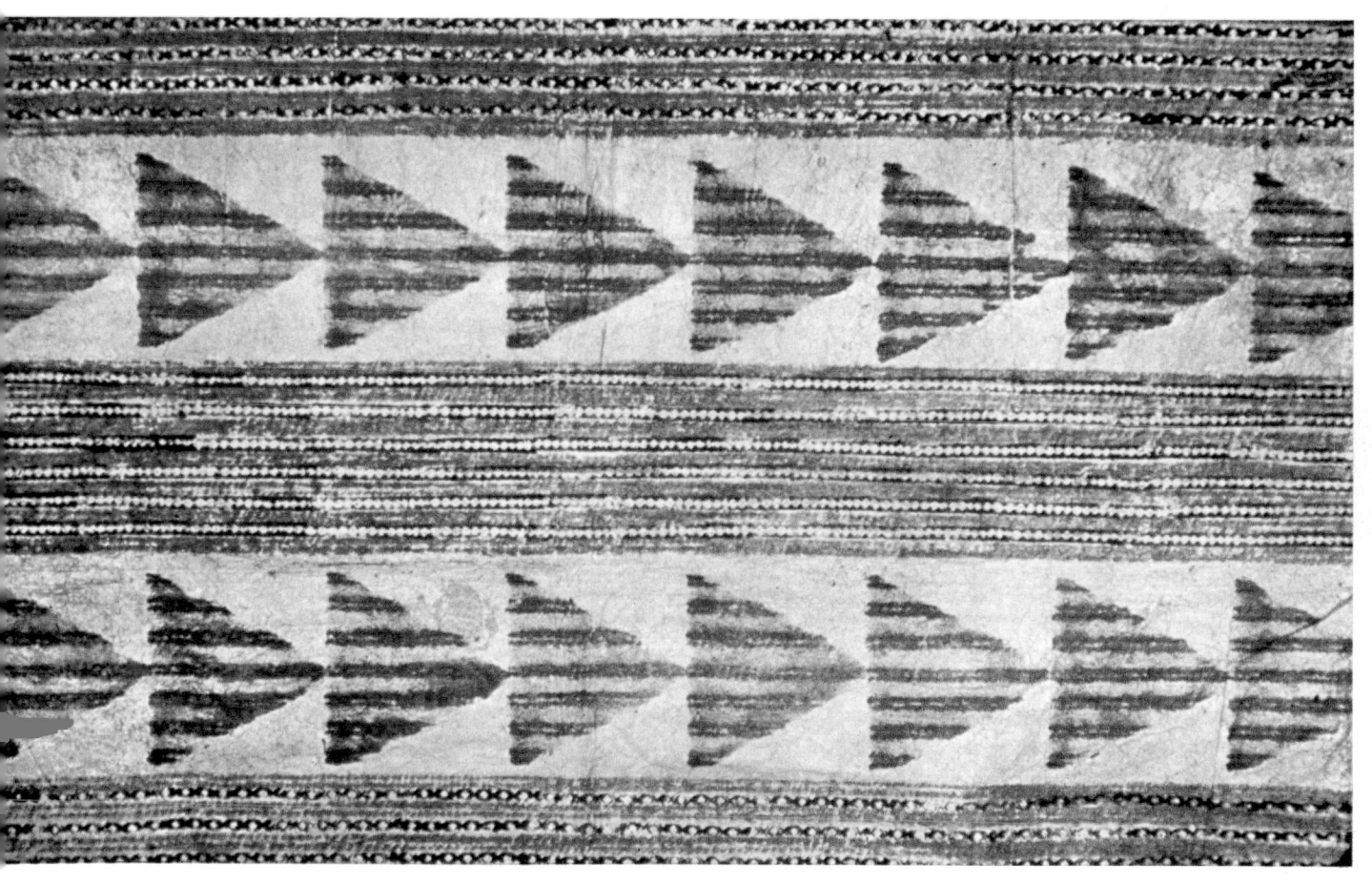

04. Hawaiian Islands. *Tapa*. Honolulu.

391

MICRONESIA

Life on the atolls of Micronesia was particularly difficult and precarious owing to the lack of natural resources, of fresh water, even of the soil necessary to grow crops. Hence perhaps the simplicity and uniformity of the material culture of these islands, even of the higher and larger islands of the area. Yet these conditions did not prevent the development, on the more thickly populated islands, of a highly complex social structure.

Of all peoples of Oceania, these were the ones whose arts and crafts most clearly reveal former knowledge of metals and metal-working, and the only ones of whom we can be certain that they formerly had a more advanced technology. Those Micronesians who had settled on Mally and Durour Islands close to New Guinea were the best wood-workers in all Oceania, and had a profound knowledge of the techniques of carpentry. Their dishes and stools, the latter forming part of the coconut scraper, show functional forms remarkable for their purity of line.

Only a few pieces of sculpture have survived, of which the *tino* figure in the Musée de l'Homme, Paris, is probably the best specimen. It bears a certain resemblance to Polynesian statuettes. The body is indicated simply by curved surfaces intersected by sharp ridges. Only the volume of the head is indicated, without any anatomical detail; spindly arms hang from the shoulders.

Another classic example is the gable ornament of the men's houses in the Caroline Islands which shows a human face or mask set on a sort of escutcheon. Against a white ground the thin lips and the eyebrows stand out in dark red, as does the outline of the face streaked with white. A circular ornament is attached to the right side of the mask.

In the Palau Islands, a local school of craftsmen, still flourishing today, produces mythological scenes with flat painted figures whose silhouettes appear in relief; these scenes, sometimes of an erotic nature, are treated with engaging realism. The Palau Islanders also make wooden bowls, charmingly decorated in inlaid mother-of-pearl with a bird as the principal motif.

Geometric decoration is either in braided or woven material; the attention to detail recalls Indonesian work.

The art of the Santa Cruz islands, which lie between the New Hebrides and the Solomons may conveniently be treated with that of Micronesia. The carving has, in fact, much the same simplicity. The clubs and representations of fish in white wood are enhanced with details and a geometric decoration painted in thin lines. But the undoubted masterpiece is the local variant of the Melanesian *kapkap* with its interpretation of the frigate-bird theme.

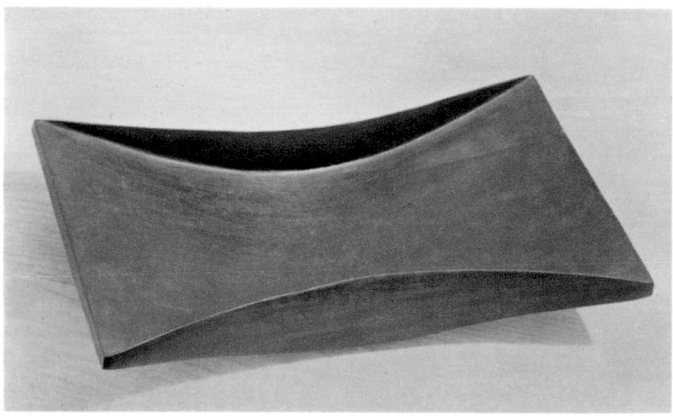

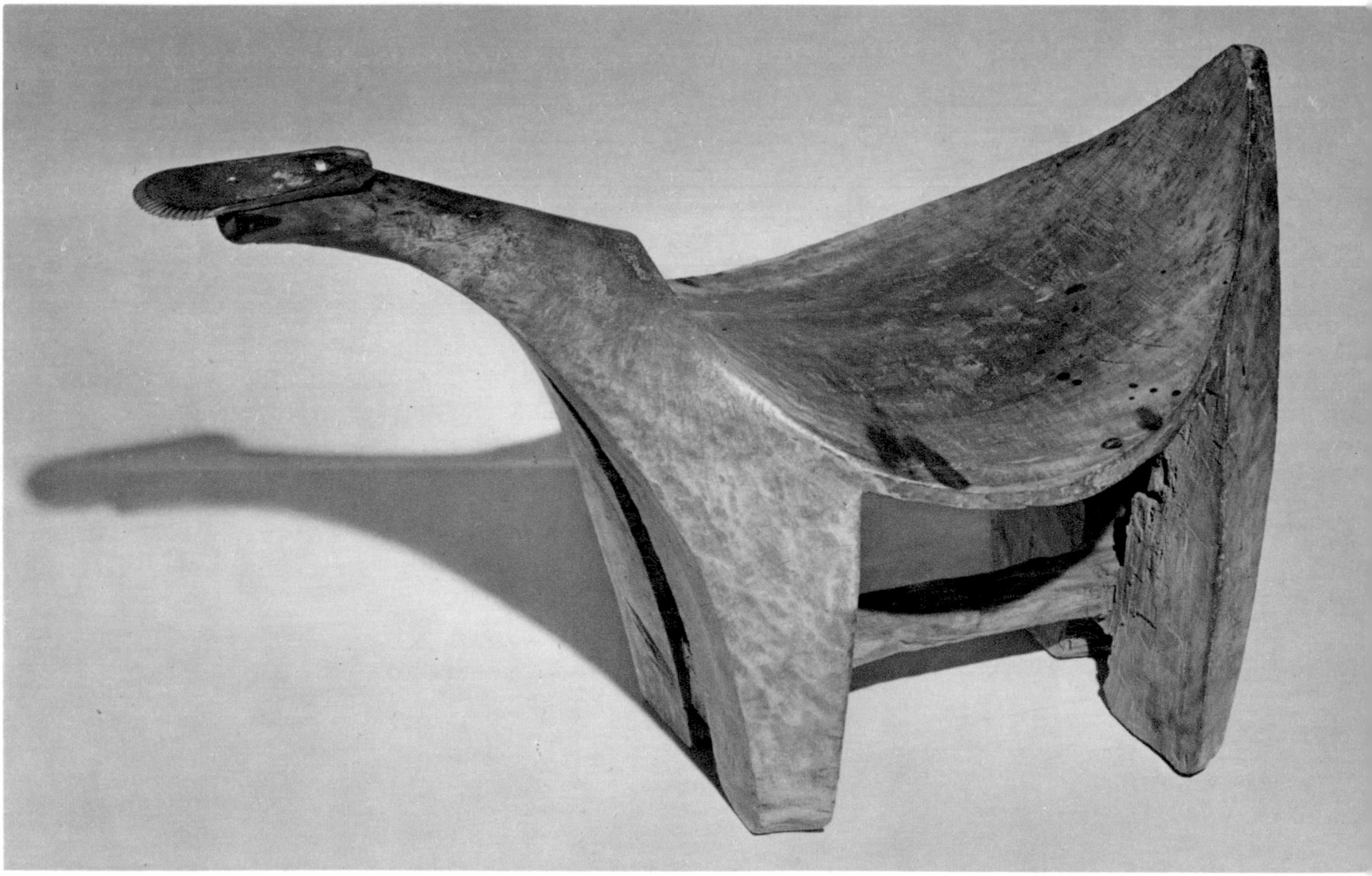

406. Matty Island. *Wooden plate*. Mus. of Primitive Art, New York.
407. Caroline Islands, Nukuoro. *Coconut grater in the form of a stool*. Mus. of Primitive Art, New York.
408. Caroline Islands, Nukuoro. *Female figure*. Honolulu.

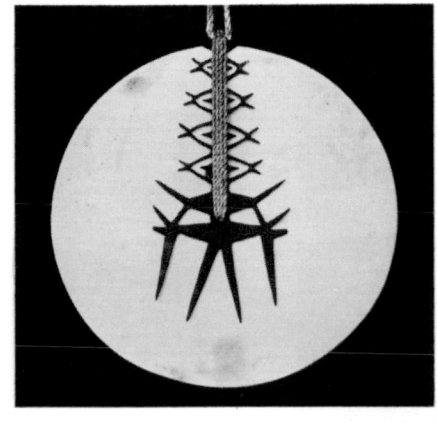

409. Caroline Islands, Ponape (?). *Tino figure*. Musée de l'Homme, Paris.
410. Santa Cruz Islands, Nitendi. *Pendant*. Basle.
411. Gilbert Islands. *Basketwork armour*. Brussels.

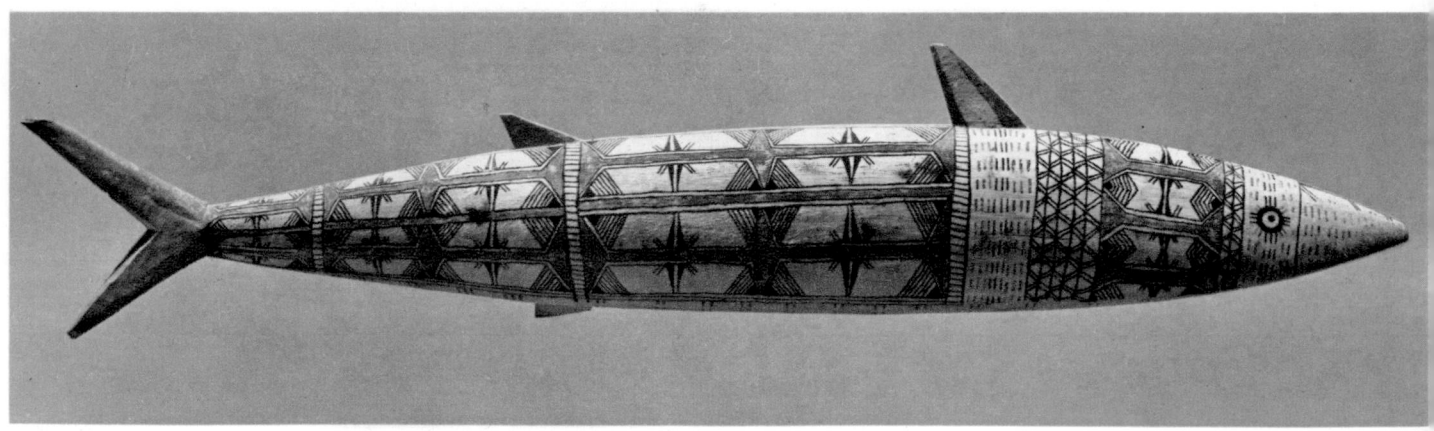

412. *Detail of* 414.
413. Santa Cruz Islands. *Representation of fish*. Basle.
414. Santa Cruz Islands. *Male figure*. Mus. of Primitive Art, New York.

415. Palau Islands. *Plank incised with a mythical scene.* M.A.A.O., Paris.

416. Palau Islands. *Bowl with mother-of-pearl incrustation.* British Museum.

400

417. Caroline Islands. *Gable-end ornament*. Honolulu.

GLOSSARIAL INDEX

BIBLIOGRAPHY

AND

LIST OF ILLUSTRATIONS

418. New Guinea. Papua. Era-Maipura River. *Irivake figure*, Amsterdam - 419. New Guinea. Papua. Koiravi. Era River. *Incised figure*, Brooklyn Museum - 420. New Guinea. Papua. Ikunu. Namau coast. *Feminine figure*, Basle.

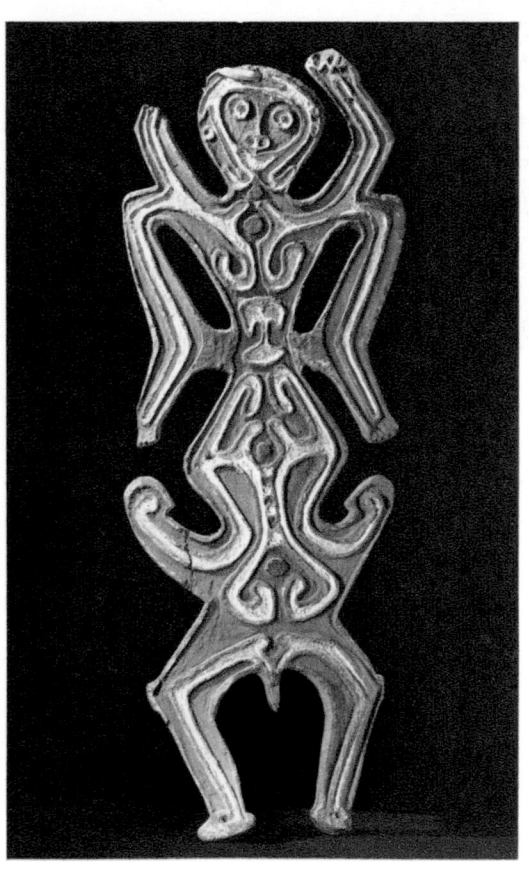

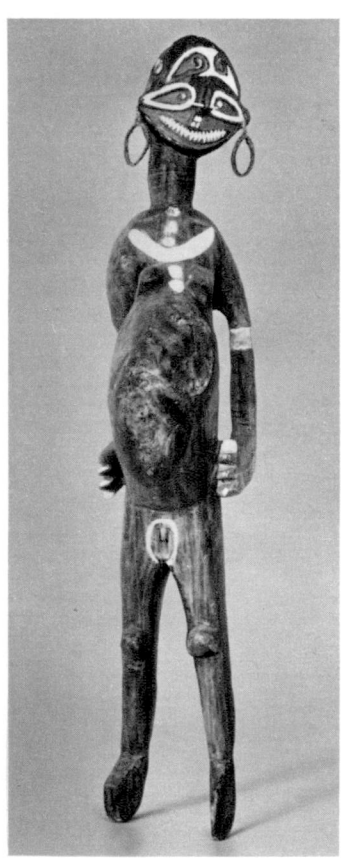

GLOSSARIAL INDEX

ABELAM. People of the Prince Alexander Mountains region, eastern New Guinea, dominating the left bank of the Sepik. *P.* 170 *fig.* 138, 144.

ADALBERTHAFEN. A former German administrative centre to the east of the mouth of the Sepik, eastern New Guinea. *P.* 179.

ADMIRALTY (Islands). Discovered by Schouten in 1615. Consist of Manus Island and a great number of small islands. The work of Margaret Mead, R. Fortune and Schwartz has demonstrated the essential cultural unity of the group. *P.* 96, 98, 103, 104, 112, 229, 315, 320-321 *fig.* 67, 70, 320-323, 325-327.

AITAPE (Region). Australian administrative sub-division, to the west of the mouth of the Sepik, eastern New Guinea. *P.* 179 *fig.* 201-203.

AMBAT (Deity). Divinity responsible for the introduction of culture; represented as the youngest of five brothers named after the five fingers of the hand. *P.* 133.

AMBRIM. Island in the Melanesian New Hebrides archipelago: volcanic, with two active craters. Population approx. 3,000. Famous for its traditional sculpture. *P.* 134.

ANATOM (or Aneiteum Island). Most southerly of the New Hebrides. The name is that used by the people of the south of neighbouring Tanna. The coming of Christianity coincided with a decline in population from 3,000 to 300. Captain Paddon and the Marist missionaries found refuge here after being driven from Balade, north-east New Caledonia. Anatom used traditionally to maintain relations with the Loyalty Islands, southern New Caledonia, where it was known as Kiamu. *P.* 29.

ANIWA (Island). A partly submerged coral atoll with a lagoon. Its 200 inhabitants speak a Polynesian language although the social organization is very similar to that of the neighbouring island of Tanna. *P.* 22, 66.

AOBA (or Omba). Called Leper Island by Cook on account of the light colour of some of its inhabitants who now number about 4,000. Dominated by an extinct crater filled by a warm-water lake. Its extremely independent population has been able to avoid all expropriation by Europeans and all outside authority in a most modern manner. *P.* 86, 91, 231 *fig.* 205, 223.

ARCHEY (Gilbert). New Zealand anthropologist. Director of the War Memorial Museum, Auckland. *P.* 352, 353.

ARNHEM LAND. Peninsula in the extreme north of Australia (Northern Territory), famous for its aboriginal inhabitants (reserve, paintings, life). *P.* 120, 139, 140. *fig.* 30, 34, 39, 40, 41, 42, 102, 103, 104.

ARUNTA. A central Australian tribe. Famous for the remarkable studies by Spencer and Gillen. *P.* 127.

ASMAT. A people adapted to life in the marshy lowlands in the south-east of western New Guinea. Thanks to the efforts of Catholic missionaries, the work of explorers in their region has been greatly eased in recent years. Long famous for their sculpture. *P.* 66, 79, 104, 154 *fig.* 15, 19, 32, 43, 49, 78, 79, 119-125, 424, 427.

ASTROLABE (Bay). Named after the French ship in which Dumont d'Urville made his scientific voyages. To the south-east of Port Moresby, Papua. *P.* 104, 264-265. *fig.* 249-256.

AURID (Island). One of the islands in the Torres Straits. *P.* 60.

AUSTRAL (Islands). The most southerly of the archipelagos of French Polynesia, consisting of Tubuai, Rurutu, Raivavae, Rimatara and Rapa Islands, with a total population of about 4,000. *P.* 18, 25, 336, 338, 339 *fig.* 349, 355, 361-363.

BAINING. Little-known people in northern central New Britain. The rugged country and their dispersal into tiny groups, following a sharp fall in number, have led to their being almost ignored by the administration. They are occasionally called on to present their Snake Dance to distinguished visitors. *P.* 282, 294 *fig.* 276, 278, 280.

BANKS (Islands). Northern part of the New Hebrides archipelago; named by Captain Bligh, of the *Bounty*, after the naturalist Sir Joseph Banks (1743-1820). These islands, which were once very troublesome, have remained under the control of their engaging and highly conservative people who number about 3,000. *P.* 22, 29, 60, 63, 91, 229, 231 *fig.* 64, 207, 208, 212, 234.

BARRAU (Jacques). French scientist (born in 1925) of New Caledonian origin, famous for his work in applied botany. *P. 28.*

BATESON (Gregory). American anthropologist, who specialised in the Sepik valley. *P. 172, 173, 175.*

BATIK. An Indonesian reserve-dyeing technique in which the cloth is plunged into successive baths of dye-stuffs, the areas which are not to be dyed being protected by a layer of wax. *P. 85.*

BERNICE PAUAHI BISHOP MUSEUM. A famous Museum in Honolulu, specialising in Polynesian culture and natural history. Named after a Hawaiian princess who married a Bishop, a member of a missionary family whose fortune was based upon large-scale expropriation of real estate. *P. 21.*

BERTRAND (Island). A small island situated just off the north coast of New Guinea to the west of the mouth of the Sepik. *P. 178.*

BETEL. Kind of climbing pepper. A mixture of substances, of which betel leaves form the base, which is used in tropical areas as an astringent tonic 'chew'. *P. 92, 101, 316 fig. 429.*

BISMARCK (Melanesian archipelago). This group includes the Admiralty Islands, New Ireland and New Britain. With Buka and Bougainville it makes up the island region of Papua/New Guinea. *P. 21, 24, 25, 293, 320.*

BODROGI (Tibor). Hungarian anthropologist whose analytical ability and professional skill compensate for his lack of field experience. Director of the Ethnographic Museum, Budapest. *P. 264.*

BOESOU EURIJISI. Melanesian pastor and former carver of masks. One of the best informants of Maurice Leenhardt, who taught him to read. *P. 115, 136.*

BORA BORA. Island in the Leeward group, French Polynesia; 1,632 inhabitants in 1956. *fig. 3.*

BOSTON MISSION. American nonconformist mission which evangelised Hawaii and parts of Micronesia. *P. 7.*

BOUGAINVILLE (Island). One of the largest and most mountainous islands of the Solomons with over 25,000 inhabitants. Discovered in June 1768 by Bougainville, whose name it preserves, it became a German colony and was mandated to Australia. Has been studied by Father Patrick O'Reilly and Douglas Oliver. *P. 34, 137, 326. fig. 328, 344.*

BRETON (André). French writer, born 1896. With Tristan Tzara and Paul Eluard was responsible for the cult of primitive art. *P. 116.*

BUCK (Sir Peter H.). Known also by his Maori name: Te Rangi Hiroa. A doctor of partly Maori origin and one-time member of the New Zealand parliament. Best known for his anthropological work and as Director of the Bernice Pauahi Bishop Museum, Honolulu. Knighted several years before his death in 1951. *P. 21.*

BÜHLER (Alfred). Born 1900. Has made his career at the Ethnographic Museum, Basle, of which he has been Conservator and later Director. Much field-work in New Guinea. *P. 170.*

BUKA (Island). Next island north from Bougainville. Studied by Beatrice Blackwood. About 15,000 inhabitants. *P. 136, 137, 326 fig. 100, 101, 343.*

BULOTU (Island). Mythical island to which, according to Fijian and Polynesian belief, the dead go. At the same time it is believed that the dead exist beside the living. *P. 68.*

CANALA. Formerly Napoleonville. One of the earliest French naval and military bases in New Caledonia. Situated on a deep bay with marshy shores and surrounded by mountains which leave little cultivable land. Population 3,000. *P. 116, 252 fig. 240, 241, 244.*

CAROLINE (Islands). Micronesian archipelago. Partially colonised by the Portuguese in 1527 and subsequently occupied by the Spanish, the Germans, the Japanese. Now under American administration. 35,000 inhabitants. *P. 392 fig. 407-409, 417.*

CARPENTARIA (Gulf of). North coast of Australia. *P. 24.*

CHAMBULI (or Lake Tchambuli). Flows into the middle Sepik and is famed for the artistic achievements of the people in the villages on its banks, studied particularly by Margaret Mead. *P. 171-172, 174, 175 fig. 28, 148, 152.*

CHAUVET (Stephen). French physician, owner of very fine Oceanian collections. An enlightened amateur anthropologist. *P. 370.*

CHOISEUL (Island). One of the medium-sized Solomon Islands (4,000 inhabitants). Important deposits of nickel which are being surveyed. *P. 326.*

CODRINGTON (Robert Henry). 1830-1922. Anglican missionary of the Melanesian Mission. Principal of the college established on Norfolk Island, between Australia and New Caledonia. The first to use large numbers of informants whom he encouraged to write in the light of their knowledge and inclination, instead of in reply to a prepared questionnaire. The best of the old ethnographers of Melanesia. (*The Melanesians. Studies in their anthropology and folklore*, Oxford, 1891). *P. 60, 64, 68, 135, 231, 325, 326.*

CONCEPTION. Site of a Marist missionary centre in New

Caledonia, the foundation of which was prompted by the reduction of the Jesuits in Paraguay. The congregation consisted mainly of emigrants from Balade, Poneso and Hienghene. *P.* 253.

COOK (or Hervey Islands). Discovered by James Cook in 1775. A considerable part of the population originated in New Zealand (of which they were a dependency), Tahiti and the Leeward Islands. Under 2,000 inhabitants. *P.* 25, 28, 88, 125, 135, 336, 337, 338, 339, 352, 353, 364 *fig.* 10, 25, 351, 356, 357, 359.

COWRIE. A regularly shaped shell used both for ornament and as money. *P.* 34, 103, 172, 173, 174, 176.

CYCAS. A gymnosperm tree, resembling a palm. Its leaf, held up, is a symbol of peace. *P.* 36.

DARIEN. Eastern part of the Isthmus of Panama, north-west of Colombia and south of the gulf which bears the same name. *P.* 27.

DENSHERING. Slash-and-burn. The practice of clearing a patch of ground of bushes and grass, piling the debris on top of the cleared patch and firing it. The ashes are then spread to provide a fertiliser and the patch is taken into cultivation. *P.* 5, 8.

D'ENTRECASTEAUX (Islands). A group immediately to the east of the eastern New Guinea peninsula, with which it is included to form the Massim cultural region. *P.* 315, 316 *fig.* 312.

DUMONT-D'URVILLE (Island). Now known officially as Kairirn. Off the north coast of eastern New Guinea, opposite the Prince Alexander Mountains. *P.* 179.

DUROUR (or Aua). With MATTY Island the most easterly of the Admiralty Islands; typically Micronesian islands despite their proximity to New Guinea. *P.* 22, 392.

EASTER (Island). A Chilean dependency in the Pacific. (300 inhabitants). *P.* 18, 25, 125, 135, 336, 352, 370-371 *fig.* 89, 90, 384-391.

EI AO (Island). In the north-west of the Marquesas. Discovered by Marchand in 1791. *P.* 364.

ELLICE (Islands). Archipelago forming part of the administrative group of Gilbert and Ellice Islands. Polynesian population of about 5,000. *P.* 22, 28.

EMAE (or Three Hill Island). With 400 inhabitants; in the Shepherds group, New Hebrides. *P.* 22, 39.

EPI. One of the large islands of the New Hebrides. Was a centre of French civilisation: now in decay. The native population is much depleted, as a result of alienation of land. *P.* 39.

ESPIRITU SANTO. The largest island of the New Hebrides.

Relatively small population (6,000, of whom 4,000 are Melanesian) despite its size. The least known and least administered, except for the south-east fringe, where the coral ledge is occupied by European plantations. (Cf. Jean Guiart: *Espiritu Santo.* Plon, Paris, 1957.) *P.* 8, 22, 77, 99, 104, 230, 231 *fig.* 4, 219.

FATU HIVA (Island). Most southerly of the Marquesas, discovered by Mendaña de Neira in 1595, when he called it Santa Madalena. One of the most depopulated of the group. *P.* 364.

FIJI (Islands). An archipelago with 400,000 inhabitants to the west of the Tonga islands of which the eastern part, Lau Islands, were a political and cultural dependency. It was the seat of one of those ephemeral monarchies which came into being through the efforts of the Europeans and the political shrewdness and warlike qualities of the chief of the island of Bau (in the eastern part of Viti Levu), the Vunivalu named Thakoban. The Fiji islands were ceded to the British Crown in 1870 under certain conditions which included the payment of the islands' international debts. It was the scene of the first British experiments in indirect rule. The nobles of the eastern islands took advantage of this to affirm their authority over the western part of Viti Levu. This situation had been developing over the centuries although the social structure there was very different from the semi-Polynesian hierarchies of the regions which were in contact with the Europeans. The growing and processing of sugar cane is responsible for the presence of Indian labourers, who today form the majority of the population. *P.* 8, 15, 18, 25, 42, 57, 77, 92, 95, 104, 336, 337, 338 *fig.* 12, 345-348, 360.

FLY (River). One of the chief water systems of eastern New Guinea, explored by Alberti in 1876. *P.* 137, 146 *fig.* 425, 433.

FOX (C.E.). Anglican missionary, anthropologist and linguist. An enlightened director of the Melanesian Mission, like Codrington and Ivens, between whose tenures he held office. Devoted himself to the evangelisation and study of the south-eastern Solomons. *P.* 135.

FUTUNA (Islands). There are two Futuna, one known also as Hoorne (Futuna and Alofi with a population of 3,000). North-west of Fiji, they are part of the French Wallis and Futuna Islands. Traditionally linked with Samoa. In the New Hebrides, Futuna is the name of a volcanic island 45 miles east of Tanna. Also known as Eronan, it has a population of 300, held to be Polynesian. *P.* 22, 25, 28, 29, 87, 92, 229, 336.

GAMBIER (Islands). Volcanic archipelago in French Polynesia on the axis and to the south-east of the coral group of Tuamotu. Seriously depopulated, its traditional history is well known thanks to the publication by Alfred Métraux of the manuscripts of Father Laval. *P.* 25.

GEELVINK (Bay). An immense re-entrant in the north

coast of western New Guinea which is partly closed by the line of Schouten Islands. Well populated, although the coast, covered with houses on piles, is largely marshy. A good early account of the region in Dumont d'Urville's account of his voyages. *P.* 104, 307 *fig.* 300-302.

GILBERT (Islands). Form with the Ellice Islands a vast British territory, consisting of coral islands, virtually without humus. Their population (40,000) of hardy sailors draws most of its food from the sea. These warriors, with vegetable armour, have been strongly influenced from Samoa, although they should be classed as Micronesians. *P.* 7, 22 *fig.* 411.

GILLEN (Francis James, 1856-1912). Former employee of the Australian Telegraph Service. Stationed at Alice Springs, he collaborated with Spencer (q.v.), a university teacher, in one of the most detailed studies ever made of the aboriginals. *P.* 127.

GIRARD (Françoise). Head of the Oceanian Department, Musée de l'Homme, Paris. *P.* 172.

GIZO (Island). One of the smallest of the Solomons; a coral formation, it is an administrative centre. *P.* 325.

GOMAWE (Deity). A New Caledonian divinity in the Patyi language. Is identical with Pijèva, the lord of the land of the dead. Both are represented by masks. *P.* 64, 75.

GOMEN. Locality on the north-west coast of New Caledonia *fig.* 5, 235.

GOODENOUGH (Ward C.). American anthropologist and professor at the University of Pennsylvania. *P.* 137.

GUILBERT (Island). A small island on the north coast of eastern New Guinea, to the west of the Sepik. *P.* 179.

HANDY (Mrs. Willowdean C.). American anthropologist noted for her connection with the Bernice P. Bishop Museum of Honolulu and for her work in the Marquesas. *P.* 121, 364.

HAWAII (Archipelago). A Polynesian archipelago in the Northern Hemisphere which forms one of the States of the U.S.A. Formerly known under the name of Sandwich Islands. *P.* 18, 25, 45, 66, 74, 79, 84, 89, 125, 336, 352, 353, 380 *fig.* 20, 21, 390-405.

HENRI (Teuira). Granddaughter of the missionary L.M.S. Ormond and an excellent linguist who reconstructed and published his notes on the customs and traditions of Polynesia, *Ancient Tahiti*. *P.* 74.

HERMIT. One of a small group of islands, to the west of the Admiralty Islands, which show Micronesian influence. *P.* 321.

HEYERDAHL (Thor). Norwegian, born in 1914. His daring raft voyage, remarkable as a feat of sport, required exceptional courage. As an ethnologist, he employed comparative methods believed to be out of date. He nonetheless drew attention to the undoubted link between the Americas and Oceania. *P.* 18, 27, 371.

HINA. Polynesian goddess who fled to the moon in order to avoid incest with her brother. She can be seen there working pandanus leaves and making mats. *P.* 68.

HIVA OA (or Domenica Island). Discovered by Mendaña de Neira in 1595. Long opposed French rule. Headquarters of the Atuona archipelago, and the scene of Paul Gauguin's last years. *P.* 364.

HUAHINE. One of the Leeward Islands little frequented by Europeans; 2,700 inhabitants. The London Missionary Society established a press there in the 18th century. *P.* 337 *fig.* 6, 358.

HUAILU (Valley). One of the narrow, impoverished valleys on the east slopes of New Caledonia with 3,000 inhabitants. Known through the work of Maurice Leenhardt (q.v.) who established a flourishing mission station at Do Neva which his successors neglected. *P.* 22, 52 *fig.* 8, 26, 99, 238, 242.

HUMBOLDT (Bay). Near the boundary between the two parts of New Guinea. The capital of the western part, Hollandia or Kota Baru, lies on it. *P.* 160, 307 *fig.* 309.

HUON (Gulf or Bay). One of the principal bays of eastern New Guinea into which the Marckham river flows. Its mouth is the start of a route to the Highlands. Formerly district headquarters. *P.* 96, 271-272 *fig.* 51, 258, 259-265.

IATMÜL. A tribe on the middle Sepik known through the work of Bateson (q.v.). *P.* 172-173 *fig.* 96, 149, 151, 154-156.

IMANDA. A locality in Aranda district, Central Australia, the centre of a religious rite. *P.* 127.

IUMORAN. A place on the island of Tomman with religious significance of particular importance in the symbolism of south-west Malekula, New Hebrides. *P.* 133.

IVENS (Walter G.). Anthropologist and Anglican missionary noted for his remarkable studies of the south-east of the Solomons. *P.* 135, 326.

KALABU. Locality in eastern New Guinea, in the Maprik region of the Sepik river valley. *fig.* 27.

KAMBRIMAN. A people of the middle Sepik valley. *P.* 173.

KAMBRINGI. A people of the middle Sepik valley. *P.* 173-174 *fig.* 158-164.

KANIGARA. A people of the middle Sepik living near the junction with the Yuat river.   *P.* 174-175.

KARKAR. A medium-sized island lying off the north coast of eastern New Guinea. Traditionally linked with the Admiralty Islands further to the north as well as with the mainland.   *P.* 108.

KAVA. A traditional drink obtained by cold infusion of the fibres of the root of *piper methysticum*. Its distribution in Polynesia as well as Melanesia gave rise to various theories of migration put forward by Rivers. Still in use in Fiji, the New Hebrides and western Polynesia.   *P.* 46, 92, 96, 98, 229, 337.

KIHO TUMU. A Polynesian deity whose existence and attributes have led to thirty years of bitter disputes between specialists on eastern Polynesia.   *P.* 68.

KIWAI. A tribe living at the mouth of the Fly river, Papua.   *P.* 137   *fig.* 113, 114.

KOOIJMAN (S.). Dutch anthropologist and Director of the Leiden Ethnographic Museum.   *P.* 160.

KOKOYAO. An Australian tribe living in Cape York, Queensland.   *P.* 133.

KULA. The cyclical exchange of local products on a ceremonial basis in the Massim region. Bronislaw Malinowski's account of this system was one of his major works.   *P.* 95.

KULKA (Deity). A local divinity of Aurid Island, Torres Strait.   *P.* 60.

LAROCHE (Mme Marie). French anthropologist, secretary of the Société des Océanistes.   *P.* 307.

LAU. A large number of coral islands which make up eastern half of Fiji. Of Polynesian, especially Tongan, influence.   *P.* 28, 338.

LAVACHERY (Henri). Formerly curator-in-chief of the Musées Royaux d'Art et d'Histoire, Brussels. Known for his archaeological work on Easter Island.   *P.* 370, 371.

LEENHARDT (Maurice). French anthropologist and Protestant missionary (1878-1954) whose influence on the Pacific can be seen and felt today. Built a brilliant academic career on his experience as a missionary.   *P.* 115, 136, 252.

LÉVI-STRAUSS (Claude). French anthropologist, born 1908. Professor at the Collège de France. One of keenest intellects that French anthropology has produced in the last half-century.   *P.* 28.

LIBER. The phloem or inner bark which lies nearest to the alburnum or sapwood; one of the three layers which make up the bark of pteridophytes.   *P.* 79.

LIFU. The largest and most populous (7,000) of the Loyalty Islands.   *P.* 22, 29.

LINTON (Ralph). American anthropologist noted for his tendency to offer psychological interpretations of social phenomena.   *P.* 271.

LOBSIGER-DELLENBACH (Marguerite Elisabeth). Swiss anthropologist and Director of the Ethnographic Museum and Institute of Geneva.   *P.* 115.

LONDON MISSIONARY SOCIETY. A non-denominational association of Protestant missions. Responsible, in the 18th century, for the first successful evangelisation in Oceania, starting from Tahiti and reaching as far as Papua. It later handed over its responsibilities in French Polynesia and New Caledonia to the Société des Missions de Paris.   *P.* 28.

LOUISIADE (Archipelago). Group of islands to the east of New Guinea.   *P.* 315.

LOYALTY (Islands). Group of high coral atolls to the east of New Caledonia (13,000 inhabitants). Converted to Christianity early, they played a part in the conversion of the neighbouring group for which they also provide large numbers of industrial and mine workers. A lack of ports and good communications and of markets for their primary products (the soil is rich), contribute to their poverty which in turn leads to a marked devotion to traditional forms of society.   *P.* 11, 15, 22, 25, 42.

LUOMALA (Katharine). American anthropologist of Finnish origin and Professor at the University of Hawaii. Has specialised in Polynesian mythology.   *P.* 73.

MABUIAG. One of the islands of Torres Strait.   *P.* 60   *fig.* 46.

MACCLUER (Gulf). A large re-entrant on the western peninsula of New Guinea.   *P.* 307.

MACLAY (Count Miklucho). 19th-century Russian explorer who visited New Guinea in 1874. Successful in gaining the confidence of the people of the Rai coast by his humane attitude. Despite his efforts they were annexed by Germany, since the Tsarist government would not accept responsibility for so remote a colony.   *P.* 264.

MAEWO (Or Aurora Island). Discovered by Bougainville in 1768. Earlier (1606) Quiros had thought it formed part of Raga or Pentecost to the north of which it lies. The population has seriously decreased.   *P.* 35, 91.

MAIU. Semi-divine hero whose myth links Cape York peninsula with certain islands of the Torres Strait (Yam).   *P.* 60.

MAKEMAKE. A divinity—half man, half bird—whose

personification by a man formed the theme of the year's most important ritual cycle on Easter Island. (Cf. Métraux: *Easter Island. A stone-age civilization of the Pacific*, London 1957.)   *P.* 135, 370.

MALEKULA (Or Mallicolo).   One of the largest and most populous (12,000) islands of the New Hebrides: includes the islets on its east and south coasts whose inhabitants cultivate on the main island.   Except for a large, pagan population (1,500) on the Big Nambas plateau of the north peninsula, the centre of the island is virtually empty, the main population being found in Christian (mostly Presbyterian) coastal villages.   *P.* 35, 42, 50, 64, 71, 79, 91, 104, 112, 117, 121, 133, 229, 231   *fig.* 54, 81, 85, 93-95, 209, 210, 221, 222, 224-229, 231, 233.

MALINOWSKI (Bronislaw) (1884-1942).   British anthropologist of Polish origin.   Founder of social anthropology in England.   He revolutionised field-work, but his total mistrust of historical perspective has not found acceptance except, perhaps, in England.   He even sought to disregard the structural aspects of kinship, wishing to concentrate upon their functional aspect alone, but this idea too died with him.   All his publications on the Trobriand Islands are of the highest value.   *P.* 3, 73, 95.

MALO (Island).   In the New Hebrides, to the south-east of Espiritu Santo, whose native inhabitants, reduced to a mere 400, live in scattered hamlets in the interior, the coast being alienated to European colonists.   Malo was an important link between the east coast of Espiritu Santo, north-east Malekula and western Aoba.   *P.* 229   *fig.* 211.

MAMAIA.   A messianic movement, pagan revivalist and anti-European, in Tahiti, at the beginning of the 19th century. (Cf. Segalen, Victor: *Les immémoriaux*. Plon, Paris, 1956.)   *P.* 49.

MANSIP (Deity).   A local divinity of south-east Malekula. His main role is as son-in-law of the ogress Nevinbumboau in the puppet display called Nevinbür.   *P.* 133, 134.

MAPRIK.   A region on the left bank of the middle Sepik, in the Prince Alexander Mountains area of eastern New Guinea.   *P.* 170-171   *fig.* 58, 61, 73, 140-143, 146, 147.

MARAKIHAU.   Marine goddess who eats men, in Maori mythology.   *P.* 352.

MARIANAS (Islands).   One of the most important archipelagos in Micronesia; under U.N. Trusteeship.   The best known island is Guam (American) which prospers as a result of the large military base, and has the highest population, (60,000), the other islands having no more than 8,000.   The islands were discovered by Magellan in 1521; his officers called them Ladrones (Islands of Robbers) but the sailors preferred Islas de las Velas Latinas, from the lateen sails of the local canoes.   The Spanish conquest of the archipelago was long and costly for the local people, the Chamorros, whose resistance reduced their numbers

from 100,000 to 5,000.   The islands have since been ruled by the Germans and the Japanese.   *P.* 18, 21.

MARQUESAS (Islands).   Archipelago in French Polynesia consisting of two groups of islands, the north-western includes Nuku Iva and the south-eastern Hiva Oa.   *P.* 18, 25, 77, 108, 120, 125, 135, 336, 352, 364, 371, 380   *fig.* 377-383.

MARSHALL (Archipelago).   A Micronesian group under American trusteeship.   The islands are named after their discoverer in 1788.   Under nominal Spanish rule, then German and later Japanese.   Among the hundreds of coral islets which form the 34 atolls are Eniwetok and Bikini, the atomic test sites.   *P.* 21.

MASSIM.   The name given to the cultural zone consisting of the eastern tip of New Guinea and the archipelagos which lie off it in the Coral Sea, d'Entrecasteaux, Louisiade, Trobriands, and Woodlark.   *P.* 101, 104, 175, 283, 315, 316, 320, 325   *fig.* 74.

MATTY (Or Wavulu island).   A Micronesian island immediately to the west of the Admiralty Islands.   *P.* 22, 394   *fig.* 406.

MAUSS (Marcel) (1872-1950).   French sociologist and anthropologist.   The true founder of the French school of anthropology, whose first professional workers he trained.   *P.* 134.

MAUTIKITIKI.   A Polynesian hero, centre of a highly developed cycle of myths found both in Polynesia and in parts of Melanesia (particularly the New Hebrides). Although never the centre of a cult, in Polynesia at least, he is the god of the yam first-fruits in Melanesia and the origin of fire is ascribed to him.   He paid with his life for his attempt to save human beings from death.   *P.* 68

MEAD (Margaret).   American anthropologist, born in 1901, who gained a reputation among a wide public for her hypotheses on the social origin of sexual behaviour.   Her scientific work has been concerned with Samoa, the Admiralty Islands and the valley of the Sepik.   *P.* 175.

MEALDEI.   Student at a teacher training school in Papua whose illustrations of a kiwai creation myth were preserved by Ward Goodenough of Philadelphia University·   *P.* 137.

MELANESIAN MISSION.   An Anglican mission, linked with the Anglican diocese of New Zealand.   Founded in 1841 by Bishop George Augustus Selwyn.   The first mission in the Pacific to train Melanesians for the Church.   *P.* 135.

MENDAÑA de NEIRA (Alvaro) (1549-1595).   Spanish sailor and explorer.   Responsible for the discovery of the southern part of the Marquesas in 1595, particularly of Hiva Oa and Fatu Hiva.   *P.* 325.

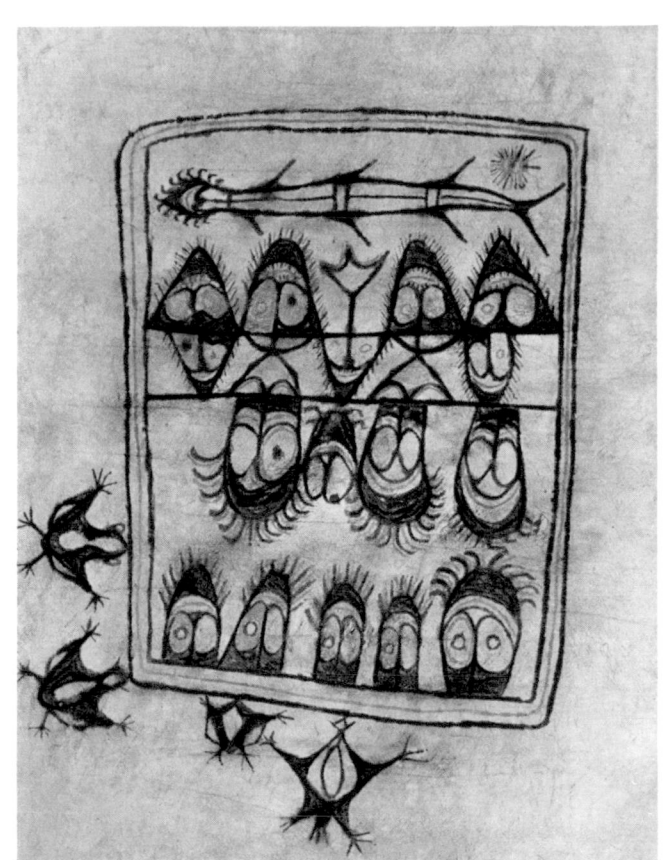

421. Lake Sentani. *Skirt*, Amsterdam - 422, 423. New Guinea. Papua. Turama river delta. *Door of a long-house*, Basle.

411

MERAT (or Samma Island). Situated off the north coast of western New Guinea and noted for its canoe-prows carved in the form of frigate birds. Visited by Prince Roland Bonaparte. *fig.* 303-306.

MÉTRAUX (Alfred). Swiss explorer and anthropologist, best known for his work on Easter Island and South America, and for long one of the directors of the UNESCO Amazonia project. Became a French citizen and director of studies at the École Pratique des Hautes Études. One of the best of the first generation of French-trained anthropologists. Recently published an important work on Haitian voodoo. Died 1963. *P.* 370.

MOAI KAVAKAVA. Name of the incurved male statues of haggard aspect from Easter Island. *P.* 125, 370 *fig.* 89, 90.

MOAI PAEPAE. Name of the flat female statues from Easter Island. *P.* 125, 370.

MOERENHOUT (Jacques-Antoine) (1796-1879). United States consul, then French consul at Tahiti as well as a trader. One of the most important of the early writers on French Polynesia, with a two-volume work: *Voyage aux îles du Grand Océan* (1837). *P.* 60, 68.

MOTONUI. A small inhabited islet at the south-west point of Easter Island. Each year the first person to take a sea-swallow's egg from a nest on the island becomes the temporary representative of the god Makemake. *P.* 135.

MUNDUGUMOR. A people living on the banks of the Yuat, a tributary of the Sepik, known through the work of Margaret Mead (q.v.). *P.* 175, 176 *fig.* 181-187, 431.

MURCHISON (Mountains). A chain of rocky peaks springing from the desert and separating central Australia from the Northern Territories. The range occupies an important place in local ritual. *P.* 128.

MUSCHU (Island). Off the north coast of Eastern New Guinea, to the west of the mouth of the Sepik. *P.* 179.

NANGGA. A semi-esoteric ritual of sexual connotation dedicated to the cult of ancestors. Confined to the west part of the island of Viti Levu, Fiji. *P.* 57.

NEW BRITAIN. The largest island off the north coast of eastern New Guinea. Its population, estimated at more than 100,000, is administered in inverse ratio to their distance from the administrative centre Rabaul, the old German administrative headquarters, located in an extinct volcanic crater on the tip of the Gazelle peninsula. The population, Tolai, a Melanesian people, is one of the richest, through owning cocoa plantations, and one of the most mobile in the territory. *P.* 9, 77, 104, 176, 230, 271, 282, 283, 294, 295 *fig.* 277, 281.

NEW CALEDONIA. Pacific archipelago. A French terri-

tory with 72,500 inhabitants. *P.* 8, 10, 11, 12, 15, 16, 17, 18, 21, 22, 24, 25, 41, 44, 55, 64, 79, 80, 89, 92, 95, 101, 104, 114, 115, 122, 124, 252-254, 265, 316 *fig.* 2, 5, 22, 88, 99, 137, 236, 239-241, 243, 245, 246.

NEW GUINEA. A Pacific island bordered on the south by the Coral and Arafura Seas which, together with Torres Strait, separate it from Australia. The eastern part was administered by Australia, the western by the United Nations until 1 May 1963. *P.* 2, 3, 4, 5, 8, 10, 11, 14, 15, 16, 21, 22, 24, 25, 28, 32, 76, 77, 92, 95, 99, 104, 108, 135, 139, 140, 176, 177, 282, 283, 320, 392 *fig.* 9, 27, 50, 71, 91, 307, 316, 319.

NEW HEBRIDES. Pacific archipelago to the north-east of New Caledonia; an Anglo-French condominion. (65,000 inhabitants). *P.* 10, 11, 15, 21, 22, 25, 29, 34, 52, 77, 79, 91, 92, 99, 104, 108, 110, 112, 114, 117, 118, 229-231, 282, 392 *fig.* 211, 216, 218.

NEW IRELAND. This island, with its 38,000 inhabitants, is one of the more densely populated of the New Guinea group under Australian trusteeship. It is famous for its sculpture which was popularised between the wars by avant-garde European artists. *P.* 50, 51, 103, 134, 283, 293-295, 320, 321, 326 *fig.* 35, 36, 38, 72, 274, 283-297.

NEW ZEALAND. Pacific archipelago, to the south-east of Australia, which forms a dominion of the British Commonwealth (2,400,000 inhabitants). *P.* 5, 14, 15, 18, 25, 28, 49, 68, 89, 120, 125, 336, 352-353, 364, 380 *fig.* 16, 76, 92, 365-376.

NISSAN (Island of). A coral atoll lying off south-east New Ireland and near to Buka. Also known as Sir Charles Hardy Island or Ile Verte (1,500 inhabitants). *P.* 22, 294.

NOGUGU. An island of potters on the north-west coast of Espiritu Santo, New Hebrides. *P.* 77.

NOTU. A black pigeon of the New Caledonian and New Hebridean forests. *P.* 52, 89, 92, 253.

NUKU HIVA. One of the larger islands of the Marquesas, though having less than 1,000 inhabitants. Visited in 1791 by Ingraham and Marchand. Once attached to Taiohae, the headquarters of the group. Famous in the literature for the wars between the Haopa and the Taipi and the adventures of Herman Melville. *P.* 18, 364.

NUR TOMBOI. An island lying across the southern end of Suroit, or South West Bay, Malekula. Also known as Ten Stick Island from the value in sticks of tobacco of this small fragment of land. *P.* 133.

OLIVER (Douglas). American anthropologist, professor at Harvard University. Studied in Vienna and worked before the war in south-east Bougainville. His studies on the Siuai are among the most detailed and comprehensive which we have on this region. Intellectually he ranks with Malinowski and Raymond Firth. Later, after working on development plans for Micronesia under American trusteeship, he undertook a long series of investigations in French Polynesia, assisted by a team of researchers, to whom we are indebted for the change from fantasy with which Tahitian studies had been previously encumbered. *P*. 34, 56.

ONTONG JAVA. A Polynesian atoll (600 inhabitants) to the north of the Solomons. Discovered by Mendaña (q.v.), in 1568. Its present name was given to it by the Dutch navigator Tasman in 1634. Also called Lord Howe Island. Studied by Australian anthropologist Ian Hogbin. *P*. 22.

O'REILLY (Father Patrick). Anthropologist, born 1900, of the Society of Mary. His work on Bougainville unfortunately remains unpublished, but he is known as a historian of the Pacific and as Secretary General of the Société des Océanistes in Paris. A booklover and scholar who occupies a special place in his Order and in the small world of scholars concerned with the Pacific. *P*. 135, 136, 325.

ORO (Deity). Polynesian god of war and patron deity of the Arioi in their public rituals on esoteric beliefs, according to the published material. Well before the first European contacts an attempted unification of Tahiti and the Leeward Islands was made in his name. *P*. 58, 125, 338.

PALAU (Or Peleu Islands). Part of the Carolina Islands. The native name for Palau is Babelthuap. Discovered by Villalobos in 1543; a group of more than 200, whose headquarters is Koror. The whole group has less than 9,000 inhabitants. *P*. 18, 392 *fig*. 415, 416.

PANDANUS. Monocotyledon plant. Much sought for ornamental purposes. Its leaves, cut into ribbons and treated, are used to make baskets. *P*. 79, 85, 88.

PAPUA. Part of Australian New Guinea; Port Moresby is the administrative headquarters. *fig*. 110-118, 418-420, 422, 423, 426, 432, 434, 435, 438.

PARKINSON (R.). Anthropologist, noted for his work on the former German territories of eastern New Guinea and the northern Solomons. *P*. 112.

PATA. Native name for a traditional dance on Ambrim, New Hebrides. Mainly connected with circumcision ceremonies, the dance has satirical elements. *P*. 72.

PATTESON (John Coleridge) (1827-1871). Missionary and subsequently Anglican bishop in Melanesia where he succeeded G. Selwyn. Like the latter he avoided the superiority complex of his contemporaries and organised the church in such a way that Melanesians as well as Europeans were ordained. He was killed in Santa Cruz by the natives in revenge for brutalities committed by a labour recruiter who used to dress in episcopal robes. *P*. 63.

PATYI. A language spoken in the Kone Ponerihuen—Poindimie and Poya regions of New Caledonia. *P*. 252.

PENTECOST (Or Raga Island). Discovered by Quiros in 1606, named Pentecost by Bougainville in 1768. A coral formation, relatively densely populated (5,000), especially in the north. Pentecost is very mountainous and includes a number of groups who resist European influence. *P*. 101, 117, 229, 230, 231 *fig*. 232.

PIG. Employed as currency in commerce. 36, 37, 38, 103, 117, 118.

PIJEVA. A protean divinity and lord of the undersea world of the dead, for central and northern New Caledonia. He has eyes all over his body, and he may appear as a shark, a lizard, a turtle or in the form of the air bubbles at the foot of a waterfall. He is impersonated by a masker. *P*. 64.

PINES (Isle of). An extension, to the south-east, of French New Caledonia. With 600 inhabitants. Consists of an ironstone mass surrounded by a heavily dissected coral plateau. Visited by Cook who gave it its name. The chieftainship, which was of Loyalty Islands origin, was one of the most important in the region because of its political and military dynamism and maintained relations of varying degrees of hostility with the first Europeans who were attracted to the island by its sandalwood. The existence of this commodity, of great value in the Chinese market, was first disclosed by a sailor on the *Undine*, the ship of Bishop Selwyn of the Melanesian mission. *P*. 22, 29, 42 *fig*. 1, 237.

PONERIHUEN. A region in the middle of the east coast of New Caledonia. The French form of *Pwêhê*, head, *iriwê*, of the river, one of the centres of the Patyi language speakers (q.v.). *P*. 75.

POTLATCH. A term from the north-west coast of North America, applied to the ceremonial display of goods of which part is destroyed and the other given to an adversary whose prestige diminishes unless he can offer and destroy goods to a greater value than those originally displayed. By extension the term is applied to all similar forms of institutionalised exchanges. *P*. 34.

POTSDAMHAFEN. Former German administrative centre on the north coast of eastern New Guinea east of the Sepik. *P*. 177, 178 *fig*. 191, 192, 196.

PURARI. The second longest river in Papua, navigable for 120 miles. *P*. 132, 146.

QUATREFAGES DE BREAU (Jean-Louis-Armand) (1810-1892). French naturalist and anthropologist. *P*. 16.

QUEENSLAND. A state in Australia which covers the north-east part of the continent. The aboriginal tribes of the north coast, especially of Cape York Peninsula, were in contact with Papua through the inhabitants of the island in Torres Strait. *P*. 2.

RAI (coast). Name of a coastal region between Wewak and Madang on the north of eastern New Guinea. Was studied by the first specialist in New Guinea, the Russian, Count Miklucho Maclay, before the territory became a German possession. *fig.* 69.

RAMBARAMB. South and south-east Malekula. A funerary figure constructed from vegetable matter six months after the death of the man whose body it represents. The dried skull with a face modelled on it is placed on top. The figure carries all the material symbols of the dignities and grades occupied by the man in his lifetime. *P.* 50, 122, 133, 230 *fig.* 221, 222.

RAMU. River in the north part of eastern New Guinea. Its mouth is close to that of the Sepik. *P.* 177 *fig.* 194, 197, 198.

RAROTONGA. The largest but not the most highly populated (7,500) of the Cook Islands. Has always maintained close relations with French Polynesia. *P.* 68 *fig.* 352, 353.

RENNELL (Island). Polynesian island, 100 miles south of Solomons. A coral formation like its neighbour Bellona. Has a fresh-water lake. Discovered by Butler in 1801: long protected against outside influences by the British Government. Unfortunately only Tikopia has been completely studied, by Raymond Firth. 1,500 inhabitants. *P.* 22.

RIVERS (W.H.R.) (1864-1922). The British founder of modern Pacific anthropology. Harshly criticised by his successors and now re-established. The quality and speed of his investigations is astonishing when one realises how little time he spent on each project. His great work *History of Melanesian Society* is still of value and the chapter on the Banks Islands is the best that has been written on this group. *P.* 31.

RIVET (Paul) (1876-1958). French anthropologist, professor at the Musée d'Histoire Naturelle de Paris. Founder of the Musée de l'Homme, who, by his acumen, was able to obtain the necessary funds for it. He attracted as his associates in this project the leading men of the day: Marcel Mauss, Georges-Henri Rivière, Lucien Levi-Bruhl, Maurice Leenhardt and Marcel Griaule. *P.* 27, 28.

ROTUMA. Polynesian island, (4,500 inhabitants), 300 miles north of Fiji, formerly a tributary of the maritime empire of Tonga: a British possession. Discovered by Edwards, in the *Pandora*, in 1791, during his fruitless search for the Bounty mutineers. *P.* 25, 28, 92.

RURUTU. Island in the Austral group, French Polynesia, discovered by Cook in 1777. 1,300 inhabitants. *P.* 337 *fig.* 354.

SAGO PALM. Group of Malaysian palms, especially of the Metroxylon genus, which yields sago, and is cultivated as a food producer. *P.* 10, 77, 84, 96, 99, 161, 174, 230, 307.

SAMOA. One of the main Polynesian archipelagos, first visited by the Dutchman Roggeveen in 1722. Now divided into Western Samoa, originally German, then under New Zealand trusteeship and now independent (100,000), and Eastern Samoa which is American. *P.* 18, 22, 25, 28, 40, 41, 77, 88, 92, 336, 337, 338.

SAN CRISTOBAL. One of the main islands in the south-east of the Solomons group (8,500 inhabitants). *P.* 135, 136 *fig.* 329, 334, 335, 339, 342.

SANTA CRUZ (Islands). A group lying to the north of the New Hebrides, but coming under the British protectorate of the Solomons. Discovered by Carteret in 1767 and the scene of the shipwreck of the French navigator Lapérouse in 1788. (6,000 inhabitants). *P.* 103, 104, 392 *fig.* 62, 410, 412-414.

SENIANG. Name given on Malekula to a cultural region stretching from Tomman island in the south to the southern part of Suroît or South West Bay. Very detailed study by the British anthropologist A.B. Deacon (1903-1927) whose grave dominates the bay on the northern edge of the region. *P.* 134.

SENTANI (Lake). North-east of western New Guinea, overlooking Humboldt Bay and the site of the territory's capital, Hollandia or Kota Baru. *P.* 154, 160-161, 177, 307 *fig.* 63, 126-136, 421, 436, 437.

SEPIK. The principal river of New Guinea which flows for much of its course through a marshy plain. Formerly called Empress Augusta River. *P.* 79, 85, 92, 96, 101, 104, 110, 140, 160, 170-179, 229, 230, 271, 282, 325 *fig.* 13, 18, 29, 31, 37, 44, 45, 55, 56, 65, 77, 96, 97, 145, 149, 150, 151, 153, 157, 161-163, 166-171, 173-180, 188-190, 193, 195, 199, 200, 204, 428-430.

SHARP (Andrew). A New Zealand writer who has stated the problem of Oceanian migrations in fruitful and concrete terms in his book *Ancient voyagers in the Pacific*. 1956. *P.* 29.

SHEPHERDS (Islands). A group of small volcanic islands scattered between Epi and Efate in the centre of the New Hebrides. *P.* 39, 230.

SIGAI. Divine hero whose myth records the links between the islands of the Torres Strait and Cape York peninsula. *P.* 60.

SIOVILI. Name of the founder of a syncretistic sect in Samoa which represented a reaction against missionary authoritarianism at the beginning of the 19th century. *P.* 49.

SIAUI. A people in the south-east of Bougainville known through the work of Oliver (q.v.). *P.* 34, 35, 56.

SOCIETY (Islands). Name of a volcanic archipelago, the principal island being Tahiti (22,500 inhabitants). *P.* 25, 28, 57, 66, 68, 89, 92, 122, 352.

SOLOMON (Islands). Discovered by Alvaro de Mendana (q.v.) in 1567, and one of most important archipelagos in Melanesia. Ten large islands and dozens of small ones, stretching in an arc from the northern New Hebrides in the south-east to New Guinea in the west. 110,000 inhabitants. *P.* 8, 15, 21, 22, 25, 91, 92, 98, 99, 104, 135, 136, 315, 320, 325-326, 392 *fig.* 66, 75, 98, 100, 101, 330-333, 336, 341.

SOMUK. A part-time Melanesian artist, born at Buka in about 1900. Brought to notice by Father O'Reilly. *P.* 136.

SPEISER (Felix) (1880-1949). Swiss anthropologist. Known for his studies on the New Hebrides and New Guinea. From 1942 Director of the Ethnographic Museum, Basle. One of the great figures of Oceanian anthropology. *P.* 173.

SPENCER (Sir Baldwin). Australian anthropologist, Director of the National Museum of Victoria at Melbourne. Famous for his work with Gillen (q.v.), on the Arunda and Warramunga peoples of central Australia. *P.* 127.

SPOEHR (Alexander). Formerly Director of the Bernice Pauahi Bishop Museum, and now chancellor of the East-West Center, University of Hawaii. A noted archæologist, whose scientific gifts are equalled by his organisational ability and his receptivity to new ideas. A great Oceanist. *P.* 21.

STOLPE (Knut H.). Swedish museum curator. See bibliography. *P.* 338.

SULKA. Name of a cultural zone in the north of New Britain. *P.* 79, 104, 282 *fig.* 47, 271, 272, 275, 279.

SWEET POTATO (*Ipomaea batatas*). Its name throughout almost the entire Pacific area is a variant on the Polynesian *kumula*. Its distribution includes South America. The sweet potato is an important factor in the study of migrations. Its distribution in the Pacific is in fact irregular and related to two systems of diffusion, one from classical Polynesia and the other, thanks to the Portuguese, from America to Indonesia and thence from west to east. *P.* 10, 12, 28.

TAHITI. Principal island of the Society archipelago. *P.* 45, 49, 125, 336, 338, 352 *fig.* 24, 52.

TAMBANUM. Locality on the Sepik. *P.* 174, 175 *fig.* 139, 165.

TAMI (Island). Small island in Huon Gulf, eastern New Guinea, famous for the products of its sculptors who work for the whole region. *P.* 99, 271 *fig.* 257, 266-269.

TANE (Deity). Polynesian demiurge, son of Rangi (Sky) and Papa (Earth). *P.* 67.

TANGAROA (Deity). Mistress of the Sea, among the Polynesians. In the south New Hebrides appears in the form of a turtle. *P.* 66, 67, 68, 337.

TANNA (Island). Not the largest, but the most populated (8,000) of the New Hebrides. Noted for the persistence since 1941 of a neo-pagan movement called 'John Frum', from the name of the Messiah who is its main mythical figure. Studied by Jean Guiart. *P.* 92, 229.

TAPA. Bark cloth widely used in Oceania. *P.* 79-85, 87-89, 92, 125, 127, 146, 161, 254, 265, 282, 336, 337, 371, 380 *fig.* 57, 63, 136, 256, 404, 421.

TARO. A tuber used as a staple foodstuff. Botanically the *Colocasia*, but in practice the term includes *Cyrtosperma*, *Xanthosoma* and *Amorphophallus* with lanceolate leaves and edible tubers. *P.* 10, 11, 12, 13, 34, 96, 99, 230, 364.

TENMARU. A locality in Big Nambas, Malekula. The name applies also to the associated anchorage. *P.* 71.

TEREI. Region in south-east Bougainville, adjoining that of the Siuai studied by Oliver. *P.* 326.

TIDORE (Sultanate of). A traditional Muslim sultanate in eastern Indonesia which used to receive a tribute of women and birds of paradise from western New Guinea. This tribute is put forward as proof of Indonesia's claims to that region. *P.* 307.

TIKI. Name of a human figure in eastern Polynesia which became a god in Maori mythology. *P.* 103, 108, 121, 125, 307, 364.

TIKOPIA (Island). Polynesian island off the eastern Solomons. Known through the detailed studies of Raymond Firth, which are remarkable for their accuracy and for the fact that he made a follow-up study thirty years later. Discovered by Quiros in 1606. Usually overpopulated (1,500) and consequently a base for repeated small-scale migrations, traces of which are to be found in the Solomons and New Hebrides. *P.* 22, 29.

TOKELAU (Or Union Islands). A small Polynesian archipelago belonging to New Zealand and situated 270 miles to the north of Western Samoa. (1,700 inhabitants). *P.* 28.

TOMMAN. Small island at the south-east tip of Malekula which plays an important role in local tradition as the centre of the myth of the god Ambat and his four brothers. *P.* 133 *fig.* 33, 84.

TONGA. An extensive Polynesian archipelago, neither coral nor volcanic, which was the centre of an important maritime empire. Has been able to remain independent till today. War parties from Tonga made their presence felt as far as the Ellice Islands, Rotuma, Samoa and Fiji. *P.* 18, 22, 25, 28, 29, 39, 41, 66, 77, 88, 92, 104, 336, 337, 338, 353 *fig.* 14, 350, 364.

TONGARIKI. A small island (400 inhabitants) in the Shepherds archipelago. *P.* 39.

TORRES (Straits). Between New Guinea and Australia. The numerous small islands serve as stepping-stones between the two areas. *P.* 60, 132, 139, 143, 283 *fig.* 107-109.

TRIDACNA. A genus of lamellibranch molluscs which in the case of *t. gigas*, the giant clam, attain enormous size. *P.* 46, 76, 230, 254, 326 *fig.* 340.

TROBRIAND (Islands). An archipelago which lies off the eastern point of New Guinea. Famous through the work of the Anglo-Polish anthropologist Malinowski (q.v.). Administratively part of Papua. *P.* 3, 73, 315, 316, 326 *fig.* 68, 310, 311, 313-315, 317, 318.

TUAMOTU. A chain of atolls lying off north-east and east French Polynesia. The smallest island, Hereheretue, has 35 inhabitants, the largest, Rangiroa, 667. There are 38 administrative units but hundreds of islands (7,600 inhabitants). Studied by F. Stimson, K. Emory and B. Danielsson. *P.* 25, 67.

TUI TONGA. Name of the religious ruler of Tonga whose undoubted historical political power was transferred to palace chamberlains, the Tui Hakalaua, later the Tui Kanokupolu. The latter regained the title Tui Tonga, to their profit after their conversion to Methodism and their elevation to royalty in the 19th century. *P.* 66.

TUKA. An anti-European messianic movement, centred in Viti Levu, Fiji, about 1880. *P.* 49.

UA HUKA. Island in the Marquesas (300 inhabitants). *P.* 364.

UA PU. Island in the Marquesas (900 inhabitants). *P.* 364.

UEN. Island lying off the south-west coast of New Caledonia and consisting almost entirely of iron-pan. Less than 100 inhabitants. Its former importance stemmed from a deposit of serpentine, used for making discoidal blades of ceremonial axes. *P.* 254.

ULAWA (Island). Medium-sized (1,000 inhabitants) in the centre of the Solomons, culturally close to the large island of Malaita. *P.* 118 *fig.* 337, 338.

URUPWE (Deity). Name of the person figuring on the heads of the shell money of New Caledonia, who is none other than Pijeva the lord of the undersea world of the dead (q.v.). *P.* 64, 122.

UVEA (Island). The most northerly and most Polynesian of the Loyalty Islands. Its 3,000 inhabitants are partly descended from a migration in the second half of the 18th century from the Wallis Islands. The name Uvea derives, in the vernacular, from Wallis, which is also called Uvea. The inhabitants of the latter call the island from the Loyalty group *Uvea lalo.* *P.* 29.

VATGANAY. A rocky islet 22 miles north of Ureparapara in the Banks Islands which served as a landing point for canoes travelling between Banks and Tikopia. *P.* 29.

WAHGI. A high valley of eastern New Guinea which is densely inhabited by the Chimbu who are noted for dynamic economy in recent years. *fig.* 11, 17, 23.

WALLIS (Archipelago). A Polynesian group discovered by the British captain whose name it bears, in 1767. (6,000 inhabitants). *P.* 22, 25, 28, 88, 92, 336 *fig.* 57, 59, 60.

WARRAMUNGA. A people living to the north of the Arunda in central Australia and studied by Spencer and Gillen. *P.* 128.

WASHKUK. A tribe on the middle Sepik in eastern New Guinea. *P.* 170 *fig.* 137.

WILEMB. A linguistic region on the coast of the north part of Suroît Bay, south-west Malekula. *P.* 134.

WINGERT (Paul S.). American authority on primitive art and professor at Columbia University. If he had not been ill he would have been the author of this book, which would then have had the benefit of a life devoted to this subject. *P.* 271.

WIRZ (Paul). Anthropologist and collector of primitive art. See bibliography. *P.* 173.

WITU (Or French Archipelago). A group of small islands off south-west New Britain (4,000 inhabitants). *P.* 283 *fig.* 273, 282.

WUSI. A village of potters on the west coast of Espiritu Santo, New Hebrides. *P.* 77.

YAM. An island in Torres Straits. *P.* 60.

YEDYEBAN (Island). A small island in Pum Bay, in the north of New Caledonia, whose population consists of Lords of the Soil of the large island of Baaba which is a north-easterly extension of New Caledonia. *fig.* 48.

YUAT (River). A tributary on the right bank of the lower Sepik. *P.* 174, 175 *fig.* 181-187.

424. New Guinea Asmat. *Full-length male figures*. Michael C. Rockefeller collection - 425. New Guinea. Papua. Lower Fly river. *Figure for moguru rite*, British Museum - 426. New Guinea Papua. Turama river delta. *Figure for moguru rite*, Amsterdam.

 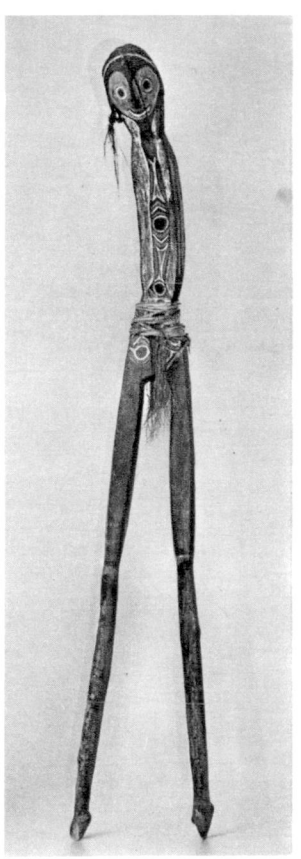

417

BIBLIOGRAPHY

Mlle Nicole Echard and M. Daniel de Coppet have assisted in the compilation of the bibliography.

ABBREVIATIONS

Genera

Bibliog.	Bibliography
Bull.	Bulletin
Fasc.	Fascicule
p.	Page
t.	Tome
vol.	Volume

Periodicals

Amer. Anthrop.	American Anthropologist, Menasha
Aust. Mus. Mag.	Australian Museum Magazine, Sydney
Aust. Mus. Rec.	Australian Museum Records, Sydney
B.P.B.M.	Bernice Pauahi Bishop Museum, Honolulu
B.S.E.O.	Bulletin de la Société d'Études Océaniennes, Papeete
Ethnol. Cran.	Ethnologia Cranmorensis, Chislehurst
I.A.E.	Internationales Archiv für Ethnographie, Leiden
J.A.I.	Journal of the Royal Anthropological Institute of Great Britain and Ireland, London
J.P.S.	Journal of the Polynesian Society, Wellington
J.S.O.	Journal de la Société des Océanistes, Paris
J.S.T.	Journal of Science and Technology, Wellington
M.A.G.W.	Mitteilungen der anthropologischen Gesellschaft in Wien
NZ Inst. Trans.	New Zealand Institute Transactions, Wellington
P.I.M.	Pacific Islands Monthly, Sydney.
Z.f.E.	Zeitschrift für Ethnologie

(The) Alan Wurtzburger Collections of Oceanic Art. *Baltimore Museum of Art, January 7 to March 4, 1956, foreword by Adelyn D. Breeskin, text by Paul S. Wingert and Douglas Fraser. A private collection containing very fine classical specimens.*

ANDRÉE (Richard). Holzfiguren von den Salomon-Inseln in *Globus, vol. 59, p. 6-8. Brunswick, 1891. Very fine decorated and carved pieces.*

ANTZE (Gustav). Ahnenfiguren aus Kreide von Neu-Mecklenburg in *Jahrbuch des Museums für Völkerkunde zu Leipzig, vol. 4, p. 37-42. Leipzig, 1911.*

ARCHER (W. G.) *and* MELVILLE (R.). 40.000 years of modern art. *A comparison of primitive and modern art. The Institute of Contemporary Arts. London, 1949.*

ARCHEY (Gilbert). Evolution of certain Maori carving patterns in *J.P.S., vol. 42, p. 171-190. Wellington, 1933. The characteristic forms of Maori art sprang from a development peculiar to New Zealand.*

ARCHEY (Gilbert). Wood carving in the North Auckland area in *Records of the Auckland Institute and Museum, vol. 1, no 4, p. 209-218. Auckland, 1933. Well illustrated.*

ARCHEY (Gilbert). Maori carving patterns in *J.P.S., vol. 45, p. 49-62. Wellington, 1936.*

ARCHEY (Gilbert). Maori carvings from the Three Kings Islands in *Records of the Auckland Institute and Museum, vol. 3, p. 207-209. Auckland, 1948. Article in a volume exclusively concerned with these islands.*

ARCHEY (Gilbert). South Sea folk in *Handbook of Oceanic Ethnology, Auckland War Memorial Museum. Auckland, 1949. This catalogue of a famous museum contains some brilliant and convincing notes on certain Maori art motifs.*

ARCHEY (Gilbert). Sculpture and design: an outline of Maori art in *Handbook of The Auckland War Memorial Museum. Auckland, 1955. A good introduction to Maori art.*

ARCHEY (Gilbert). Maori decorative art. Comment in *J.P.S. vol. 66, p. 60-63. Wellington, 1957.*

ARMATTOE (R. E. G.). An unusual food bowl from Melanesia in *Man, vol. 44, p. 46-47. London, 1944.*

L'Art des Océaniens in *Cahiers d'Art, vol. 4, nos 2-3, p. 57-119. Paris, 1929. Fasc. edited in collaboration with Tristan Tzara. Articles of varied merit covering the whole of the Pacific. Good photographs with careful notes.*

AUSTEN (Leo). Native handicrafts in the Trobriand Islands in *Mankind, vol. 3, no 7, p. 193-198. Sydney, 1945.*

Australian Aboriginal Art: bark paintings, carved figures, sacred and secular objects. *An exhibition arranged by the State Art Gallery of Australia, 1960-1961. Sydney, 1960.*

BAILEY (B. A. de Vore). Notes on Oceanian war clubs in *J.P.S., vol. 56, p. 3-17. Wellington, 1947. Collections of the University of Michigan Museum.*

BALFOUR (Henry). On the evolution of a characteristic pattern on the shafts of arrows from the Solomon Islands in *J.A.I., vol. 17. p. 328-332. London, 1887.*

BALFOUR (Henry). Evolution of decorative art of modern races of mankind. *Percival. London, 1893.*

BALFOUR (Henry). Bird and human designs from the Solomon Islands, illustrating the influence of one design over another in *Man, vol. 5, p. 81-83. London, 1905. Cf.: Records of the Past, August 1906, p. 253-255.*

BARRET (Ch.) and CROLL (R. H.). Art of Australian Aboriginal *(with a foreword by A. P. Elkin). The Bread and Cheese Club. Melbourne, 1943.*

BARROW (Terry). Maori decorating carving - an outline in *J.P.S., vol. 65, p. 305-331. Wellington, 1956. A good summary of Maori art and account of the various answers put forward to the problems which it poses.*

BARROW (Terry). Free-standing Maori images in *Anthropology in the South Seas. Essays presented to H. D. Skinner. Edited by J. D. Freeman and W. R. Geddes, p. 111-120. New Plymouth, 1959. A useful, new article showing what the persistence of a museum curator has to offer us.*

BARROW (Terry). Maori godsticks collected by the Reverend Richard Taylor in *Dominion Museum, Records in Ethnology, vol. 1, no 5, p. 183-211. Wellington, 1959. An interesting and accurate monograph on a subject which deserved an exhaustive study.*

BARTELS (Max). Über Schädelmasken aus Neu-Britannien, besonders über eine mit einer Kopfverletzung in *Festschrift für Adolf Bastian, Reimer, p. 231-246. Berlin, 1896.*

BARTHEL (Thomas S.). Female stone figures on Easter Island in *J.P.S., vol. 67, p. 252-255. Wellington, 1958.*

BASLER (Adolpho). L'Art chez les peuples primitifs. *Afrique, Océanie, Archipel Malais, Amérique et Terres Arctiques. Styles et Civilisations. Librairie de France. Paris, 1929. A general study of primitive art.*

BASTIAN (Otto). Sammlung aus Adamaua... der Osterinsel... in *Verhandlungen der Berliner Gesellschaft für Ethnologie, vol. 15, p. 301-302. Berlin, 1885.*

BATESON (Gregory). Social Structure of the Iatmül people in *Oceania, vol. 2, p. 245-291, 401-453. Sydney, 1932. Interesting illustrated notes on sculpture in the Sepik.*

BATESON (Gregory). Arts of the South Seas in *The Art Bulletin, n° 28, p. 119-123, New York, 1946. Comments on the arts of the Pacific at the exhibition organised by René d'Harnoncourt, Paul S. Wingert and Ralph Linton at the Museum of Modern Art, New York, 1940.*

BATESON (Gregory). Naven, a survey of the problems suggested by a composite picture of the culture of a New Guinea tribe drawn from three points of view. *1° ed.: Cambridge University Press, 1936. 2° ed.: Stanford University Press, Stanford, Calif., 1958. One of the fundamental works on the ethnology of New Guinea, regrettably marred by a psychoanalytical vocabulary. Excellent descriptions of rituals.*

BEASLEY (Harry Geoffrey). Rapa Nui: a stone image in *Man, vol. 23, p. 113. London, 1923.*

BEASLEY (Harry Geoffrey). A human and lotus form club in *Man, vol. 29, p. 181. London, 1929.*

BEASLEY (Harry Geoffrey). A carved wooden figure from Hawaii in *Man, vol. 32, p. 33. London, 1932.*

BEASLEY (Harry Geoffrey). Notes on a feather head-dress from the Cook group in *Ethnol. Cran., vol. 1, p. 13-16. Chislehurst, 1937.*

BEGOUËN (Le Comte H.). Deux bambous pyrogravés modèles pour tatouages des Iles Marquises in *Bulletin. Société d'Histoire Naturelle de Toulouse, vol. 57, p. 223-232. Toulouse, 1928.*

BEGOUËN (Le Comte H.) and DELLENBACH (Marguerite). Deux modèles de tatouages pyrogravés sur bambou, provenant des Iles Marquises in *Archives Suisse d'Anthropologie Générale, t. 6, p. 191-200. Geneva, 1932-1934.*

BERGMAN (Bengt). Easter Island in the Ethnographical Museum of Sweden in *Ethnos, vol. 2, n° 4, p. 102-115. Stockholm, 1937.*

BERNDT (Ronald M.). The evolution of the human motif in Papuan arrow designs in *Records of The South Australian Museum, vol. 6, p. 297-308. Adelaide, 1939.*

BEST (Elsdon). Evolution of the tautau, a Maori pendant in *Man, vol. 15, p. 2-5. London, 1915.*

BEST (Elsdon). Two greenstone pendants in *J.S.T., vol. 3 p. 169. Wellington, 1921.*

BEST (Elsdon). Notes on the occurrence of the lizard in Maori carvings in *J.S.T., vol. 5, p. 321-335. Wellington, 1923.*

BIRÓ (Ludwig). Beschreibender Katalog der ethnographischen Sammlung... aus Deutsch Neu-Guinea (Astrolabe Bai und Berlinshagen). *Hungarian Academy and Museum, Hornyánszky, 2 vol. Budapest, 1899-1901.*

BODROGI (Tibor). Oceanian Art. *Corvina. Budapest, 1952. An incomplete account of the rich Oceanian collections of Budapest Museum, with excellent plates. A handsome volume which shows Bodrogi to be a versatile and scrupulous author.*

BODROGI (Tibor). Some notes on the ethnography of New Guinea in *Acta Ethnographica Academiae Scientiarum Hungaricae, t. 3, fasc. 1-4, p. 91-150. Budapest, 1953. The first important work of a productive writer who is fortunate to be working in a museum with rich collections of ancient Oceanian material.*

BODROGI (Tibor). Art in New Guinea. IV. Tago masks from the Tami Islands in *Acta Ethnographica, t. 5, fasc. 1-2, p. 189-193. North east of Huon Gulf.*

BODROGI (Tibor). Ein Beitrag zur Kunst der Gunantuna in *Acta Ethnographica Academiae Scientiarum Hungaricae, t. 8, fasc. 3-4, p. 345-348. Designs on flutes from Gazelle Peninsula, New Britain.*

BODROGI (Tibor). New Guinea style provinces, the style province 'Astrolabe Bay' in *Opuscula Ethnologica Memoriae Ludovici Biro Sacra, p. 39-99. Budapest, 1959. One of the best regional monographs available.*

BODROGI (Tibor). Art in North East New Guinea. *Publishing House of the Hungarian Academy of Sciences. Budapest, 1961. The author's best piece of work to date and the best documented regional art monograph that we have.*

BODROGI (Tibor). Kapkap in Melanesien in *Beiträge zur Völkerforschung, Hans Damm zum 65. Geburtstag. Veröffentlichungen des Museums für Völkerkunde zu Leipzig, Heft 11, p. 50-65. Berlin, 1961. Useful comparison between kapkap themes and certain ornamental motifs in malanggan bas-reliefs.*

BOUGE (Louis-Joseph). Notes sur trois statuettes de forme humaine, recueillies à Lifou, Iles Loyalty in *Revue d'Ethnographie et de Sociologie, t. 5, p. 65-67. Paris, 1914. 3 rare and interesting pieces.*

BOUGE (Louis-Joseph). Contribution à l'étude des pilons océaniens. *Larose. Paris, 1931. A note made interesting by its illustrations. A more complete version issued by the Bernice P. Bishop Museum,*

Honolulu (*Occasional Papers of the Bernice P. Bishop Museum, Honolulu, vol. 9, n° 2, p. 1-11).* Notes on the Polynesian Pounders. *Translated from the French by Kenneth Emory, Honolulu, 1930.*

BOUGE (Louis-Joseph). Poissons magiques des Iles Marquises. *Bibliophiles de la Société des Océanistes série documentaire n° 1. Paris, n. d. A useful presentation, in an unusual format, of some little-known objects.*

BRAUNHOLTZ (H.J.). An ancestral figure from New Ireland in *Man, vol. 27, p. 217-219. London, 1927.*

BRIGHAM (William T.). A preliminary catalogue of The Bernice Pauahi Bishop Museum of Polynesian Ethnology and Natural History. *Bishop Museum Special Publications, n° 1. Honolulu, 1892-1893.*

BRIGHAM (William T.). Old Hawaiian carvings found in a cave on the Island of Hawaii in *Bernice Pauahi Bishop Museum Memoir, vol. 2, n° 2. Honolulu, 1906.*

BRIGHAM (William T.). Hawaiian kapas from the collection in the Bernice Pauahi Bishop Museum, Honolulu. *Only three copies: British Museum, U.S. National Museum, Australian Museum.*

British Museum. Handbook to the Ethnographical Collections. 2nd ed. London, 1925. *An out-of-print work, most useful on account of its many illustrations.*

BROWN (J. Macmillan). Raivaivai and its statues in *J.P.S., vol. 27, p. 72-77. Wellington, 1918.*

BROWN (Rev. H. A.). Elema traditional art. *Papua and New Guinea Scientific Society, Annual Report and Proceedings. Port-Moresby, 1959. Valuable and rare data on the symbolism of motifs.*

BRYAN (E. H.). Artistic stone work in Hawaii in *Ipek vol. 7, p. 61-63. Klinkhardt und Biermann, Leipzig, 1931.*

BÜHLER (Alfred). Dyeing among primitive peoples in *Ciba review, n° 68, p. 2478-2512. Basle, 1948. A well documented study.*

BÜHLER (Alfred). Schmuck aus Muschel- und Schneckenschalen in Neu-Guinea in *Kosmos, 53e année, cahier 5, p. 231-236. Stuttgart, 1957. The author deals with an aspect of the art of New Guinea which is too often thought to be of minor importance.*

BÜHLER (Alfred). Heilige Bildwerke aus Neu-Guinea. *Führer durch das Museum für Völkerkunde und das Schweizerische Museum für Volkskunde Basel, Sonderausstellung. Basle, 1958. Reading this booklet, we can only regret that the Director of*

the Basle Museum has not yet produced his full-scale book. He has so much to tell us and so many beautiful things to show.

BÜHLER (Alfred). Kunststile am Sepik. *Sonderausstellung, Museum für Völkerkunde Basel, 1960. The first attempt to integrate the art of the upper Sepik into a general synthesis of the valley's art.*

BÜHLER (Alfred), BARROW (Terry) and MOUNTFORD (Charles P.). Ozeanien und Australien. Die Kunst der Südsee. *Holle-Verlag. Baden-Baden, 1962.* Oceania and Australia. The Art of the South Seas. *Methuen. London, 1962. The best book to date on Oceanian art, which is also the most complete; well presented. Barrow's contribution is a comprehensive chapter on New Zealand, though to some extent at the expense of other parts of Polynesia. Professor Bühler has contributed all his knowledge of New Guinea. An irritating omission is that of the museum numbers.*

BÜLOW (W. von). Die Tapa-Bereitung in *Internationales Archiv für Ethnologie, vol. 12, p. 66-75. Leiden, 1899. Technical analysis with ethnobotanical notes.*

BUREAU (G.). Les Masques. *Essai. Éditions du Seuil (Collection "Pierres Vives"), Paris. n.d.*

CAMPBELL (J.D.). The paru matau of Rarotonga in *Mankind, vol. 1, n° 5, p. 112-114. Sydney, 1932. About a fish-hook for shark, bonito and barracuda.*

Catalog der ethnologischen Sammlung der Neu Guinea-Compagnie. *Museum für Völkerkunde, vol. 46. Berlin, 1886.*

CHAPMAN (F. R.). On the working of greenstone or nephrite by the Maoris in *NZ. Inst. Trans., vol. 24, p. 479-539. Wellington, 1892.*

CHAUVET (Stephen). Les arts indigènes des colonies françaises. *Maloine & Fils. Paris, 1923. General study*

CHAUVET (Stephen). Sur l'art de l'archipel des Salomon en général et celui, inconnu, d'une de ses îles : île Trésorerie in *Cahiers d'art, vol. 4, n°s 2-3, p. 83-87, Paris, 1929. Noting the resemblance between the art of Treasury Island and of certain Indo-European peoples of Afghanistan, the author strays into a migration theory starting from some point in Eurasia. Good illustrations.*

CHAUVET (Stephen). Les arts indigènes en Nouvelle-Guinée *Société d'Éditions Géographiques, Maritimes et Coloniales. Paris, 1930. An essential work on account of its illustrations and the wonderful accuracy of the index to these.*

CHAUVET (Stephen). L'Ile de Pâques et ses mystères. *Éditions Tel. Paris, 1935. A collection of all the evidence before the Métraux-Lavachery Expedition. Still useful on account of its illustrations.*

CHEESEMAN (T.F.). An ancient carved pare in *J.P.S.,
vol. 28, p. 160. Wellington, 1919.*

CHRISTENSEN (Erwin Ottomar). Primitive art. *A Studio
Publication, Thomas & Crowell. New York, 1955.
A well-illustrated general work. South Seas and
Australia: chapter V, p. 265-312.*

CHURCHILL (William). Club types of nuclear Polynesia
in *Carnegie Institution of Washington, publication
n⁰ 255. Washington, 1917. A useful detailed paper.*

CLAUSEN (Raymond). Slit drums and ritual in Malekula,
New Hebrides in *Three Regions of Melanesian
Art: New Guinea and the New Hebrides, p. 16-20,
New York, 1960. An interesting attempt to base
an explanatation, in psychological terms, of the
function of the drum on unpublished material from
John Layard.*

CLOUZOT (H.) and LEVEL (A.). L'art nègre et l'art océanien. *Devambez. Paris, 1919.*

CLOUZOT (H.) and LEVEL (A.). Sculptures africaines et
océaniennes. *Colonies françaises et Congo belge.
Librairie de France. Paris, 1927.*

Collection André Breton et Paul Eluard. Sculptures d'Afrique,
d'Amérique et d'Océanie. *Hôtel Drouot, Paris,
1931. Oceania, Nos. 31-165, pls IV-XVI.*

Collection océanienne du voyage de la 'Korrigane'. Hôte
Drouot, Paris, 4-5 décembre 1961. *Lamentable
conclusion of a so-called scientific expedition.*

Collection Paul Ruppaley. Arts primitifs. *Hôtel Drouot,
Paris, 1930. 125 Oceanian specimens.*

Collection Roland Tual. Arts primitifs. *Hôtel Drouot, Paris,
1930. 68 Oceanian pieces.*

COOK (James). A catalogue of the different specimens of
cloth collected in the three voyages of Captain
Cook... with... account of the... manufacturing.
Alexander Shaw. London, 1787.

COWAN (James). The art craftmanship of the Maori in
*Art in New Zealand, vol. 2, p. 121-129, Wellington,
1929.*

CRANSTONE (B.A.L.). Melanesia: a short ethnography.
*British Museum. London, 1961. An unpretentious
and useful account of the Melanesian collections
in the British Museum. A long-awaited tool for
research.*

CRAWFORD (M. D. C.). Tapas of the South Seas in *Asia,
vol. 19, p. 1148-1153, New York, 1919.*

DAMM (Hans). Zeremonial-schemel vom Sepik (Kaiser
Wilhelmsland), in *Kultur und Rasse, Festschrift
zum 60. Geburtstag Otto Reches, p. 274-289,
Lehmans Verlag. Munich, 1939.*

DAMM (Hans). Unbekannte Zeremonial-Geräte von Rubiana
(Salomo-Inseln) in *Zeitschrift für Ethnologie, vol. 73,
p. 29-33. Berlin, 1941. Excellent technical descriptions. Figures of crocodiles with men or animals
between their jaws.*

DAMM (Hans). Polynesien. *Die Schatzkammer. Bd. 1.
Prisma-Verlag. Leipzig, 1959. A well-illustrated
presentation of a series of Polynesian pieces.*

DANIELSSON (B.). A unique Tahitian stone figure in
J.P.S., vol. 66, p. 396-397. Wellington, 1957.

DAVIDSON (Daniel Sutherland). Aboriginal Australian
and Tasmanian rock carvings and paintings in
*Memoirs American Philosophical Society, vol. V.
Philadelphia, 1936. Stressing that, in the present
day, Australia is the only continent where engraving
and painting on rock are normal means of expression,
the author summarises the styles and techniques
and examines the different sites by regions, with
an analysis of each.*

DAVIDSON (Daniel Sutherland). A preliminary consideration of Aboriginal Australian decorative art in
*Memoirs American Philosophical Society, vol. IX.
Philadelphia, 1937. General study of decorative
techniques, the objects decorated and the distribution
of themes and motifs.*

DAVIDSON (Daniel Sutherland). Oceania. *The Oceanic
collections of the University Museum in University
Museum Bull. 12, n⁰ˢ 3-4. Philadelphia, 1947.
A guide-book for museum visitors.*

DEACON (Arthur Bernard). Geometrical drawings from
Malekula and other islands of the New Hebrides
in *J.A.I., vol. 64, p. 129-175. London, 1934. Geometric designs carried out with the finger in the sand;
the line is unbroken and never crosses itself.*

DELLA SANTA (Elizabeth). Une exposition d'art primitif
aux Musées Royaux d'Art et d'Histoire in *Bulletin
des Musées Royaux d'Art et d'Histoire, vol. 4,
n⁰ 20, p. 1-15. Brussels, 1948.*

DELLA SANTA (Elizabeth). Figures jumelées et adossées
dans l'art du Pacifique in *Bulletin et Mémoire de
la Société Royale Belge d'Anthropologie et de
Préhistoire, t. 63, p. 94-104. Brussels, 1952. The
author advances the hypothesis that the figures
travelled by way of the Sunda Islands.*

DELLA SANTA (Elizabeth). La Galerie du Mercator.
Les collections polynésiennes et micronésiennes
des Musées Royaux d'Art et d'Histoire. *De Sikkel.*

423

Antwerp, 1952. Detailed presentation of a series of objects which marked the beginning of the author's fruitful work in Oceanian studies. The illustrations are inadequate.

DELLA SANTA (Elizabeth). Mélanésie. *Éditions de la Connaissance. Brussels, 1954. Catalogue of a pleasantly organised exhibition, with numerous illustrations which are well produced.*

DELLA SANTA (Elizabeth). L'oiseau qui lacère une tête humaine : un thème d'art commun à la côte occidentale des Amériques et à l'Océanie in *Mélanges Pittard, offerts au Professeur Pittard par ses collègues et ses amis en l'honneur de son 90e anniversaire, le 15 juin 1957, p. 331-358. Brive 1957. Comparison between American specimens and those from New Zealand, New Guinea and New Ireland. The author concludes that the theme travelled from America to Oceania.*

DELLA SANTA (Elizabeth). Arts de la Mélanésie. Catalogue de la salle n° 90 aux Musées Royaux d'Art et d'Histoire à Bruxelles. *A.C.L. Brussels, 1958. A comprehensive and well-illustrated catalogue which is a contribution to the study of the material. It is a pity that the author did not use more detailed descriptions than the usual 'ancestor figure', 'mask' which tend to mislead the reader.*

DELLENBACH (Marguerite) and LOBSIGER (Georges). Traité d'agriculture néo-calédonienne (igname et taro) gravé sur un bambou in *Archives Suisses d'Anthropologie Générale, t. 8, p. 55-70. Geneva, 1938. Detailed study of a design incised on bamboo.*

DELLENBACH (Marguerite) and LOBSIGER (Georges). Quelques scènes de la vie sociale, religieuse et matérielle des Néo-Calédoniens, gravées sur bambou in *Archives Suisses d'Anthropologie Générale, t. 8. v. 336-350, Geneva, 1939.*

DELLENBACH (Marguerite) and LOBSIGER (Georges). Essai d'interprétation de gravures néo-calédoniennes incisées sur bambou. Étude de onze bambous gravés inédits in *Archives Suisses d'Anthropologie Générale, t. 8, p. 105-148. Geneva, 1939.*

DELLENBACH (Marguerite) and LORIGER (Georges). Description d'un bambou gravé néo-calédonien des collections ethnographiques du Musée de Berne in *Archives Suisses d'Anthropologie Générale, t. 9, p. 320-324. Geneva, 1941.*

DELLENBACH (Marguerite) and LOBSIGER (Georges). Les bambous gravés néo-calédoniens du Musée de Bâle in *Verhandlungen der Naturforschenden Gesellschaft in Basel, vol. 52, p. 101-126. Basle, 1941.*

DELLENBACH (Marguerite) and LOBSIGER (Georges). Quelques aspects de l'existence des Néo-Calédoniens d'après leur bambous gravés in *Globus, vol. 81, p. 1-42. Geneva, 1942.*

DELLENBACH (Marguerite) and LOBSIGER (Georges). Les bâtons messages en Australie in *Archives Suisses d'Anthropologie Générale, t. 12, p. 108-115. Geneva, 1947.*

DELLENBACH (Marguerite) and LOBSIGER (Georges). Trois bambous gravés de Nouvelle-Calédonie in *Archives Suisses d'Anthropologie Générale, t. 15, n° 2, p. 154-172. Geneva, 1950.*

DELLENBACH (Marguerite) and LOBSIGER (Georges). Dessins réalistes et motifs symboliques gravés sur les bambous de Nouvelle-Calédonie in *Études sur l'Océanie, p. 318-329. Basle, 1951.*

DELLENBACH (Marguerite) and LOBSIGER (Georges). Description de trois bambous gravés de Nouvelle-Calédonie de la collection M. Ratton in *J.O.S., t. 6, p. 105-121. Paris, 1951.*

DELLENBACH (Marguerite) and LOBSIGER (Georges). Quelques aspects de la civilisation européenne gravés sur les bambous par les Néo-Calédoniens in *J.S.O., t. 7, p. 229-243. Paris, 1953.*

DELLENBACH (Marguerite) and LOBSIGER (Georges). Trois bambous gravés de Nouvelle-Calédonie in *Archives Suisses d'Anthropologie Générale, t. 22, p. 76-92. Geneva, 1957.*

DELLENBACH (Marguerite) and LOBSIGER (Georges). Deux bambous gravés de Nouvelle-Calédonie. *Collection de Lausanne in J.S.O., t. 14, p. 37-50. Paris, 1958. A sustained effort to make available a little known category of objects providing a mass of graphic material upon which we shall draw for a long time to come.*

DICKSON (T. Elder). Ceremonial lime spatulae from British New Guinea in *Man, vol. 43, p. 25-26. London, 1943.*

DIGBY (A.). A fisherman's chest from Tokelau and an inlaid coconut shell vessel from the Solomon Islands in *British Museum Quarterly, vol. 13, p. 48-50. London, 1938-1939.*

DODGE (Ernest Stanley). The Hervey Island adzes in the Peabody Museum of Salem. *Peabody Museum. Salem, 1937. 32 specimens.*

DODGE (Ernest Stanley). The Marquesas Islands collection in the Peabody Museum of Salem. *Peabody Museum. Salem, 1939. 155 specimens.*

DODGE (Ernest Stanley). Austral Islands tapa in *J.P.S., vol. 50, p. 107-113. Wellington, 1941.*

DODGE (Ernest Stanley). The New Zealand Maori collection in the Peabody Museum of Salem. *Peabody Museum. Salem, 1941. 156 specimens.*

DORMAN (P.) and MEIER (Josef). P. Matthäus Rasher, M.S.C., und Baining (Neu-Pommern) Land und Leute. I. Der Sammlung aus der deutschen Südsee. *Aschendorffscher Verlag. Münster, 1909.*

Easter Island wood carvings in *University Museum of Pennsylvania, Bull. vol. 6. Philadelphia, 1935.*

EDGE-PARTINGTON (James). Objects from the New Hebrides in *Cambridge University Museum, 17th report, p. 14. Cambridge, 1902.*

EDGE-PARTINGTON (James). A 'domestic idol' from Easter Island (Rapa Nui) in *Man, vol. 4, p. 73-74. London, 1904.*

EDGE-PARTINGTON (James) and HEAPE (Charles). An album of the weapons, tools, ornaments, articles of dress etc., of the natives of the Pacific Islands drawn and described from examples in public and private collections in England. *Privately printed by J. C. Norbury, 3 albums. Manchester, 1890-1898. Still the best documentary source for the material culture of Oceania despite a certain number of errors of attribution.*

EDGE-PARTINGTON (James) and JOYCE (Thomas Athol). Note on funerary ornaments from Rubiana and a coffin from Santa Anna in *Man, vol. 4, p. 129-131. London, 1904.*

EICHHORN (August). Alte Maori-Holzskulpturen in *Baessler-Archiv, vol. 2, p. 216-220. Berlin, 1911. Excellent account of ancient pieces with good photographs.*

EICHHORN (August). Die Herstellung von «Muschel-Perlen» aus Conus auf der Insel Ponam und ihre Verwendung im Kunsthandwerk der Admiralitäts-Insulaner in *Baessler-Archiv, vol. 5, p. 257-283. Berlin, 1916. Remarkable article on the manufacture and anthropological significance of shell money. The technology of the ornaments is less interesting.*

EICHHORN (August). Neuhebridische Spinngewebs-Masken mit Rudimenten eines Wangenschmucks und dessen Verbreitung in Melanesien in *Baessler-Archiv vol. 5, p. 284-292. Berlin, 1916. Illustrations and valuable notes.*

EICHHORN (August). L'art chez les habitants du fleuve Sepik (Nouvelle Guinée) in *Cahiers d'Art, vol. 4, nº 2-3, p. 73-78. Paris, 1929. Summary account of Sepik art based on the accompanying photographs.*

EINSTEIN (Carl). Plastiek uit den Bismarck Archipel in *Bijdragen tot de Taal-, Land- en Volkenkunde. Nederlandsch Indie, vol. 13, p. 209-216, 1928.*

ELKIN (Adolphus Peter) and BERNDT (Catherine and Ronald). Art in Arnhem Land. *London, Melbourne, 1950. The Australian edition suffers from the lack of the resources required for a work which should have been in colour. The text is as substantial and sound as usual with its authors. The first account of true sculpture in Arnhem Land.*

EMORY (Kenneth Pike). Hawaii: godsticks in *Ethnol. Cran., vol. 3, p. 9-10. Chislehurst, 1938.*

EMORY (Kenneth Pike). Hawaii: notes on wooden images in *Ethnol. Cran., vol. 2, p. 2-7. Chislehurst, 1938.*

ENGLAND (Peter). The Ramu Stones: notes on stone carvings found in the Annaberg-Atemble Area, Ramu Valley, New Guinea in *Mankind, vol. 3, nº 8, p. 233-236, Sydney, 1946.*

Exhibition of the art of primitive peoples at the Berkeley Galleries. *London, 1945. Catalogue: 30 examples of Oceanian art.*

FAGG (William). Traditional sculpture from the colonies. An illustrated handbook for the exhibition of traditional art from the Colonies held in the Art Gallery of the Imperial Institute, May to September 1951. *Colonial Office. London, 1951. Excellent photographs including 5 Oceanian pieces.*

FINSCH (Otto). Ethnologische Erfahrungen und Belegstücke aus der Südsee in *Annalen des Kaiserlich Königlichen Naturhistorischen Hofmuseums, Vienna, vol. 3, p. 293-364, 1888; vol. 6, p. 1-106, 1891; vol. 8, p. 293-383, 1893. Account of museum collections concerned with New Guinea, Bismark and Admiralty Islands.*

FINSCH (Otto). Tanzmaske von Südost-Neu Guinea in *Verhandlungen der Berliner Gesellschaft für Anthropologie, vol. 22, p. 423-425. Berlin, 1890.*

FINSCH (Otto). Ethnologische Erfahrungen und Belegstücke aus der Südsee in *Annalen des Kaiserlich Königlichen Naturhistorischen Hofmuseums, vol. 6, p. 2, p. 1-130. Vienna, 1891.*

FINSCH (Otto). Ethnologische Erfahrungen und Belegstücke aus der Südsee in *Annalen des Kaiserlich Königlichen Naturhistorischen Hofmuseums, vol. 8, pt. 2, Kusaie und Ponape, p. 1-436. Vienna, 1893.*

FINSCH (Otto). Papua-Töpferei in *Globus, vol. 84, p. 329-334. Brunswick, 1903.*

FINSCH (Otto). Südsee-Arbeiten. Gewerbe und Kunstfleiss. Tauschmittel und «Geld» der Eingeborenen in *Abhandlungen des Kolonial-Instituts, vol. 14. Hamburg, 1914. Remarkable work of classification and reproduction with extremely precise details.*

FIRTH (Raymond W.). The Maori carver in *J.P.S., vol. 34, p. 277-291. Wellington, 1925. On the origin, social status, methods of work and tools of the Maori sculptor.*

FIRTH (Raymond W.). Maori material in the Vienna Museum (Collected by A. Reischek) in *J.P.S., vol. 40, p. 95-102. Wellington, 1931.*

FIRTH (Raymond W.). Art and life in New Guinea. *Studio. London, 1936.*

FIRTH (Raymond W.). Bark cloth in Tikopia, Solomon Islands in *Man, vol. 47, p. 69-72. London, 1947.*

FISCHER (V.F.). Maori decorated sinkers in *Auckland Institute and Museum, Records, vol. 1, n° 3, p. 163-167. Auckland, 1932.*

FORGE (Anthony). Notes on Eastern Abelam designs painted on paper - New Guinea in *Three regions of Melanesian art, p. 12-15. The Museum of Primitive Art, New York, 1960. Interesting experiment with local artists, demonstrating the process of elaboration of decorative groups in the Abelam style.*

FORGE (Anthony). Three Kamanngabi figures from the Arabak people of the Sepik people, New Guinea. *Ibid. p. 6-9. A useful study of a particular type of sculpture which is localised and presented in context.*

FORMAN (Werner and B.). L'art des pays lointains. Égypte, Afrique, Amérique, Océanie, Indonésie. *Artia. Prague, 1956. An art volume with modest texts related to the illustrations and revealing the wealth of museum and private collections in Czechoslovakia. 45 specimens from Oceania.*

FOX (L.E.). The Threshold of the Pacific. *New York, London, 1924. Melanesian anthropology in the manner of Rivers but without his genius. Very useful for its non-theoretical sections.*

FREEMAN (J.D.). The Polynesian collection of Trinity College, Dublin, and the National Museum of Ireland in *J.P.S., vol. 58, p. 1-18. Wellington, 1949.*

FROBENIUS (Leo). Über oceanische Masken. Notizen über Masken und Maskeraden von Neu-Pommern und Duke of York in *I.A.E., vol. 10, p. 69-70. Leiden, 1897.*

FROBENIUS (Leo). Über oceanische Masken. 2. Über Fische in melanesischen Masken in *I.A.E., vol. 10. p. 206-209. Leiden, 1897-1898.*

FROBENIUS (Leo). Über oceanische Masken. 3. Über die Eidechsen in melanesischen Masken, 4. Über die Vögel in melanesischen Masken. 5. Schädelmasken in *I.A.E., vol. 11, p. 82-85, 130-132, 162-164. Leiden, 1898. In addition to a large number of magnificent plates, an attempt to classify masks which shows a great understanding of forms.*

FUHRMANN (Ernst). New Guinea in *Kulturen der Erde. Material zur Kultur- und Kunstgeschichte aller Völker, Bd. XIV. Folkwang Verlag. Hagen-in-W., 1922. A slight text but useful illustrations because comprehensive. The numbers of the specimens are lacking. The photographs are excellent.*

GARDI (René). Sepik. Land der sterbenden Geister. *Alfred Scherz-Verlag. Berne, Stuttgart, Vienna, 1958. An album of coloured photographs which are technically splendid; the choice of illustrations is admirable.*

GEISLER (W.). Die Kampfschilde der Jabim aus Deutsch Neu-Guinea in *Globus, vol. 94, p. 126. Brunswick, 1908. The technique of the manufacture of curved shields by fire-treatment.*

GIGLIOLI (Enrico Hillyer). Su due nuovi Hei-Tiki litici della Nuova Zelanda in *Archivio per l'Antropologia e la Etnologia, vol. 23, p. 83-86. Florence, 1893.*

GIGLIOLI (Enrico Hillyer). Delle ascie litiche di Mangaia e più specialmente della «toki mahia», simbolo di pace, e della triplice «tokitane-mata ariki» (Tabernacolo di Dio) in *Archivio per l'Antropologia e la Etnologia, p. 291-301. Florence, 1902.*

GIGLIOLI (Enrico Hillyer). La collezione etnografica del Prof. Enrico Hillyer Giglioli, Parte I. Australasia. *Soc. tipografica. Città di Castillo, 1911.*

GIRARD (Françoise). Deux sculptures maories au Musée de l'Homme in *J.S.O., t. 6, p. 279-282. Paris, 1951.*

GIRARD (Françoise). L'Océanie. In *André Malraux: Le Musée Imaginaire de la Sculpture Mondiale. Texte p. 748-751; ill. p. 419-441. Paris, 1952.*

GIRARD (Françoise). Les riches collections néo-calédoniennes du Musée de l'Homme in *J.S.O., t. 9, p. 302-306. Paris, 1953.*

GIRARD (Françoise). L'importance sociale et religieuse des cérémonies exécutées pour les malanggan sculptés de Nouvelle-Irlande in *L'Anthropologie, t. 58, n° 3-4, p. 241-267. Paris, 1954. An excellent museum study which is perhaps a little conventional in its conclusions.*

GIRARD (Françoise). Nouvelle-Guinée, Haut Morobé, Bas Sépik. *Musée de l'Homme. Paris, 1956. It is a pity that neither time nor funds allowed Mlle Girard to prepare a proper guide to this admirable exhibition to which this pamphlet does scant justice.*

GIRARD (Françoise). Acquisitions nouvelles du Département d'Océanie in *Objets et Mondes, t. 1, fasc. 2, p. 41-48. Paris, 1961. An incised bamboo, a New Caledonian gable-end and a figurine from the Lower Sepik.*

GOODENOUGH (Ward H.) and LITTLE (Keith). My father the crocodile in *University Museum Bulletin, vol. 17, n° 1, p. 38-47. Philadelphia, 1952. Shows that no document should be neglected. It would have been a pity if this text and drawings had not been published.*

GRAEBNER (Felix). Holztrommeln des Ramu-distriktes auf Neu Guinea in *Globus, vol. 82, p. 299-305. Brunswick, 1902. Study of the decorative motifs on the drums from Ramu and a comparison with Malayan drums.*

GRAHAM (Geo). «Rei puta», a Maori pendant in *J.P.S., vol. 32, p. 29-34. Wellington, 1923.*

GRAHAM (Geo). Te Kaoreore... as narrated by Pirika Te Miroi Tiniraupeka (Ohinemutu, January, 1936) in *J.P.S., vol. 52, p. 46-64. Wellington, 1943.*

GRIMBLE (Arthur). Canoe crests of the Gilbert islanders in *Man, vol. 21, p. 81-85. London, 1921.*

GROVES (William C.). Tabar to-day: a study of a Melanesian community in contact with alien non-primitive cultural influences in *Oceania, vol. 5, p. 346-360. Sydney, 1934-1935.*

GROVES (William C.). Secret beliefs and practices in New Ireland in *Oceania, vol. 7, p. 220-245. Sydney, 1936. Useful notes on the malanggan. Unfortunately we are still waiting for the monograph promised by the author who has been forced to change his career by the lack of research funds.*

GUIART (Jean). Les effigies religieuses des Nouvelles-Hébrides. Étude des collections du Musée de l'Homme in *J.S.O., t. 5, p. 51-86. Paris, 1949. A version, reduced in length by a third, of a monograph written in the author's youth.*

GUIART (Jean). Sociétés, rituels et mythes du Nord Ambrym (Nouvelles-Hébrides) in *J.S.O., t. 7, p. 5-103. Paris, 1951. A young anthropologist's first contact with his area. A museum training meant that objects were not forgotten in the study of institutions.*

GUIART (Jean). L'art autochtone de Nouvelle-Calédonie. *Éditions des Études Mélanésiennes. Nouméa, 1953. A popular study seeking to facilitate the survival of traditional artistic themes until they are renewed.*

GUIART (Jean). Notes sur les tambours d'Ambrym in *J.S.O., t. 12, p. 334-336. Paris, 1956. A note on a drum presented to the Musée de l'Homme by the author.*

HADDON (Alfred Cort). The decorative art of British New Guinea. A study in Papuan ethnography. *Cunningham Memoir n° 10, Royal Irish Academy. Dublin, 1894.*

HADDON (Alfred Cort). Evolution in art: as illustrated by the life histories of designs. *London, 1895. The author used illustrative material from British New Guinea above all. A whole chapter is concerned with the decorative art of that region.*

HADDON (Alfred Cort). Drawings by natives of British New Guinea in *Man, vol. 4, p. 33-36. London, 1904.*

HADDON (Alfred Cort). Decorative, pictorial and glyptic art in *Reports of the Cambridge Anthropological Expedition to Torres Straits, vol. 4, (Arts and Crafts), p. 342-393. Cambridge, 1912.*

HADDON (Alfred Cort). A new form of mask from the Sepik, Papua in *Man, vol. 23, p. 81-82. London, 1923.*

HADDON (Alfred Cort). The interpretation of Melanesian design in *Amer. Anthrop., vol. 37, p. 164-167. Menasha, 1935.*

HADDON (Alfred Cort) and BRAUNHOLTZ (H.J.). Notes on carved gopi boards from the Papuan Gulf area in *Man, vol. 31, p. 58. London, 1931.*

HAGEN (Karl). Die ornamentik der Matty-Insulaner in *Correspondenz-Blatt der Deutschen Gesellschaft für Anthropologie, vol. 28, p. 155-157; vol. 29, p. 62. Berlin, 1897-1898.*

HALL (Henry Usher). New Ireland masks in *The Museum Journal, vol. 10, n° 4, p. 184-187. Philadelphia, 1919 Two masks.*

HALL (Henry Usher). Maori woodcarving and moko in *The Museum Journal, vol. 11, p. 212-242. Philadelphia, 1920.*

HALL (Henry Usher). Woodcarvings of the Austral Islands in *The Museum Journal, p. 179-199. Philadelphia, 1921. One of the good articles on this subject.*

HALL (Henry Usher). Art of the Marquesas Islanders in *The Museum Journal, p. 252-292. Philadelphia, 1921. An old but still useful catalogue of a museum* collection. *Very detailed with a remarkably fine set of illustrations.*

HALL (Henry Usher). The orator's staff in *The Museum Journal, p. 293-309. Philadelphia, 1924. Interesting monograph on a set of Maori orators' staffs.*

HALL (Henry Usher). A woodcarving from Easter Island in *The Museum Journal, p. 125-131. Philadelphia, 1925. A lizard man.*

HALL (Henry Usher). A Maori feeding funnel in *The Museum Journal, vol. 19, p. 85-99. Philadelphia, 1928.*

HALL (Henry Usher). Malangan of New Ireland in *The University Museum Bulletin, vol. 5, nº 4, p. 3-11. Philadelphia, 1935. Brief presentation of a museum series.*

HAMILTON (Augustus). The art workmanship of the Maori race in New Zealand. *New Zealand Institute. Dunedin, 1896. The classic work on the subject in spite of its date.*

HAMILTON (H.). The Kaitaia carving in *J.P.S., vol. 30, p. 91-95. Wellington, 1921.*

HAMILTON (H.). *The Kaingaroa Carvings* in *J.P.S., vol. 34, p. 356-362. Wellington, 1925.*

HAMY (E.T.). Bambou gravé de la Nouvelle-Calédonie in *Magasin Pittoresque, Série 11, t. 1, 340-342. Paris, 1883.*

HANDY (Willowdean Chatterson). Tattooing in the Marquesas in *B.P.B.M., Bull. nº 1; Layard Dominick Expedition Publication nº 3. Honolulu, 1923.*

HANDY (Willowdean Chatterson). Handcrafts of the Society Islands in *B.P.B.M., Bull. 21, Honolulu, 1927.*

HANDY (Willowdean Chatterson). L'art des Iles Marquises. *Éditions d'Art et d'Histoire. Paris, 1938. Next to the definitive work by Karl von den Steinem this is a minor classic on the art of the Marquesas which retains its value on account of the aptness of many of the judgments.*

HESSE (Irene). Die Darstellung der menschlichen Gestalt in Rundskulpturen Neu-Mecklenburgs. *Welzel. Köln, 1933.*

HORNELL (James). The ornaments and decorative carvings of outrigger canoes on the north coast of Netherlands New Guinea in *J.P.S., vol. 32, p. 70-78. Wellington, 1923.*

HORNELL (James). The artistic degradation of Easter Island woodcarvings in *J.P.S., vol. 49, p. 282-284. Wellington, 1940.*

HOUSTON (John). Taranaki Maori carvings in *J.P.S., vol. 57, p. 301-303. Wellington, 1948.*

ISHIBASHI (B.). Hawaiian Art. Illustration of the creative art of Hawaii from the Bishop Museum Collection. *Honolulu Lithograph Co. Honolulu, 1951.*

IVENS (Walter G.). Melanesians of the South East Solomon Islands. *London, 1927. One of the best works on the Solomons. Retains its value on account of the descriptions of local institutions. The author loved the objects and the colours: his book reflects this love.*

IVENS (Walter G.). Solomon Islands clubs called «wari-ihau» in *Ethnol. Cran., vol. 2, p. 8-18. Chislehurst, 1938.*

JOYCE (Thomas Athol). A ceremonial 'mask' from the Sepik River, New Guinea in *Man, vol. 26, p. 1-2. London, 1926.*

KJERSMEIER (Carl). Ny Guineas Kunst. *Copenhagen, 1948. A good account of an exhibition centring on New Guinea.*

KNAPP (C.). Deux statuettes de l'Ile de Pâques in *Société Neuchâteloise de Géographie, Bull., vol. 20, p. 465-466. Neuchâtel, 1909-1910.*

KNOCHE (Walter). Waren die Toromiro der Osterinse Marionetten in *Zeitschrift für Ethnologie, vol. 59, p. 95-98. Berlin, 1927.*

KOOIJMAN (S.). Art of the Southwestern New Guinea, a preliminary survey in *Antiquity and Survival, nº 5, p. 343-372. The Hague, 1956. The author is particularly interested in decorated shields.*

KOOIJMAN (S.). De Kunst van Nieuw-Guinea. *Servire. The Hague, 1955. Excellent but insufficient illustrations with a text in Dutch.*

KOOIJMAN (S.). The Art of Lake Sentani. *Museum of Primitive Art. New York, 1959. One of the first post-war monographs on the art of Oceania which leaves little more to be said about the art of Lake Sentani.*

KRAEMER (Augustin). Die ornamentik der Kleidmatten und der Tatauierung auf den Marshall-Inseln, nebst technologischen, philologischen und ethnologischen Notizen in *Archiv für Anthropologie, vol. 29, p. 1-28, Brunswick, 1904.*

KRAEMER (Augustin). Die Malanggane von Tombara. *Müller. Munich, 1925.*

KRAEMER (Augustin). Die Malaiisch-Pazifische Kunst. In *Anton Springer: Handbuch der Kunstgeschichte, vol. 6, p. 657-696. Kröner-Verlag. Leipzig, 1929.*

427. New Guinea. Asmat. *Funerary figures*. Michael C. Rockefeller collection - 428. New Guinea. Sepik. Arambak. *Kamanggabi figure*, Basle - 429. New Guinea Tambanum Sepik. *Lime spatula detail*, Basle.

429

KRIEGER (Herbert W.). Design areas in Oceania based on specimens in the United States National Herbarium. *United States National Museum Proceedings, vol. 79. Washington, 1932.*

KÜHN (Herbert). Die Kunst der Primitiven. *Delphin-Verlag. Munich, 1923.*

KUPKA (Karel). Un art à l'état brut. Peintures et sculptures aborigènes d'Australie. *Édition Clairefontaine. Lausanne, 1962. An excellent presentation for the general public of a beautiful collection of bark paintings from Arnhem Land.*

LANDTMAN (Gunnar). Ethnographic collection from the Kiwai district of British New Guinea in the National Museum of Finland. *Commission of the Antell Collection. Helsingfors, 1933.*

LAROCHE (Marie-Charlotte). Notes sur quelques ornements de pirogue de la Nouvelle-Guinée Hollandaise - Baie de Walkener in *J.S.O., t. 5, p. 105-115. Paris, 1949. If Mme Laroche had been able to pursue this topic, we should have had the comprehensive study of the bird in New Guinea which we lack.*

LAROCHE (Marie-Charlotte). Petits outils Hawaiiens en bambou sculpté servant à décorer les tapas, conservés au Musée de l'Homme in *J.S.O., t. 7, p. 181-186. Paris, 1951. This article is the best we have until the material from the Bernice P, Bishop Museum is published.*

LAROCHE (Marie-Charlotte). Collection calédonienne du Muséum de Rouen in *J.S.O., t. 9, p. 320-322. Paris, 1953.*

LAROCHE (Marie-Charlotte). Société des Océanistes. Nouvelle-Guinée in *Objets et Mondes, t. 1, fasc. 3-4, p. 87-89. Paris, 1961. A collection of Papuan masks of recent manufacture presented to the Musée de l'Homme by the Australian Government.*

LAROCHE (Marie-Charlotte). Collection d'objets calédoniens du Musée de Toulouse in *J.S.O., t. 9, p. 307-319. Paris, 1953.*

LAVACHERY (Henri). Contribution à l'étude des statuettes en bois de l'Ile de Pâques in *Bulletin de la Société des Américanistes de Belgique, p. 13-47. Brussels, 1932.*

LAVACHERY (Henri). Les bois employés dans l'Ile de Pâques in *Bulletin de la Société des Américanistes de Belgique, nº 13, p. 67-71. Brussels, 1934.*

LAVACHERY (Henri). Les pétroglyphes de l'Ile de Pâques. *Ouvrage publié avec le concours de la Fondation Universitaire de Belgique. De Sikkel, 2 vol. Antwerp.*

1939. The second volume consists entirely of plates. The first includes descriptions of the petroglyphs and in addition the interpretations which can be made of them.

LAVACHERY (Henri). L'art vivant de l'Ile de Pâques in *J.S.O., t. 5, p. 163-170. Paris, 1949.*

LAVACHERY (Henri). Notes sur l'art plastique de l'Ile de Pâques in *Mélanges Georges Smets, p. 481-495. Brussels, 1952.*

LEENHARDT (Maurice). Notes d'Ethnologie Néo-Calédonienne. *Paris, 1930. The anthropological classic on the Grande Terre. The clearness of presentation and reliability of its matter will maintain it as the best book on the subject for many years to come.*

LEENHART (Maurice). L'habitation indigène dans les possessions françaises. *Société d'Éditions Géographiques, Maritimes et Coloniales. Paris, 1931. Oceania, p. 91-111.*

LEENHARDT (Maurice). Le masque calédonien. *Bull. Musée d'Ethnographie du Trocadéro, nº 6, p. 3-21. Paris, 1933. This fundamental work could have been better.*

LEENHARDT (Maurice). Gens de la Grande Terre. *Gallimard. Paris, 1937. The best account of New Caledonia as it used to be.*

LEENHARDT (Maurice). Arts de l'Océanie. *Editions du Chêne. Paris, 1947 (1948). This work attempts the difficult task of an aesthetic synthesis for Oceania. By a philosopher of religion, who presents to a wider public, people who are neither savage nor primitive. His language and humanity make a lively text convincing. The only fault is the undue importance given to the explanation of forms and themes in Le Havre terms of religious phenomena.*

LEM (F.H.). L'art décoratif des peuples océaniens in *Art et Décoration, nº 23, p. 13-20. Paris, 1951. On three simultaneous exhibitions.*

LENNIER (Gustave). Description de la collection ethnographique océanienne qu'a offerte à la ville du Havre M. Le Mescam, négociant de Nouméa... *Mirer, Muséum d'Histoire Naturelle et d'Ethnographie du Havre. Le Havre, 1896. The only published record of the collection which was partly destroyed when Le Havre burned in 1944.*

LEWIS (Albert B.). New Guinea masks. *Field Museum of Natural History. Chicago, 1922. A note by one of the great collectors of Oceanian material.*

LEWIS (Albert B.). Decorative art of New Guinea. *Anthropology Design series nº 4, Field Museum of Natural History. Chicago, 1925. Very useful.*

LEWIS (Albert B.). Carved and painted designs from New Guinea. *Anthropology Design series nº 5, Field Museum of Natural History. Chicago, 1931. 52 plates of excellent and useful illustrations including a number of views of the interiors of Papuan long houses.*

LEWIS (Albert B.). The Melanesians. People of the South Pacific. *Chicago Natural History Museum. Chicago, 1951. (New edition completed by A. Spoehr) A. B. Lewis gives one of the few useful introductions to this part of the world, firmly based on material culture. The illustrations are excellent, though unevenly distributed. No museum numbers are given.*

LINDBLOM (Gerhard). Crescent-shaped lime spatulas from British New Guinea in *Man, vol. 43, p. 143. London, 1943. Complements an article by T. Elder Dickson.*

LINTON (Ralph). The material culture of the Marquesas Islands in *B.P.B.M., Memoir vol. 8, nº 5. Honolulu, 1923.*

LINTON (Ralph) and WINGERT (Paul S.). Arts of the South Seas. *Museum of Modern Art. New York, 1946. In collaboration with René d'Harnoncourt. A synthetic study which clears the ground. The Polynesian chapters are best. The liens between themes and institutions are not sufficiently clear to allow the psycho-sociological conclusions of the authors to be accepted as proven. An indispensable reference book.*

LOMMEL (Andreas). Kunst der Südsee. *Munich, 1952. Summary catalogue of a temporary exhibition mounted when there was still a shortage of material.*

LOMMEL (Andreas and Catherine). Die Kunst des fünften Endteils - Australien. *Staatliches Museum für Völkerkunde. Munich, 1959. A book notable both for its accuracy and for its method, both in text and in the copious illustrations. It is based upon a comprehensive knowledge of the region. A perfect piece of work.*

LOPPE (Étienne). Note sur une sculpture en pierre de l'Ile de Pâques in *L'Homme Préhistorique, nº 6-8, p. 172-174. Paris, 1928. A small stone figurine.*

LUDERS (C.W.). Holzfiguren und Schnitzereien von den Salomo-Inseln in *Globus, vol. 26, p. 198-200. Brunswick, 1892.*

LUQUET (Georges Henri). L'art néo-calédonien. *Documents recueillis par Marius Archambault. Travaux et Mémoires de l'Institut d'Ethnologie II. Paris, 1926. The first attempt at an analysis of New Caledonian art. Especially concerned with the petroglyphs and psychological interpretations.*

LUQUIENS (H.M.). Hawaiian Artotet. *Bernice P. Bishop Museum Special Publication, vol. 18. Honolulu, 1931.*

LUSCHAN (Felix von). Das Wurfholz in Neu Holland und in Oceanien in *Festschrift für Adolf Bastian, p. 129-156. Reimer. Berlin, 1896.*

LUSCHAN (Felix von). Schilde aus Neu-Britannien in *Verhandlungen der Deutschen Gesellschaft für Anthropologie, p. 496-504. Berlin, 1900. Excellent reproductions of objects whose technology is minutely investigated. A valuable study.*

LUSCHAN (Felix von). Eine neue Art von Masken aus Neu-Britannien in *Globus, vol. 80, p. 4-5. Brunswick, 1901. A mask in the form of a sunshade. Excellent description.*

MAC CARTHY (Frederic D.). The Shell Inlay Decoration of the Southern Solomon Islands in *Australian Museum Magazine, vol. 7, p. 154-159. Sydney, 1943.*

MAC CARTHY (Frederic D.). Smoking and Art in New Guinea in *Aust. Mus. Mag., vol. VIII, nº 8, p. 255-259. Sydney, 1944. Designs on bamboo pipes.*

MAC CARTHY (Frederic D.). The Art of Malangan in New Ireland. *Aust. Mus. Mag., vol. 8, p. 397-403. Sydney, 1945.*

MAC CARTHY (Frederic D.). The Malangan Masks of New Ireland in *Aust. Mus. Mag., vol. 9, p. 50-56. Sydney, 1946.*

MAC CARTHY (Frederic D.). Australian Aboriginal Decorative Art. *Sydney, 1948. Straightforward, useful and accurate. A museum guidebook, based on a single topic. It is a pity that there are not more like it.*

MAC CARTHY (Frederic D.). Sepik River Face Masks in *Aust. Mus. Mag., vol. 10, nº 1, p. 3-8. Sydney, 1949. An interesting series of masks, including two from Mundugumor.*

MAC CARTHY (Frederic D.). A Circumcision Ceremony and Stone Arrangement on Groote Eylandt in *Aust. Mus. Rec., vol. 23, nº 3, p. 97-103. Sydney, 1953. A bark painting and its context.*

MAC CARTHY (Frederic D.). The Snake Woman, Siningbirna in *Aust. Mus. Rec., vol. 23, nº 3, p. 105-109. Sydney, 1953. The myth which explains a bark painting.*

MAC CARTHY (Frederic D.). Australian Aboriginal Rock Art. *Foreword by A. P. Elkin. The Australian Museum. Sydney, 1958. The most recent and complete study of this subject, using both anthropological and archaeological methods.*

MANNZEN (W.). Primitive Art of Arnhem Land in *South West Pacific, new series, n° 24, p. 29-35. Canberra, 1950.*

MARQUARDT (Carl). Verzeichnis einer ethnologischen Sammlung aus Samoa. *Reimer. Berlin, 1902.*

MEAD (Margaret). The Maoris and Their Arts. *American Museum of Natural History, guide leaflet, series 7, n° 71. New York, 1928. A short, general pamphlet on Maori art, both clear and well illustrated. Unfortunately it does not tackle the main problems of this art.*

MEIER (Josef). Steinbilder des Iniet-Geheimbundes bei den Eingeborenen des nordöstlichen Teiles der Gazelle-Halbinsel Neu Pommern in *Anthropos, vol. 6, p. 837-867. Vienna, 1911. A remarkable ethnographic study, based on a limited collection. Transcription of an initiation ceremony.*

MENZIES (J.H.). Maori patterns, painted and carved. *Smith and Anthony. Christchurch, 1910. A collection of coloured plates.*

METAIS (Élyane). Quelques symboles de l'art primitif. Étude d'une hache ostensoir néo-calédonienne in *Cahiers internationaux de Sociologie, 8ᵉ année, vol. 13, p. 78-93. A good study, vitiated in part by an error of interpretation as the result of confusion between the god Kong Hulup and the Polynesian deity Rongo.*

METAIS (Élyane). Étude comparative d'expressions graphiques d' « étendues concrètes » canaques in *Cahiers internationaux de Sociologie, vol. 15, 8ᵉ année, p. 115-131. Paris, 1953. A sociological interpretation of the scenes on two incised bamboos from New Caledonia.*

MÉTRAUX (Alfred). Relief carving on stone in Polynesia in *Ethnos, vol. 2, p. 340-344. Stockholm, 1937.*

MEYER (Adolf Bernard). Masken von Neu Guinea und dem Bismarck-Archipel. *Abhandl. aus dem Königlichen Ethnographischen Museum zu Dresden, n° 7. Dresden, 1889.*

MEYER (Adolf Bernard) and PARKINSON (Richard). Schnitzereien und Masken von Bismarck-Archipel und Neu Guinea. *Abhandl. aus dem Königlichen Ethnographischen Museum zu Dresden, n° 10. Dresden, 1900.*

MIKLUCHO-MACKLAY (N. von). Vestiges de l'art chez les Papouas de la côte Maclay en Nouvelle-Guinée in *Bulletin de la Société d'Anthropologie, vol. 1, 3ᵉ série, p. 524-531. Paris, 1875.*

MOSCHNER (Irmgard). Die Wiener Cook-Sammlung. Südsee-Teil in *Archiv für Völkerkunde, Bd 10,* *p. 135-253. Stuttgart, 1955. If all the museums of the world produced work like this, we should have much more material on the historical ethnography of the Pacific and comparative studies would be greatly facilitated. An excellent piece of work whose value is reduced by the inadequacy of certain drawings.*

MOSCHNER (Irmgard). Katalog der Neuseeland-Sammlung (A. Reischek) in *Archiv für Völkerkunde, Bd. 13, p. 51-131. Vienna, 1958. A useful catalogue of a rich, specialised collection.*

MOUNTFORD (Charles P.). Art, myth and symbolism. *American Australian Scientific Expedition to Arnhem land 1948, records vol.1. University Press. Melbourne, 1956. After a general introduction to the art of Australian aboriginals, the author studies the art of different regions of Arnhem Land. There is a chapter on human representations.*

Musée Guimet. Le Masque. *Décembre 1959-mai 1960. Éditions des Musées nationaux. Paris, 1959. Short articles by F. Girard and J. Guiart on Oceania, with three photographs.*

The Museum of Primitive Art. Second exhibition: carvings from Melanesia and Polynesia. *Museum of Primitive Art, Selected Works n° 2. New York, 1957.*

The Museum of Primitive Art. Second exhibition: color in sculpture and ceramics. *Museum of Primitive Art, Selected Works n° 3. New York, 1957.*

NEWMAN (A.K.). On a stone carved ancient wooden image of a Maori Eel God in *NZ Inst. Trans., vol. 38, p. 130-134. Wellington, 1906.*

NEWTON (Douglas). Art styles of the Papuan Gulf. *The Museum of Primitive Art. New York, 1961. A needed account of an art of which little was accurately known because its products were often too fragile to have survived. The best chapters are concerned with the definition of local styles.*

NGATA (Sir Apirana T.). Maori arts and crafts. In *Sutherland (I.L.G.) The Maori People to-day, p. 307-335. New Zealand Council for Educational Research. Wellington, 1940.*

NOULET (J.B.). Bambous gravés de la Nouvelle-Calédonie in *Revue d'Ethnographie, vol. 3, p. 353-354. Paris, 1885. Specimens in the Musée d'Histoire Naturelle, Toulouse.*

Oceania. Catalogue d'une exposition d'art océanien. *Andrée Olive. (Avant-propos et poèmes inédits d'André Breton; introduction au catalogue de F.H. Lem.). Paris, 1948. 116 Oceanian pieces from various private collections.*

OLDMAN (W.O.). Skilled handwork of the Maori, Collection of Maori artifacts. *Memoirs of the Polynesian Society, nᵒ 14 2nd ed. Wellington, 1946.*

O'REILLY (Patrick). Description sommaire d'une collection d'objets ethnographiques de l'Ile de Bougainville, groupe des Iles Salomon in *Annali Lateranensi, vol. 4, p. 163-198. Rome, 1940. Objects given to the Musée de l'Homme, Paris, by the Marist Mission in 1934.*

O'REILLY (Patrick). Statuette bicéphale masculine de l'Ile de Pâques conservée à La Rochelle in *J.S.O., t. 3, p. 118-121. Paris, 1947. A figurine in the Musée Lafaille (La Rochelle).*

O'REILLY (Patrick). Une statuette de bois découverte à Tahiti et conservée au Musée d'Ethnographie de Neuchâtel (Suisse) in *Bulletin de la Société Neuchâteloise de Géographie, t. 55, fasc. 2, nouvelle série nᵒ 7, p. 77-81. Neuchâtel, 1948. On the rarity of wooden figures from Tahiti.*

O'REILLY (Patrick). Les Nouvelles-Hébrides au Musée de la France d'Outre-Mer in *La Vie de la France et de l'Union française, 47ᵉ année, nᵒ 8, p. 101. Paris, 1949.*

O'REILLY (Patrick). Une sculpture des Nouvelles-Hébrides (Vao) au Musée de la France d'Outre-Mer in *J.S.O., t. 5, p. 192-194. Paris, 1949.*

O'REILLY (Patrick). Jeunesse de l'art océanien. *Missions des Iles, 4ᵉ année, nᵒ 27. Paris, 1950. An attempt to claim the survival of an art style, after christianisation, based upon the exceptional surviving pieces. A kind of remorse.*

O'REILLY (Patrick). Art Mélanésien. Somuk, Hikot, Tsumomok, Tsimès, Ketanon. *Nouvelles Éditions Latines. Paris, 1951. A scarce booklet by a man of taste presenting a collection of coloured drawings by artists from the Solomons. We would have preferred more comments by artists other than Somuk, since their drawings seem at least as rich in symbolism.*

O'REILLY (Patrick). Nouvelles-Hébrides. Mallicolo. Sculpture de faîtage en racine de fougère in *J.S.O., t. 8, p. 289-290. Paris, 1952. A specimen from the Musée des Missions Maristes at Sainte-Foy-les-Lyon.*

Other Faces: An Exhibition of Masks. *Arranged for the Auckland Festival 1955. With an introduction by Olwyn Turbott. Auckland War Memorial Museum. Auckland, 1955. Short catalogue of a temporary exhibition. Excellent photographs.*

PADOVAN (R.). The Maori as an Artist. *Plates and an Essay; Preface by R.A. Falla. Reed. Wellington, 1957.*

PARAVICINI (Eugen). Zwei Holzfiguren von San Cristobal (Salomo-Inseln) in *Ethnologischer Anzeiger, vol. 3 p. 283-284. Stuttgart, 1933.*

Peabody Museum of Salem. The Hawaiian Portion of the Polynesian Collections in the Peabody Museum of Salem. *Special Exhibition (2nd ed. E.S. Dodge, 1937). Salem, 1920. 381 pieces.*

PEEKEL (Gerhard). Die Ahnenbilder von Nord - Neu Mecklenburg in *Anthropos, vol. 21, 1926, p. 807-824; vol. 22, p. 16-44. Vienna, 1927. Review of a book by Kraemer (Augustin):* Die Malanggan von Tombara. *Müller. Munich, 1925. Numerous anthropological details.*

PHILLIPPS (William J.). Maori Carving in *Art in New Zealand, vol. 10, p. 199-206. 1938.*

PHILLIPPS (William J.). Carved Maori houses of the Eastern districts of the North Island (New Zealand) in *Records of the Dominion Museum, vol. 1, nᵒ2 p. 69-119. Wellington, 1944.*

PHILLIPPS (William J.). Maori Spirals in *J.P.S., vol. 57, p. 30-40. Wellington, 1948. Copy by a modern Maori sculptor of 48 types of spiral found in traditional carvings.*

PHILLIPPS (William J.). Carved pumice box from Waikato in *J.P.S., vol. 59, p. 76-77. Wellington, 1950.*

PHILLIPPS (William J.). Sculpture inédite des Iles Chatham in *J.S.O., t. 6, p. 273-274. Paris, 1951. Carving in haematite.*

PHILLIPPS (William J.). Maori houses and food stores. *Dominion Museum. (Dominion Museum Monograph nᵒ 8.) Wellington, 1952. A detailed commentary on each house or granary reproduced.*

PHILLIPPS (William J.). Carved Maori houses of Western and Northern areas of New Zealand. *(New Zealand Dominion Museum Monograph nᵒ 9). Wellington, 1955.*

PHILLIPPS (William J.). Maori carving illustrated. *A.H. and A.W. Reed. Wellington, 1958. An excellent introduction to Maori art. The writer does not share Archey's views on the manaia motif.*

PHILLIPPS (William J.) and MAC EWEN (J.M.). Carved houses of Te Arawa (New Zealand) in *Dominion Museum Records in Ethnology, vol. 1, nᵒ 1, 1946, p. 1-46; nᵒ 2, 1948, p. 47-112. Wellington, 1946-48. Detailed study of each house discussed.*

PLISCHKE (Hans). Geister-Trompeten und Geister-Flöten aus Bambus vom Sepik, Neu Guinea in *Jahrbuch des Museums für Völkerkunde zu Leipzig, vol. 8, p. 57. Leipzig, 1922.*

Polynesian Artifacts. The Oldman Collection. *Memoirs of the Polynesian Society, vol. 15. Wellington, 1953. (2nd ed.) A marvellous collection of photographs of Polynesian art.*

PONCETTON (François) and PORTIER (A.). Décoration océanienne. *Calavas. Paris, 1930.*

PONCETTON (François) and PORTIER (A.). Les arts sauvages. Océanie. *Éditions Albert Morancé. Paris, 1930. A de luxe volume which brings to our notice above all pieces in private collections. No. 12 (from the Musée de l'Homme) comes from New Ireland and not, as is stated, from the New Hebrides.*

POWDERMAKER (Hortense). Mortuary rites in New Ireland (Bismarck Archipelago) in *Oceania, vol. 2, no 1, p. 26-43. Sydney, 1931. The context o malanggan.*

POWELL (Guy). Notes on a Maori whale ivory pendant in *J.P.S., vol. 59, p. 273-274. Wellington, 1950.*

POWELL (Jane P.) and FRIEDMAN (Martin L.). Primitive art of the Pacific Islands. *Brooklyn Museum. New York, 1957. The pieces illustrated are housed in the Brooklyn Museum.*

PREUSS (Konrad Theodor). Künstlerische Darstellungen aus Kaiser-Wilhelmsland in ihrer Bedeutung für die Ethnographie in *Zeitschrift für Ethnologie, vol. 29, p. 77-139; vol. 30, p. 74-120. Berlin, 1897-98. An attempt to establish a typological system for the art of the north coast of New Guinea.*

PREUSS (Konrad Theodor). Über einige Ornamente vom Kaiserin-Augusta-Fluss in Deutsch Neu-Guinea in *I.A.E., vol. 11, p. 145-153. Leiden, 1898. A good account of certain motifs which extend from the human figure to the abstract.*

PREUSS (Konrad Theodor). Künstlerische Darstellungen aus dem Deutsch-Holländischen Grenzgebiet in Neu-Guinea in *I.A.E., vol. 12, p. 161-185. Leiden, 1899. A good, illustrated account of painted motifs.*

READ (Charles H.). On the origin and sacred character of certain ornaments of the South Eastern Pacific in *J.A.I., vol. 21, p. 139-159. London, 1891-92.*

READ (Charles H.). An account of a collection of ethnographical specimens formed during Vancouver's voyage in the Pacific Ocean 1790-1795 (in the British Museum) in *J.A.I., vol. 21, p. 90-108. London, 1892.*

READ (Charles H.). Note on a carved canoe head from New Zealand in *J.A.I., vol. 29, p. 305. London, 1899. Cf. Edge-Partington. Ibid. vol. 30, no 42, 1900, for some corrections.*

READ (Sir Herbert). Australia. Aboriginal Paintings - Arnhem Land. *Preface by Charles B. Mountford. New York Graphic Society, U.N.E.S.C.O. New York, 1954.*

REAL (Daniel). La décoration primitive. 2e partie - Océanie. *Librairie des Arts Décoratifs. Paris, 1923.*

REICHHARD (Gladys Amanda). Melanesian Design. A study of style in wood and tortoise-shell carving. *Columbia University Press, 2 vol. New York, 1933.*

RIVERS (William Halse). The statues of Easter Island in *Folklore, vol. 31, p. 294-306. London, 1920.*

ROTH (Geo. Kingsley). The manufacture of bark cloth in Fiji (Navatusila, Viti Levu) in *J.A.I., vol. 64, p. 289-303. London, 1934.*

ROTH (Geo. Kingsley). Pottery making in Fiji in *J.A.I., vol. 65, p. 217-233. London, 1935.*

ROTH (Henry Ling). Some unrecorded Maori decorative work in *Man, vol. 20, p. 70-73. London, 1920.*

ROTH (Henry Ling). The Maori mantle. *Bankfield Museum. Halifax, 1923. Comprehensive, illustrated monograph.*

ROUSSEAU (Madeleine). L'art et la philosophie des Océaniens in *L'Age nouveau, no 60, p. 55-60. Paris, 1951. About three exhibitions held simultaneously in Paris.*

ROUSSEAU (Madeleine) and others. L'Art océanien. Sa présence. *Le Musée Vivant, no 38. Paris, 1951. This 'private enterprise' publication is praiseworthy and richly illustrated, and would be of fundamental importance were it not for its numerous eccentricities.*

ROWE (W. Page). Maori artistry. *Board of Maori Ethnological Research Memoir, vol. 3, 16. New Plymouth, 1928.*

ROWE (W. Page). Some unorthodox reflexions on the spiral in Maori ornament in *J.P.S., vol. 44, p. 112-123. Wellington, 1935. Against Archey's hypothesis which derives the double spiral from the crossing of manaia loops.*

ROWE (W. Page). A study of the geometrical drawings from the New Hebrides in *J.A.I., vol. 66, p. 117-128. London, 1936. The method of executing drawings and an analysis of their elements.*

434

ROWE (W. Page). The origin of the Maori spiral in *J.P.S.,* vol. 47, p. 129-133. Wellington, 1938. *Against Archey's hypothesis.*

ROY (Claude). Les arts sauvages in *Encyclopédie essentielle, Robert Delpire. Paris, 1957. 18 plates of Oceanian material. A delightful piece of literary skill which is, unfortunately, without scientific value. It throws far more light upon Claude Roy than upon so-called primitive art, but is not without charm. The presentation, in an extraordinary format, is perfect.*

SARFERT (Ernst). Ausgrabung von Nanmatol auf Ponape : Masken aus dem Bismarck-Archipel : Masken von Nissam ; Eine Kanuplanke aus Kaiser Wilhelmsland; *Jahrbuch des Museums für Völkerkunde zu Leipzig, vol. 5. Leipzig, 1913.*

SARFERT (Ernst) and DAMM (Hans). Luangiua und Nukumanu. 1.) Allgemeiner Teil und materielle Kultur. 2. Mikronesien in *Ergebnisse der Südsee-Expedition II, Ethnographie, vol. 12. Friedrichsen. Hamburg, 1929.*

SCHELLER (A.). Aufhängehaken aus Indonesien und der Südsee in *Ethnologica, vol. 5, p. 73-171. Cologne 1941.*

SCHELLONG (O.). Über die Herstellung einiger ethnographica der Gegend Finschhafens in *I.A.E., vol. 1, p. 220-222. Leiden, 1888. A fine plate with detailed illustrations.*

SCHELLONG (O.). Notizen über das Zeichnen der Melanesier in *I.A.E., vol. 8, p. 57-61. Leiden, 1895. A plate of extremely interesting pencil drawings.*

SCHLAGINHAUFEN (Otto). Eine ethnographische Sammlung vom Kaiserin Augusta-Fluss in Neu-Guinea. *Abhandlungen aus dem Königlichen Ethnologischen Museum zu Dresden, vol. 13, n° 2. Dresden, 1910.*

SCHMIDT (E.W.). Die Schild-Typen vom Kaiserin Augusta-Fluss und eine Kritik der Deutung ihrer Gesichts-Ornamente in *Baessler-Archiv, vol. 13, p. 136-177. Berlin, 1929. A collection of great interest on account of its geographical coverage. Superficial interpretation.*

SCHMITZ (Carl A.). Die Jawik-Figuren der Pasum in Nordwest Neu-Guinea. *Jahrbuch des Museums für Völkerkunde zu Leipzig, vol. 17, p. 30-51. Leipzig, 1959.*

SCHMITZ (Carl A.). Style provinces and Style elements. A study in method in *Mankind, vol. 5, n° 3, p. 107-116. Sydney, 1956. Should be read.*

SCHURTZ (Heinrich). Schnitzereien der Maori aus dem Städtischen Museum in Bremen in *Globus, vol. 77, p. 53-58. Brunswick, 1900. A good account of the collection in the Bremen Museum.*

SCHUSTER (Carl). Prehistoric stone objects from New Guinea and the Solomons in *Mankind, vol. 3, n° 9, p. 247-251. Sydney, 1946. Presentation of undated archaeological material. The mystery remains unsolved.*

Sculpture monumentale d'Océanie. Nouvelle-Guinée et Nouvelles-Hébrides. *Texte de Christian Zervos, Pierre Loeb, Tristan Tzara, Marcel Evrard; photographies de Luc Joubert. Éditions Jeanne Bucher. Paris, 1961. Remarkable photographic studies of an exhibition of sculpture of very variable value which achieved astonishing prices at the sale. As far as the New Hebrides are concerned (North Malekula), where I saw most of the pieces in situ, I can say that none of the pieces is earlier than 1930 and Nos. 17, 30, 31, 32, 33, 34, and 35 are very recent. Nos. 32-35 are the unskilled work of men living to the north of the Big Nambas region who lack the tradition of this style of sculpture. The first seven pieces should have no market value, having been made, as far as I know, at the suggestion of the Director of 'Plantations Réunies,' Norsup, Malekula, for sale overseas.*

SEBBELOV (Gerda). The E.W. Clark Collection. New Zealand in *Museum Journal, vol. 2, n° 2, p. 30-42. Philadelphia, 1911.*

SEBBELOV (Gerda). The E.W. Clark Collection. Polynesia in *The Museum Journal, vol. 2, n° 3, p. 60-67. Philadelphia, 1911. Interesting photographic study of engraved maces from Tonga spacing which have too often been overlooked. Adzes from Mangaia.*

SEBBELOV (Gerda). The E.W. Clark Collection. New Caledonia in *Museum Journal, vol. 2, n° 4, p. 78-82. Philadelphia, 1911.*

SELIGMANN (Charles Gabriel). A type of canoe ornament with magical significance from South Eastern British New Guinea in *Man, vol. 9, p. 33-35. London, 1909.*

SELIGMANN (Charles Gabriel). A lime spatulae from Rossel Island, British New Guinea in *Man, vol. 16, p. 6-7. London, 1916.*

SHEPPARD (T.). A carved drum from Raivavae, High Islands in *Man, vol. 39, p. 108-109. London, 1939.*

SKINNER (H. Devenish). Evolution of Maori art in *J.A.I., vol. 46, I: p. 184-196; II: p. 309-321. London, 1916. Patu, onewa and mere.*

SKINNER (H. Devenish). The Maori Hei Tiki in *Man, vol. 17, p. 162-163. London, 1917. On the relation between the reduced size of the axe and the position of the tiki portrayed on it.*

SKINNER (H. Devenish). A type of Maori carved wooden bowl in *J.P.S.*, *vol. 31, p. 182-184. Wellington, 1922.*

SKINNER (H. Devenish). Notes on the "Rei Puta" type of pendant in *J.P.S.*, *vol. 32, p. 31-34. Wellington, 1923.*

SKINNER (H. Devenish). On the patu family and its occur: rence beyond New Zealand in *J.P.S.*, *vol. 40, p. 183-196. Wellington, 1931. Main varieties of the patu in the region of New Zealand and Chatham Islands; date of the spread of patu in the Pacific and study of pieces discussed in an article by J. Imbelloni-Origin and relationships of patu, onewa and mere.*

SKINNER (H. Devenish). Maori amulets in stone, bone and shell in *J.P.S.*, *vol. 41, p. 202-211, 302-309, 1932; vol. 42, p. 1-9, 107-113, 191-203, 310-320, 1933; vol. 43, p. 25-29, 106-117, 198-215, 271-279, 1934; vol. 44, p. 17-25, 1935; vol. 45, p. 127-141, 1936; vol. 52, p. 132-152, 1943; vol. 56, p. 357-363, 1947. Wellington, 1932-1947. An accurate and detailed study.*

SKINNER (H. Devenish). A patu representing a human face in *J.P.S.*, *vol. 43, p. 130. Wellington, 1934.*

SKINNER (H. Devenish). A Ngaitahu carved skull-box in *J.P.S.*, *vol. 45, p. 63-66. Wellington, 1936.*

SKINNER (H. Devenish). The Maori Hei-Tiki. *Otago-Museum, Booklet, nº 1. Dunedin, 1946.*

SKINNER (H. Devenish) and PHILLIPPS (William J.). Necklaces, pendants and amulets from the Chatham Islands and New Zealand in *J.P.S.*, *vol. 62, p. 169-195. Wellington, 1953.*

SMITH (S. Percy). Note on the Manaia in Maori carvings in *J.P.S.*, *vol. 26, p. 130-131. Wellington, 1917.*

SÖDERSTRÖM (Jan). Die Figurstühle vom Sepik-Fluss auf Neu Guinea; mit einem Anhang von Georg Höltker. Drei Zeremonial-Schemel vom Sepik. *Statens Ethnographiska Museum, Smärre Meddelander, nº 18. Stockholm, 1941.*

South Sea Islands Art Portfolio in *Magazine of Art, vol. 39, p. 143-147. Washington, 1946.*

SPEISER (Felix). Pfeile von Santa Cruz in *Archiv für Anthropologie, vol. 8, p. 308-311. Brunswick, 1909.*

SPEISER (Felix). Die Ornamentik von Santa Cruz in *Archiv für Anthropologie, vol. 13, p. 323-334. Brunswick, 1915.*

SPEISER (Felix). L'art plastique des Nouvelles-Hébrides in *Cahiers d'Art, vol. 4, p. 91-94. Paris, 1929. The religious conditioning of New Hebridean art and symbolism. The illustrative pieces are almost all from the Basle Museum.*

SPEISER (Felix). Über Kunststile in Melanesien in *Zeitschrift für Ethnologie, vol. 68, p. 304-369. Berlin, 1936. An attempt to classify Melanesian art and establish its geographical distribution.*

SPEISER (Felix). Kunststile der Südsee. *Führer durch das Museum für Völkerkunde. Basle, 1941.*

SPEISER (Felix). Malereien aus Nord-Neu Guinea im Museum für Völkerkunde in Basel in *Phoebus, vol. 1, nº 1, p. 3-15. Munich, 1946.*

SPEISER (Felix) and WIRZ (Paul). Kult und Kunst auf Neu Guinea. *Sammlungen des Gewerbe-Museum. Basle, 1931.*

SPENGEMANN (W.). Holzschnitzereien von Neu-Mecklenburg in *Jambo, vol. 4, p. 1-4. Leipzig, 1927.*

STEINEN (Karl von den). Die Marquesaner und ihre Kunst. Bd. I: Tatauierung. *Dietrich Reimer, Ernst Vohsen. Berlin, 1925.*

STEINEN (Karl von den) in Die Marquesaner und ihre Kunst. Studien über die Entwicklung primitiver Südsee-Ornamentik. *Dietrich Reimer. Berlin, 1925-1928. The two definitive works on the subjects; factually sound and exhaustive.*

STEPHAN (Emil). Südsee-Kunst. Beiträge zur Kunst des Bismarck-Archipels und zur Urgeschichte der Kunst überhaupt. *D. Reimer. Berlin, 1907.*

STEVENSON (G.B.). Waitaki Maori Paintings in *J.P.S., vol. 52, p. 191-198. Wellington, 1943.*

STEWART (Anthony B.). Great Stone Faces of Easter Island in *National Geographic Magazine, t. 85, p. 225-232. London, 1944.*

STOLPE (Knut Hjalmar). Entwicklungserscheinungen in der Ornamentik der Naturvölker. Eine ethnographische Untersuchung. *M.A.G.W., vol. 22 (N.S. vol. 12), p. 19-60. Vienna, 1892. One of the best detailed studies of the evolution of themes and motifs, especially of the human figure.*

STOLPE (Knut Hjalmar). Collected essays in ornamental art. Atlas. *Privately printed. Stockholm, 1927.*

STRAUCH (H.). Allegemeine Bemerkungen ethnologischen Inhalts über Neu Guinea, die Anachoreten-Inseln, Neu-Hannover, Neu-Irland, Neu Britannien und Bougainville im Anschluss an die dort gemachten Sammlungen ethnologischer Gegenstände in *Zeitschrift für Ethnologie, vol. 9 p. 9-63, 81-105. Berlin, 1877. A mass of anthropological details of variable value, but excellent reproductions of New Ireland masks.*

SURRIDGE (Margaret N.). Decoration of Fiji water jars in *J.P.S.*, vol. 53, p. 17-36. *Wellington, 1944.*

SYDOW (Eckart von). Die Kunst der Naturvölker und der Vorzeit. *Oceania, p. 163-242. Propyläen-Verlag. Berlin, 1927.*

SYDOW (Eckart von). Polynésie et Mélanésie. L'art régional des mers du Sud in *Cahiers d'Art, vol. 4, n° 2-3, p. 61-64. Paris, 1929. Comparison between the regional arts of the Pacific.*

TAYLOR (William Anderson). Maori Art in Canterbury. *Ellesmere Guardian. Leeston, 1946.*

TE RANGI HIROA (Peter H. BUCK). Maori decorative art. House panels in *NZ Inst. Trans., vol. 53, p. 452-470. Wellington, 1921.*

TE RANGI HIROA (Peter H. BUCK). Mangarevan images in *Ethnol. Cran., n° 4, p. 13-19. Chislehurst, 1939.*

TE RANGI HIROA (Peter H. BUCK). The feather cloak of Tahiti in *J.P.S., vol. 52, p. 12-15. Wellington, 1943.*

TE RANGI HIROA (Peter H. BUCK). Arts and crafts of the Cook Islands in *B.P.B.M., bull. 179. Honolulu, 1944. Remarkable analyses of techniques.*

TE RANGI HIROA (Peter H. BUCK). Arts and crafts of Hawaii. *B.P.B.M. Special Publication, n° 45. Honolulu, 1957. A posthumous work, the fruit of 25 years as Director of the Bernice P. Bishop Museum, Honolulu. An essential tool for the study of the material culture of Hawaii.*

TE RANGI HIROA (Peter H. BUCK). The coming of the Maori. *Whitcombe and Tombs. Wellington, 1949. The best scientific work of this writer. A balanced and comprehensive study of ancient Maori life. An indispensable tool which is also a scientific testament.*

THORPE (W.W.). A tomako or head hunter's canoe from the Solomon Islanders in *Aust. Mus. Mag., vol. 1, p. 289-292. Sydney, 1923.*

THORPE (W.W.). An inscribed wooden gorget from Rapanui in *J.P.S., vol. 33, p. 149-150. Wellington, 1924.*

THORPE (W.W.). Carved gopi boards from the Papuan Gulf area in *Man, vol. 31, p. 57-58. London, 1931.*

TISCHNER (Herbert). Eine ethnographische Sammlung aus dem östlichen Zentral-Neu Guinea (Hagen-Gebirge, Wagital, Ramu). *Mitteilungen aus dem Museum für Völkerkunde in Hamburg, vol. 21. Hamburg, 1939. An excellent museum study, with the risks that that implies. Very good drawings, but old-fashioned photographs which are not always clear.*

TISCHNER (Herbert). Oceanic Art. *Pantheon. New York, 1954. Remarkable for the quality of the pictures and their presentation. Text too short to be of use. Well documented.*

TURBOTT (Olwyn). A carved canoe ornament from the Marquesas in *J.P.S., vol. 52, p. 210-211. Wellington, 1943.*

TURNER (Sir William). Decorated and sculptured skulls from New Guinea in *Proceedings of the Royal Society of Edinburgh, vol. 22, p. 553-572. Edinburgh 1898-1899. Ten skulls.*

TZARA (Tristan). L'Art et l'Océanie in *Cahiers d'Art, vol. 4, n° 2-3, p. 59-60. Paris, 1929. A literary text which urges the poetic approach to Oceanian art in particular and to primitive art in general as the only valid method open to modern man.*

VALENTINE (C.A.). Masks and men in a Melanesian society. The Valuku or Tubuan of the Lakalai of New Britain. *University of Kansas Publications, Social Science Studies. Lawrence, Kansas, 1961. A reasonable work with curious gaps. Total omission of the technique of masks. Well illustrated.*

VAN RENSELAAR (H.C.). Asmat. Art from South West New Guinea. *Royal Tropical Institute N° 121, Department of Cultural and Physical Anthropology, n° 55. Amsterdam, 1961. A well-produced booklet, in English. Numerous illustrations. An essential work until the exhaustive study announced is available.*

VINSKY (Zdenko). Une idole Moai-Kava-Kava de l'Ile de Pâques au Musée Ethnographique de Zagreb. in *Anthropos, vol. 37-40, n° 1-3, p. 329-331. Freiburg, 1942-1945.*

VON HAAST (Julius). A few remarks on the carved stone bird named Korotangi by the Maoris in *NZ Inst. Trans., vol. 14, p. 104-105. Wellington, 1882.*

WALCOTT (R.H.). Note on the Fijian clubs ornamented with Maori patterns in *Melbourne National Museum Memoirs, vol. 4, p. 54-57. Melbourne, 1912.*

WEBSTER (W.D.). Catalogue of ethnographical specimens from Australia, New Zealand, Hervey Island, Marquesas, New Guinea, New Ireland, Tahiti, Samoa, Tonga, Solomon Islands, New Caledonia, Norfolk Island, Admiralty Island and other parts of Polynesia. *Halliday, 3 vols. Leicester, 1911.*

WILITSCH (Gottfried). Betrachtungen über die Bildende Kunst Melanesiens und daraus sich ergebende Folgerungen für die Ethnologie in *Zeitschrift für Ethnologie, vol. 67, p. 331-348. Berlin, 1935. An attempt at historical reconstruction based upon artistic evolution.*

WILLIAMS (F.E.). The collection of curios and the preservation of native culture. *Territory of Papua, Anthropology Report, nº 3. Port Moresby, 1923.*

WILSON (Major). On the Korotangi or stone bird in *NZ Inst. Trans., vol. 22, p. 499-508. Wellington, 1890.*

WINGERT (Paul S.). Outline guide to the art of the South Pacific. *Columbia University Press. New York, 1946.*

WINGERT (Paul S.). Human forms in the art of Melanesia in *Records of the Auckland Institute and Museum, vol. 4, nº 3, p. 145-151. Auckland, 1952.*

WINGERT (Paul S.). Art of the South Pacific Islands. *Thames and Hudson. London, 1953.*

WIRZ (Paul). Über die Entwicklung einiger ornamentaler Formelemente in der Kunst von Holländisch Nord-Neu Guinea in *Tijdschrift, Indische Taal-, Land- en Volkenkunde, vol. 61, p. 508-518. Amsterdam, 1922.*

WIRZ (Paul). Kunstwerke vom Sepik. *Introduction by A. Bühler. Führer durch das Museum für Völkerkunde und Schweizerische Museum für Volkskunde Basel. Sonderausstellung 1. Oktober bis 31. Dezember 1954. Basle, 1954. A text intended for the general public which is too brief. But the illustrations are admirable.*

WIRZ (Paul). The exhibition 'Art from the Sepik' at the Ethnographical Museum in Basle in *Antiquity and Survival, nº 1, p. 67-82. The Hague, 1955.*

WIRZ (Paul). Neu Guinea. *Koninklijk Instituut voor de Tropen, Medeling, nº 133 - Afdeling Culturele en Physische Anthropologie, nº 62. Amsterdam, 1959. The last testament of one of the greatest experts on New Guinea. Excellent illustrations. Mainly Sepik valley. Most of the illustrations are of pieces in the Wirz collection which is now housed in the Tropical Institute, Amsterdam.*

WOODFORD (Charles Morris). Further note on funerary ornaments from the Solomon Islands in *Man, vol. 5, p. 38-39. London, 1905. Complements the article by Edge-Partington and Joyce: note on funerary ornaments from Rubiana and a coffin from Santa Anna.*

WORSLEY (Peter M.). Material symbols of human beings among the Wanindiljaugwa in *Man, vol. 54, p. 165-167. London, 1954. Australia.*

WORNSNOP (Thomas). The prehistoric arts, manufactures, works, weapons of the Aborigines of Australia. *Adelaide, 1897. Good general work on the art and techniques of the aboriginals.*

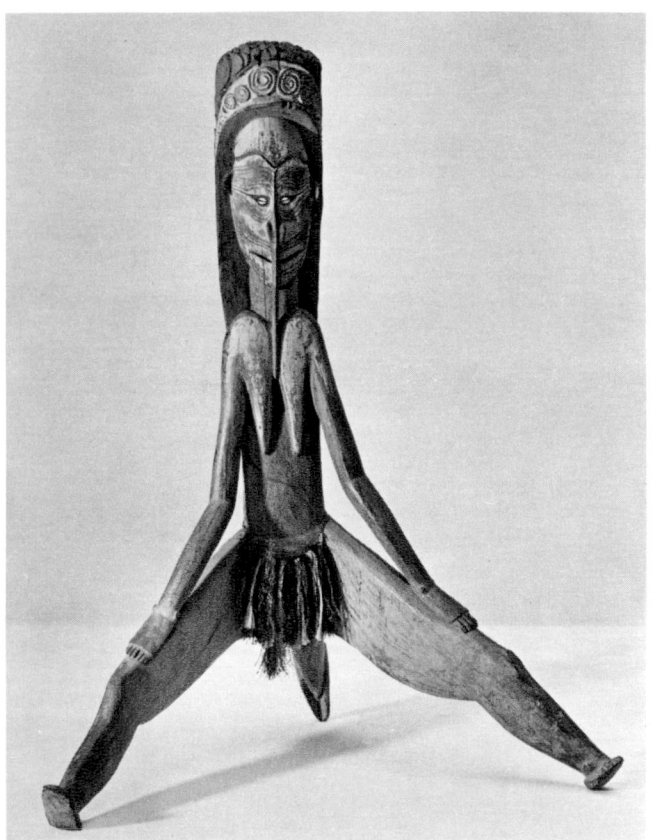

430. New Guinea. Palimbei, middle Sepik. *Ridge figures*, Basle - 431. New Guinea Mundugumor. *Mouthpiece of flute*, Basle - 432. New Guinea Papua. Numobawi. *Stool*, Amsterdam.

439

LIST OF ILLUSTRATIONS

Frontispiece: Hawaian Islands, Oahu. *The God of War « Ku ».* (Detail of 392.) British Museum. *(Museum Photo.)*

1. New Caledonia, Isle of Pines. *Coral Landscape* (Ph. Jean Guiart.)

2. New Caledonia. *Typical countryside: savana with paper-mulberries on fire.* (Ph. Jean Guiart.)

3. French Polynesia, Bora-Bora. *Coral beach with volcanic relief.* (Ph. Aubert de la Rüe, Agence Rapho.)

4. New Hebrides, Naleyto, Espiritu Santo. *Mountain village at 2,200 ft.* (Ph. Jean Guiart.)

5. New Caledonia, Gomen (Bwaganda). *Village in a poor region with mud-walled huts.* (Ph. Jean Guiart.)

6. French Polynesia, Huahine. *Fishing village on a lagoon.* (Ph. Aubert de la Rüe, Agence Rapho.)

7. Loyalty Islands, Uvea (Fayawe). *Tribal meeting house, Hwenegei.* (Ph. Jean Guiart.)

8. New Caledonia, Huailu. (Nerheughakwea). *Method of growing yams on a hillside.* (Ph. Jean Guiart.)

9. Western New Guinea, Baliem Valley. *Irrigated sweet potato cultivation at 9,000 ft.* (Ph. Jean Guiart.)

10. Cook Islands. *Mangaian man* (From: Voyages round the world by Byron, Carterets, Willis and Cook: Plate XI.) London, 1773.

11. *Art of New Guinea,* Wahgi Tribe. *Mourning woman with white-painted face.* (Ph. Jacques Villeminot.)

12. *Fijian.* (From: Atlas pour servir à la relation du voyage à la recherche de La Pérouse par le citoyen Labillardière.) Paris, 1800.

13. *Sepik Art.* Washkuk. *Man's head with ceremonial adornment.* Hibiscus flowers; cassowary and cockatoo feathers; locks of dead father's hair; cowries and snail-shells, rubbed down to discs, fixed to a netting base. Adze on left shoulder. (Ph. René Gardi.)

14. *Art of western Polynesia.* Tonga, Friendly Islands. *King Pulako.* (From: Byron et al.: Plate XVIII.) London, 1773.

15. *Art of New Guinea (South-west),* Pirimapun. *Skull worn as breast ornament* (Ph. Tony Saulnier.)

16. New Zealand *Maori.* (From: Byron et al.: Plate XII.)

17. *Art of New Guinea.* Wahgi Tribe. *Tattooing a young girl.* 1960. (Ph. Jacques Villeminot.)

18. *Sepik Art.* Timbunke. *Overmodelled skull of ancestor.* 1955. The ornament consists of flowers and decorative leaves, feathers, dogs' teeth, snail and other shells, which were worn by the man in his lifetime. (Ph. René Gardi.)

19. *Art of New Guinea (South-west).* Asmat. *Nose ornament, worn through the septum.* 1959. (Ph. Tony Saulnier.)

20. Hawaiian Islands. *Sandwich Islander* (From: Byron et al.: Plate LXVI.)

21. Hawaiian Islands. *Double canoe with paddles and sails* (From: Byron et al.: Plate LXV.)

22. New Caledonia. *Double canoe, with furled sails, being poled.* (From: Atlas pour servir à la relation du voyage à la recherche de La Pérouse par le citoyen Labillardière, Plate XLIV.)

23. *Art of New Guinea.* Wahgi Tribe. *Heavy ceremonial head-dress.* 1960. Bark, covered with clay, and painted, edged with beetles and bird-of-paradise plumes. (Ph. Jacques Villeminot.)

24. *Art of eastern Polynesia.* Tahiti. *Male dance costume.* The otea dance, with men wearing saffron-coloured more. (Ph. Bernard Villaret.)

25. *Art of central Polynesia.* Atiu, Cook Islands. *Chief's stool.* New York Museum of Primitive Art (no: 56-24) Wood: height: 16 1/4 ins.

26. New Caledonia, Huailu. *Monumental alley of the Tyibey clan.* (Ph. Jean Guiart.)

27. *Sepik Art.* Kalabu. *Great men's ceremonial house,* (*tambaran*). 1961. End view. The frontispiece is decorated with painted bark. (Ph. Jacques Villeminot.)

28. *Sepik Art.* Lake Chambuli. *Orator's stool* 1960. (Ph. S. Diczbalis).

441

29. *Sepik Art*. Eastern New Guinea, Tambanaman, Sepik valley. *Anthropomorphic design, forming part of a men's house.* 1960. (Ph. S. Diczbalis.)

30. *Australian Art*. Liverpool River, Arnhem Land. *Body painting, marking the lifting of a taboo.* 1952. Mineral colours mixed with spittle. (Ph. Axel Poignant.)

31. *Sepik Art*. South Maprik, Numbungai. *Basketwork mask.* 1955. The cape is of sago palm leaf ribbons. The mask is decorated with fruit, leaves, and mineral colours. The word tumbuan, used to describe this mask, is pidgin english and not the local name. The mask is used during the initiation of adolescents, and therefore could not be approached by women. (Ph. René Gardi.)

32. *Art of New Guinea (South-west)*. Eastern New Guinea, Asmat region (Aworket). *Mask for jipae funerary rite.* (Ph. Tony Saulnier.)

33. *New Hebridean Art*. Tomman Island, Malekula. *Over-modelled skulls: the mannikin, which was in poor condition, has been removed.* 1950. (Ph. Jean Guiart.)

34. *Australian Art*. Melville Island, Arnhem Land. *Cut-off funerary posts: incised and painted.* 1948. (Ph. Axel Poignant.)

35. *Art of New Ireland*. North-east coast. *Detail of the face of a figure called muligau.* Basle, Museum für Völkerkunde. Collected by A. Bühler in 1932. Height: 6 ft. (Ph. Hans Hinz.)

36. *Art of New Ireland*. North-east coast, Medina. *Malanggan mast.* Basle, Museum für Völkerkunde. Collected by A. Bühler in 1932. Height: 7 ft 5 1/2 ins. The scene refers to the legend of a man who died after having stepped on a fish. The woman (at top) fills water gourds and gives water to protector birds. (Ph. Hans Hinz.)

37. *Sepik Art*. Eastern New Guinea, Sepik Valley. *Over-modelled skull.* Dried skull covered with clay. *Korrigane* collection, 1939. Sold by auction in 1962 in the course of the dispersal of a collection made on allegedly scientific grounds. (Ph. Ina Bandy.)

38. *Art of New Ireland*. North New Ireland, Fessoa. *Open-work malanggan bas-relief.* Basle, Museum für Völkerkunde. Collected by F. Speiser in 1930. Length: 4 ft. 3 ins, height, 20 1/2 ins. Represents bird devouring a serpent, flanked by two small birds. (Ph. Hans Hinz.)

39. *Australian Art*, Oenpelli, Arnhem Land. *Bark painting: the night fishing-spirit Dignuk.* (From: Australia. Aboriginal Paintings, Arnhem Land. The New York Graphic Society by arrangement with UNESCO, Plate XXVIII, left), 1954.

40. *Australian Art*. Oenpelli, Arnhem Land. *Painting on bark: the kangaroo spirit Kandarik* (Op. cit. sup. Plate XXXII, right).

41. *Australian Art*. Goulburn Island, Northern Arnhem Land. *Undergroud tuber with its root system.* (Op. cit. sup. Plate XVII).

42. *Australian Art*. Oenpelli, Arnhem Land. *Bark painting: the spirits called Namarakain.* (Op. cit. sup. Plate XXVIII, right).

43. *Art of New Guinea (South-west)*. Western New Guinea, Asmat. *Statue of unknown purpose;* so-called ancestor figure. Brussels, Musées Royaux d'Art et d'Histoire. *Arts of Melanesia,* by Mme Della Santa, 1958 (ET, 658). Height: 31 3/4 ins. Gift of Le Coq d'Armandville. (Ph. A.C.L., Brussels.)

44. *Sepik Art*. Eastern New Guinea, Sepik Valley. *Wooden mask.* New York, Museum of Primitive Art (56-66), Height: 21 ins. (Ph. Museum - Charles Uht.)

45. *Sepik Art*. Eastern New Guinea, Tambanaman, Sepik Valley. *Mask-robe.* 1960. Mantle of basketwork and fibre, mask of wood enhanced with shells and boars' tusks (Ph. S. Diczbalis.)

46. *Art of Torres Strait*. Mabuiag Island. *Tortoise-shell mask.* British Museum (A.M. Franks, 3278). Length: 4 ft. 1 1/4 ins; breadth: 22 7/8 ins. Collected by the Rev. MacFarlane in 1885. (Ph. British Museum.)

47. *Art of New Britain*. Sulka. *Ceremonial head-dress of great size, made from light vegetable material.* Basle, Museum für Völkerkunde. Collected by Hamburger Südsee Expedition 1908-1910; exchanged in 1914. Diameter 6 ft. 7 ins. (Ph. Hans Hinz.)

48. *Art of New Caledonia*. Yedyeban Island, Pum District. *Fragment of an old mask called Jawaraba Mapi, from the Tijin tribal area.* Coll. Maurice Leenhardt. 1959. Height: 6 1/4 ins. (Ph. Draeger.)

49. *Art of New Guinea (South-west)*. Western New Guinea, Asmat. *Mask and heavy woven costume for the jipae funerary rite.* Amsterdam, Koninklijk Instituut voor de Tropen (2882-10). Height: 35 3/8 ins; width: 35 3/8 ins. (Ph. Ina Bandy.)

50. *Papuan Art*. Eastern New Guinea, Aikora River. *Carved stone pestle.* British Museum (1908-4-23-1). Height: 14 ins. Collected in 1908. An undated archæological specimen. (Ph. British Museum.)

51. *Art of Huon Gulf*. Huon Peninsula. *Head of stone pestle.* Chicago, Natural History Museum (138592-2). Height: 9 7/8 ins. Archæological specimen, undated. Collected by A.B. Lewis in 1909-13. (Ph. Museum.)

52. *Art of central Polynesia*. Tahiti. *Carving in volcanic stone: mother and child.* (Ph. Bernard Villaret.)

53. *New Hebridean Art*. Ambrim. *Full-length statue: grade

symbol. Paris, Musée de l'Homme (X 46-13). Height: 7 ft. 6 ins. Tree-fern enhanced with white paint. (Ph. Sougez.)

54. *New Hebridean Art.* South Malekula. *Heavy headdress in overmodelled tree-fern.* Collection A. Malraux. The blue is an ordinary launderer's 'blue'. (Ph. Roger Parry.)

55. *Sepik Art.* Eastern New Guinea, Kararau, Sepik Valley. *Incised pottery enhanced with colours.* Chicago, Natural History Museum (138006). Height: 3 7/8 ins; diameter: 10 1/4 ins. Collected by A.B. Lewis, 1909-13. (Ph. Nat. Hist. Museum.)

56. *Sepik Art.* Eastern New Guinea, Amuim Klinjam, Sepik Valley. *Detail of incised and coloured pottery.* Chicago, Natural History Museum (138020). Height: 6 3/4 ins; diameter: 10 1/2 ins; Collected by A.B. Lewis, 15909-13. (Ph. Museum.)

57. *Art of western Polynesia.* Wallis Islands. *Young woman beating tapa.* 1960. (Ph. Bernard Villart.)

58. *Sepik Art.* North Maprik, Ulupu. *Painters at work.* The surface consists of flattened rib-sheaths of palm-leaves sewn together and covered with grey clay. The colours: kaolin, red and yellow ochre, wood charcoal mixed with water and, in the case of charcoal, chewed with special leaves. Red is also obtained from the pith of the rose-laurel fruit. The chief artist, the man on the left with long ear-loops, fixes the position of the eyes with the aid of pieces of bamboo and reed, and then paints himself. His assistants help with the rest of the face. (Ph. René Gardi.)

59. *Art of central Polynesia.* Wallis Islands. *Carved wooden stamp for impressing design on tapa (detail).* Paris, Musée de l'Homme. Collected by Dr Renaud. (Ph. Giraudon.)

60. *Art of central Polynesia.* Wallis Islands. *Vegetable stamp for impressing tapa.* Paris, Musée de l'Homme. (Ph. Museum - José Oster.)

61. *Sepik Art.* North Maprik, Ulupu. *Sculptor at work* 1955. (Ph. René Gardi.)

62. *Micronesian Art.* Nitendi, Santa Cruz Islands. *Fine matting used for boys' skirts.* Basle, Museum für Völkerkunde (Vb. 2710). Width: 5 7/8 ins. Collected by F. Speiser, 1912. (Ph. Museum.)

63. *Lake Sentani Art.* Lake Sentani. *Tapa skirt.* Amsterdam, Koninklijk Instituut voor de Tropen (666-320). (Ph. Museum - R.L. Mellema.)

64. *New Hebridean Art.* Banks Island, Mota (?) *Ceremonial cape, called malosaru, of woven matting and decorated with feathers.* British Museum (7929). Length, excluding fringes: 22 1/2 ins. Collected by the Rev. R.H. Codrington, 1873. (Ph. Museum.)

65. *Sepik Art.* *Incised double hook, painted and decorated with cowries.* Philadelphia, University Museum. (29-50-339). (Ph. Museum.)

66. *Art of the Solomon Islands.* San Cristobal (?) *Large wooden bowl, encrusted with mother-of-pearl.* Honolulu, Bernice Pauahi Bishop Museum. (Ph. Museum.)

67. *Art of the Admiralty Islands.* Admiralty Islands. *Large wooden bowl with incurving openwork handles.* Honolulu, Bernice Pauahi Bishop Museum. (Ph. Museum.)

68. *Art of Massim.* Trobriand Islands, Kiriwana. *Lime spatula with anthropomorphic figure.* Basle, Museum für Völkerkunde. (Vb 1031.) Gift of P.G. Blach, Sydney. Black wood, enhanced with lime. Length: 11 3/4 ins. (Ph. Museum.)

69. *Art of New Guinea.* Eastern New Guinea, Rai coast. *Lime gourd of incised bamboo.* Leningrad, Museum of Anthropology and Ethnology (168-84). Length: 8 ins; width : 1/4 in. Collected by Miklucho Macklay, 1870-1885. (Ph. Museum.)

70. *Art of the Admiralty Islands.* Anchorite Islands (?) *Carved wood comb, with a frieze of human heads whose hair is arranged in a crest.* Honolulu, Bernice Pauahi Bishop Museum. Registered, probably erroneously, as from New Hebrides. (Ph. Museum.)

71. *Papuan Art.* Papua. *Bark belt, incised and enhanced with lime.* Budapest, Ethnographic Museum (72-074). Height: 6 1/8 ins; diameter: 8 1/2 ins. Collected by the German warship *Panther* before 1905. (Ph. Museum.)

72. *Art of Solomon Islands.* New Georgia, Marovo Lagoon. *Tortoise-shell and tridacna shell pendant, Kapkap.* Basle, Museum für Völkerkunde (Vb. 8072). Collected by E. Paravicini, 1931. Diameter: 4 ins. (Ph. Museum.)

73. *Sepik Art.* North Maprik, Yemal. *Maprik dancer in full costume.* 1955. The colouring matter on the dancers' forehead and eyelids is so thick that they have to be led to the dancing place. A dance performed at the opening of a school at Maprik itself. (Ph. René Gardi.)

74. *Art of Massim.* Tip of eastern New Guinea. *Parade mace, incised and enhanced with lime.* Leningrad, Museum of Anthropology and Ethnology (3117-35). Length: 2 ft. 2 ins. Collection H.R. Pulleine, formerly at the Stockholm Museum, 1925. (Ph. Museum.)

75. *Art of Solomon Islands.* Santa Isabel Island. *Mace in light relief carving.* New York, Museum of Primitive Art (56-29). Length: 4 ft. 2 ins. (Ph. Museum.)

76. *Maori Art.* New Zealand. *Short whalebone patu mace.* Honolulu, Bernice Pauahi Bishop Museum (1458). Length: 15 ins; width: 5 1/4 ins; thickness: 3/4 in. Collected by Eric Craig, 1888. (Ph. Museum.)

77. *Sepik Art.* Eastern New Guinea, Banaro, Sepik Valley. *Ceremonial shield, of semi-human, semi-animal symbolism.* Rome, Lateran Museum, 'Monumenti Musei e Gallerie Pontificie' Stato della città del Vaticano (Au. 2262 Av.). Basket-work covered with clay and decorated with cassowary feathers, nassa shells, and cowries, as well as boartusks. The head with its trunk is modelled on a piece of human skull: the eyes are of mother-of-pearl. A hole in the back houses a miniature bow and arrows. Height: 5 1/8 ins. (Ph. Friedrich Hewicker.)

78. *Art of New Guinea (South-west).* Asmat. *Manufacture and decoration of shields.* 1959. (Ph. Tony Saulnier.)

79. *Art of New Guinea (South-west).* Western New Guinea, Asmat. *Shield with painted decorations in champlevé.* New York, Museum of Primitive Art (59-10). (Ph. Museum-Charles Uht.)

80. *New Hebridean Art.* South-east Ambrim. *Tree-fern carving : symbol of the mage lon bul grade.* Hamburg, Museum für Völkerkunde und Vorgeschichte. Height: 5 ft. 4 ins. (Ph. Fr. Hewicker.)

81. *New Hebridean Art.* South-east Malekula (Port Sandwich?). *Grade symbol carving.* Paris, Musée de l'Homme (90-27-4). Height: 10 3/8 ins; diameter at chevrons: 12 1/4 ins; diameter at front: 14 1/8 ins. Tree-fern collected by Higginson in 1890. (Ph. Museum.)

82. *New Hebridean Art.* Ambrim. *Female carving, symbol of the mage lon bul.* Basle, Museum für Völkerkunde (53-90). Base of tree-fern trunk. (Ph. Museum.)

83. *New Hebridean Art.* Ambrim. *Carving: symbol of the grade wurwur: mage ne urur (detail of bust and face).* Basle, Museum für Völkerkunde (53-90). (Ph. Hans Hinz.)

84. *New Hebridean Art.* Tomman Island, Malekula. *Monumental drum: detail of head.* 1950. (Ph. Jean Guiart.)

85. *New Hebridean Art.* Mendu, south-west of Malekula. *Group of monumental drums set up on the dance place,* 1950. (Ph. Jean Guiart.)

86. *New Hebridean Art.* Ambrim (Lolubulo). *Sand-drawing, tu, made by Tokon in 1949. Special name: havate, the moon.* A man sits on a bowl and with a staff pushes away the clouds which obscure the light of the moon. (Ph. Jean Guiart.)

87. *New Hebridean Art.* Ambrim (Lolubulo). *A sand-drawing, tu, made by Tokon in 1949. Special name: loruwer, taro-cake (lap lap).* The taro being a feminine symbol, the metaphor of taro grated into porridge, and cooked in the oven, links the description of the details of the drawing : man and woman in position of coitus. (Ph. Jean Guiart.)

88. *New Caledonian Art.* New Caledonia, Canala region. *Incised bamboo tube: a round dance.* Geneva, Musée et Institut d'Ethnographie. (Ph. Museum.)

89. *Art of Easter Island.* Easter Island. *Male statue, moai kava-kava (detail of the head).* British Museum. Height: 1 ft. 5 3/8 ins. In red taromiro wood: the eye-socket is made from a hollow bird-bone, and the pupils of fragments of obsidian. (Ph. Fr. Hewicker.)

90. *Art of Easter Island.* Easter Island. *Male statue, moai kavakava.* Philadelphia, University Museum. (Ph. Museum.)

91. *Papuan Art.* Papua. *Incised votive plaque.* Leningrad, Museum of Anthropology and Ethnology (1186-18). Height: 4 1/2 ins. Enhanced with red and black.

92. *Maori Art.* New Zealand. *Wall panel of a meeting house.* Hamburg: Museum Für Völkerkunde und Vorgeschichte. Height: 8 1/2 ins. Central carving and interwoven white, black and red reeds. The figure's eyes are made from the green shell of a marine gasteropod (Haliotis). Tischner explains that it is an allusion to the myth of Maui fishing the islands out of the sea. We may also think of a sexual symbol which occurs elsewhere, that of a fish nibbling the phallus: here the figure is sexless, but the fish is normally a male symbol. (Ph. Ursula Jonas.)

93. *New Hebridean Art.* South Malekula. *Heavy tree-fern head-dress, with an overmodelled face, which supports a figure.* Paris, Musée des Arts Africains et Océaniens (1018). Height: 2 ft. 8 5/8 ins; width: 1 ft. 6 7/8 ins. The face of the mask is that of the ogress Nevinbumbaau and the figure, that of her son or husband. (Ph. Ina Bandy.)

94. *New Hebridean Art.* South Malekula. *Temes nevinbür figure, from a marionette show.* Paris, Musée de l'Homme. (Ph. Museum-José Oster.)

95. *New Hebridean Art.* South Malekula. *Temes nevinbür figure.* Paris, Musée de l'Homme. (Ph. Museum-José Oster.)

96. *Sepik Art.* Eastern New Guinea, Iatmül (Kararau?) *Carved ridge-board from a men's long-house.* New York, Museum of Primitive Art (58-343). (Ph. Museum.)

97. *Sepik Art.* Eastern New Guinea, Kaminimbit, Sepik Valley. *Canoe shield.* Basle, Museum für Völkerkunde (9367). Height: 2 ft. 7 1/2 ins; width: 3 ft. 5 3/4 ins. Head carved, with vegetable panels. Collected by F. Speiser, 1930. (Ph. Moeschlin and Baur.)

98. *Art of Solomon Islands.* San Cristobal. *Drawing of a marine divinity, an adaro ni Matawa, called Tararamanu. By Saunitiku, of Fagani village.* These divinities travel by sliding on a rainbow, a gust of wind or a waterspout. Fishermen attacked by them feel as if they have been struck on the back of the neck and fall unconscious. If they survive the first shock, they can be saved by offering a flying-fox tooth to the adaro. Specific diseases are attributed to particular adaro, while others protect the fields or treasures of chiefs. In San Cristobal the adaro Tararamanu was the

object of a cult designed to ensure the success of the bonito fishing. (From: C.E. Fox: *The Threshold of the Pacific*, p. 126.)

99. *New Caledonian Art.* Huailu (Nerheughakwea). *King-post of a house being dragged from the forest. By Boesou Eurijisi, 1920.* The commoners pull while the priests give them strength by their rites. (From Maurice Leenhardt: *Notes d'ethnologie néo-calédonienne,* fig. 2, p. 5.)

100. *Art of the Solomon Islands.* Buka. *Search for the soul after death. Detail of a drawing by Somuk, 1939.* Collection: Father O'Reilly. Ink drawing (10 *1/2* × 13 *3/4* ins.). The chief is shown holding the branch which is to be replanted. The adzes were used to cut down the dead man's plantations. (Ph. Draeger.)

101. *Art of the Solomon Islands.* Buka. *Funeral dance in front of a body laid on a platform. By Somuk, 1939.* Collection: Father O'Reilly. Drawing in ink and coloured pencil (6 3/4 × 8 1/4 ins.). (Ph. Draeger.)

102. *Australian Art.* Wellington Mountains, Arnhem Land. *Rock painting,* 1952. (Ph. Axel Poignant.)

103. *Australian Art.* Wellington Mountains, Arnhem Land. *Rock painting of a fish in the x-ray style.* (Ph. Axel Poignant.)

104. *Australian Art.* Inagurduwil, Arnhem Land. *Rock painting.* Armed Mimi spirits running. (From: Australia, Aboriginal paintings, Arnhem Land, The New York Graphic Society by arrangement with UNESCO, Plate VI, 1954.)

105. *Australian Art.* Cape Stewart, near Millingimbi, Arnhem Land. *Ceremonial representation of a fish, a clan symbol.* 1952. Made of human hair consolidated with vegetable gum round a wooden core. Very rare, because it is usually destroyed at the end of the ritual. (Ph. Axel Poignant.)

106. *Australian Art.* Victoria. *Incised wood panel.* Melbourne, National Museum of Victoria. (Ph. K. Lommel.)

107. *Art of Torres Strait.* Torres Strait. *Portable drum.* New York, Museum of Primitive Art (56-260 B). Length: 3 ft. 4 1/2 ins. (Ph. Museum.)

108. *Art of Torres Strait.* Torres Strait. *Mask.* Private collection, New York. Length: 15 ins. width: 5 1/2 ins. Tortoise-shell. (From: Linton and Wingert: *Arts of the South Seas,* p. 125.)

109. *Art of Torres Strait.* Torres Strait. *Mask.* Collection: Lecorneur-Roudillon. Tortoise-shell. (Ph. Ina Bandy.)

110. *Papuan Art.* Eastern New Guinea, Goari Bari. *Incised and painted votive tablet.* Chicago, Natural History Museum (142697). Height: 4 ft. 2 3/4 ins; breadth: 8 1/2 ins. Collected by A.B. Lewis, 1909-13. (Ph. Museum.)

111. *Papuan Art.* Eastern New Guinea, Purari delta. *Painted votive plaque.* Budapest, Ethnographic Museum (72-153). Length: 4 ft. 4 3/4 ins; breadth: 8 7/8 ins; thickness: 14 to 20 ins. Collected by the warship *Panther* before 1905. (Ph. Museum.)

112. *Papuan Art.* Eastern New Guinea. *Detail of a painted votive plaque.* Coll: Paul Vérité. (Ph. Giraudon.)

113. *Papuan Art.* Kiwai (?). *Detail of full-length figure.* New York, Museum of Primitive Art. Incised and painted decoration. (Ph. Museum - Ch. Uht.)

114. *Papuan Art.* Kiwai (?). *Full-length figure.* New York, Museum of Primitive Art. Incised and painted decoration. (Ph. Museum - Ch. Uht.)

115. *Detail* of 116.

116. *Papuan Art.* Papua. *Painted bark belt.* Budapest, Ethnographic Museum (72-012). Paint on champlevé. Collected by the warship *Panther* before 1905. (Ph. Museum.)

117. *Papuan Art,* Papua. *Tapa Mask.* Budapest, Ethnographic Museum. Tapa on a rattan frame. Height: 9 1/2 ins. (Ph. Museum.)

118. *Papuan Art.* Elema (Orokolo Bay). *Tapa mask on a light framework.* New York, Museum of Primitive Art (5894). Height: 4 ft. 3 3/4 ins. (Ph. Museum - Ch. Uht.)

119. *Art of New Guinea.* South-west, western New Guinea, Asmat. *Kneeling figure (carved canoe-prow).* Basle, Museum für Völkerkunde (Vb. 6165). (Ph. Moeschlind Baur.)

120. *Art of New Guinea. (South-west).* Western New Guinea, Eilanden River, Asmat. *Carved canoe-prow.* Collection: Paul Wirz, 1923. Basle, Museum für Völkerkunde (Vb 6155). Brown wood, red ochre and white paint. Height: 2 ft. 9 1/2 ins; dimension of square portion: 17 × 15 ins. (Ph. Friedrich Hewicker.)

121. *Art of New Guinea (South-west).* Western New Guinea, Asmat. *Carved prow of a canoe.* Coll. Horst Bandat. Budapest, Ethnographic Museum (136-897). Length: 2 ft. 2 ins; height: 12 1/4 ins; thickness: 4 1/4 ins. (Ph. Museum.)

122. *Detail of* 120.

123. *Detail of* 121.

124. *Art of New Guinea (South-west).* Western New Guinea, Asmat. *Shield.* Coll. Horst Bandat, 1935-39. Budapest, Ethnographic Museum (136-783). Paint and champlevé. Length: 4 ft. 4 1/8 ins; breadth: 16 3/8 ins. (Ph. Museum.)

125. *Art of New Guinea (South-west).* Western New Guinea, Asmat. *Painted shield.* New York Museum of Primitive Art (56-324). Height: 13 1/4 ins; champlevé. (Ph. Museum.)

445

126. *Art of Lake Sentani.* Western New Guinea, Kabiterau, Lake Sentani. *Carved centre-post of a house.* Amsterdam, Koninklijk Instituut voor de Tropen (2202-75). Height: 6 ft. 0 ins. (Ph. Museum-R.L. Mellema.)

127. *Detail of 129.* (Ph. Fr. Hewicker.)

128. *Art of Lake Sentani.* Western New Guinea, Lake Sentani. *Carved ridge-pole.* Amsterdam, Koninklijk Instituut voor de Tropen (574-14). Painted in black, white and dark red ochre. Length: 9 ft. 7 5/8 ins. (Ph. Museum-R.L. Mellema.)

129. *Art of Lake Sentani.* Western New Guinea, Kabiterau, Lake Sentani. *Motherhood.* Basle, Museum für Völkerkunde (Vb 6559). Height: 3 ft. 1/4 ins. (Ph. Fr. Hewicker.)

130. *Art of Lake Sentani.* Western New Guinea, Asei, Lake Sentani. *Carved ridge-pole.* Coll. Paul Wirz, 1927. Basle, Museum für Völkerkunde (Vb 6666). Length: 8 ft. 7 3/4 ins. (Ph. Moeschlin and Baur.)

131. *Art of Lake Sentani.* Western New Guinea, Lake Sentani. *Dish with carved bottom.* Amsterdam, Koninklijk Instituut voor de Tropen (1302-9). Length: 20 7/8 ins. Frog motif. Comparative study shows that it also represents a human being. (Ph. Museum.)

132. *Art of Lake Sentani.* Western New Guinea, Lake Sentani. *Dish with carved bottom.* Basle, Museum für Völkerkunde (Vb 6649). Length: 2 ft. 2 3/8 ins; width: 8 1/8 ins. Used for serving fish. (Ph. Museum.)

133. *Art of Lake Sentani.* Western New Guinea, Lake Sentani, (Netar). *Carved portable drum.* Coll. Paul Wirz, 1927. Basle, Museum für Völkerkunde (Vb 6654). Head of cassowary skin, lashings of rattan. Height: 2 ft.; breadth: 9 1/16 ins. (Ph. Museum.)

134. *Art of Lake Sentani.* Western New Guinea, Lake Sentani. *Double hook.* Coll. Paul Wirz, 1921. Basle, Museum für Völkerkunde (Vb 5563). Height: 2 ft. 2 3/4 ins. The arms of the figure form the hooks. (Ph. Moeschlin and Baur.)

135. *Art of Lake Sentani.* Western New Guinea, Ajafo, Lake Sentani. *Decoration of a longhouse gable-end: solar disc.* Coll. Paul Wirz, 1927. Basle, Museum für Völkerkunde (Vb. 6657). Red, black and white paint. Diameter: 2 ft. 3 1/2 ins. (Ph. Museum.)

136. *Art of Lake Sentani.* Western New Guinea, Saboiboi. Lake Sentani. *Piece of ritual tapa.* Coll. Paul Wirz, 1927. Basle, Museum für Völkerkunde (Vb 6658). Black and red painted motifs. Length: 5 ft. 8 7/8 ins; breadth: 3 ft. 8 1/8 ins. Tapa of this sort was hung by the tombs of women. Smaller pieces of the same type were worn by girls at feasts. (Ph. Museum.)

137. *Sepik art.* Eastern New Guinea, Washkuk, Sepik valley. *Painted vegetable plaques.* Coll. Alfred Bühler, 1955. Basle,

Museum für Völkerkunde (unnumbered). This is not bark but the lower part of the casing of an areca-palm trunk. (Ph. Hans Hinz.)

138. *Sepik art.* Eastern New Guinea, Abelam, Sepik Valley. *Ridge-pole ornament.* New York, American Museum of Natural History (800-6682). Height: 14 ins. Polychrome face. (Ph. Museum.)

139. *Sepik art.* New Guinea, Tambanum, Middle Sepik. *Human face; detail of the backrest of an orator's stool.* (1955). Covered with clay and red ochre; decorated with cassowary plumes, tufts of human hair, boar tusks and snail shells (chin, forehead and eyes). These stools were not to be sat upon, but the orator struck them with leaves or placed on them a single leaf from time to time in the course of his speech. This ritual attested that the words spoken were true. (Ph. René Gardi.)

140. *Sepik art (Abelam).* Eastern New Guinea, South Maprik (Numuoaka, near Numdungai). *Painted plaques.* Coll. Alfred Bühler, 1955-56. Basle, Museum für Völkerkunde (Vb 13931-2). Painted in white, red, black, light brown and blue-green. Height: 5 ft. 1 7/8 ins; breadth: 2 ft. 6 3/4 ins. (Ph. Hans Hinz.)

141. *Sepik art.* Kalabu, Maprik. *Detail of a frieze of faces painted on the fronton of a longhouse.* 1961. (Ph. Jacques Villeminot.)

142. *Sepik art.* Kalabu, Maprik. *Detail of a frieze of carved and painted heads on the lower part of a longhouse fronton.* 1961. (Ph. Jacques Villeminot.)

143. *Sepik art.* South Maprik, Bogmuken. *Carvings from inside a men's longhouse.* Coll. Alfred Bühler, 1955. Basle, Museum für Völkerkunde (Vb 13855 and 13862). (Ph. Hans Hinz.)

144. *Sepik art.* Eastern New Guinea, Abelam (Bogmuken), Sepik valley. *Carved figure: one of the series inside a monumental longhouse, tambaran.* Coll. Alfred Bühler, 1955-56. Basle, Museum für Völkerkunde (Vb 13857). Height: 4 ft. 2 7/8 ins. (Ph. Museum.)

145. *Sepik art.* Eastern New Guinea, mouth of the Sepik. *Beaked mask.* Brussels, Musées royaux d'Art et d'Histoire, *Arts de la Mélanésie,* by Mme Della Santa. 1958. (Et. 43-5.) Height: 15 3/8 ins. Red ochre with white and brown accents. (Ph. A.C.L., Brussels.)

146. *Sepik art (Abelam).* Eastern New Guinea, Maprik. *Basketwork mask.* New York, Museum of Primitive Art (59-206). (Ph. Museum.)

147. *Sepik art (Abelam).* North Maprik. *Carved polychrome frieze from the lower part of a longhouse fronton.* New York, Museum of Primitive Art (58-246). (Ph. Museum.)

148. *Sepik art (Chambuli).* Eastern New Guinea, Uambong, Lake Chambuli. *Ornamental head, gable-end, longhouse.*

Paris, Musée de l'Homme (55-76-377). Height: 2 ft. 3 1/2 ins; width (at ears): 13 3/4 ins. Collected by Françoise Girard in 1954-55. (Ph. Museum - José Oster.)

149. *Sepik art (Iatmül)*. Eastern New Guinea, Kararau (?), Middle Sepik. *Ornamental head, gable-end, longhouse.* New York, Museum of Primitive Art (56-411 A). (Ph. Museum.)

150. *Sepik art.* Eastern New Guinea, Kararau, Middle Sepik. *Ornamental head, gable-end, longhouse.* Chicago, Museum Natural History (141236). Height: 2 ft. 10 5/8 ins; breadth : 18 1/8 ins. Collected by A.B. Lewis in 1909-13. (Ph. Museum.)

151. *Sepik art (Iatmül).* Eastern New Guinea, region of contact between Iatmül and Chambuli. *Polychrome carved wood plaque.* New York, Museum of Primitive Art, (56-372). (Ph. Museum.)

152. *Sepik art (Chambuli).* Eastern New Guinea, Lake Chambuli. *Human face in flattened pottery, used as a hearth in pile-dwellings.* Coll. Alfred Bühler, 1955-56. Basle, Museum für Völkerkunde (Vb 14720). Diameter : 24 3/4 ins. (Ph. Moeschlin and Baur.)

153. *Sepik art.* Middle Sepik. *A symbolical carving of a human figure, Kamanggabi.* Budapest, Ethnographic Museum. Height: 8 7/8 ins. (Ph. Museum.)

154. *Sepik art (Iatmül).* Eastern New Guinea, Middle Sepik. *Overmodelled and painted skull.* New York, Museum of Primitive Art (57-245). (Ph. Museum.)

155. *Sepik art (Iatmül).* Eastern New Guinea, Middle Sepik. *Canoe-prow carved into a cayman's head.* New York, Museum of Primitive Art (55-1 A). Length: 5 ft. 4 3/4 ins. (Ph. Museum.)

156. *Sepik art (Iatmül).* Eastern New Guinea, Middle Sepik. *Human-headed multiple hook.* New York, Museum of Primitive Art. (Ph. Museum - Ch. Uht.)

157. *Sepik Art.* Eastern New Guinea, Middle Sepik. *Basket-work mask, surmounted by a bird with spread wings.* Philadelphia, University Museum. (Ph. Museum.)

158. *Sepik art (Kambringi).* Eastern New Guinea, Kabriman, middle loop of the Sepik. *Ornamental head, gable-end, longhouse.* Coll. Paul Wirz, 1954. Basle, Museum für Völkerkunde (Vb. 2897). Height: 5 ft. 3 3/4 ins; width: 22 1/4 ins. (Ph. Moeschlin and Baur.)

159. *Sepik art (Kambringi).* Eastern New Guinea, River Karawari (or Kwolawoli), right bank of Sepik, to south-east of the Iatmül. *Orator's stool.* New York, Museum of Primitive Art, (59-291). Height: 3 ft. 8 1/8 ins. (Ph. Museum.)

160. *Detail of* 159.

161. *Sepik Art.* Eastern New Guinea, Middle Sepik. *Pot decorated with human faces in relief.* Formerly in Munich Museum. Basle, Museum für Völkerkunde (Vb 11909). Height: 17 3/8 ins. (Ph. Museum.)

162. *Sepik art (Kambringi).* Eastern New Guinea, Middle Sepik. *Pottery ridge ornament.* Basle, Museum für Völkerkunde (Vb 9417). Height : 18 7/8 ins. Collected by Felix Speiser in 1930. (Ph. Moeschlin and Baur.)

163. *Sepik art.* Töpfer River. *Shield covered with feather mosaic.* Steyl Museum (14). Length: 3 ft. 9 5/8 ins; width: 11 ins. A human face motif can be detected. (Ph. Hans Hinz.)

164. *Sepik art (Kambringi).* Eastern New Guinea, Middle Sepik. *Pottery ridge ornament.* Basle, Museum für Völkerkunde (Vb. 9356). Red ground, white decoration. Height: 13 3/4 ins. Collected by Felix Speiser in 1930. (Ph. Hans Hinz.)

165. *Sepik art.* Eastern New Guinea, Tambanum, Middle Sepik. *Small mask used for decorating cult objects.* Basle, Museum für Völkerkunde (Vb. 8620). Height: 5 ins. Collected by Felix Speiser in 1930. (Ph. Moeschlin and Baur.)

166. *Sepik art.* Eastern New Guinea, Kaminimbit, Middle Sepik. *Standing figure.* Basle, Museum für Völkerkunde (Vb. 9389). Height: 6 ft. 7 1/2 ins. Collected by Felix Speiser in 1930. (Ph. Moeschlin and Baur.)

167. *Detail of* 168.

168. *Sepik art.* Eastern New Guinea, Mandanan, Middle Sepik. *Orator's stool.* Basle, Museum für Völkerkunde (Vb 9403). Height: 5 ft. 2 1/4 ins. Collected by Felix Speiser in 1930. (Ph. Moeschlin and Baur.)

169. *Detail of* 166.

170. *Sepik art.* New Guinea, Sepik. *Stopper for a lime gourd.* Honolulu, Academy of Arts. Polychrome, carved wood. (Ph. Museum.)

171. *Sepik art.* New Guinea, Sepik. *Lime-container with carved stopper.* New York, Museum of Primitive Art (575) Height: 22 1/4 ins. (Ph. Museum.)

172. *Art of New Guinea (South-west).* Mimika, Avea. *Open-work canoe-prow.* New York, Museum of Primitive Art. At once related to, and contrasted with, the forms in 170. (Ph. Museum - Ch. Uht.)

173. *Sepik art.* Kebiang, Middle Sepik. *Carved ridge ornament: man and bird.* New York, Museum of Primitive Art (59200). Height: 4 ft. 1/8 ins. (Ph. Museum.)

174. *Sepik art.* Poropolo. *Mask.* New York, Museum of Primitive Art. (Ph. Museum - Ch. Uht.)

175. *Sepik art.* Eastern New Guinea, Middle Sepik. *Bas-relief: female figure whose genitals are offered to two fishes.* Coll.

Paul Wirz. Height: 4 ft. 2 3/8 ins. Door panel. Since the fish is a male sex symbol, the sexual theme here is capable of various interpretations. (Cf. Wirz, Paul: *Kunstwerke vom Sepik*, Basle, 1954, fig. 31.)

176. *Sepik art.* Eastern New Guinea, Mindimbit, Middle Sepik. *Mythical scene.* Coll. Paul Wirz. Amsterdam, Koninklijk Instituut voor de Tropen. Carved, openwork wood. Height: 7 ft. 3 3/8 ins. The figure is called Betman-Gambi. (Ph. Museum - R.L. Mellema.)

177. *Sepik art.* Eastern New Guinea, Middle Sepik. *Wooden plaque: carving and openwork.* New York, Museum of Primitive Art (56-320). Height: 6 ft. 2 3/8 ins. (Ph. Museum.)

178. *Sepik art.* Eastern New Guinea, Kanduonum, Lower Sepik. *Carved and painted shield.* New York, Museum of Primitive Art (56-269). (Ph. Museum.)

179. *Sepik art.* Eastern New Guinea, Kambrambo, Middle Sepik. *Vegetable panel with a painting of two cassowaries.* Basle, Museum für Völkerkunde (Vb 9409). Height: 3 ft. 2 1/8 ins; width: 3 ft. 1/4 ins. Decoration of a longhouse. Collected by Felix Speiser in 1930. (Ph. Hans Hinz.)

180. *Sepik art.* Eastern New Guinea, Kambrambo, Middle Sepik. *Painted vegetable panel.* Basle, Museum für Völkerkunde (Vb 4915). Height: 3 ft 6 1/8 ins; width: 3 ft. 2 ins. Collected by Felix Speiser in 1930. (Ph. Hans Hinz.)

181. *Sepik art* (*Mundugumor*). Eastern New Guinea, Yuat River. *Mouthpiece of a ritual flute, surmounted by a human figure.* Coll. Eckert, Basle. Height: 20 1/2 ins. (Ph. Moeschlin and Baur.)

182. *Sepik art* (*Mundugumor*). Eastern New Guinea, Yuat River. *Polychrome carved head-rest.* New York, American Museum of Natural History (80-1-201). Length: 13 ins; height: 3 7/8 ins. Collected by Margaret Mead in 1933. (Ph. Museum.)

183. *Sepik art* (*Mundugumor*). Eastern New Guinea, Yuat River. *Protean figure.* New York, Museum of Primitive Art (59-170). (Ph. Museum.)

184. *Sepik art* (*Mundugumor*). Eastern New Guinea, Yuat River. *Carved polychrome head-rest.* New York, American Museum of Natural History (80-1-199). Length: 19 ins; width: 3 1/4 ins. Collected by Margaret Mead in 1933. (Ph. Museum.)

185. *Sepik art* (*Mundugumor*). Eastern New Guinea, Yuat River. *Representation of a human face.* New York, Museum of Primitive Art (57-296-A). Height: 11 1/4 ins. Fragments of cowrie and shell inserted in vegetable gum; cassowary plumes. (Ph. Museum.)

186. *Detail of* 187.

187. *Sepik art* (*Mundugumor*). Eastern New Guinea, Yuat

River. *Squatting figure.* New York, Museum of Primitive Art. (Ph. Museum - Ch. Uht.)

188. *Sepik art* (*coastal region*). Eastern New Guinea, Seleo Island. *Vertical frieze : carving and openwork.* Bremen, Völkerkundliche Abteilung, Übersee-Museum (D. 4721). Height: 8 ft. 7 1/2 ins. Brown wood, unpainted. (Ph. Fr. Hewicker.)

189. *Sepik art.* Eastern New Guinea, Lower Sepik. *Wooden panel with carving and openwork.* Formerly Hamburgisches Museum. New York, Museum of Primitive Art (58-330). Height: 5 ft. 10 7/8 ins. (Ph. Museum.)

190. *Sepik art* (*coastal region*). Eastern New Guinea, to the east of the mouth of the Sepik. *Wooden mask with trunk.* Budapest, Ethnographic Museum (54-352). Height: 17 1/2 ins; width: 3 1/2 ins. Collected by Giovanni Bettanin before 1904. (Ph. Museum.)

191. *Sepik art* (*coastal region*). Eastern New Guinea, Potsdamhafen. *Beaked wooden mask.* Budapest, Ethnographic Museum (54-348). Height: 17 1/2 ins; width: 3 1/2 ins. Collected by Giovanni Bettanin before 1904. (Ph. Museum.)

192. *Sepik art* (*coastal region*). Eastern New Guinea, Potsdamhafen. *Wooden mask.* Budapest, Ethnographic Museum (72-066). Height: 15 3/4 ins; width: 6 3/4 ins. Collected by the warship *Panther* before 1905. (Ph. Museum.)

193. *Sepik art.* Sepik. *Water drum.* Basle, Museum für Völkerkunde. Used by striking vertically on the surface of the water which serves both as skin and as resonator. (Ph. Moeschlin and Baur.)

194. *Sepik art.* Eastern New Guinea, Ramu river valley. *Standing figure.* Leningrad, Museum of Anthropology and Ethnology (599-10). Height: 7 7/8 ins. Collected by Hans Meyer in 1900. (Ph. Museum.)

195. *Sepik art* (*coastal region*). Eastern New Guinea, mouth of the Sepik (?). *Standing figure with trunked face: detail.* Coll. P. Vérité, Paris. (Ph. Giraudon.)

196. *Sepik art* (*coastal region*). Eastern New Guinea, Potsdamhafen. *Carved and incised shield, enhanced with lime.* Budapest, Ethnographic Museum (54-325). Length: 4 ft. 4 3/8 ins; thickness: 8 1/4 ins. Collected by Giovanni Bettanin before 1904. (Ph. Museum.)

197. *Sepik art.* Eastern New Guinea, Ramu river valley. *Ceremonial drum.* New York, Museum of Primitive Art (5799). Diameter: 3 ft. 6 1/2 ins. Carved handles, sides incised and enhanced with lime. (Ph. Museum.)

198. *Sepik art.* Eastern New Guinea, Ramu river valley. *Wooden panel.* New York, Museum of Primitive Art (59-13). Height: 2 ft. 3/8 ins. Champlevé decoration, enhanced with lime. (Ph. Museum.)

199. *Sepik art.* Eastern New Guinea, Manam Island. *Head-rest.* New York, Museum of Primitive Art (58-113). Height: 5 1/2 ins. (Ph. Museum.)

200. *Sepik art (coastal region).* Eastern New Guinea, Taravaj Island (Aitape District). *Head-rest.* Budapest, Ethnographic Museum (9-836). The feet are drawn back and held by tension. Length: 17 ins; height: 6 3/4 ins; thickness: 2 ins. Collected by Lajos Biro in 1896. (Ph. Museum.)

201. *Sepik art (coastal region).* Eastern New Guinea, Aitape. *Statuette.* Budapest, Ethnographic Museum (11-892). Height: 4 1/4 ins. Collected by Samuel Fenichel in 1892-93. (Ph. Museum.)

202. *Sepik art (coastal region).* Eastern New Guinea, Aitape. *Statuette (profile).* Budapest, Ethnographic Museum (54-368). Height: 9 ins. Collected by Giovanni Bettanin before 1904. (Ph. Museum.)

203. *Three-quarter view of* 202.

204. *Sepik art.* Eastern New Guinea, Lower Sepik. *Polychrome vegetable panel.* New York, Museum of Primitive Art (56-264). Height: 3 ft. 4 1/8 ins; width: 5 ft. 3 3/4 ins. (Ph. Museum - Ch. Uht.)

205. *New Hebridean art.* Aoba. *Stone dish.* Basle, Museum für Völkerkunde (Vb. 11885). Coll. Meier und Stähelin. Originally: Me G. Des Granges, Port Vila. Dish used in the preparation of kava. Volcanic tufa. The raised cups inside help to fray the roots; the tusks are painted black. Length: 2 ft. 1 1/4 ins; height: 13 3/8 ins. (Ph. Moeschlin and Baur.)

206. *New Hebridean art.* Metamli, Ambrim. *Carved head used in the pig magic wüü ne bu.* Paris, Musée des Arts Africains et Océaniens (D-62-1-1). Dense volcanic tufa. Length: 14 ins; width: 6 1/4 ins. Collected by Jean Guiart in 1949. Former collection of the Institut français d'Océanie, depository of the Office de la Recherche scientifique et technique d'outre-mer, M.A.A.O. 'Found by Mweleun Kòn of Mèlwar in a hollow tree where the owner had hidden it, charging that it had made his son ill. Bought for £A 4. When it was left in a house, the inhabitants claimed to have heard it moving. It had to be shifted.' (Ph. Service de Documentation photographique, Réunion des Musées nationaux - Ina Bandy.)

207. *New Hebridean art.* Banks Islands, Gaua. *Grade sculpture.* Basle, Museum für Völkerkunde (Vb 4450). Height: 6 ft. 1 ins. Tree fern. Collected by Felix Speiser in 1912. The number of heads and birds indicates the grade. (Ph. Fr. Hewicker.)

208. *Detail of* 207.

209. *New Hebridean art.* Malekula (East coast). *Wooden sculpture symbol of a grade obtained.* Geneva, Museum and Institute of Ethnography (20938). (Ph. Museum.)

210. *New Hebridean art.* Pao, West Malekula. *Carved and painted post.* Basle, Museum für Völkerkunde (Vb 4822). Collected by Felix Speiser in 1912. (Ph. Hans Hinz.)

211. *New Hebridean art.* Malo (?). *Standing figure: detail.* Paris, Musée de l'Homme (38-42-8). Surmounted by a vertical extension carrying the lower jaws of pigs. Entirely coated with washing blue. Height: 9 ft. 10 1/4 ins; width at shoulders: 13 3/8 ins. Gift of Me G. Des Granges, Port Vila. (Ph. Museum - José Oster.)

212. *New Hebridean art.* Banks Islands, Gaua. *Carving.* Paris, Musée de l'Homme (20-27-2). Tree-fern. Height: 5 ft. 11 5/8 ins; diameter at face: 14 5/8 ins; diameter at belly: 11 3/8 ins. Collected by Higginson in 1890. (Ph. Museum - José Oster).

213. *New Hebridean art.* Fanu, Ambrim. *Ceremonial drum: detail of the head.* Paris, Musée de l'Homme (50-79-1). Breadfruit tree wood. Height: 11 ft. 9 ins; maximum depth of cavity: 1 ft. 7 5/8 ins; height of face: 4 ft. 6 3/4 ins; height of the slit: 5 ft. 4 5/8 ins; cross-section diameter of body: 2 ft. 1 3/4 ins. Collected by Jean Guiart in 1949. Bought from Simon Setap, son of a dignitary of the Mal grade, for £A 10. Made by Naim Bebe (Mèlbülbül. (Ph. Museum - René Pasquino.)

214. *Back of the head shown in* 213.

215. *New Hebridean art.* West Ambrim. *Ceremonial drum.* Basle, Museum für Völkerkunde (Vb 4020). Height: 13 ft. 9 1/4 ins. Collected by Felix Speiser in 1912. The number of faces indicates the rank of the individual who paid for its manufacture. (Ph. Moeschlin and Baur.)

216. *New Hebridean art.* New Hebrides, Achin. *Canoe with its prow carved in the form of a frigate bird.* (Ph. Bernard Villaret.)

217. *New Hebridean art.* Ambrim. *Ritual bludgeon for pigs, atata wanten.* Basle, Museum für Völkerkunde. (Ph. Museum.)

218. *New Hebridean art.* Central south New Hebrides (Paama ?). *Adze.* Honolulu, Bernice P. Bishop Museum. Blade: tridacna shell. (Ph. Museum.)

219. *New Hebridean art.* Espiritu Santo. *Carved wooden dish.* Paris, Musée de l'Homme (29-14-45). Length: 1 ft. 7 1/2 ins; breadth: 10 ins. Collected by Dr. Capitan. (Ph. Museum - José Oster.)

220. *New Hebridean art.* West Ambrim. *Dish for the pounding of breadfruit: lower surface.* New York, Museum of Primitive Art (58-331). Length: 2 ft. 9 1/2 ins. Collected by P. Langlois (?) in 1957. (Ph. Museum).

221. *New Hebridean art.* South Malekula, *Rambaramb funerary figure.* Paris, Musée de l'Homme (39-82-1). Vegetable paste, without clay, on a dried skull, body of tree

449

fern, limbs of rolls of banana leaf, prepared by retting. Gift of Me G. Gomichon Des Granges, Port Vila in 1939. (Ph. Museum - José Oster.)

222. *New Hebridean art.* South Malekula. *Rambaramb funerary figure.* Paris, Musée des Arts Africains et Océaniens (AF-62-1-2). Height: 5 ft. 10 ins; breadth at shoulders: 1 ft. 10 ins. Legs of wood. (Ph. Draeger.)

223. *New Hebridean art.* Aoba. *Mask in light vegetable materials.* Paris, Musée de l'Homme (94-9-6). Cloak of banana trunk fibres. Height: 3 ft. 3 3/8 ins. Collected by Dr. Jollet in 1894. (Ph. Museum.)

224. *New Hebridean art.* South Malekula. *Temes nevinbür figurine.* Paris, Musée de l'Homme. (Ph. Museum - José Oster.)

225. *New Hebridean art.* South-east Malekula (?). *Lozenge-shaped mask with lateral wings, rom.* Paris, Musée de l'Homme (X-44-28). (Ph. Museum - José Oster.)

226. *New Hebridean art.* South Malekula. *Mask to cover the head and shoulders.* Basle, Museum für Völkerkunde (Vb 4776). Height: 3 ft. 11 1/4 ins. Tree fern. Attribute of the semi-public ritual known as Nalawan. Collected by Felix Speiser in 1912. (Ph. Hans Hinz.)

227. *New Hebridean art.* South Malekula. *Polychrome mask.* Paris, Musée des Arts Africains et Océaniens (AF-62-1-1). Height: 3 ft. 10 1/2 ins; width at nose level: 11 3/8 ins. Tree fern. (Ph. Ina Bandy.)

228. *Detail of* 227.

229. *New Hebridean art.* North Malekula (Big Nambas). *Human face motif placed just below the point of a spear.* Paris, Musée de l'Homme (93-22-18). Length of spear: 9 ft. 4 3/4 ins. Collected by Higginson in 1893. (Ph. Roger Parry.)

230. *New Hebridean art.* Ambrim (Mèlwar). *Light, polychrome mask, rom kòn.* Made by Mweleun Kòn (Mèlwar), 1949. Paris, Musée des Arts Africains et Océaniens (D-62-1-4). Overall height: 2 ft. 7 1/2 ins; height of mask: 13 3/4 maximum width: 8 1/2 ins. Former collection of the Institut français d'Océanie, depository of the Office de la Recherche scientifique et technique d'outre-mer, M.A.A.O. Bought from Mweleun Kòn for £A 4 and a shirt. Normally burnt after use. (Ph. Ina Bandy.)

231. *New Hebridean art.* Hebierr (?), South West Bay, Malekula. *Small mask on a spider's web, nabiki, worn in the head-dress.* Paris, Musée de l'Homme (62-1-122). Height: 4 1/2 ins; diameter: 4 3/4 ins. Collected by the *Korrigane* expedition in 1937. 'Badge of the grade of Mweleun... bought at anchor.' (Mme de Ganay). (Ph. Museum - José Oster.)

232. *New Hebridean art.* Pentecost. *Wooden mask with tenon.* Paris, Musée de l'Homme (34-186-229). Total height:

13 ins; height of face: 9 ins; diameter at eye level: 5 1/4 ins. Collected by Aubert de la Rüe in 1934. (Ph. Museum.)

233. *New Hebridean art.* South Malekula. *Head-dress for ceremony, with symmetrical extensions which bear human faces.* Paris, Musée des Arts Africains et Océaniens. Tree fern. (Ph. Service de Documentation photographique des Musées nationaux - Ina Bandy.)

234. *New Hebridean art.* Banks Islands. *Ritual head-dress of light material, tamate.* British Museum (1305). Length: 1 ft. 9 1/2 ins. Collected by the Rev. R.H. Codrington (?) in 1883. (Ph. Museum.)

235. *New Caledonian art.* North Zone (Gomen-Uebia). *Carved entrance from a longhouse.* Paris, Musée de l'Homme (32-55-91-92-94-96-99). Lefthand *jovo*: maximum diameter: 1 ft. 8 ins; height: 5 ft. 10 1/8 ins. Righthand *jovo*: maximum diameter: 1 ft. 8 ins; height: 5 ft. 6 1/2 ins. Lefthand door-jamb: diameter: 9 1/16 ins; height of opening: 3 ft. 9 1/2 ins. Righthand door-jamb: diameter: 7 1/2 ins; height of opening: 3 ft. 9 1/2 ins. Threshold: Height: 20 5/8 ins; breadth: 19 1/4 ins; width at faces: 9 1/3 ins. The threshold piece is an old *jovo*, much worn and reshaped to fill a new function. Collected by Archambault. (Ph. Museum.)

236. *New Caledonian art.* Yambe (Ubatche). *Carved door-jamb, jovo.* Basle, Museum für Völkerkunde (Vb 26-29). Collected by Fritz Sarasin. (Ph. Museum.)

237. *New Caledonian art.* Isle of Pines (Vao). *Carved door-jamb.* 1960 (Ph. Bernard Villaret).

238. *New Caledonian art.* Huailu-Burail. *Carved jamb, tale.* Paris, Musée de l'Homme (31-50-2). Height: 6 ft.; maximum breadth: 1 ft. 9 1/4 ins. The beard motif is unusual. The squared mouth points to a date of manufacture after the arrival of Europeans. Collected by Philippe Rey-Lescure in 1931. (Ph. Museum-José Oster.)

239. *New Caledonian art.* Pote (Burail). *Ridge decoration, go mwê.* Basle, Museum für Völkerkunde. Height: 7 ft. 2 5/8 ins. The projecting and bulging cheeks are typical of this region. Collected by Fritz Sarasin. (Ph. Museum.)

240. *New Caledonian art.* Kwede (Canala). *Ridge decoration.* Basle, Museum für Völkerkunde. Height: 11 ft. 5 3/4 ins. The emphasis is on the lower part of the ear-lobe and the motif of multiple arms attached to the shoulders and wrists. Kwede is on the western limit of this style which belongs more specifically to Canala. Collected by Fritz Sarasin. (Ph. Moeschlin and Baur.)

241. *New Caledonian art.* Mwaregu (Canala). *Ridge ornament on a geometrical theme.* Basle, Museum für Völkerkunde. Height: 7 ft. 4 5/8 ins. The central motif is called fish-belly, *pweshembe*; the thin plaques on either side of it: conus bracelets, *sinja*; the double-pointed motif at top and bottom: wings of the bird of prey, *menekio.* (F. Sarasin.) Collected by F. Sarasin. (Ph. Moeschlin and Baur.)

242. *New Caledonian art.* Warai (Huailu). *Carved beam, bedu, placed horizontally.* Basle, Museum für Völkerkunde (Vb 26-50). Height: 6 ft. 10 5/8 ins. These pieces of wood frame a niche, the height of a man, in the clan house, in which one awaits a divinatory dream. Collected by F. Sarasin. (Ph. Museum.)

243. *New Caledonian art.* Cape Colnett. *House post.* Basle, Museum für Völkerkunde. Height: 5 ft. 1 ins. The carving faces inwards. Collected by F. Sarasin. (Ph. Moeschlin and Baur.)

244. *New Caledonian art.* Canala-Thio region. *Finial.* New York, Museum of Primitive Art (56-302-A). Height: 12 3/4 ins. (Ph. Museum.)

245. *New Caledonian art.* North of the Mainland. *Representation of a child in a traditional cradle.* Numea, Musée Néo-Calédonien. (Ph. Bernard Villaret.)

246. *New Caledonian art.* North of the Mainland. *Pwemwa mask.* Collection: Bischoffsheim, 1880. Paris, Musée de l'Homme (80-39-4). Overall height: 5 ft. 6 7/8 ins; diameter at cheekbones: 6 7/8 ins; height of hair: 1 ft. 6 7/8 ins; height of face: 11 ins; height of nose: 10 1/2 ins; diameter of the nape: 11 3/4 ins. (Ph. Museum - José Oster.)

247. *New Caledonian art.* East coast. *Detail of a spear.* Paris, Musée des Arts Africains et Océaniens (AF-62-2-1). Length of spear: 7 ft. 1 ins; height of human face: 1 1/4 ins; breadth of face: 1 3/8 ins. The face is surrounded by tapa (*awa*), twists of flying-fox hair, and esparto grass on the upper part. (Ph. Ina Bandy.)

248. *New Caledonain art.* New Caledonia. *Ceremonial axe, gi o kono.* Coll. Maurice Leenhardt (Ph. Draeger.)

249. *Art of Astrolabe Bay.* Eastern New Guinea, Astrolabe Bay. *Standing figure.* Budapest, Ethnographic Museum (11-882). Height: 1 ft. 8 1/8 ins. Collected by Samuel Fenichel in 1892-3. (Ph. Museum.)

250. *Art of Astrolabe Bay.* Eastern New Guinea, Astrolabe Bay. *Standing figure, telum.* Budapest, Ethnographic Museum (34-654). Height: 4 ft. 2 3/4 ins. Collected by Lajos Biró in 1896-8. (Ph. Museum.)

251. *Art of Astrolabe Bay.* Eastern New Guinea, Astrolabe Bay. *Standing figure, telum, with bird.* Budapest, Ethnographic Museum (11-852). Height: 4 ft. 1 5/8 ins. (Ph. Museum.)

252. *Art of Astrolabe Bay.* Eastern New Guinea, Astrolabe Bay. *Armlet of incised shell.* Budapest, Ethnographic Museum (7685). Height: 6 5/8 ins; circumference: 9 3/4 ins. Probably originated in Huon Gulf; collected in Astrolabe Bay by Samuel Fenichel in 1892-3. (Ph. Museum.)

253. *Art of Astrolabe Bay.* Eastern New Guinea, Astrolabe Bay. *Polychrome shield.* Collection: Wandres, 1896-9.

Basle, Museum für Völkerkunde (Vb 469). Very heavy wood. Red, white and black paint. Diameter: 2 ft. 6 3/4 ins. The flashes may symbolise lightning. (Ph. Museum.)

254. *Art of Astrolabe Bay.* Eastern New Guinea, Bongu or Bogajim, Astrolabe Bay. *Mask.* Budapest, Ethnographic Museum (8920). Wood, Collected by Samuel Fenichel in 1892-3. (Ph. Museum.)

255. *Art of Astrolabe Bay.* Eastern New Guinea, Astrolabe Bay. *Mask.* Budapest, Ethnographic Museum. Height: 1 ft. 6 1/8 ins. Hard wood which is reddened or blackened in places. (Ph. Museum.)

256. *Art of Astrolabe Bay.* Eastern New Guinea, Astrolabe Bay. *Tapa cover.* Budapest, Ethnographic Museum (12-879). Length: 5 ft. 5 3/8 ins; maximum width: 3 ft. 3 3/4 ins. Collected by Samuel Fenichel in 1892-3. (Ph. Museum.)

257. *Art of Huon Gulf.* Eastern New Guinea, Tami Island. *Tapa mask on a light framework, tago.* Budapest, Ethnographic Museum (64-277). Height: 2 ft. 3 1/8 ins. Collected by Lajos Biró in 1899-1900. Published in colour in Bodrogi, Tibor: *Oceanic Art* p. 45. (Ph. Museum.)

258. *Art of Huon Gulf.* Eastern New Guinea, Huon Gulf. *Polychrome wooden mask.* Honolulu, Bernice P. Bishop Museum. Height : 1 ft. 7 1/2 ins ; breadth : 8 ins. (Ph. Museum.)

259. *Art of Huon Gulf.* Eastern New Guinea, Apo, Huon Gulf. *Polychrome wooden mask.* Chicago, Natural History Museum (138432). Height: 1 ft. 11 5/8 ins; breadth: 11 3/4 ins. Collected by A. B. Lewis in 1909-13. (Ph. Museum.)

260. *Art of Huon Gulf.* Eastern New Guinea, Huon Gulf. *Polychrome bas-relief of a standing figure.* Honolulu, Bernice P. Bishop Museum. (Ph. Museum.)

261. *Art of Huon Gulf.* Eastern New Guinea, Tami Island (?). *Standing figure.* Basle, Museum für Völkerkunde (Vb 2915). Height: 4 ft. 7 1/8 ins. White, red and black paint. Coll.: Miss H. P. Wenzel, Rabaul. Bought near Finschhafen. (Ph. Museum.)

262. *Art of Huon Gulf.* Eastern New Guinea, Molu, Huon Gulf. *Polychrome standing figure.* Budapest, Ethnographic Museum. (64-729.) Height: 1 ft. 4 7/8 ins. Collected by Lajos Biró in 1899-1900. (Ph. Museum.)

263. *Art of Huon Gulf.* Eastern New Guinea, Huon Gulf. *Carved head-rest.* Budapest, Ethnographic Museum (56-819). (Ph. Museum.)

264. *Art of Huon Gulf.* Eastern New Guinea, Huon Gulf. *Head-rest.* Budapest, Ethnographic Museum (63-911). Height: 4 7/8 ins; breadth: 6 ins. Collected by Lajos Biró in 1899-1900. (Ph. Museum.)

265. *Detail of 264.*

266. *Art of Huon Gulf.* Eastern New Guinea, Tami Island. *Portable drum.* Budapest, Ethnographic Museum (37-918). Height: 2 ft. 1 5/8 ins; circumference at head: 1 ft. 11 1/4 ins; circumference at foot: 1 ft. 10 7/8 ins. Collected by Lajos Biró in 1899-1900. (Ph. Museum.)

267. *Art of Huon Gulf. Detail of the decoration on the upper edge of a wooden bowl.* Paris, Musée des Arts Africains et Océaniens (D-61-2-2-). Coll.: Helen Sheils. Total length 11 1/2 ins; maximum width: 4 5/8 ins; height: 1 3/4 ins; length of central motif: 4 ins. (Ph. Ina Bandy.)

268. *Art of Huon Gulf.* Eastern New Guinea, Tami Island. *Food scoop with carved handle.* Paris, Musée des Arts Africains et Océaniens (D-61-2-1). Coll: Helen Sheils, Length: 2 ft. 1/4 ins; width of scoop 3 3/4 ins. (Ph. Ina Bandy.)

269. *Art of Huon Gulf.* Eastern New Guinea, Tami Island. *Carved double bowl.* Paris, Musée des Arts Africains et Océaniens (D-61-2-3). Coll: Helen Sheils. Length 1 ft. 7 5/8 ins; height 3 3/4 ins; width at centre: 5 3/8 ins. (Ph. Ina Bandy.)

270. *Detail of 271.* (Ph. Museum.)

271. *Art of New Britain.* New Britain, Sulka. *Polychrome canoe-prow.* Budapest, Ethnographic Museum (72063). Height: 4 ft. 11 7/8 ins; width: 12 1/4 ins. Portrayal of a seated pig. Collected by the warship *Panther* before 1905. (Ph. Museum.)

272. *Art of New Britain.* New Britain, Sulka. *Carved canoe prow with anthropomorphic figure.* Budapest, Ethnographic Museum (72070). Total height: 6 ft. 8 3/4 ins; height of figure: 1 ft. 6 1/8 ins; width: 5 3/4 ins. Collected by the warship *Panther* before 1905. (Ph. Museum.)

273. *Art of New Britain.* Witu (or French) Islands. *Tapa mask on a rattan frame.* Budapest, Ethnographic Museum. Height: 2 ft. 6 3/4 ins. (Ph. Museum.)

274. *Art of New Ireland.* Tanga Island. *Mask.* Budapest, Ethnographic Museum. Tapa on a rattan frame: the eyes are half coconut shells, whitened with lime. Height: 15 3/4 ins. (Ph. Museum.)

275. *Art of New Britain.* New Britain, Sulka. *Polychrome mask of sewn basketry.* Bremen. Völkerkundliche Abteilung Übersee Museum. Covered with threads of dyed pith, and cassowary feathers. Height: 3 ft. 11 1/4 ins. (Ph. Hed Wiesner.)

276. *Art of New Britain.* New Britain, Baining. *Tapa mask on a light frame.* Hamburg, Museum für Völkerkunde und Vorgeschichte (1188-33). Height: 3 ft. 3 1/2 ins. (Ph. Friedrich Hewicker.)

277. *Art of New Britain.* New Britain. *Incised motif on a bamboo rod.* Budapest, Ethnographic Museum. Overall length of rod: 2 ft. 9 1/4 ins. (Ph. Museum.)

278. *Art of New Britain.* New Britain Baining. *Mask with blow-pipe.* Basle, Museum für Völkerkunde (Vb 296). Formerly in Hamburg Museum. Red and black on a white ground. Height: 2 ft. 7 1/2 ins; width: 10 1/2 ins; length of tube: 3 ft. 7 1/4 ins. It is not worn on the head but fixed on a pole which is supported in a pocket on the front of the dance costume. Gift of F. Sarasin. (Ph. Moeschlin and Baur.)

279. *Art of New Britain.* New Britain, Sulka. *Polychrome wooden shield.* New York, Museum of Primitive Art (59-158). Height: 4 ft. 2 1/4 ins. (Ph. Museum.)

280. *Art of New Britain.* New Britain, Baining. *Features modelled on the facial part of a dried skull.* Budapest, Ethnographic Museum (104490). Collected by Janos Pauer, before 1913. (Ph. Museum.)

281. *Art of New Britain.* South coast of New Britain. *Wooden mask.* Chicago, Natural History Museum (B7-685). Height: 1 ft. 10 ins; width: 11 3/4 ins. Collected by A.B. Lewis in 1909-13. (Ph. Museum.)

282. *Art of New Britain.* Witu Islands. *Polychrome wooden mask.* Budapest, Ethnographic Museum (67819). Predominantly green. Height: 17 ins. Collected by Lajos Biró in 1900. (Ph. Museum.)

283. *Art of New Ireland.* New Ireland. *Polychrome mask, with carving and openwork.* Basle, Museum für Völkerkunde. (Ph. Hans Hinz.)

284. *Art of New Ireland.* New Ireland. *Polychrome openwork bas-relief.* Basle, Museum für Völkerkunde. (Ph. Hans Hinz.)

285. *Art of New Ireland.* North coast of New Ireland, Lonan. *Standing figure, totok: a figure standing on a pig's head.* Budapest, Ethnographic Museum (64251). Height: 4 ft. 4 1/2 ins; breadth: 10 1/4 ins. Collected by Lajos Biró in 1900. (Ph. Museum.)

286. *Art of New Ireland.* New Ireland, Fatmilak. *Openwork bas-relief with human figures, muligan.* Basle, Museum für Völkerkunde (Vb 10584). Height: 9 7/8 ins; length: 7 ft. 1 1/2 ins. In the centre "the great fire" (Sun?), surrounded by a snake which is held by two men with added heads. The *muligan* ends in two fishes. Collected by Alfred Bühler, in 1932. (Ph. Hans Hinz.)

287. *Art of New Ireland.* New Ireland, Lesu. *Openwork bas-relief with anthropomorphic figures, muligan.* Basle, Museum für Völkerkunde (Vb 10583). Height: 1 ft. 4 1/2 ins; length: 6 ft. 11 1/2 ins. A snake in the centre: four figures framing a flying fish; a fish-head at the end. Collected by Alfred Bühler in 1932. (Ph. Hans Hinz.)

288. *Art of New Ireland.* New Ireland, Medina. *Piece with relief carving and openwork: fish and mythical figures, muligan.* Basle, Museum für Völkerkunde (Vb 10561). Height: 16 1/2 ins; length: 6 ft. 11 1/2 ins. Piece depicting a mythical scene: The gods, "Solanang" in male and female form; the man god "Lamesisi"; fish, flying fish and snake. Lamesisi, the two other heads, the woman's breasts and the ventral fin of the fish have been added after carving. Collected by Alfred Bühler in 1932. (Ph. Hans Hinz.)

289. *Art of New Ireland.* Northern New Ireland. *Polychrome wooden mask with vertical extensions.* Budapest, Ethnographic Museum (54330). Height: 3 ft. 4 1/2 ins; width: 6 ins. Collected by Giovanni Bettanin before 1904. (Ph. Museum.)

290. *Art of New Ireland.* New Ireland, north-east coast, Medina. *Polychrome wooden mask called tatanua.* Basle, Museum für Völkerkunde (Vb 10533). Collected by Alfred Bühler in 1932. Vernacular name: *belerafkof.* Height: 1 ft. 7 5/8 ins. The central "caterpillar" is painted fibres, supplemented by a lime-plaster on the lateral faces. (Ph. Hans Hinz.)

291. *Art of New Ireland.* New Ireland, Fisher Island. *Wooden mask; carving and open work.* Presented by Mrs. K. and R. Geigy, bought in Sydney. Basle, Museum für Völkerkunde (Vb 76). Height: 2 ft. 5 1/2 ins. (Ph. Hans Hinz.)

292. *Art of New Ireland.* North of New Ireland. *Polychrome mask with openwork.* Budapest, Ethnographic Museum (13437). Height: 1 ft. 10 1/2 ins; width 10 1/4 ins. Collected by Giovanni Bettanin before 1904. (Ph. Museum.)

293. *Art of New Ireland.* New Ireland. *Pendant of tridacna and tortoise-shell, kapkap.* Coll. Wandres. 1896-99. Basle, Museum für Völkerkunde (Vb 547). Diameter: 5 1/4 ins. (Ph. Museum.)

294. *Art of New Ireland.* Central New Ireland, Malom; north-east coast, Lemakot. *A battery of drums with open lips, called iaunut.* Basle, Museum für Völkerkunde (Vb 5153), collected in 1920: Length: 5 1/2 ins. (Vb 10791), collected by A. Bühler: length: 1 ft. 11 3/4 ins. (Ph. Museum.)

295. *Art of New Ireland.* North-east coast of New Ireland. *Standing figure called uli.* Basle, Museum für Völkerkunde (Vb 1585). The development of the breasts represents male vigour: there is no question of hermaphroditism. Its function is in connection with ancestor-worship rites and secondary burials. (Ph. Hans Hinz.)

296. *Detail of 295.*

297. *Art of New Ireland.* New Ireland, north of the island. *Mask.* Budapest, Ethnographic Museum. Tapa stretched on a rattan frame. (Ph. Museum.)

298. *Korovar art.* North of western New Guinea. *Korovar with a child.* Copenhagen, National Museum. (Ph. Museum - Lennart Larsen.)

299. *Korovar art.* North of western New Guinea, Mansiman. *Korovar statuette with arabesque decoration.* Leningrad, Museum of Anthropology and Ethnology (190 B 1). Height: 12 1/4 ins. Collected by V. A. Band, Russian Consul at Batavia in 1889. (Ph. Museum.)

300. *Korovar art.* North of western New Guinea, Geelvink Bay. *Carved canoe-prow.* Brussels, Musées royaux d'Art et d'Histoire, *Arts de la Mélanésie* by Mme Della Santa 1958. (Et. 47-26-1). Height: 1 ft. 8 3/4 ins. (Ph. A.C.L., Brussels.)

301. *Korovar art.* North of western New Guinea, Geelvink Bay. *Korovar statue of figure placed against a background of arabesques.* Frankfurt-on-Main, Museum für Völkerkunde. Height: 12 ins. (Ph. Fr. Hewicker.)

302. *Korovar art.* North of western New Guinea, Jendee, Roon Island, Geelvink Bay. *Carved canoe prow.* Cambridge (Mass.), Peabody Museum of Archaeology and Ethnology (72754-5). Collected by Thomas Barbour in 1907. (Ph. Museum.)

303. *Three-quarter detail view of 304.*

304. *Art of the north of western New Guinea.* Merat Island. *Stern ornament of a canoe.* Paris, Musée de l'Homme (87-31-63). Height: 9 3/4 ins; diameter: 5 ins. Collected by Prince Roland Bonaparte in 1887. (Ph. Museum-José Oster.)

305. *Art of the north of western New Guinea.* Merat Island. *Stern ornament of a canoe, fafore.* Paris, Musée de l'Homme (28-25-4). Overall height: 11 ins; breadth at the transverse bar: 6 ins. Collected by Prince Roland Bonaparte in 1928. (Ph. Museum-José Oster.)

306. *Art of the north of western New Guinea.* Merat Island. *Polychrome carved canoe prow, mani.* Paris, Musée de l'Homme (87-31-57). Height: 1 ft. 6 ins; breadth: 8 ins. Collected by Prince Roland Bonaparte in 1887. (Ph. Museum-José Oster.)

307. *Art of the north of western New Guinea.* North of western New Guinea. *Carved figure.* Leningrad, Museum of Anthropology and Ethnology (190-B-94). Height: 9 ins. Collected by V.A. Band, Russian Consul in Batavia in 1889. (Ph. Museum.)

308. *Art of the north of western New Guinea.* McCluer Gulf. *Polychrome mask (?).* Budapest, Ethnographic Museum (56-27-1). Height: 13 3/4 ins; width: 8 ins. Collected by Horst Bandat in 1935-39. (Ph. Museum.)

309. *Art of the north of western New Guinea.* Humboldt Bay. *Painted pottery.* Chicago, Natural History Museum (148029). Height: 10 ins; diameter: 11 1/2 ins. Collected by A.B. Lewis in 1909-13. (Ph. Museum.)

310. *Massim art.* Trobriand Islands (?). *Carved and openwork canoe prow.* Gift of the Amis du Trocadéro. Paris, Musée de l'Homme (28-13-1). Height: 15 1/2 ins; width: 1 ft. 11 1/4 ins; diameter of the projection: 1 ft. 5 3/4 ins. (Ph. Museum-José Oster.)

311. *Massim art.* Trobriand Islands. *Dance shield for kaydiba.* Leningrad, Museum of Anthropology and Ethnology (168-102-2). Collected by Miklucho Macklay in 1870-85. (Ph. Museum.)

312. *Massim art.* D'Entrecasteaux archipelago, Duan Island, Sigasiga. *Lime spatula.* Budapest, Ethnographic Museum (131560). Length: 11 1/2 ins; width: 7/8 ins. Collected by Geza Róheim in 1929-30. (Ph. Museum.)

313. *Massim art.* Trobriand Islands. *Figure of a pig.* Budapest, Ethnographic Museum (127557). Height: 5 ins; length: 12 1/4 ins; width: 3 3/4 ins. Collected by Károly Verebélyi before 1928. (Ph. Museum.

314. *Massim art.* Trobriand Islands. *Lime spatula.* Budapest, Ethnographic Museum (127665). Length: 12 ins; width: 1 1/4 ins. Collected by Károly Verebélyi before 1928. (Ph. Museum.)

315. *Massim Art.* Trobriand Islands, Kiriwana. *Lime spatula.* Basle, Museum für Völkerkunde (Vb 1032). Black wood. Height: 11 5/8 ins. Collected by P.G. Black in 1903. Anthropomorphic figure with two openwork wings. (Ph. Museum.)

316. *Massim Art.* Eastern New Guinea. *Lime spatula.* Honolulu, Bernice P. Bishop Museum. (Ph. Museum.)

317. *Massim Art.* Trobriand Islands. *Lime spatula, detail.* Budapest, Ethnographic Museum (127-674). Length: 13 3/4 ins; width: 1 1/2 ins. Collected by Károly Verebélyi before 1928. (Ph. Museum.)

318. *Massim Art.* Trobriand Islands. *Axe.* New York, Museum of Primitive Art (5927). Stone blade and carved, crooked handle. (Ph. Museum.)

319. *Massim Art.* Eastern New Guinea, south-east coast. *Betel mortar.* Leningrad, Museum of Anthropology and Ethnology (406-16). Collected by Miklucho Macklay in 1870-1885. (Ph. Museum.)

320. *Art of the Admiralty Islands.* Admiralty Islands. *Food ladle.* Budapest, Ethnographic Museum (32-095). Overall height: 8 5/8 ins; height of figure: 7 1/4 ins; diameter of bowl: 4 1/2 ins. Half coconut shell with handle. Collected by Rudolf Festetics de Tolna, in 1896. (Ph. Museum.)

321. *Art of the Admiralty Islands.* *Standing figure.* Bremen, Völkerkundliche Abteilung übersee Museum (D 10787). Height: 5 ft. 8 1/8 ins. (Ph. Hed Wiesner.)

322. *Art of the Admiralty Islands.* Admiralty Islands. *Carved socket of a spear point.* Budapest, Ethnographic Museum (36286). Stone. Overall length: 6 ft. 7 1/8 ins; length of figure: 11 3/4 ins; breadth of figure: 1 7/8 ins; thickness of spear: 1 in. Collected by Rudolf Festetics de Tolna. (Ph. Museum.)

323. *Art of the Admiralty Islands.* Admiralty Islands. *Polychrome canoe prow.* Budapest, Ethnographic Museum (36114). Length: 1 ft. 7 1/4 ins; height: 4 ins; thickness: 5 5/8 ins. Collected by Rudolf Festetics de Tolna in 1896. (Ph. Museum.)

324. *Art of the Admiralty Islands.* Hermit Islands. *Wooden spatula with openwork decoration.* Leningrad, Museum of Anthropology and Ethnology (402-49). Length: 1 ft. 8 1/2 ins. Collected by Miklucho Macklay in 1891. (Ph. Museum.)

325. *Art of the Admiralty Islands.* Iru Manus Island. *Monumental dish with incurved openwork handles.* Basle, Museum für Völkerkunde (Vb. 10520). Diameter: 3 ft. 8 7/8 ins; height: 1 ft. 8 1/8 ins. Collected by Alfred Bühler in 1932. (Ph. Moeschlin and Baur.)

326. *Art of the Admiralty Islands.* Admiralty Islands. *Carved dish.* *Korrigane* collection. Wood. Length: 1 ft. 8 1/2 ins. Auctioned in 1962. (Ph. Sougez.)

327. *Art of the Admiralty Islands.* Admiralty Islands. *Monumental dish in the form of a bird.* New York, Museum of Primitive Art (56-87). Length: 15 3/4 ins. (Ph. Museum.)

328. *Art of the Solomon Islands.* North of Bougainville. *Bust of a woman, detail.* Basle, Museum für Völkerkunde (Vb. 8234). (Ph. R. Spreng.)

329. *Art of the Solomon Islands.* San Cristobal, Suafulia, Mali village, Star Harbour district. *Crucifixion.* Coll. Father O'Reilly, Mission des Iles. (Ph. Draeger.)

330. *Art of the Solomon Islands.* Rubiana. *Anthropomorphic canoe prow.* Budapest, Ethnographic Museum (72086). Height: 8 1/4 ins; breadth: 3 1/2 ins. Collected by the warship *Panther* before 1905. (Ph. Museum.)

331. *Art of the Solomon Islands.* *Full-length carving of a squatting figure.* 1895. Budapest, Ethnographic Museum (36125). Height: 1 ft. 6 1/2 ins; breadth: 5 1/2 ins. (Ph. Museum.)

332. *Art of the Solomon Islands.* New Georgia, Marovo. *Carved canoe prow.* Basle, Museum für Völkerkunde. (Vb 7525). Wood coloured black encrusted with mother-of-pearl and nautilus shell. Height: 6 3/4 ins. (Ph. Fr. Hewicker.)

333. *Art of the Solomon Islands.* Santa Anna. *Sculptured group with two figures.* Basle, Museum für Völkerkunde

(Vb. 6819). Surface of stone grey and white; eyes set with mother-of-pearl. Height: 11 3/4 ins. Collected by E. Paravicini in 1929. (Ph. Museum.)

334. *Art of the Solomon Islands.* San Cristobal. *Dish in the shape of a frigate bird.* Basle, Museum für Völkerkunde (Vb 2668). Wood enhanced with mother-of-pearl inlays. Length: 2 ft. 10 1/4 ins. An old piece obtained from missionaries by Felix Speiser in 1915. (Ph. Museum.)

335. *Art of the Solomon Islands.* San Cristobal. *Dish carved in the form of a pig.* Basle, Museum für Völkerkunde (Vb 7182). Wood enhanced with mother-of-pearl inlays and painted black. The body is hollowed out. Overall length: 18 1/2 ins; height at the head: 8 ins; height of body: 7 1/2 ins. Collected by E. Paravicini in 1929. (Ph. Museum.)

336. *Art of the Solomon Islands.* North-western part of the archipelago. *Club with carved handle.* British Museum (150). Height: 3 ft. 2 3/4 ins. (Ph. Museum.)

337. *Art of the Solomon Islands.* Ulawa. *Carving of a shark.* British Museum. (1944 Cc2, 1315). Wood enhanced with mother-of-pearl inlay. Length: 3 ft. 8 1/2 ins. Acquired in 1944. (Ph. Museum.)

338. *Art of the Solomon Islands.* Ulawa. *Drawing of the god Ngorieru seated on a rainbow.* After Ivens, W.G. *Melanesians of the South East Solomon Islands*, New York, 1924, p. 201.

339. *Art of the Solomon Islands.* San Cristobal. *Pendant.* Basle, Museum für Völkerkunde (Vb. 7248). Mother-of-pearl and tortoise-shell. *Stylised frigate-bird and fish (bonito?).* Length: 7 1/8 ins; height 2 1/2 ins. Collected by E. Paravicini in 1929. (Ph. Museum.)

340. *Art of the Solomon Islands.* Choiseul. *Openwork tridacna plaque.* Basle, Museum für Völkerkunde (Vb. 7731). Ornament from a men's house. Length: 11 3/4 ins; height: 9 ins. Collected by E. Paravicini in 1929. (Ph. F. Hewicker.)

341. *Art of the Solomon Islands.* Solomon Islands. *Shield.* New York, Museum of Primitive Art (59-111). Pieces of nautilus shell bedded in a vegetable gum. Height: 2 ft. 9 1/4 ins. (Ph. Museum.)

342. *Art of the Solomon Islands.* San Cristobal. *Ceremonial club with an anthropomorphic handle.* New York, Museum of Primitive Art (56-28). Height: 3 ft. 10 1/4 ins. (Ph. Museum.)

343. *Art of the Solomon Islands.* Buka (?). *Detail of a painted paddle.* Budapest, Ethnographic Museum (54386). Overall length: 5 ft. 6 1/4 ins; width at top: 5 1/4 ins; width at centre: 2 5/8 ins. Collected by Giovanni Bettanin before 1904. (Ph. Museum.)

344. *Art of the Solomon Islands.* Bougainville. *Polychrome dance shield.* Budapest, Ethnographic Museum (54343). Diameters: 19 7/8 × 17 3/4 ins. Collected by Giovanni Bettanin before 1904. (Ph. Museum.)

345. *Art of central Polynesia.* Fiji. *Water pot; sangga drua tola.* (Triple-hulled canoe). Coll. Chauvel. Gift of G.H. Rivière. Paris, Musée de l'Homme (30-29-388). Length of a hull: 8 1/4 ins; width of pot 6 3/4 ins; height: 5 7/8 ins. Glazed with cowrie gum. (Ph. Museum-José Oster.)

346. *Art of central Polynesia.* Fiji. *Cup for ritual oil.* New York, Museum of Primitive Art (58241). (Ph. Museum.)

347. *Art of central Polynesia.* Fiji. *Water pot, in the form of eight joined coconuts.* Gift of Mason. Paris, Musée de l'Homme (87-13-1). Height: 7 7/8 ins; equatorial diameter: 9 1/2 ins. (Ph. Museum-José Oster.)

348. *Art of central Polynesia.* Fiji. *Oil cup in the form of a tortoise (underside).* Budapest, Ethnographic Museum (72088). Length: 13 ins; breadth: 10 5/8 ins. Collected by the warship *Panther* before 1907. (Ph. Museum.)

349. *Art of central Polynesia.* Austral Islands, Raivavae. *Finely incised cup.* New York, Museum of Primitive Art (56-102). Length: 13 1/8 ins. (Ph. Museum.)

350. *Art of central Polynesia.* Haapai Islands, Tonga. *Female figurine.* New York, Museum of Primitive Art (57108). Whale ivory. Height: 5 1/4 ins. Collected in Fiji in the 19th century. (Ph. Museum.)

351. *Art of central Polynesia.* Cook Islands. *Male figure.* British Museum (9866). Height: 3 1/4 ins; breadth at shoulders: 6 1/4 ins. Collected in 1876. A similar image in the collection of the London Missionary Society is said to be Tarianui, the god of fishermen. (Ph. Fr. Hewicker.)

352. *Art of central Polynesia.* Rarotonga, Cook Islands. *The god Te Rongo and his three sons.* British Museum (L.M.S. 169). Height: 2 ft. 3 3/8 ins; breadth at shoulders: 6 1/4 ins. Acquired by the London Missionary Society in 1890. Collected in the field at the end of the 18th century. (Ph. Fr. Hewicker.)

353. *Side view of 352.* (Ph. Fr. Hewicker.)

354. *Art of central Polynesia.* Austral Islands, Rurutu. *The god Tangaroa creating gods and men.* British Museum (L.M.S. 19). Height: 3 ft. 8 1/2 ins; breadth at shoulders: 12 3/4 ins. Acquired by the London Missionary Society in 1890. Collected in the field at the end of the 18th century. Cf. Ellis, W.: *Polynesian Researches*, London, 1829, Vol. II frontispiece and p. 20. (Ph. Fr. Hewicker.)

355. *Art of central Polynesia.* Austral Islands, Raivavae. *Image of female divinity.* Collection bought by the New

Zealand Government. Height: 21 ft. 7 7/8 ins. Breadth at shoulders: 8 ft. 2 3/8 ins. Formerly Col. W.O. Oldman, London (n° 413). Collected by John Williams who gave it to Rev. Timothy East of Birmingham. End of 18th century. (Ph. Hans Sibbelee.)

356. *Art of central Polynesia.* Cook Islands, Mangaia. *Detail of the beginning of the functional part of a ceremonial spoon.* Budapest, Ethnographic Museum. Overall length: 3 ft. 1 3/8 ins. (Ph. Museum.)

357. *Detail of 356.*

358. *Art of central Polynesia.* Leeward Islands, Huahine. *Handle of ritual fly-whisk.* New York, Museum of Primitive Art (58-57 A). Length: 2 ft. 8 ins. (Ph. Museum.)

359. *Art of central Polynesia.* Cook Islands, Mangaia. *Ritual adze.* Leningrad, Museum of Anthropology and Ethnography (402-11). Height: 1 ft. 8 1/8 ins. Collected by Miklucho Macklay in 1891. (Ph. Museum.)

360. *Art of central Polynesia.* Fiji. *Lipped club.* New York, Museum of Primitive Art (56-31). Height: 3 ft. 9 5/8 ins. (Ph. Museum.)

361. *Art of central Polynesia.* Austral Islands. *Ceremonial paddle.* New York, Museum of Primitive Art (56-1). Length: 4 ft. 7 1/2 ins. (Ph. Museum.)

362. *Art of central Polynesia.* Austral Islands. *Ceremonial bailer.* New York, Museum of Primitive Art (56-23). Length: 4 ft. 6 ins. (Ph. Museum.)

363. *Art of central Polynesia.* Austral Islands. *Vertical drum.* New York, Museum of Primitive Art (57251). Height: 4 ft. 3 1/8 ins. (Ph. Museum.)

364. *Art of central Polynesia.* Tonga. *Head-rest.* New York, Museum of Primitive Art (57110). Feet of wood: cross-piece in whalebone. (Ph. Museum.)

365. *Maori art.* New Zealand. *Standing figure of a man with a short club, mere.* New York, Museum of Primitive Art (56100). Height: 2 ft. 2 1/4 ins. (Ph. Museum.)

366. *Maori art.* New Zealand. *Fragment of a lintel.* Philadelphia University Museum. Christensen, Erwin O.: *Primitive Art*, New York, 1955, p. 306. (Ph. Museum.)

367. *Maori art.* New Zealand. *Bas-relief with a double figure.* New Zealand Embassy, Washington, U.S.A. (Ph. Embassy.)

368. *Maori art.* New Zealand. *Bas-relief with standing figure.* Leningrad, Museum of Anthropology and Ethnography (1279-75). Formerly in the Dominion Museum, Wellington, 1908. (Ph. Museum.)

369. A-B-C. *Maori art.* New Zealand. *Relation between the face theme and the manaia motif.* Transition from a front view to a distorted, profile one. Drawing, **after** Archey, Gilbert: *South Sea Folk*, Auckland, 1949, fig. 8a, 9a, 11a.

370. *Maori art.* New Zealand. *Manaia frieze.* Hamburg, Museum für Völkerkunde und Vorgeschichte. Height: 1 ft. 9 5/8 ins. Here the manaia gives an impression of bird-headed monsters. (Ph. Fr. Hewicker.)

371. *Maori art.* New Zealand. *Figure in realistic manner.* Glasgow, The Hunterian Museum, The University (E. 341). Height: 15 3/4 ins. (Ph. Museum.)

372. *Maori art.* New Zealand. *Carved parts of a war canoe: stem and stern.* Honolulu, Bernice Pauahi Bishop Museum. *Sternpiece* (1426): length: 2 ft. 8 5/8 ins; height: 15 ins; width: 12 1/4 ins. Stempiece (1429): length: 1 ft. 8 1/2 ins; width at centre: 11 3/4 ins; width at base: 15 ins. Collected by Eric Craig in 1888. (Ph. Museum.)

373. *Maori art.* New Zealand. *Casket for feathers; viewed from below.* New York, Museum of Primitive Art (54103). Length: 1 ft. 10 ins. (Ph. Museum.)

374. *Maori art.* New Zealand. *Adze of a chief.* New York, Museum of Primitive Art (56-15). Jade blade. Height: 12 3/4 ins. (Ph. Museum - Ch. Uht.)

375. *Maori art.* New Zealand, Taranaki. *Wahaika club.* Honolulu, Bernice Pauahi Bishop Museum (1458). Whalebone. Length: 15 ins; maximum width: 3 1/2 ins; thickness: 1/2 in. Collected by Eric Craig in 1888. Belonged to Ropata Ngarongomaka, one of the principal chiefs of Taranaki. (Ph. Museum.)

376. *Maori art.* New Zealand. *Jade pendant, hei tiki* Coll. Pierre Vérité, Paris. (Ph. Giraudon.)

377. *Marquesan art.* Marquesa Islands. *Stone net-weight with double figure.* Col. Pierre Vérité, Paris. (Ph. Giraudon.)

378. *Marquesan art.* Fatu Hiva Island. *Stone figure.* Munich, Staatliches Museum für Völkerkunde. (Ph. Museum.)

379. *Marquesan art.* Marquesa Islands. *Carved housepost.* Coll. Pierre Vérité, Paris. (Ph. Giraudon.)

380. *Marquesan art.* Marquesa Islands. *Carved piece placed at an angle in the prow of a canoe for the mooring rope.* Geneva, Museum and Institute of Ethnography (8937). (Ph. Museum.)

381. *Marquesan art.* Marquesa Islands. *Feminine ear ornament.* Philadelphia, University Museum. Bone. (Ph. Museum.)

382. *Marquesan art.* Marquesa Islands. *Handle of a fan.* Philadelphia, University Museum. Bone. (Ph. Museum.)

383. *Marquesan art.* Marquesa Islands. *Diadem.* New York, Museum of Primitive Art (58-3). Plates of tortoise-shell and shell. Length: 1 ft. 5 3/4 ins. (Ph. Museum.)

384. *Easter Island art.* Easter Island. *Male figure, moa¹ kavakava (seen from the side).* 1928. Leningrad, Museum of Anthropology and Ethnology (3701-1). (Ph. Museum.)

385. *Easter Island art.* Easter Island. *Female figure, moai paepae.* Leningrad, Museum of Anthropology and Ethnology (402-1). Height: 1 ft. 11 1/4 ins. Collected by Miklucho Macklay in 1891. (Ph. Museum.)

386. *Easter Island art.* Easter Island. *Tangata manu, man-bird.* 1928. Leningrad, Museum of Anthropology and Ethnology (736-204). Height: 12 ins. (Ph. Museum.)

387. *Easter Island art.* Easter Island. *Human figure covered in tapa.* Cambridge (Mass.), Peabody Museum, Harvard University (53543). Boston Museum collection. Collected by David Kimball. (Ph. Museum.)

388. *Easter Island art.* Anakena Bay. *Monumental head.* Paris, Musée de l'Homme (35-611). Height: 4 ft. 11 ins. Collected by the Métraux-Lavachery expedition. (Ph. Sougez.)

389. *Easter Island art.* Easter Island. *Tapa head-dress.* Cambridge (Mass.), Peabody Museum, Harvard University (53541). Diameter: 11 3/4 ins. Wingert, Paul: *Art of the South Pacific Islands,* London, 1953, pl. 96. (Ph. Museum.)

390. *Easter Island art.* Easter Island, Orongo. *Stone sculpture called Hoa hake hapa ia, waves breaking.* 1868. British Museum. Height: 8 ft. 4 3/8 ins; breadth at elbows: 3 ft. 5 3/4 ins. Found in a hut at Orongo village. Cf. Palmer, J.L.: "A Visit to Easter Island in 1868." in *Journal of the Royal Geographical Society,* vol. 40, 1870, p. 177. (Ph. Museum.)

391. *Easter Island art. Petroglyphs.* (Ph. Musée de l'Homme - A. Métraux.)

392. *Hawaiian art.* Hawaiian Islands, Oahu. *The god of war, Ku.* British Museum (L.M.S. 223). Overall height: 4 ft. 1 1/8 ins; height of figure: 2 ft. 5 7/8 ins; breadth at elbows : 14 7/8 ins. Collected by the London Missionary Society in 1890. Two accounts exist of its acquisition: a) it was one of the idols adorning the *marae* of Kaili at Kawailae; b) it was taken from the wall of the old *marae* of Kailua with the permission of the governor Kuakene. (Ph. Fr. Hewicker.)

393. *Hawaiian art.* Hawaiian Islands, Kawaihae. *Female figurine.* Honolulu, Bernice Pauahi Bishop Museum (9072). Height: 2 ft. 4 1/2 ins. Found in a cave by Forbes and Wagener in 1902. Bought from W. Wagener in 1907. (Ph. Museum.)

394. *Hawaiian art.* Hawaiian Islands. *Figurine.* Honolulu, Bernice Pauahi Bishop Museum (C. 9595). Height: 15 1/2 ins; maximum width: 7 1/2 ins. Long in the possession of the family of Mrs. Geo. H. Wright, Washington. (Ph. Museum.)

395. *Hawaiian art.* Hawaiian Islands. *Cup with human supporters.* British Museum. In brown, hard wood; the eyes are mother-of-pearl, the teeth fragments of bone. Height: 9 7/8 ins; length 1 ft. 6 7/8 ins. (Ph. Fr. Hewicker.)

396. *Hawaiian art. Cup with human supporters.* British Museum. Height: 7 1/2 ins. (Ph. Fr. Hewicker.)

397. *Hawaiian art.* Hawaiian Islands. *Double dish with a central figure.* 1890. British Museum (Haw. 47). Length: 11 ins; height: 4 1/2 ins. *Pa inamona,* probably to hold salt and cooked nuts. (Ph. Museum.)

398. *Hawaiian art.* Hawaiian Islands, Honaunau. *Full-length temple figure.* Honolulu, Bernice Pauahi Bishop Museum (C. 10189). Height of image: 5 1/2 ins; height of pedestal: 8 3/4 ins. Collected by Rev. Andrew Bloxam in 1825. Bloxam, of H.M.S. *Blonde,* Lord Byron captain, took it with the authority of Kalaimoku, governor of Hawaii. It formed part of the royal mausoleum, *Hale-o-keawe,* at Honaunau, Kea la kokua Bay.

399. *Hawaiian art.* Hawaiian Islands. *Bracelet.* Honolulu, Bernice Pauahi Bishop Museum (1304). Tortoise-shell and bone carved into heads. External circumference: 6 3/4 ins. (Ph. Museum.)

400. *Hawaiian art.* Hawaiian Islands. *The goddess Pele with a comb.* Paris, Musée de l'Homme (C-61-834-493). (Ph. Museum - José Oster.)

401. *Hawaiian art.* Hawaiian Islands. *Image of the god of war, Ku Kailimoku.* End of the 18th century. Goettingen, Institut für Völkerkunde, Universität. Basketry covered with feathers. Height: 18 1/2 ins. (Ph. Wollscheid.)

402. *Hawaiian art.* Hawaiian Islands. *Image of the god of war, Ku Kailimoku.* Berlin-Dahlem, Museum für Völkerkunde (VI-253). Basketry and feathers. Mother-of-pearl eyes, human hair and polished dog teeth. Height: 2 ft. 9 1/2 ins. (Ph. Museum - Walter Steinkopf.)

403. *Hawaiian art.* Hawaiian Islands. *Divine figure: the netting and plumes are missing.* Paris, Musée de l'Homme (78-30-15). Height: 2 ft. 2 ins. (Ph. Sougez.)

404. *Hawaiian art.* Hawaiian Islands. *Tapa with printed motifs.* Honolulu, Bernice Pauahi Bishop Museum. Mulberry tree, *wanke,* bark. (Ph. Museum.)

405. *Hawaiian art.* Hawaiian Islands. *Feather cape.* British Museum, Height: 5 ft. 8 7/8 ins; overall diameter: 9 ft. 5 3/4 ins. The wearing of such capes was restricted to the highest nobility. (Ph. Museum.)

406. *Micronesian art.* Eastern New Guinea, Matty Island. *Dish.* New York, Museum of Primitive Art (56-91). Wood. Length: 12 ins. (Ph. Museum.)

407. Micronesian art. Caroline Islands, Nukuoro. *Stool for grating coconuts.* New York, Museum of Primitive Art (56-93). Length: 22 1/4 ins. (Ph. Museum.)

408. *Micronesian art.* Caroline Islands, Nukuoro. *Female figure.* Honolulu, Academy of Arts (4752). Height: 15 3/8 ins. (Ph. Museum.)

409. *Micronesian art.* Caroline Islands, Ponape (?). *Tino figure.* Paris, Musée de l'Homme (33-2-1). Height: 13 ins. Collected by G. H. Rivière in 1933. (Ph. Museum-René Pasquino.)

410. *Micronesian art.* Santa Cruz Islands, Nitendi (South Solomons). *Pendant.* Basle, Museum für Völkerkunde (Vb 1838). Shell and tortoise-shell. Collected by Felix Speiser in 1912. (Ph. Museum.)

411. *Micronesian art.* Gilbert Islands. *Body armour.* Brussels, Musées royaux d'Art et d'Histoire. *Art de la Mélanésie* by Mme Della Santa. 1958. (E.T. 537 and 2072). Basketry enhanced with black twigs to give a lozenge effect. Height: 3 ft. 1 3/8 ins. (Ph. A.C.L., Brussels.)

412. *Detail of 414.* (Ph. Museum - Ch. Uht.)

413. *Micronesian art.* Santa Cruz Islands (South Solomons.) *Representation of a fish with coloured designs.* Basle, Museum für Völkerkunde (Vb 1885). (Ph. Moeschlin and Baur.)

414. *Micronesian art.* Santa Cruz Islands (South Solomons). *Male figure.* New York, Museum of Primitive Art (56-58). Height: 16 3/8 ins. (Ph. Museum - Ch. Uht.)

415. *Micronesian art.* Palau Islands. *Incised board enhanced in colours—mythical scene.* Paris, Musée des Arts Africains et Océaniens (62-2-1). Length: 1 ft. 11 7/8 ins; breadth: 6 7/8 ins. Collected by Jacques Barrau in 1956. (Ph. Ina Bandy.)

416. *Micronesian art.* Palau Islands. *Bowl.* British Museum. Mother-of-pearl inlay. Length: 3 ft. 1 ins; height: 20 1/2 ins. Given by King Abba Thule of the Palau Islands to Captain Wilson (H.M.S. *Antelope*) in 1793. (Cf. Wilson, Henry: *An account of the Pelew Islands*, London, 1803, Pl. 1.) (Ph. Museum.)

417. *Micronesian art.* Mortlock Island, Nomoi, Caroline Islands. *Rafter ornament.* Honolulu, Bernice Pauahi Bishop Museum (5620). Height: 1 ft. 9 ins; width: 11 7/8 ins; thickness: 5 1/2 ins. Collected by the American Board of Foreign Missions in 1874. (Ph. Museum.)

418. *Papuan art.* Era-Maipua river. *Irivake figure; champlevé motifs.* Coll. P. Wirz. 1930. Amsterdam, Koninklijk Instituut voor de Tropen (2670-282). Wood, fibres, bark belt. Height: 4 ft. 2 ins. (Ph. Museum-R.L. Mellema.)

419. *Papuan art.* Koiravi, Era river. *Champlevé figure, bioma.* Coll. John W. Vandercock. 1929. Brooklyn Museum (51-118-9). Height: 2 ft. 2 1/2 ins. (Ph. Museum.)

420. *Papuan art.* Ikunu, Namau coast. *Female figure.* Coll. P. Wirz. Basle, Museum für Völkerkunde (Vb 7785). Wood, fibres, red and white paint. Height: 4 ft. 10 5/8 ins. (Ph. Museum.)

421. *Art of Lake Sentani.* *Tapa skirt.* Amsterdam, Koninklijk Instituut voor de Tropen (1772-726). Black and reddish brown. Length: 4 ft. 7 1/2 ins. (Ph. Museum-R.L. Mellema.)

422. *Papuan art.* Turama delta. *Door of a long-house.* Coll. P. Wirz. 1930. Basle, Museum für Völkerkunde (Vb 7987). Black and white painted wood. Height: 4 ft. 1 1/4 ins. (Ph. Museum.)

423. *Papuan art.* Turama delta. *Door of a long-house.* Coll. P. Wirz. 1930. Basle, Museum für Völkerkunde (Vb. 7987). Wood painted black and white. Height: 4 ft. 1 1/4 ins. (Ph. Museum.)

424. *Art of South-west New Guinea.* Asmat. *Standing male figures.* Coll. Michael C. Rockefeller. 1961. (Ph. Eliot Elisofon.)

425. *Papuan art.* Lower Fly river. *Figure used in the moguru ritual.* British Museum. (Ph. Museum.)

426. *Papuan art.* Turama delta. *Figure for the moguru ritual.* Coll. P. Wirz. 1930. Amsterdam, Koninklijk Instituut voor de Tropen (2670-302). Red and white. Height: 5 ft. 7 3/4 ins. The *moguru* is a complex ritual whose connotations range from agrarian magic to the sexual initiation of the young: it always includes head-hunting. (Ph. Museum - R.L. Mellema.)

427. *Art of South-west New* Guinea. Asmat. *Bis figures used at funerals.* Coll. Michael C. Rockefeller. 1961. (Ph. Eliot Elisofon.)

428. *Sepik art.* Arambak, Korewori river. *Kamanggabi figure.* Basle, Museum für Völkerkunde (409). Length: 7 ft. 10 1/2 ins. Collected by Alfred Bühler in 1959. (Ph. Moeschlin and Baur.)

429. *Sepik art.* Tambanum. *Lime spatula; detail of bird carving.* Coll. Bühler. 1955. Basle, Museum für Völkerkunde (Vb 14-924). Carved human bone. Length: 15 3/4 ins. (Ph. Moeschlin and Baur.)

430. *Sepik art.* Palimbei, Middle Sepik. *Female figure from the roof-crest of a men's house.* Coll. Bühler. 1955.

Basle, Museum für Völkerkunde (Vb. 14-717). Height: 4 ft. 9 1/2 ins. (Ph. Moeschlin and Baur.)

431. *Sepik art*. Mundugumor. *Mouthpiece of flute with female figure*. Basle, Museum für Völkerkunde. Collected by S. Brignoni. Height: 13 3/4 ins. (Ph. Moeschlin and Baur.)

432. *Papuan art*. Numobawi. *Stool*. Amsterdam, Koninklijk Instituut voor de Tropen (2670-295). Painted wood. Length: 3 ft. 6 7/8 ins. (Ph. Museum - R.L. Mellema.)

433. *Papuan art*. Lower Fly river. *Drum in human shape*. Chicago, Natural History Museum (142777). Height: 2 ft. 11 7/8 ins. (Ph. Museum.)

434. *Papuan art*. Namau region (interior). Koriki (?). *Aiaimunu mask*. Before 1890. Dublin, National Museum of Ireland (349-90). Tapa on a rattan framework. Black and white paint. Height: 4 ft. (Ph. Museum.)

435. *Papuan art*. Gogodara. *Painted mask*. Coll. A.B. Lewis. 1912. Chicago, Natural History Museum (142766). Light wood with edge of rattan and red, black, brown and white fruit. Height: 2 ft. 6 ins. The *iobo* variant of the *tao* theme. (Ph. Museum.)

436. *Detail of 437*.

437. *Art of Lake Sentani*. Western New Guinea, Lake Sentani. *House-post*. Amsterdam, Koninklijk Instituut voor de Tropen (2202-101). Iron wood. Height: 7 ft. 2 5/8 ins. (Ph. Museum - R.L. Mellema.)

438. *Papuan art*. Wapo. *Male figure*. Coll. P. Wirz. 1930. Amsterdam, Koninklijk Instituut voor de Tropen (2670-299). Piece of wood painted black and white and decorated with shell. Height: 3 ft. 1 3/8 ins. (Ph. Museum-R.L. Mellema.)

Maps by Jacques ROCHETTE

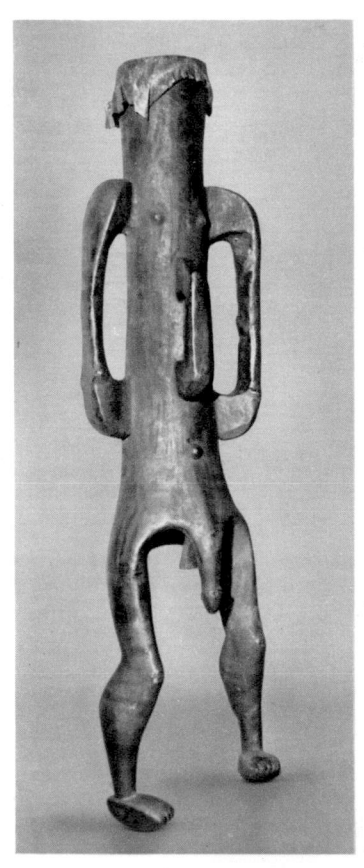

433. New Guinea, Papua, lower Fly river. *Drum.* Natural History Museum, Chicago - 434. New Guinea, Papua, Namau region. *Mask.* National Museum, Dublin - 435. New Guinea, Papua, Gogodara. *Painted mask.* Natural History Museum, Chicago.

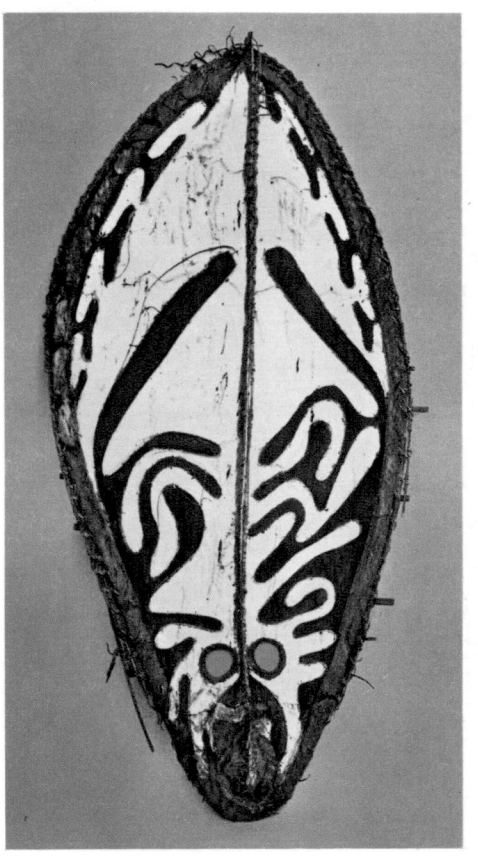

460

436 *detail and* 437. New Guinea, Lake Sentani. *House-post*, Amsterdam - 438. New Guinea, Papua, Wapo. *Male figure*, Amsterdam.

461

MAPS

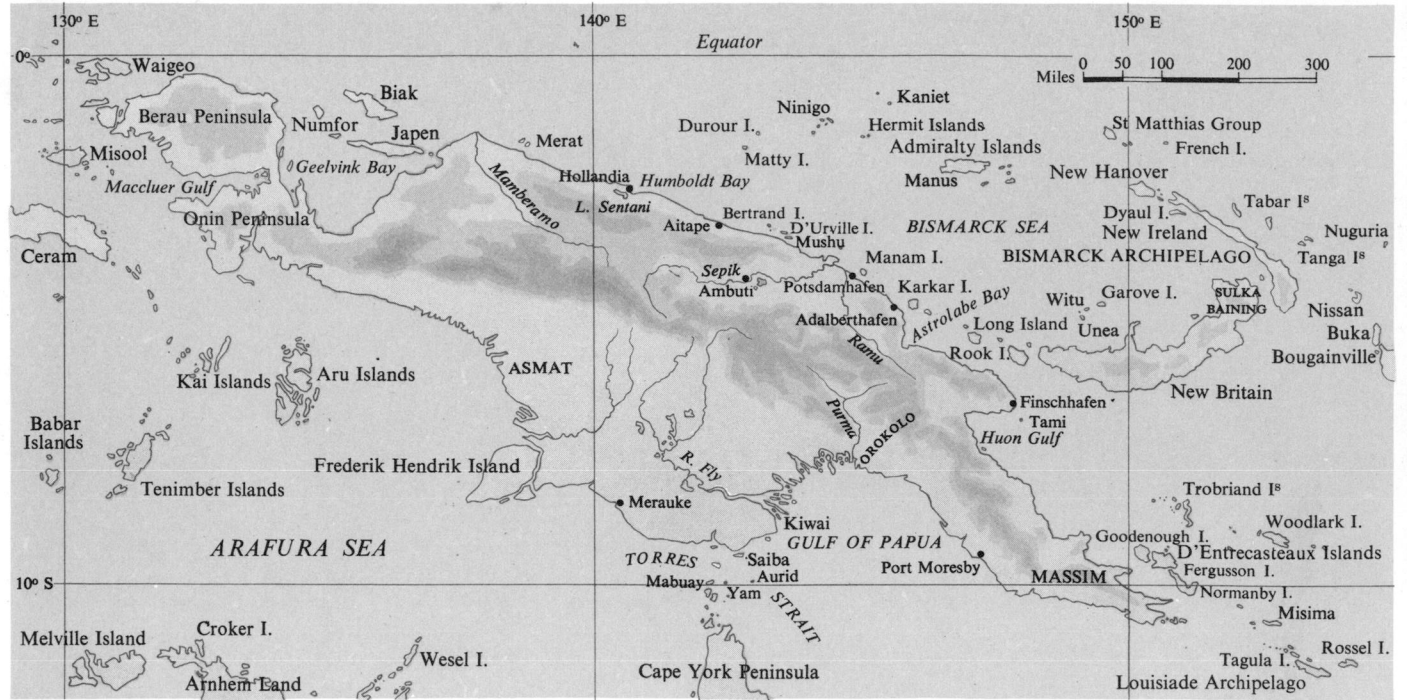

New Guinea

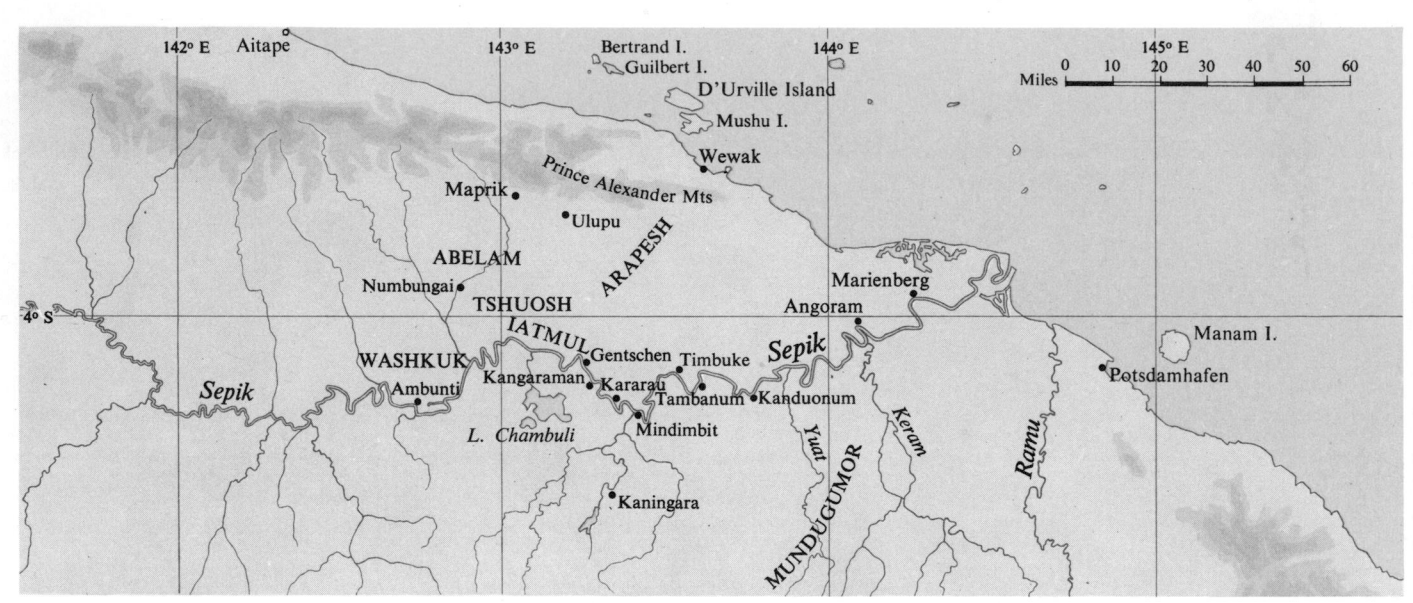

Sepik River Valley

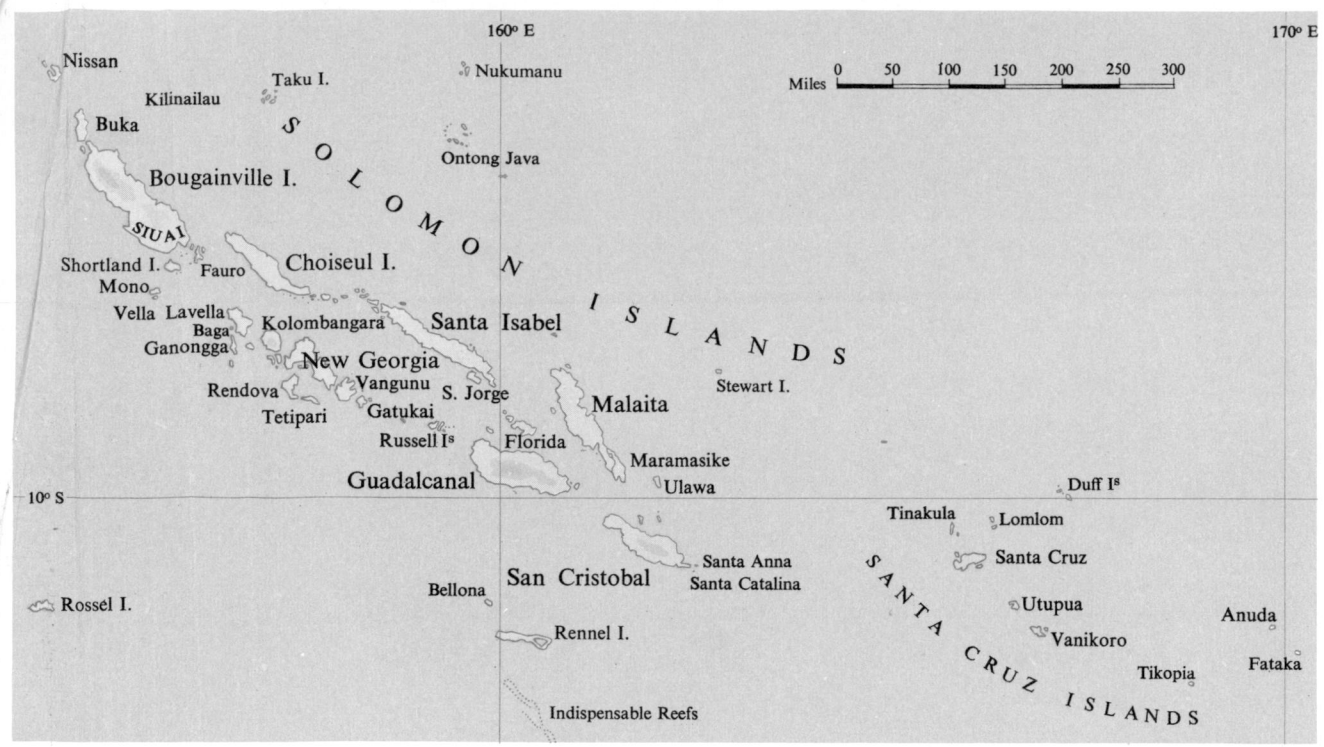

Solomon Islands and Santa Cruz Islands

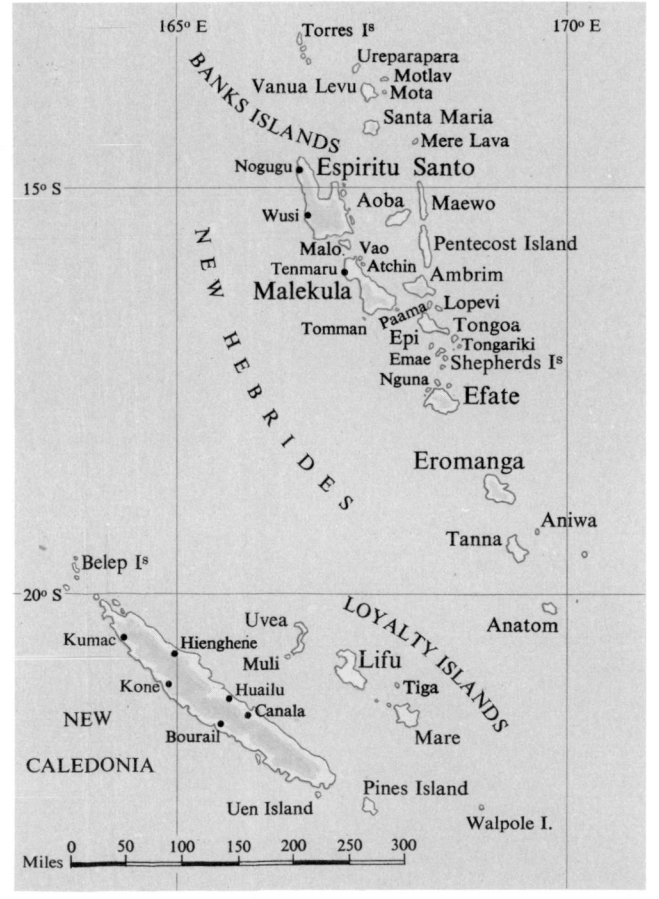

New Hebrides
New Caledonia

165° W 150° W 135° W 120° W

Guadalupe I.

CALIFORNIA

R SANDWICH ISLANDS

Gardner I.

Necker I.

Cancer

Kauai
Niihau Oahu
Honolulu Maui

Hawaii

Revilla Gigedo Is

Clipperton I.

Palmyra Island
Washington I.
Fanning I.

O C E A N

Christmas I.

uator

Jarvis I.

NDS
n I.

LINE ISLANDS

Malden I.

Y
I.

N

Starbuk I.

E

S

Hatutu MARQUESAS
Nuku-Hiva Hiva-Oa

au Is

Penrhyn I.

I

Danger Is Humphrey I. Vostok I. Caroline I. Tahuata Fahu-Hiva

Nassau I. Flint I.

A

anua Suvarov Is

Rangiroa Takaroa Puka-Puka

Bellinghausen I. Bora-Bora Raroia TUAMOTU
Scilly I. aiatea Toau Makemo Tatakoto
Palmerston I. Tahiti Anaa Amanu
Niue I. Aitutaki Marokau Parao Reao
Hervey Is SOCIETY ISLANDS Nengonengo

COOK ARCHIPELAGO Rarotonga Maria I. AUSTRAL ISLANDS Amanu-Raro Pinaki Tureia
Mangaia Mururoa
Rurutu Morane Gambier Is

pricorn Tubuai Vavitu Oneo I. Elisabeth I.
Pitcairn I. Ducie I.

Lancaster Rf Easter Island

Rapa

Maria-Theresa Rf

0 300 600 900 1200
Miles

Map labels

HAWAIIAN

Morell I.
Midway I^s
Lisiansky I.
Laysan I.

Tropic o[f]

Krusenstern R^f

Ogasawara Arch.

Kasan I^s

Minami Tori

Wake I.

Schjetmar R^f

Johnston I[.]

MARIANAS
Assumption
Pagan
Sariguan
Saipan
Tinian
Rota
Guam

Pokaaku

Eniwetok   Bikini

MARSHALL ISLANDS

Likiep
Wotje
Kuezyerin I.
Malulap
Arno

M I C R O N E S I A

Urusi
Yap   Huaesu   Gurinesu   Ororu I^s
Kurru   Sororu   Horu I^s
Palau Islands

C A R O L I N E   I S L A N D S

Yorupikku   Ifalik I^s Syukku   Ororukku   Ponape
Namoluk   Motorokku I^s

Jaluit

Morotai

M E L A N E S I A

P A C I F I [C]

Halmahera

Eq[uator]

Tarawa
Apamama
Nonuti

GILBERT ISLANDS

Schouten I^s

Nauru   Paanopa

PHŒNIX ISLA[NDS]

Misool
Ceram

Admiralty Islands
Hollandia

Bismarck
Archipelago

New Ireland

SOLOMON ISLANDS

P O L [Y]

Mc Kean I.   Canto[n]

Nanomea I^s Gardner I.   Sydne[y]

Aru Islands

NEW GUINEA

New Britain
Bougainville I.   Choiseul I.

ELLICE ISLANDS

Vaitupu
Funafuti

Tok[elau]

Tenimber I^s

Port Moresby

ARAFURA SEA

TORRES STRAIT

Guadalcanal
S. Cristobal

Santa Cruz
Islands

Rotuma   Wallis I^s Savaï   SAMO[A]
Futuna   Upolu   Tu[tuila]

Melville I.   Wesel I.

Cape York
York Peninsula

Louisiade Archipelago

Banks Islands
Espiritu Santo I.

Gulf of
Carpentaria

Wellesley I^s

CORAL

Malekula

NEW HEBRIDES

Ambrim
Efate
Eromanga

Vanua Levu

Viti Levu   Lau I^s

Vavao I^s

Chesterfield I^s

FIJI

TONGA   Hapaï I^s

Ono i Lau I^s Tongatabu

LOYALTY ISLANDS

Uvea

New
Caledonia

Pylstaart I.

Tropic of C[apricorn]

A U S T R A L I A

SEA

Brisbane

Norfolk I.

Raoul I.

30° S

Lord Howe I.

Kermadec Islands
Esperance R^f

Newcastle
Sydney

Adelaïde   Canberra

T A S M A N

North Cape

Auckland   North Island

Melbourne

NEW
ZEALAND

BASS STRAIT

S E A

TASMANIA

Wellington

South Island   Christchurch   Chatham Island[s]

45° S

THIS, THE FOURTH VOLUME OF THE SERIES 'THE ARTS OF MANKIND'
EDITED BY ANDRÉ MALRAUX AND GEORGES SALLES, HAS BEEN
PRODUCED UNDER THE SUPERVISION OF ALBERT BEURET,
EDITOR-IN-CHARGE OF THE SERIES. THE BOOK WAS DESIGNED BY
JEANINE FRICKER ASSISTED BY MICHEL MUGUET. THE TEXT AND
PLATES IN BLACK AND WHITE WERE PRINTED BY L'IMPRIMERIE
GEORGES LANG, PARIS; PLATES IN COLOUR BY L'IMPRIMERIE
DRAEGER, MONTROUGE. DESIGNED BY MASSIN, THE BINDING WAS
EXECUTED BY BABOUOT, GENTILLY.

PRINTED IN FRANCE